Praise for *Black Vinyl White Powder*

'One of the most authoritative, intelligent, diligently researched, conscientiously indexed, and thoroughly unpretentious disquisitions on the history of the British pop scene yet written'

Sunday Telegraph

'Probably the greatest book ever written about English pop'
Julie Burchill, *Spectator*

'The cold-print equivalent of a sparkling evening in the company of a world-class raconteur'

Charles Shaar Murray, *Independent*

'Funny, entertaining and even shrewd'

Sunday Times

'Bitchy, glib, fun and shrewd ... His honesty in writing such an engaging exposé of the business is to be cherished'

Daily Telegraph

'His preoccupation with trivia is what makes his book so compelling and informative. Napier-Bell knows that if you scratch the surface of pop music you will find more surface'

Times Higher Education Supplement

Simon Napier-Bell has been a composer, songwriter, record producer and author, but he is best known for having managed such artists as the Yardbirds, Marc Bolan, Japan and Wham!. Under his management, Wham! became the first Western pop group ever to play in communist China. He is the author of three other acclaimed books about the music industry – *You Don't Have to Say You Love Me*, *I'm Coming to Take You to Lunch* and *The Business* – as well as a memoir, *Sour Mouth, Sweet Bottom*. He is CEO of the Pierbel Entertainment Group, and continues to consult, write and broadcast, most recently directing documentary films on subjects ranging from Frank Sinatra to the decriminalisation of homosexuality in Britain. Simon lives in Thailand.

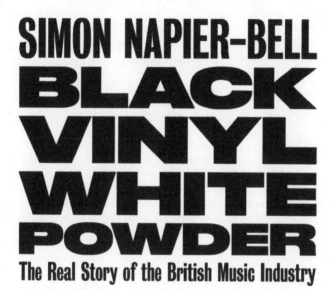

SIMON NAPIER-BELL

BLACK VINYL WHITE POWDER

The Real Story of the British Music Industry

unbound

First published in Great Britain by Ebury Press in 2001
This paperback edition first published in 2023

Unbound
Level 1, Devonshire House, One Mayfair Place, London W1J 8AJ
www.unbound.com

© Simon Napier-Bell, 2001

Text design by PDQ Digital Media Solutions Ltd

A CIP record for this book is available from the British Library

ISBN 978-1-80018-165-6 (paperback)
ISBN 978-1-80018-166-3 (ebook)

Printed and bound in Great Britain by Clays Ltd, Elcograf S.p.A.

1 3 5 7 9 8 6 4 2

CONTENTS

FOREWORD

This is a history of the British music business.

I didn't set out to write anything as grandiose as that – I simply went to see literary agent Julian Alexander to discuss writing a novel. He said it would be a good idea for me first to write a substantial book on my experiences in the music business, something more serious than my previous, rather flippant book, *You Don't Have to Say You Love Me*. And he suggested a history of the British music industry.

To me that sounded like an impossible task, something a journalist or social historian should undertake. So instead, while I agreed that Julian could call it a history of the music business if he wanted to, I said I would write an insider's look at the business over the last forty years. I would divide the subject into categories – Management, Publishing, Sex, Drugs, Money, etc., and that way, I wouldn't have to write it in chronological order. Neither would I have to base it on music or artists. For the truth is, my fascination with the music business has always been for the trivia, the gossip, the outrage and the surface gloss – the actual music has just been a backdrop, however diverting.

Julian liked the idea and asked me to write a forty-page presentation, which I did. Jake Lingwood at Ebury Press commissioned the book and we were in business.

I decided the best way to tackle the book was to make writing it as much fun as possible. I would spend three months having lunch with fifty or sixty old friends – managers, pop stars, A&R men – reminisce a bit and get things sorted out in my memory. I started with Harold Pendleton, the creator of the Reading Festival and the owner of the Marquee Club. The result was a four-hour lunch during which we consumed five bottles of the best wine known to man. The next day I was unable to remember anything from our conversation that would contribute to a serious history of the music business (or even a flippant one), except perhaps the story of how Harold, having announced Dizzy Gillespie to 3,000 expectant jazz fans at the Royal Festival Hall, decided the best way back to his seat in the stalls was to jump over the orchestra pit in which he landed arse upwards to tumultuous applause.

For a while, I continued to enjoy myself eating lunch with old friends every day, but I soon came to realise that by using this less-than-scientific method of research the book could take five years to write and cost upwards of £50,000 on food and fine wine. So I stayed at home for a month and settled down to write a first chapter, basing it on the subject of drugs, which seemed to me an integral part of the music industry. I wrote it chronologically from the mid-fifties to the present day, interweaving stories about artists with information on the recreational substances they most enjoyed. I intended this first chapter to act as a reference point for everything that happened in the book thereafter. That way, nothing else would need to be written in chronological order. I could write the rest of the book from memory and I expected the whole job to take no longer than six months.

But, when they read the first chapter, both Julian and Jake said, 'That's it! That's how the book should be. Forget about your idea of dividing the industry into different subjects. Take this chapter and expand it into a full book!'

Once they'd said it, I realised they were right, of course. The more I looked at that first chapter, the more I realised that drugs and drug culture had been absolutely central to the development of the British music business. But as I proceeded with the book, I also began to see that of almost equal importance was the influence of gay culture. In fact, in the British music business gay culture seemed to have played the same creative role as black culture had in the American music business. Examples of this were to be found everywhere – in the fifties with Larry Parnes's stable of homo-erotic rock 'n' roll stars, in the sixties with Mick Jagger's androgynous stage projection and the extraordinary prevalence of gay managers, in the seventies with glam rock and David Bowie's proud flaunting of his bisexuality, in the eighties with Boy George and the New Romantics, and in the nineties with Elton John and George Michael receiving very different rewards for having made one of the world's best-selling charity records together – for Elton, a knighthood – for George, arrest by the Los Angeles police.

But there was a problem. By having to write the book in chronological order, I soon realised I'd thrown away my chances of finishing it quickly. I was now stuck with researching everything that had happened in the music business during the last forty years. Instead of finishing the book in six months, it took me three years.

The only way to pack everything in was to focus on the most visible trends in each decade. Nowhere would I linger on people who'd made it big in the previous decade unless they were still hitting the headlines in the next one (except, perhaps, when I was writing about myself).

Nevertheless, it was still a daunting prospect. On several occasions I thought about quitting. To keep myself going I thought back to a slim Penguin paperback I once picked up at an airport – *A Short History of the World* by H.G. Wells. If Wells had squeezed 5,000 years into 300 pages, surely I could do the same with a mere forty years of pop music.

In doing so, I tried hard to put aside the usual clichéd perceptions of the industry and come up with something fresh. But the more I wrote, the more it became clear that the popular view of the music industry is the right one, especially in relation to drugs. As if to confirm this, last year, with the book finished and me back in business as a manager, I found myself sitting with a group of record company executives. They were discussing the promotion of dance music in South East Asia and they pointed out that the strongest sales were coming from the countries that had the highest incidence of ecstasy usage – Indonesia, Singapore, Malaysia and Thailand. One of the executives explained, 'Because ecstasy's a designer drug it's mostly used by the middle classes, so it tends to be the Chinese kids who introduce it into each territory. Consequently they turn out to be our target audience for dance music.'

To some people it might seem shocking that a group of serious middle-aged company executives should casually discuss the potential for record sales in terms of the popularity of an illegal drug. But if you look back at the history of the music industry you'll see that's how it's always been – especially in Britain.

So here it is… money, sex and drugs. What more could you ask for, except perhaps a little music?

Simon Napier-Bell
London, January 2001

PART ONE

PART ONE

CHAPTER ONE

1956

In 1956 I was seventeen. Big bands were still the main draw in Britain and I'd got myself a roadie's job with the Johnny Dankworth Orchestra. The Dankworth band was one of the top three big bands in the country and went from town to town playing in dance halls. There was Dankworth himself, two singers and sixteen musicians, five of them jazz soloists. Fresh out of public school I was their posh bandboy, something of an amusement to them. I'd taken on the job because I intended eventually to earn my living as a jazz musician and wanted to be around other jazz musicians.

Before each show I had to unload the instruments from the bus and set them up on the stage. Afterwards I had to pack them away again. I was also expected to look after the musicians and get them anything they wanted – sandwiches, cigarettes, beer, or 'something special' to smoke. The Dankworth band was trendier than other big bands, it was more jazz-orientated, and where there were jazz musicians there was marijuana.

To provide the guys in the band with a smoke whenever they needed it, I kept in my pocket a chunk of hash, the hard brown resin of the female cannabis plant, much easier to carry around than a bag full of grass. The technique was to sit on the floor at the back of the bus, hack a small piece from my master chunk, wrap it in foil from a cigarette pack and heat the outside with a match. The dried hash crumbled easily onto a Rizla cigarette paper and was mixed with tobacco to be rolled into a joint, which in those days was called a reefer.

I was much better at making them than smoking them. I was a trumpet player, and if I was to succeed in my chosen career as a jazz musician smoking reefers was obviously essential. But the truth was, they set my throat on fire.

In the end it didn't matter. I discovered that the real fascination of being with the Dankworth band didn't come from hanging out with the band's half-dozen jazz musicians, it came from gossiping with all the others – regular musicians and singers whose main career was in popular music, not jazz. From them I learnt about the music business, a huge private club where everyone talked about everyone else as if they were all best friends. Whether someone was a star, the head of a record company, an agent or a manager – everyone else in the music business referred to them by their first names and knew everything there was to know about them. Deals, drugs, sex, health – problems at home or problems with money – where there was a story to be told there was always somebody ready to tell it.

My obsession with jazz faded, replaced by a fascination with the behind-the-scenes world of pop. It wasn't so much the music that interested me, it was what went on around it. If this was the music business, I was hooked. The flow of information was endless.

CHAPTER TWO

OH BOY!

This is how Britain got started in the record business.

John Kennedy was a young adventurer from New Zealand who came to London and hung out at La Caverne, an illicit after-hours drinking club in Soho. Larry Parnes was the owner of a women's clothing shop in Essex and had a share in La Caverne. He also had an investment in the West End play *Women of the Streets* which John Kennedy offered to publicise for him. John told two of the actresses to stand outside the stage door during the interval and look like prostitutes. When a passing policeman arrested them, John got the story on the front page of every paper in England and the play became a smash.

Another regular at La Caverne was Lionel Bart who wrote comedy songs for the *Billy Cotton Band Show*, the Sunday lunchtime radio show that was a British institution in the fifties. The three men became good friends. They were in their mid-twenties and all of them fancied the same type of good-looking young guy.

Tommy Hicks was a cabin boy on the ocean liner *Mauritania*. In September 1956 he took two weeks off from work to visit his sick mum in London. One evening – cocky, blond and just nineteen – he was playing guitar in a Soho coffee bar when Lionel Bart walked in.

Lionel was dazzled by Tommy and decided at once to form a group with him – the Cavemen. They played at the 2i's, a tiny basement coffee shop that served cappuccino and Coke. Lionel painted the walls black with two large eyes over the stage but he left the thinners out of the paint and people kept turning up with dry-cleaning bills.

Lionel talked about the group to John Kennedy and persuaded him to come and see them. John took an instant fancy to Tommy and came back the next night with Larry Parnes who was equally taken with the lad. Kennedy and Parnes knew nothing about pop music but they decided to manage Tommy and change his second name from Hicks to Steele. Kennedy phoned Hugh Mendl, a talent scout at Decca, and when Hugh saw Tommy perform he agreed to record him the next day.

The song they recorded started out as one of Lionel's comedy numbers. 'We were called the Cavemen,' Tommy explains. 'We played country songs and comedy. Our theme song was "Rock With The Cavemen", and it was a joke, a spoof, the sort of thing Monty Python might have done.' But Kennedy pulled one of his stunts. He booked Tommy at a debutantes' ball and persuaded the girls to scream. The press were on hand to witness it and the next day Tommy hit the tabloids – 'Deb's delight' – 'Posh girls scream for cockney Tom'.

When 'Rock With The Cavemen' became a smash, Tommy Steele found himself dubbed 'Britain's Elvis'. This was far from the truth. Novelist Colin MacInnes called him 'a thoroughly English singer', and TV producer Jack Good was puzzled by his strange stage costume, 'a pale-blue bellboy outfit'. But what impressed Good was Tommy's sparkling personality and the fact that 'his eyes twinkled and his mouth was full of wonderful shining teeth'.

British teenagers had a preference for American music but they wanted someone of their own age and nationality to sing it. Tommy's biggest hit wasn't a British song, it was 'Singing

The Blues', a cover version of an American record. The US version got to No. 1 first, then Tommy's version replaced it.

To the press, Larry Parnes boasted 'Tommy Steele is a better performer than Elvis.'

The kids weren't fooled. They knew Tommy was no match for Presley – his sex appeal was nothing more than a sweet dumb grin. But they didn't care. They didn't love Tommy Steele because he was sexy, they loved him because he'd managed to do something never done before in the British music business. Be young!

Before the mid-fifties the British music industry had been under the control of a select group of people – the music publishers. The biggest hits were from Broadway shows. Middle-aged people bought sheet music to take home with the evening paper. For music publishers it was a comfortable business and they thought it would go on forever.

Singers from the USA like Guy Mitchell and Johnnie Ray could pull huge audiences, but home-grown talent was something of a joke. Dickie Valentine, one of Britain's biggest artists, had an act that consisted of impressions of American stars. David Whitfield sang songs like 'The Book' and 'I Believe' and claimed to communicate directly with God as he did so. Frankie Vaughan performed wearing a top hat and looked like Victor Mature imitating Al Jolson. Ronnie Carroll looked like Victor Mature imitating Judy Garland.

Broadcasting in Britain was controlled by the BBC. There were only ten hours a week during which pop records were allowed to be played but there were endless programmes of live music. On these, different bands and singers would perform all the currently popular songs. Because of this, it was the *songs* not the singers that became popular.

Every hit song would be recorded by several singers. Wally Ridley was an A&R man at EMI, the person responsible for choosing the right song for the right artist. 'Every month each record company had an A&R meeting to which they would invite all the publishers. At EMI, we sat around and chose the songs we wanted to record. Then the publishers went on to Decca where most of the best songs would get chosen again. If a song was really good it would end up with four versions – one by each company.'

New Musical Express published a weekly list of the Top Ten songs compiled from sales of sheet music. These were sung live by different performers each week on a Friday evening radio show called *Hit Parade*. Alternatively, on Sunday evenings the Top Ten could be heard played from records on Radio Luxembourg, a programme with wavering reception from mainland Europe.

At that time, a recording artist's income came from live performances; making records was just a way of getting better known. Frank Coachworth worked at Chappell's, one of the biggest publishing companies. 'Mostly, we got big American songs. Whenever we got a new one, we'd phone a few artists and they'd come rushing in and beg to be the first to record it. But when it came to recording, artists weren't given much of a say in things.'

Lita Roza was proud of being a quality big-band singer. She was signed to Decca where her A&R man was Dick Rowe, later to become famous for turning down the Beatles. Among singers he worked with, Dick was well-known for his lack of sensitivity. One day he called Lita to say he had a new song for her. 'He had an American hit by Patti Page that he wanted me to cover for the English market. When I got to the studio and heard the song, I said: 'I'm not recording that rubbish.''

Dick insisted that she sing it, so Lita sang it through just once, then told him: 'I'm never going to sing that ever again.'

The song was 'How Much Is That Doggie In The Window'. Lita's once-sung version went to No. 1, the first time ever for a British female vocalist, but as promised, she never sang the song again. Later she told the collective heads of Decca how upset she was about the way they treated their artists. 'To try to calm me down they sent me a new Hoover.'

Whenever a song was played on the radio, or whenever a piece of sheet music or record was sold, the publisher received a royalty. Individually these payments were minimal but collectively they amounted to millions. The big publishers, like Boosey & Hawkes or Keith Prowse, were content with slowly accumulating royalties of less than a penny a record and made their real income from printing and distributing sheet music. But the big four record companies – Decca, EMI, Philips and Pye – wanted quick profits. Their raw material was vinyl which was cheap. With a hit song pressed into it, vinyl could be sold at a mark-up of twenty times its original cost, but record sales had reached a ceiling. To sell larger quantities of them record companies needed new avenues of promotion.

At EMI, Wally Ridley made hit after hit, but he was aware that most people in the industry still thought of records as secondary to sheet music. 'Publishers saw records as just another way to boost sales of sheet music. Artists thought of them as a way of making themselves better known. No one saw them as the major focus of the music industry. This was because there were so few opportunities to hear records on the radio. I would produce a big hit record, but nearly every time I heard the song on the radio it would be someone performing it live.'

In 1955 the BBC finally agreed to introduce *Pick of the Pops*, a new programme which would play currently popular records, but it still wasn't the Top Ten chart programme the record companies wanted. It was ten records chosen at random from the best-selling twenty-five and presented by Franklin Englemann, as old and square as they come.

Then, for the record companies, a miracle happened. Rock 'n' roll arrived.

'Rock Around The Clock' wasn't only a record and a movie, it was also a message. Across Britain, kids stood in the aisles at their local cinema and shouted choruses back at the screen.

'See ya later alligator,' sang Bill Haley.

'In a while crocodile,' the kids yelled back.

In 1956, most of these kids lived in houses without central heating, many with outdoor loos. Parents had no spare money. New clothes were bought when old ones wore out and having fun was reserved for special occasions like birthdays or Christmas.

At school, discipline took precedence over education. Billy Fury, who became a rock 'n' roll star five years later, remembered being beaten by his teacher during the last minute of his last day at school. 'He thrashed me six times on my hand. With each stroke I laughed louder, until the bell rang as he brought down the cane for the sixth time. Then I was free. I hated school: it was like being in jail. Now I was being released, a free man. I went wild, running out of school shouting 'I'm free, I'm free, I'm free.'"

When Bill Haley sang 'Let's rip it up, we're gonna rip it up at the joint tonight', it was the best thing kids had ever heard. Whether it meant 'let's have some fun', or whether it was really a cry to 'rip things up', made little difference, it united the younger generation all over Britain.

The name rock 'n' roll had been brewing for some time. In 1924, American blues singer Trixie Smith recorded 'My Man Rocks Me With One Steady Roll', and in 1934 there was a Hollywood movie that included a song called 'Rock And Roll'. It was Alan Freed, an American DJ in the fifties, who changed the 'and' to an 'n' and started using the phrase to describe 'rhythm & blues' played by white musicians rather than black. Then Bill Haley brought rock 'n' roll to the attention of young Britons.

Haley had been a country & western singer. In 1954 he was asked to record 'Rock Around The Clock' but at the time it did nothing. A year later it was picked up by MGM and used for the title sequence of their movie *The Blackboard Jungle*. The film was about violence in the classroom and the subject matter brushed off on the song, giving it a sense of anarchy. American teenagers picked up on it; so did Columbia Pictures who cashed in on it with a low-budget movie of the same name. Six months later *Rock Around the Clock* took off around the world.

In Britain this coincided with the first ever explosion of youth spending.

Kids had discovered fashion and were dressing in Edwardian-style clothes – velvet-collared coats, tight-fitting trousers, suede shoes with thick spongy soles. These were 'teddy boys', and when they heard Bill Haley's music, they adopted it as their own.

Ten years later, Tony Calder would be running Immediate Records, but in 1955 he was a fifteen-year-old teddy boy living with his family in Southampton. 'I had a blue coat and black shoes with grey crepe soles. My grandparents used to work on the *Queen Elizabeth* and *Queen Mary*, so I knew everyone on the boats. I had this guy who brought me stuff back from New York. I had a shoe-lace tie in dark blue. The trousers were 12 inches to the bottoms, I remember that because they were 14 inches and I got my mother to take them in. And I had my hair in a duck's arse with a quiff.'

In America, rock 'n' roll was seen as white men singing black men's music. The political right thought it was a communist plot. The White Citizens Council of North Alabama denounced rock 'n' roll as part of a plot to undermine the morals of the nation. 'It is sexualistic, unmoralistic and ... brings people of both races together.'

In Britain in the mid-fifties, there was no communist paranoia and no racial tension. In teen parlance, anyone black was a spade and among hip young city-dwellers spades were welcome. Britain's first post-war black star was Shirley Bassey, totally middle-of-the-road and totally over-the-top in her projection, but her blackness made her hip for teenagers.

When singer Kenny Lynch was four his family moved to the East End. 'We were the only black family there. There was no racial prejudice. When I went to school, I was the only black boy in the classroom. It was more of a novelty than anything else, it made me feel like I was on-stage. It set me up for a career as an entertainer. By the time I was seven I was singing with a local dance band. That was the year the war ended.'

For Britons at the end of a long war, being black or white wasn't the problem; the big divide was between young and old. Adults told their children 'we fought the war for you' and kids were sick to death of hearing about it. They searched for a new identity and found it in a new word.

'Teenager' came from the slogan 'we are living in the *Teen Age*', thought up by an American advertising agency in the early fifties. Young people liked being called teenagers, it made them feel like members of an exclusive club and helped them get away from the dreary world of their parents. Rock 'n' roll helped even more, it was escapist and made things seem like they were changing. The odd thing was, Bill Haley, the person responsible for bringing it to them, was plump, in his mid-thirties, and with a kiss-curl more absurd than Hitler's moustache. When Haley toured England and arrived by boat at Southampton docks, Tony Calder and his friends were waiting to greet him dressed in their best teddy-boy gear. 'He came off the boat and the minute we saw him, someone shouted, "Fucking hell, he's old – he looks like my granddad." So we left and went home. And we never played his records again – ever.'

In 1956, while I was on the road with the Johnny Dankworth Orchestra, a new craze erupted that stemmed the tide of rock 'n' roll for a short while.

In the past trad jazz had been the only alternative to the sickly romantic pop of the day. Now with the explosion of rock 'n' roll touring bands had to adapt. To try and compete, they began to allow their rhythm sections to play a part of the set alone with a singer. From this came an enormous new craze, skiffle.

Lonnie Donegan was the banjo player with Chris Barber's band. 'We went into the studio to make a band album. Chris said he wanted to record some vocals. The engineer reluctantly said: "OK, you want to sing something, there's the mike, the tape's running, I'm going for a cup of tea."'

At that session, Donegan sang an American folk song, 'Rock Island Line', and when Chris Barber's album was completed the song was included. The record was released on Pye, the third of Britain's big four record companies, and it became Britain's first skiffle hit.

Donegan sang through his nose. When his record went to No. 1 Britain went adenoidal. Kids everywhere walked round the streets singing in nasal American accents accompanied by dustbin lids, tin pans, paper and combs. 'Rock Island Line' was even a hit in America where Donegan appeared on the *Perry Como Show* with guest-star actor Ronald Reagan.

The BBC liked skiffle; it was nicely middle-class. There were no electric guitars and it didn't seem dangerous, so they gave it a programme of its own, *Saturday Skiffle Club*, the first BBC radio programme aimed at the youth pop market.

Skiffle clubs sprang up in cellars below coffee shops, packed with sweating teenagers wearing jeans and roll-neck sweaters bought from Millets, an army surplus store which was where Lonnie Donegan had worked before he had his hit record.

Perhaps he shouldn't have left his job in such a hurry. His total income from recording 'Rock Island Line', the song that launched the skiffle boom, was his £3.50 session fee.

Shortly after skiffle started, America came up with a new rock 'n' roll singer, Elvis Presley, a teenager throbbing with sex. British kids immediately wanted one of their own. But what they got instead was Tommy Steele.

Tommy may have been a poor substitute for the real thing but when he took off every British record company wanted someone like him. Copycat rock 'n' roll stars sprang up all over the place. You pushed your arse into tight jeans, waved your credentials in the face of the audience, and became an instant front-man for the new generation. The search for rock 'n' roll stars became something of a cottage industry and leading it were Larry Parnes and Lionel Bart, both of whom had an instinctive feeling for the teenage boys that girls would fancy – the ones they fancied themselves.

Around that time, a friend of mine who knew Parnes told me about his flat. 'It's always full of boys – not Larry's singing stars, but other ones – boys who come to see him hoping to be chosen. If Larry likes the look of them, he gives them a clean white T-shirt and tells them to hang around. If a boy's wearing a black T-shirt, it means Larry's had him already and his friends can have a go if they want to. You ought to meet him. He might like you.'

I wasn't sure I wanted to be 'liked' by Larry Parnes but the chance to meet him was irresistible. We arranged to meet at a Chinese restaurant where he turned up with Lionel Bart. During most of the meal I was hardly spoken to, just stared at, but as he was paying the bill Larry asked, 'Can you sing?'

'No,' I told him, 'but I can play the trumpet, and I've been working as a bandboy for Johnny Dankworth.'

'Intriguing,' he said. 'Perhaps we could meet later.'

I turned the offer down, but it was impossible not to be fascinated by Parnes and his aura of success.

Like most managers who followed him, Larry Parnes was something of a loner. His family background made it difficult for him to be open about his homosexuality so he was unable to have a permanent relationship, but as a pop manager he had the perfect excuse for surrounding himself with the type of young men he fancied. He found himself a comfortable niche and took full advantage of it. Behind the scenes he was authoritarian. He created his artists' image, controlled their private lives, tried to keep them away from drink and drugs, and made them go to bed before midnight (sometimes, it was rumoured, with himself).

Parnes was obsessed with giving his boys new names. It was as if by changing their names he could wipe out their past and make them his very own. When singer Clive Powell turned up, Parnes told him: 'You come from the same county as George Formby, and you're going to be famous. You can be called Georgie Fame!' But when he wanted to change Joe Brown's name to Elmer Twitch, Joe refused point blank.

Parnes always liked to claim that his 'stable' of boys was one big happy family – Joe Brown, Dickie Pride, Tommy Bruce, Johnny Gentle, Duffy Power, Georgie Fame, Johnny Goode, Vince Eager – but he saw a class distinction between himself and his singers and exploited it. Joe Brown worked for three years without a single night off. 'Some of the gigs were miles apart. One night we did Bristol, the next night Torquay, and back up to Preston. Then it was in London by eight o'clock the next morning for *Saturday Club*. It was anywhere and everywhere for £15 per week. Three solid years and then my head went. I had a breakdown and got the shakes. My mother called the doctor, who said: "He's got to stop working." She phoned Larry Parnes, who said: "What d'you mean stop working. Has he broken a leg?" Within minutes he'd sent two Harley Street specialists to see me to make sure I wasn't swinging the lead. It was ridiculous – he gave me six days off, six bloody days after three years.'

Parnes's preference for boys from a working-class background fitted neatly with the outdated social etiquette of record companies. At that time George Martin worked at EMI's Abbey Road studios in Maida Vale producing records for the Parlophone label. 'In the studios, producers were expected to wear suits and ties, just as they did in the office. Engineers wore white coats to distinguish them as being of a lower class. Recording artists too were considered to be socially inferior – a bit like actors – not quite decent people – tolerated because they brought in money, but always expected to be of somewhat dubious character.'

Class distinction was deeply engrained in the record business. Companies were controlled and run by people from middle-class backgrounds, mostly from public schools, and artists were expected to come from the lower classes. For decades to come, disdain for artists within record companies would continue even though people on both sides of the fence had long stopped coming from different social backgrounds. At EMI these things started to change when a new chairman was appointed, Joseph Lockwood.

Lockwood saw at once that EMI was heading for ruin. The company had lost its licensing deals with the big American companies CBS and RCA, and Lockwood's predecessor, Sir Ernest Fisk, had failed to recognise the value of the LP to classical music. As a result most of EMI's classical artists had left and gone to Decca.

Decca had spotted the potential of the LP and now dominated the classical music market. Its chairman was Sir Edward Lewis, a pompous autocrat who in 1929 had bought a small company called Duophone, then built it up impressively. But in the field of popular music Sir Edward was lost. For pop music he relied on the advice of Bill Townsley, his general manager, who in turn relied on Decca's two most important employees, Hugh Mendl, known as 'the company gent', and Dick Rowe, known as 'the company spiv'. If these two made a wrong move, Sir Edward Lewis would have no way of knowing until it was too late.

In contrast, EMI's new chairman had an instinctive understanding of the youth market. He'd realised that the sound of rock 'n' roll guitars could not be reproduced by sheet music alone. Rock 'n' roll struck fear into the hearts of music publishers, but for record companies it was their future. George Martin found himself given a freer hand. 'When Joe Lockwood came in he changed things. He recognised where the money was coming from and did something about it. He instinctively realised that pop music was going to be more commercially important than classical music.'

Joe Lockwood's masterstroke was to buy Capitol Records in America for 8.5 million dollars. Two years later Capitol was generating sales of 35 million dollars a year and

EMI was the owner of Frank Sinatra, Dean Martin, Peggy Lee, Nat King Cole, and later, the Beach Boys. But in some things, Lockwood was surprisingly old-fashioned. He ran the company like a public school – employees dressed correctly, had their names entered in a book if they came late, and were not allowed to play music in their offices. Within the company he was feared – even George Martin felt in awe of him. 'I think he encouraged that reputation. One year, two days before Christmas, the attendants put their caps out for tips in the cloakroom. He told them the company didn't do that kind of thing and fired them on the spot, which caused a very bad feeling in the studios.'

To employees, Lockwood could seem inflexible and class-conscious, but with artists and entrepreneurs, many of whom were out of his social class, he had an easy manner. Muriel Young produced EMI's weekly radio show which went out on Radio Luxembourg. 'The Friday spectacular was an audience show recorded in the company's own studio. Joe would often wander down. I think he was bit star-struck. He was a cuddly bear – a sweetie with the artists.'

It wasn't only Muriel Young who saw him in that light; Lockwood had a whole network of friends who thought of him as humorous and easy-going. Like Larry Parnes and Lionel Bart, Joe was gay, and although he worked in an era when it was impossible in his position to be open about it, away from work he dropped his austere image and entered into the frothy social life of gay society. This played a major part in EMI's huge success with pop music in the sixties. For other gays in the music business, having easy access to its chairman made EMI an obvious first choice as record company.

*

All these things could be learned from sitting on a band bus with a bunch of singers and musicians for eight hours a day. But, for me, getting further into the business looked more difficult. When I'd originally planned to be a musician I'd chosen the trumpet, the dominant voice in jazz, but in rock 'n' roll terms that would mean being a singer which was something I couldn't even consider. At thirteen I'd sung beautifully in the school choir, but after my voice broke I could never stay in tune. So for the moment I continued to roll joints and carry musical instruments in and out of every venue in Britain that featured live bands.

Jazz clubs – just one of them at first, and then lots – found there was a market on Sundays for opening from two to six in the afternoon. They weren't allowed to sell alcohol, but the substitute attraction was darkness, and teenagers flocked to them. On-stage a band would play, but not many people stood in front of it, they would be lying around on cushions, snogging or going even further. Chas Chandler, later to become bass player with the Animals, came to London and visited the Cy Laurie Club. 'There were no lights and no alcohol ... When we saw it, we couldn't believe it. On Tyneside, people went to clubs to fight. What they did at this club was one hell of a lot more fun. It was like a huge dormitory.'

Club owners soon found that live music wasn't needed at all. Playing records was cheaper and it meant they could turn out the stage lights, which was better for smooching. Then they noticed that with records, more people were dancing, so they tried it out in the evenings. In Leeds, Jimmy Savile had known about this for years. 'I was doing my own record nights, getting over a thousand youngsters in at a shilling a head. But the Musicians' Union were so protective I had to pay a band to sit in the corner and keep quiet. Then I started lunchtime sessions for schoolkids at threepence each, playing records from midday to two in the afternoon. Teachers complained that the kids came back to class in the wrong frame of mind – which meant "happy"!'

Jimmy became Britain's first nationally known DJ, famous for his Havana cigars and tartan suits. More importantly, he influenced young people to dance to records rather than live music. It was odd – dance halls, perfectly suited to live music, were now playing records – radio, perfectly suited to playing records, continued to be obsessed with live music, and as far as rock 'n' roll was concerned, radio was a barren land.

The Musicians' Union insisted that opening the airwaves to records would destroy the livelihood of British musicians. As a result, there were just four programmes a week that played pop records, all by request – *Housewives' Choice*, Monday to Friday; *Family Favourites*, twice a week; and *Down Your Way* and *Desert Island Discs*, once a week. Don Black, now a songwriter with over fifty chart hits to his credit, was then a song plugger. 'I had to go to the BBC and talk to whoever was producing *Two-Way Family Favourites*. I had to try to persuade them to play what I was plugging, for instance, Doris Day singing "Que Sera Sera". If you got it on, it would go into next week's charts. The programme was *that* powerful. You could get a raise for getting a record on that programme.'

These programmes were supposed to be 'request' programmes, but they weren't. The producers chose the records they wanted then searched for requests that fitted them. None of these producers would consider playing more than one record a week that could even loosely be termed rock 'n' roll. Because of this, record companies persuaded their rock 'n' roll stars to become all-round entertainers. Most A&R men showed no understanding of rock 'n' roll as a youth art-form, nor did they have respect for its performers.

Record producer Mickie Most was then a teenage singer. 'The A&R man would say, "You're in the studio on Friday, this is the song you'll sing." You'd work out the key with an arranger, go to the studio and it was all done in three hours, a bit like going to the dentist. You'd sing in a booth with the band playing outside, and after a few takes, a voice would come over the PA, "That's a good take. That's it." You weren't invited upstairs to hear it. You wouldn't hear the record until it was pressed and about to come out. If you didn't like it, it was too bad. In the studio, the rule was: "Where the carpet begins, the artist stops."'

The attitude of record companies delighted the music publishers who at first had felt so threatened by the new music. It meant that rock 'n' roll singers would remain captive to the old Tin Pan Alley system – solo singers, backed by session musicians, their songs chosen for them by A&R men.

Between them, the Musicians' Union, the BBC and the big music publishers seemed to have halted the march of rock 'n' roll. When *My Fair Lady* opened in 1957, its publisher, Chappell's, announced that they were doing the biggest business ever in their hundred years of operation. But just as British rock 'n' roll was on the verge of extinction, a new champion emerged – someone who would change the history of popular music.

Jack Good was the person responsible for getting rock 'n' roll on to British television. When he left university he was a bespectacled drama student planning a career in Shakespearean theatre, but by chance he wandered into a cinema in Islington and saw *Rock Around the Clock*. 'Bill Haley was wonderful ... I'd never heard rock 'n' roll at all before. I was a snob. I used to go to promenade concerts, but when I saw those kids bopping up and down in the aisles, I was converted like St Paul on the road to Damascus.'

The BBC was planning a youth-orientated show to be called *Six-Five Special*. Jack Good was chosen as the producer 'because I was the youngest person in the building at the time. They had no intention of allowing rock 'n' roll on it, just some "suitable" pop music. The programme also had to be educational, so there was going to be a magazine section – mountain climbing for boys, make-up tips for girls, a boy's choir, a team of Hungarian acrobats.'

Jack asked if he could have teenagers dancing freely in the studio and was told, 'Certainly not. Teenagers would "break up the set"... the British public wouldn't want that sort of person "bopping" on the floor.'

Jack was determined not to be overruled so he made conventional scenery and put it on casters. Before the show he let BBC executives inspect it; when they were gone he wheeled the scenery away and waved teenage kids on to the set. 'I decided that rock 'n' roll wasn't the music itself, it was the *response* to the music. It was a riot. All those who loathed rock 'n' roll were switching on to see what horror would appear next. The head of Light Entertainment came up to the control room in the middle of the show and said: "You can't do this!" I said: "I'm doing it. Cut to Camera Five."'

It was Jack's middle-class university background that had got him into the BBC. Tommy Steele remembers that 'he always wore a suit and tie and had marbles in his mouth ... like a posh schoolteacher'. But even when Jack became Britain's 'Emperor of Rock 'n' Roll' the BBC neither approved of him nor recognised the value of the youth market he'd captured. 'We had twelve million viewers, but I was only on eighteen pounds a week.'

Among rock 'n' roll stars introduced to the public by Jack Good were Johnny Kidd, who dressed as a pirate, Wee Willie Harris, with bright red hair, and Screaming Lord Sutch, who pretended to be Jack the Ripper. But among these gimmicky British rock 'n' rollers there was one authentic American – Gene Vincent.

On his records Vincent sounded like a cut-throat street fighter. Jack decided a bit of tough imagery would enhance his show so he flew Vincent to Britain, but at the airport the American failed to live up to his evil image. 'I'm mighty pleased to meet you, suh,' he told Jack, and bowed like a Southern gentleman.

Vincent had suffered a motorcycle accident and wore leg irons which gave him a limp. Jack liked it and pictured Vincent as a character from *Hamlet*, dressed in black with a hunch and a medallion. 'On the first show I made Gene walk down a staircase so the limp would be more obvious, but he came down the stairs too carefully. I had to run round the back of the set and yell at him: 'Limp, you bugger.''

Throughout the music industry Jack Good became revered, and it sometimes amused him to take advantage of his position. One day, walking down Shaftesbury Avenue after a good lunch, he had an irresistible urge to take a nap. 'I could hardly remain on two feet and my eyelids dropped as if lead-weighted. Then it occurred to me that I was near the new offices of Lionel Bart's publishing company, Apollo Music. I staggered into the shiny reception. The smart secretary looked up from her typewriter. 'Can I help you?' she enquired. 'Yes,' I mumbled uneasily. 'My name is Jack Good and I wondered if I might sleep here for an hour?' She batted not a mascaraed eyelid and went to fetch Lionel's personal assistant, a very charming lady, and his able manager, Leslie Paul. They were kindness itself. You'd think they were quite used to people dropping in to have a doss. Ronnie Carroll in fact was there and he confessed that he'd only just woken up, such is the seductive luxury of the place. I was ushered into a lovely unoccupied room, drew up a beautiful turquoise armchair and dropped off easily into the land of Nod.'

At the height of its success, Jack Good's production of *Six-Five Special* proved too anarchic for the BBC, so Jack left and went to ITV to direct a new programme called *Oh Boy!*. 'I wanted pace and attack – next number, next number – if you were tired of someone they should be off and the next act should be on. The audience had to explode and the lights flash on cue. I wanted the whole thing to feel like a Cadillac, zooming down a freeway.'

Just then, Britain's fourth major record company, Philips, owned by the Dutch electronics firm of the same name, felt rich enough to risk investing in a little rock 'n' roll. A few years earlier, when EMI lost its contract with CBS, Philips had been quick to take it over. The company then benefited from an astonishing unbroken run of twenty-six weeks at No. 1, twenty-two of them with maudlin hits from American artists like Doris Day and Johnnie Ray, followed by four weeks of British artists Anne Shelton and Frankie Vaughan. On the back of this unprecedented success Philips had now decided to enter the youth market for the first time.

Jack Baverstock, Philips's head of A&R, asked Lionel Bart to find someone suitable and Lionel came up with a boy called Reg Smith. He was sent to Larry Parnes for assessment and Parnes agreed to manage him provided he could change his name. The boy wouldn't agree, so they settled the matter with two tosses of a coin, one for his first name and one for his second. Reg lost both times and became Marty Wilde.

Larry Parnes then persuaded Jack Good to use Marty Wilde as the resident star of his new show *Oh Boy!*. To begin with it went well, but after a few shows Wilde turned up in a grey mohair jacket that flared under the studio lights. When Jack said he couldn't wear it, Larry Parnes flew into such a rage that Good had to have him removed from the theatre by a security guard. Good's quarrel over the suit left him free to replace Marty Wilde with someone else, and he already had someone in mind. His attention had been caught by someone dark, young and sexy, someone he thought might be the future of British rock 'n' roll, a boy called Harry Webb who had rechristened himself Cliff Richard.

Cliff was olive-skinned, pouted a lot, and had beautiful thighs. Today he admits, 'I was a carbon copy of Elvis. All I had was a leg, a guitar and a lip.'

Like the Beatles, Cliff had been turned down by Decca and then signed to EMI. There, record producer Norrie Paramor chose an American hit for him to cover, 'Schoolboy Crush', which Jack Good still remembers well. 'It was a real drippy song. I hated drippy songs.'

On the 'B' side there was an original song, 'Move It'. When Jack heard it he said, 'If this record had been a product of Sun

Records [the original recording company of Elvis Presley and Jerry Lee Lewis], I should not have been surprised ... But when one considers it is the product of a seventeen-year-old boy from Cheshunt, Hertfordshire, the mind just boggles.'

So EMI turned the record over.

Jack told Cliff to curl his lip and wear outrageous clothes. 'He didn't want me to be too much like Elvis,' remembers Cliff. 'He made me cut off my sideburns.' On screen it looked as if Cliff was giving a completely spontaneous performance, something the cameramen were lucky to capture. Jack Good remembers it being the result of endless direction. 'Cliff and I spent hours getting things absolutely right for his first TV appearance. Every blink, every change in the pose of his head, every gesture had to be worked out and made meaningful.'

Particularly noticeable was Cliff's odd way of grabbing his right upper forearm with his left hand and looking anguished. Jack had told him to pretend he'd been asleep and had been woken up by someone sticking a hypodermic in his arm – an inspired vision of what rock 'n' roll was to become.

The end result of Cliff's performance was to look provocative in a totally new way. The *NME* wrote, 'His violent hip-swinging was revolting, hardly the kind of performance any parent would wish their children to see. He was wearing so much eyeliner he looked like Jayne Mansfield.'

'At that time,' Jack Good says, '*NME* and *Melody Maker* couldn't stand rock 'n' roll. The furthest they would move from Tin Pan Alley slop was trad jazz.'

Cliff's strange crotch-jerking had none of the teasing smoothness of Elvis's hip movements, it seemed to be more personal, something from his own erotic experience. To the older generation this made it both more sexual and more shocking. But by his third record, EMI had persuaded him to cut it out. They wanted to broaden his appeal and sell him to a family market.

Cliff's backing group, the Shadows, also became famous. Their speciality was to perform while walking with strange criss-cross steps as if they were trying to untangle their feet from a mike cable. Their influence was enormous. Within a year, every sixteen-year-old in Britain was capable of untangling his feet from a mike cable while playing the guitar and looking straight in front him.

Muriel Young booked Cliff and the Shadows on her EMI radio show more often than any other artist. 'When I first met Cliff he was outrageously trying to do an Elvis. He was a wriggly-hips boy. He was still singing with the Shadows, and when Jet Harris left the group they got in a new boy, Licorice Locking. Licorice was a roaring Jehovah's Witness and he started to work on the boys. He'd pretty well converted Hank Marvin before Peter Gormley, their manager, spotted what was happening and quickly sacked him. But soon after that Cliff became a born-again Christian. From then on there were no more wriggles.'

Cliff calmed down and became just another company product. When he finally got his first No. 1 he was no longer singing rock 'n' roll, it was just another pop song – 'Living Doll', provided by Lionel Bart. But for the future of British pop it didn't matter. The chain of events that had led Jack Good to move to ITV had also set in motion a chain of events that would eventually revitalise the British pop business.

With Jack Good out of the way, the BBC decided to cut back on the amount of rock 'n' roll in his old TV programme, *Six-*

Five Special. To compensate they increased the amount of their favoured 'safe' music, trad jazz, and this caused a resurgence of interest in it. Humphrey Lyttelton, Chris Barber, Acker Bilk, Mick Mulligan, Kenny Ball, all were getting regular hits, and all over London jazz clubs began to boom again. The music played in them was seen as serious and 'ethnic', quite unlike the commercialised jazz music of big bands like the Johnny Dankworth Orchestra.

The small jazz bands who played in these clubs started to book guest artists from America to come and sing with them. Bands often chose singers who were a complete mismatch for them, like Sister Rosetta Tharpe who came to perform with Mick Mulligan's Band. George Melly, the band's regular singer, enjoyed the challenge. 'She was a gospel singer, and we were a revivalist jazz band. It didn't quite fit, but she seemed to enjoy it. Off-stage, she was very flirtatious and talked a lot about Jesus. And she was pretty good at knocking back the brandy too.'

But, importantly, most of these singers were black and many sang the blues. Their presence in Britain caused the BBC to take a new interest in the history of black music. And because they regarded this as culturally superior to other forms of English and American popular music they gave it considerable airtime.

By moving away from rock 'n' roll, the resulting programmes began to build a new young audience for American rhythm & blues.

CHAPTER THREE

BEAT BOMB

Maureen was plump and rather willing, and she caused me to lose my job.

After a gig I would pack the instruments in the boot of the band bus and lay the double-bass along the back seat, but not when Maureen showed up. In the fifties, there were no floods of groupies to follow pop stars around the country. For the Johnny Dankworth band there were just one or two girls available in each regional area and one of them was Maureen. She lived in Wolverhampton and would go to any gig within a reasonable range, providing she was delivered back home afterwards. During the delivery process she would offer her services on the back seat to anyone who wanted them. If he was up to it, the bandboy would come last, but I wasn't – there was more pleasure to be had from carrying the drum kit up six flights of stairs at the Llandudno Empire, which happened to be one of the places Maureen turned up at.

After the gig that evening, in the process of organising things for the band's pleasure, I overlooked the double-bass and left it lying in the street outside the theatre. In the middle of the night, on the way to Dudley, the bass player discovered his instrument wasn't on the bus and sent me hitchhiking back to collect it. When I arrived it was mid-morning on Sunday. It was summer and there were thousands of holidaymakers in the streets, but the double bass was lying on its side on the pavement just as I'd left it with everyone walking carefully around it. I carried it to the station and set off to Dudley by train. I changed at Birmingham and Leeds and arrived at nine the next morning only to be told the band had already left. When I got to the next gig I was fired.

Back in London I picked up odd jobs here and there as a trumpet player – an East End wedding on a Saturday night or a rock 'n' roll session in a pub. Mostly, these jobs were found by going to Archer Street in Soho where musicians hung out.

Soho was changing. There was a strange mixture of people – leftover teddy boys mixing uneasily with a younger crowd who wore jeans and bright-coloured sweaters. Teenagers strummed guitars while prostitutes watched from doorways and local policemen strolled around openly picking up small bribes. Many of the old cafés had given way to espresso coffee bars which blared rock 'n' roll from their jukeboxes.

Soho had always been the haunt of the arty set, like jazz singer George Melly, who spent all his spare time there. 'It was full of wonderful failures as well as people who were having huge success. We spent our time at the Colony Club, run by Muriel Belcher, a marvellous lesbian, and it was packed with the crème de la crème of Soho, in other words, the drunks de la drunks – Francis Bacon, Dan Farson, people like that – the older set. But of course, in the streets we saw these strange new apparitions called teenagers.'

One of the apparitions George saw might have been me. At eighteen I still qualified as a teenager, but being one wasn't really my scene. Eventually though, I fell in with a crowd who'd formed their own equivalent of the Colony Club in a café in Berwick Street. Its juke box was a mix of rock 'n' roll and rhythm & blues, and its clientele was young, most of them talking about making it in music. As a way of rejecting the habits of the older generation, most of them drank coffee rather than alcohol and some of them took drugs. Watching them I became aware for the first time of the effects of drugs on musical styles. Many of the musicians who played modern jazz were hooked on heroin. The ones who liked rhythm & blues smoked grass. Rock 'n' rollers were fast and young and mad about speed.

Speed was amphetamine or Benzedrine. It raised your blood pressure and opened your bronchial tubes. Your heart raced; you took bigger breaths; you drew in more oxygen and you were instantly energised. During the Second World War both sides used it extensively. British forces were fed more than 72 million amphetamine tablets in an attempt to pep up their fighting spirit. In Japan and America even larger quantities were used, and in Germany doctors injected Hitler with methamphetamine up to eight times a day.

I used to sit around with kids who played guitars and took amphetamines. They told me, 'First it gets your stomach twitching then it spreads all over your body. You want to shout and move and dance. You feel so confident.' For me the reverse was true. When I tried one, instead of feeling confident I felt nervous and jittery and didn't sleep properly for five days.

In 1956 amphetamine tablets were withdrawn from over-the-counter sale but at chemist shops you could still buy the famous B-bomb. This was a Benzedrine inhaler intended for asthma sufferers. Inside was a soggy wad of cotton wool containing 100 times the amount of Benzedrine contained in a single tablet. For hard-up kids, one of these dunked in a cup of cappuccino could keep the party going all night. To buy one you didn't need a prescription, but you had to persuade the chemist your chest was wheezy and your nose stuffed up.

For aspiring rock 'n' roll stars, bursting open a B-bomb was hardly glamorous; the real goal was to have enough money to freak out big-time like the American stars. Young musicians back from Hamburg would recount stories told to them by Gene Vincent which gave a real insight into rock 'n' roll lifestyle in the USA.

Vincent was a speed freak, as were most of the major figures in American rock 'n' roll. One of these was Little Richard, a sexual misfit with a $1,000 a day cocaine and amphetamine habit. After gobbling down a handful of pills he would 'pay a guy with a big penis to have sex with the ladies so I could watch and masturbate while someone was eating my titties'. Another American idol, rock 'n' roll star Jerry Lee Lewis was said to be hooked on Demerol, injecting it into his arms and legs, picking it up from shady pharmacies all over the Deep South.

At the time, these things weren't revealed to the general public, but the young generation of musicians around Soho all knew what their rock 'n' roll heroes were up to. To get a taste of that sort of lifestyle many of them headed for Hamburg, an all-night port with rock 'n' roll bars full of hookers and pills, but I didn't go with them. I still felt more drawn to jazz, so I went to America instead.

I ended up with a job in a dockside pub in Montreal. We worked from 8pm to 3am, twenty minutes on, twenty minutes off, seven days a week. To keep his staff going night after night at this pace, the manager kept a box of bennies in his office. In return for twenty-five cents being knocked off their weekly money, anyone could have one whenever they wanted.

Seamen would arrive straight off a newly docked boat after six weeks at sea with a thousand dollars in their pocket. Our job was to help them spend it all in the very first place they went into. I'd come to America looking to play jazz but this wasn't the place. Here we played pop songs, four of us – bass, drums, trumpet and piano. We sat cramped on a tiny stage at the front of a pub filled with tables and chairs. Most of the clientele were sailors and the rest were prostitutes, the waiters were part-time professional wrestlers. The toilets were in front of the bandstand to the right and between 1am and 2am every night they overflowed and ran past the front of the bandstand. To go to them, every drunk in the pub would pass directly in front of us. As they came out again, Pierre, the French-Canadian pianist, solicited them for a song request. He knew every tune that ever existed and would play whatever they asked for provided they put a minimum of two dollars in the glass tumbler on the piano lid. At the end of the evening Pierre took half the proceeds and the rest of us split the other half.

If someone came in with a knife and started fighting, or with a gun and started shooting, we had strict instructions to keep playing. It happened often, but the waiters were good. In seconds, a badly behaved customer could have his facial features obliterated for life, smashed against the huge oak door that led to the kitchen.

There was an ancient whore who always sat in front of the band stand. She was in her mid-fifties with no teeth and no knickers and kept her dress pulled high enough for us to inspect the quality of the goods. One night as we played and watched, she snogged a drunken sailor who vomited in mid-kiss but continued to hold her mouth tightly to his. She allowed him to do so but simultaneously slid her hand into his trouser pocket and removed his wallet. Afterwards she simply wiped her lips and went looking for the next customer.

Another night an Irish seaman requested 'Rose Of Tralee' eleven times, putting a $50 bill into the tumbler on each occasion. When he realised he'd spent all his money he came back looking for a refund. Pierre always pocketed the tips when they reached more than $100, so the tumbler was empty. The Irishman pulled out his pockets to show he was now broke and asked if we could play 'Rose Of Tralee' again. Having already received $550 from him, Pierre obliged, and as he sang the good-humoured Irishman put his hands round Pierre's throat and jokingly pretended to strangle him. Or so we thought, because before Pierre could reach the second chorus he'd turned blue and fallen off the piano stool. That night we finished early and the next night we had a new pianist. It was that sort of place.

Later, when British rock musicians told stories about their experiences in Hamburg there was a familiar ring to them.

Like Montreal, Hamburg's bars had a rowdy dockside crowd with waiters who acted as bouncers. Customers who caused a disturbance were beaten soundly. The rule was, if there was trouble, keep playing.

Every group who worked in Hamburg had stories of the violence that went on. One club owner had a truncheon he used personally on customers after the waiters had first beaten them unconscious. Viv Prince, later of the Pretty Things, bought himself a gas gun for protection. Gene Vincent had a real one, and used it one night against Paul Raven, who later became Gary Glitter.

Paul McCartney made a point of being friendly with the staff in the bar. 'The waiters had a system, a little whistle that could be blown and there would be ten waiters where there was once one. And they were all big body-building guys. They weren't chosen for their waiting abilities.'

Tony Jackson of the Searchers was playing one night when a drunken sailor staggered on-stage and threw ice-cream. 'The bouncers dragged him out into the street and kicked him senseless.'

Tony Sheridan tried to protect himself by looking tough. 'I looked vicious, dressed vicious and said things that made people think twice about getting into an argument with me.' If there was a fight in the club, the band would have no alternative but to play on, which 'helped our own vicious image as we looked down at some guy getting kicked around like a football'.

But all the bands had fun. Apart from sex, booze and pills, there was the fun of baiting Germans. Gerry Marsden's speciality was to mess around with lyrics. 'All my life, I've been waiting – tonight there'll be no masturbating.' German musicians dropping into the club heard the songs and learnt them word for word with no idea of the meaning. Later they could be heard in other bars, straight-faced, singing the same lyrics.

Hamburg was a gestational pit for future British pop stars – the Beatles, Van Morrison, Screaming Lord Sutch, the Pretty Things, Dave Dee, Spencer Davis, Long John Baldry – all of them did their basic rock 'n' roll training in the same city. The training was part music, part sex and booze, with some speed thrown in for good measure. 'They'd be on the prellies,' says Paul McCartney, 'and I would have decided I didn't really need one, I was so wired anyway. Or I'd maybe have one pill, while the guys, John in particular, would have four or five.'

Musicians in Hamburg soon learned what American rock 'n' rollers had known for years – that amphetamine was a working drug. Marijuana slowed you down, booze could make you fall off the stage, hard drugs wrecked your life, but amphetamine kept you going all night and gave you the edge you needed.

Since the Stone Age drugs and music have gone hand in hand. Ancient man knew that singing and dancing to a continuous rhythm (which triggers the release of natural opiates in the body) could put the performers into a trancelike state, not unlike dancers on ecstasy in a modern disco. Quite apart from this, simply listening to sublime music of any sort can transport the listener into a dreamlike mood not unlike being under the influence of an hallucinogenic drug.

So music works as a drug. And since drugs are presumed to lead one to another, it's likely that music itself has often been the first step on the path to further drug exploration. For musicians, these drugs then exert an influence on the music they play.

In the case of rock 'n' roll, it was the drug itself that had originally caused the music to happen.

During the days of slavery, cocaine had been used by Southern plantation owners not only for their own well-being but also to hype up slaves and make them work harder on less food. It started in the docks in New Orleans. Slave owners found that a few cents' worth of cocaine given to the men loading and unloading ships gave them more energy than a few cents' worth of food. While slavery continued, blacks often used cocaine stored up from their daily ration for special celebrations.

But when slavery came to an end, across America blacks turned away from cocaine and took to smoking marijuana made from hemp, one of the biggest crops in the South. It calmed them and helped them to deal with poverty and abuse. As a result, black country music was usually slow and laid-back.

For Southern whites, however, the cocaine tradition continued until the drug became scarce at the time of the Second World War. During the war the US army began feeding its soldiers amphetamine tablets, a large proportion of which found their way onto the black market. Young Southern white males found they liked to finish the week on a high – getting fired up, going on the rampage, drinking, speeding, hell-raising – and amphetamine was a ready substitute for cocaine. Later, when ex-army tablets ran out, the drug could still be obtained in the form of Benzedrine, taken by truck drivers all over the South.

Every American performer's road crew had access to bennies, and so did every performer. It was this surging amphetamine energy that eventually turned country music into high-tempo rock 'n' roll. In his biography of Hank Williams, the country singer from Alabama, Chet Flippo tells of Williams visiting a radio station in 1949. 'Hank could barely stand still. He was speeding, full of bennies, the Benzedrine tablets that many touring musicians lived on so they could stay awake. Speed was wonderful for them. They could go without sleep forever.'

At the Wagon Wheel in Natchez, Mississippi, nineteen-year-old Jerry Lee Lewis had played for truck drivers who tipped him for his efforts with Benzedrine pills. And Johnny Cash had got into amphetamines by hanging out with the truckers who transported the stars of the Grand Ole Opry.

So, just as the essence of black country music was the laid-back delivery and slurred voice patterns that came from the use of marijuana, so the essence of early white rock 'n' roll became the unstoppable energy of amphetamine, taken by performers and audience alike.

Listen to the original laid-back recording of 'Hound Dog' sung by Big Mama Thornton, then listen to Elvis Presley's fired-up rendition. The marijuana version and the amphetamine version.

Same song, different drug.

CHAPTER FOUR

CHANGING VOICES

In 1959, aged twenty, I left Canada and came back to London. I'd decided playing music wasn't a suitable profession for me – it involved too much hanging out with other musicians. And I'd realised I was gay.

For some time I'd been covering it up, spending hours with the other guys ogling girls, getting stuck on dates, bullshitting, waiting for the evening somehow to end. Then I faced up to the truth. My friends had penises that stood up when ladies came into the room, mine only did so for young men. Since it obviously had no intention of changing its mind, I decided to fall in with its waywardness rather than fight it.

A few quick decisions had to be made. How open could I be about it? What career should I choose that would not be adversely affected? To whom should I tell the truth, and from whom should I hide it? Working these things out made me think how difficult it would be for a young pop star to face the same situation. With their fans and the press watching their every move, how would someone like Elvis Presley or Cliff Richard cope with a similar realisation about themselves?

For me, the best thing seemed to be to tell the truth while behaving in a perfectly normal manner. If I appeared to be straight while letting people know I wasn't, it would confuse them and leave them nothing with which to attack me. The strange thing was, once I'd established I was gay and had no further need to pretend I was straight, I found girls increasingly attractive. But although having sex with them was easy and enjoyable, being serious about it wasn't. So I mainly stuck to being gay.

I still wanted to work in the music business, probably as a producer or manager, but first I needed money. I became an assistant film editor working with people older than myself who weren't interested in what I did after 6pm. And because I knew music, it wasn't long before I was upgraded to music editor.

By being gay I'd hit the jackpot. To be inside London gay life at the beginning of the sixties was to hear gossip and inside information that made the Dankworth band bus seem like an old people's home. Bars, clubs, private invitations to dinner – the rich and famous from the entertainment world offered inside information to all ears, especially if the ears had a pretty face between them. Suddenly my knowledge of the music business (and theatre, and films and politics) became phenomenal. Famous faces were to be seen everywhere – Noël Coward, Johnnie Ray, Dan Farson, John Gielgud, Bob Boothby, Ronnie Kray, Jeremy Thorpe, Johnny Mathis – it wasn't that they were all hanging around in a gang every night, but I soon got used to seeing one or more of these famous faces in quite surprising surroundings.

Being around these people didn't mean having to be sexually compromised either. I met Billy, a boy my own age, and we moved in together. We were not available to other people, we were a couple, but an attractive one, and we were invited everywhere. Suddenly the gay element of the music industry expanded beyond the original famous three – Larry Parnes, Lionel Bart and Joe Lockwood. Now I was meeting people from record companies, from publishing companies, from booking agencies, even pop stars themselves, all ready and willing to give me an insight into the business.

Dotted around all over London were small private gay clubs – the Calabash in Fulham, run by photographer Leon Maybank, where film stars were often seen; the Festival Club off St Martin's Lane, which was mostly businessmen, and members had their own private key; the very posh Rockingham Club, which had dancing on Sunday evenings, but only for men accompanied by ladies; and in Soho, the A&B which stood for 'Arts & Battledress', a club started during the war as a meeting place for gays of different professions, and which was always full of showbusiness celebrities. But as far as the music business went, the centre of the universe was Lionel Bart's house in Reece Mews.

Lionel was having phenomenal success, discovering act after act and writing songs for all of them. He'd written a musical, *Fings Ain't Wot They Used T'Be*, and another *Oliver!*, which achieved the impossible and became the first-ever British musical to have success in America. Lionel's life was like one big party to which everyone was invited providing they were young, pretty, or in showbusiness.

Norman Newell was one of them. He was the producer at EMI who should have produced 'What Do You Want', the No. 1 record by Adam Faith, the only British rock 'n' roll artist to have got to No. 1 with his very first record. But when he heard the demo, Norman had hated the way Adam sang 'biaybee' instead of 'baby', so on the day of the session he decided to have flu. 'I thought the best solution was to send John Burgess, my assistant producer,' he explained.

The arranger that day was John Barry, who later became famous for scoring the James Bond movies. He'd scored some striking pizzicato strings to complement Adam's gimmicky voice, but when Norman first heard the finished record he thought it was dreadful and told John, 'It's horrendous. You've screwed up.'

But Jack Good loved it and Adam was booked to appear on *Oh Boy!*. A few weeks later the record was No. 1 and Norman had to climb down. 'You can't argue with success,' he told me. 'So I phoned John Barry and told him, 'It's gone rather well, hasn't it! Would you like to do the rest?''

There was another gay producer who'd established a name for himself. Joe Meek had finished his National Service as a qualified radar technician and gone to work as a balance engineer in a recording studio. Many artists who recorded there owed their hits to his unusual technique. Jazz trumpeter Humphrey Lyttelton recorded 'Bad Penny Blues' with him. 'Joe over-recorded the drum brushes, and did something very peculiar in the way of distorting the left hand of the piano ... Because I went on holiday I didn't listen back to it like I normally would. If I'd heard it, I would have had a fit, but because I didn't, it came out like that, and became a hit, I think for those reasons.'

By the end of the fifties, Joe had built his own studio in the bathroom of his flat above a North London shop and was working with electronic sounds. He became friendly with Robert Stigwood, an Australian who'd hitchhiked from Australia. On first arriving in Britain, Robert had worked in a home for unstable boys before setting himself up as a theatrical agent where he developed a passion for one of his artists, a young actor called John Leyton. Looking for ways to create an emotional response, Stigwood decided to turn him into a pop star and sent him to record with Joe Meek.

When Leyton arrived he was surprised to find he wasn't in a recording studio but in a flat above a leather shop in Holloway Road. 'I'd be in the sitting room, the string section would be in the hallway, the vocal backing group would be in the bathroom, the brass section would be on the stairs.'

Joe was famous for flooding his singers' voices with echo. On the final record, this technique made John Leyton's voice sound unlike anyone else in pop or rock 'n' roll. Stigwood took the record to EMI and tried to persuade his friend Joe Lockwood to license it. 'Joe Meek told me all I had to do was lend him a hundred quid to cover the costs and he'd fix everything himself. But after he'd made the record he lost his nerve about going to record companies and trying to license it. So I went to see Joe and did it for him.'

In America, independent production was an accepted practice. The record company organised the marketing and distribution of the record but had no control over the choice of song and the way it was produced. This had never been done in the UK and EMI's general manager, Len Wood, an unadventurous man, was unwilling to commit EMI to anything new. Joe Lockwood didn't want to overrule him so he fixed Stigwood up with a deal at Top Rank which EMI distributed. When the record got to No. 1 EMI changed their policy and agreed to accept Stigwood's future independent productions.

As for Joe Meek, he had a follow-up hit with Leyton, then went on to make 'Telstar'. It became the first British record ever to go to No. 1 in the USA, and is still the only British instrumental ever to have topped the US charts.

When Joe gave interviews to the press he taunted the major record companies. 'With their expensive studios all they can do is imitate American pop music.' But the majors rebuffed his criticism and accused him of 'making stars by twiddling knobs'. The major studios believed in recording sounds perfectly; Joe didn't. On 'Telstar', Geoff Goddard played the theme on a specially modified organ – the only clear sound in a deliberately distorted track. 'Joe would go over the top and mix all the sounds up, pumping them through different amps and coming up with a mushy sound that would lead to hands being raised in horror at major studios.'

For a while Joe had Tom Jones signed to him but they never got around to making a record together. Raymond Godfrey, one of Tom's managers at the time, visited Joe to try and sort things out. 'He was very short-tempered, very full of anxieties, very hyper and homosexual. He was very difficult to deal with – he wouldn't talk logically ... He put his hands on his head and shouted and screamed.'

It was well known in the industry, Joe Meek was unstable and could behave like a spoilt child. But he had a surprising grasp on the teenage market.

In 1960 I was surprised to read in the *Financial Times* that teenagers were now spending £500 million a year. It was this increased spending power that changed popular music into a major industry. At last, this had an effect on the BBC. Recognising the need to provide programming for this new category of consumer, the BBC started *Saturday Club*, the radio equivalent of a Jack Good TV show, and realising that the majority of teenagers in the country came from a working-class or lower middle-class background they inaugurated a change that in BBC terms was quite shocking – they allowed the programme to be hosted by someone not speaking with an Oxbridge accent, Brian Matthew.

Disc jockey David Hamilton worked for the BBC at the time. 'Brian was a Home Service newsreader. Like all of us, he read the news with an accent as posh and public school as they come. But when he started introducing *Saturday Club*, we were shocked.'

Brian hadn't been to public school and like most of the newsreaders his posh accent was a fake. 'When I got *Saturday Club*, Jimmy Grant, the producer, decided I should speak normally. We wanted to be accessible – we were aiming at youngsters. We wouldn't be allowed to use real Brummie accents, or Manchester, or even cockney, but at least we could speak in a way that wouldn't put them off. After the show had been going for a while I bumped into Frank Phillips, the BBC's senior news announcer whom I'd been working with previously. He looked me straight in the eye and said: 'I'd like to punch you on the bloody jaw, for what you're doing to the English language.''

One of the ways to cross the barriers between Britain's accent-divided classes was to use well-spoken Australians. In 1962, the BBC gave *Pick of the Pops* to presenter Alan Freeman, a DJ from Sydney. Alan not only provided an accent free of social preconceptions, he immediately changed the programme into a chart show, building tension as he went, playing the best-selling records from No. 10 to No. 1.

John Burgess, the producer at EMI who'd made Adam Faith's first record, remembered the change. 'Until then, the chart was still thought of as being best-selling songs. Music publishers held the upper hand in the business. They used to come to our offices and plug their songs by playing them on the piano and singing. But when *Pick of the Pops* became a Top Ten record chart, things began to change. At last, "hits" would mean records, not songs.'

When Brian Matthew changed his accent, he gave the BBC a voice with which they could speak to young Britain. Now *Pick of the Pops* had changed the voice that controlled the music industry, it no longer belonged to the publishers, it belonged to the record companies. The *music* business had become the *record* business.

Although the record companies had finally triumphed over the music publishers, they seemed unsure of exactly what they should be promoting. The period from 1960 to 1963 was a strange period for British pop – a hiatus, a lull before the storm. From the States there were still singers in the rock 'n' roll tradition, like Sam Cooke, Duane Eddy and Chubby Checker, but from Britain there was only one new artist who generated excitement among young people, a 14-year-old schoolgirl, Helen Shapiro. Critics called her 'mature', 'bluesy', 'rich', 'adult' and 'powerful'. Her schoolfriends called her 'the foghorn'. Helen got a No. 1 record with 'Don't Treat Me Like A Child', yet she'd been thrown out of the school choir because her voice was too deep.

Apart from Helen Shapiro, the new record chart generated by *Pick of the Pops* was full of trashy sentiment and silly jokes – 'Softly As I Leave You' by Matt Monro, a singing bus driver; 'Stranger On The Shore' by Acker Bilk, a cider-farming clarinet player; 'Hole In The Ground', by Bernard Cribbins, a comedian; and 'Toy Balloons', by Russ Conway, a nine-fingered pianist.

Jack Good's TV show looked tired and was no longer exciting. Larry Parnes had pushed his entire stable of boys into becoming 'all-round entertainers'. Maybe it made them more money but it did nothing to promote the originality or excitement of British music. Rock 'n' roll had passed and nothing new had emerged, yet there still seemed to be a feeling of expectation.

This is easy to say in hindsight for we know that something new came. But for me at the time, that expectation was always there. Perhaps it was to do with the excitement of gay social life, of being able to meet people who were really inside the music industry. One of these was Larry Parnes, whom I'd now re-met several times. He wasn't easy-going and fun like Lionel Bart, he was rather boastful and was obsessed with his principal artist of the time, Billy Fury.

Larry normally put his boys on a wage, £20 a week rising slowly according to their employment contract, but he was mad about Billy and started him off on £65 a week clear of expenses. 'After he'd had a couple of small hit records, I put it up to £130, and then £150,' Larry explained. 'At the end of 1960, I switched to a percentage basis with him. I wanted him to buy two very good properties in Balham High Street ... but he couldn't see what a good investment it would be.'

To all who knew him, Billy had a reputation for being permanently under the influence of marijuana, as did many of the other singers in Larry's stable. It was easier to keep hidden than alcohol. Lee Everett, Billy's girlfriend for eight years, had almost become part of the Parnes fraternity herself. 'Billy wanted to live with me so Larry let me move in. He had to or Billy would have quit. So there I was living in Parnes's house full of boys. A lot of them smoked grass, and did pills, thousands of them. Billy smoked grass from when he got up in the morning to when he went to bed at night. Larry hated it so much he fooled himself he didn't know about it, just refused to let himself see it.'

It was Billy Fury's apparent mental and physical fragility that appealed to the public, and it seemed to be what appealed to Larry too. One critic labelled him 'Britain's most angst-ridden pop star' and David Bowie later said that Fury was the first singer he'd ever idolised. More importantly, Billy was the only boy ever to make money out of Parnes. Larry didn't give his boys a fair cut of what they earned until they'd been with him for five years. Billy Fury was the only boy who ever stayed that long, which was only because it took him that long to get his first hit.

Larry was full of self-delusion. On one occasion, he told the press about his rules for newcomers to the 'stable'. 'I have their hair cut – that is very important. Sometimes they may have bad skin which has to be attended to. Then I get them suitable clothes and provide them with comfort. I like them to have a touch of luxury from the start ...'

Some people thought this showed a caring side to his nature, but his actions were all guided by self-interest. In fact, while I was reading a book about Selim III, an eighteenth-century sultan, I discovered that the instructions he posted for how to deal with new entrants to his royal harem at the Topkapi Palace in Istanbul were almost identical.

Despite his faults, throughout the early years of British rock 'n' roll, Larry Parnes's fame as a pop manager had spread way beyond the confines of the music industry. By the early sixties, he was as much of a celebrity as many of his artists and he was frequently on radio and TV talking about his managerial philosophy. He was the only pop manager whose name had ever been heard of by the general public.

People often made fun of him. George Martin produced a comedy album with Peter Sellers that came dangerously close to revealing the truth about this notorious pop manager and his house full of boys. But for many gays, Larry Parnes had become something of a role model. And that included me.

Throughout the fifties, homosexuality had not only been against the law, it had been actively persecuted by the police. In the aftermath of the Burgess-Maclean spy scandal, the CIA had pressured Britain into preventing such things from happening again. Plain-clothes police hung around in public toilets, masturbating, waiting for gays to reveal themselves. If they did, they were beaten up and arrested.

When the possibility of changing the law was first debated in Parliament, I was amazed at the gems of intolerance that were revealed. 'Incest is a much more natural act than homosexuality,' declared one MP, and another said, 'We should keep them out of sight of the general public.'

For decades homosexuals had hidden in the civil service or the theatre, or played out their accepted roles as waiters and hairdressers. Now they watched the success of Larry Parnes and felt encouraged. Pop management looked like a viable profession. And it was just about then that National Service came to an end.

National Service had been a two-year no-man's-land between childhood and the real world. The army snatched eighteen-year-olds out of adolescence and threw them back as adults on the other side of the generation gap. Whenever teenagers got together to form a pop group, within weeks, one of them would receive call-up papers.

In 1960 National Service had been abolished and for the first time teenagers could take serious work and earn proper money. Better still, they could hang on to their teenage dreams, which for many of them meant forming a pop group. Within a couple of years there were groups all over Britain, many of them maturing into really good musical units.

So just at the time when Larry Parnes's success had encouraged a flurry of gay entrepreneurs to go looking for talent, a reciprocal flurry of teenage boys was setting out to find managers.

And in 1963 a group emerged that made it clear that the fusion of working-class youth with middle-class homosexual had been a sensational success.

CHAPTER FIVE
SPEEDING LONDON

'Sing something,' requests a reporter at the Beatles' first US press conference.

'We need money first,' replies John.

'How do you account for your success?'

'We have a press agent.'

'What is your ambition?'

'To come to America.'

'Do you hope to get haircuts?'

'We had one yesterday.'

'Do you hope to take anything home with you?'

'The Rockefeller Center.'

'Are you part of a social rebellion against the older generation?'

'It's a dirty lie.'

'What about the movement in Detroit to stamp out the Beatles?'

'We have a campaign of our own to stamp out Detroit.'

'What do you think of Beethoven?'

'I love him,' replies Ringo. 'Especially his poems.'

Three years after National Service ended, the Beatles exploded.

It was 1963. And in London in particular anything modern was in, anyone ancient was out. Class was fading, sex was obligatory, the car to drive was a Mini. The M1 had become Britain's first motorway. The pill had been made available and was triggering a sexual revolution. The jury in the trial of *Lady Chatterley's Lover* had decided that 'fuck' was a word fit to print.

Among London's West End police, corruption flourished. Mike Gerald, who ran a late-night drinking club in Soho, told me 'Around the West End, most of the police were in the pay of the Kray twins, and Ronnie Kray was friends with Lord Boothby – they used to share the same sort of rentboys. The police knew all this and helped hush it up. I had a first-floor club which stayed open till two or three. If you found the right person at Savile Row police station and paid the right money – and providing you ran things discreetly – you could operate without interference. But you'd have to deal with the mobsters too – they'd want their cut as well.'

Soho was packed with dodgy dives where teenagers could rub shoulders with pimps and wideboys selling stolen gear. Most were dark cellars like the Last Chance, the Kilt, La Poubelle, the Coffee Pot and the Limbo. At the Roaring Twenties, a black club that played bluebeat, the smoke from the spliffs inside got so strong that kids standing on the air vent in the street could get stoned on the stale air coming out.

Bribery, kickbacks and protection rackets allowed bars to stay open after-hours, drugs to be sold openly and prostitutes to operate on the streets. This collapse in traditional police values was one of the factors that allowed London to start 'swinging', but it was the Beatles who had initially triggered it. Their music was played on every programme, at every party, in every shop. People copied their clothes, their haircuts, and their accents. Even adults who hated pop found themselves irresistibly drawn into discussions about their influence on young people, and how much money they were making.

Whatever field they worked in, everyone wanted to make it the way the Beatles had. Suddenly there were opportunities for anyone with energy and flair who could look at things in a new way. Films, theatre, fashion, music, restaurants – all of them started to boom. And it was not just in the arts that this was happening. The richest new face in town was John Bloom who had persuaded every woman in Britain that a house was not a home without one of his cut-price washing machines.

The Beatles had got people chasing success.

By now I was doing well. I owned a company hiring out film-editing equipment and was also working on each new film made by Clive Donner, Britain's trendiest new feature director. I was a cutting-room assistant and also laid the music tracks. This meant working with many of the top film composers, like Ron Grainer, Richard Rodney Bennett and John Hollingsworth.

I had a large flat which I shared with my friend Billy, my brother, and a strange girl who smoked a pipe. I also finally had enough money to try my hand at management but as yet I hadn't found a suitable artist. Like everyone else, I was hoping for something as big as the Beatles.

When the Beatles first appeared on the scene everything about them was unlike anything the pop world had seen before. It wasn't only their clothes, their accents and their way of joking with the press – it was the way they looked when they played. Paul played left-handed and the neck of his guitar rose to the right, the others rose to the left. It framed the group in an unusual way. And they held their guitars high on their chests, like Elizabethan minstrels. Even more important, they dressed with style.

In Hamburg they'd met Astrid Kirchherr, one of a group of German existentialists whom Paul McCartney called '*not* the first artsy people we'd seen... but the first *unique* artsy people'. In Astrid's silver foil-lined room, she slept on black sheets with the branch of a tree suspended from the ceiling. It was from Astrid that the Beatles got the idea for Chairman Mao collarless jackets. Those jackets, and the Beatles high-heeled flamenco-style boots, had launched Carnaby Street which was now full of fashion shops from end to end. Shoppers who searched from shop to shop for just the thing they wanted didn't realise that most of these shops were owned and supplied by the same man – John Stephen.

Stephen had opened one of the first shops on the street. When it was successful he had bought 90 per cent of the others and called them by a variety of different names, such as 'Lord John'. Even so, Stephen wasn't the man who clothed the stars. Real style meant having a jacket cut by Tommy Nutter or Dougie Millings, buying a one-off mini-skirt from Mary Quant, shopping for casual clothes at Biba in the King's Road, or buying your flared trousers from John Michael. What John Stephen did was to copy these styles and sell them to every teenager in Britain.

There was a new TV programme – *That Was the Week That Was*. It was unmissable. After dinner on Saturday night, wherever we'd eaten we would rush straight to the flat of the nearest friend to get there in time for the show. It made fun of everything and everyone. Overnight, it seemed, there were no more taboos – you could talk about anything, and *ought* to.

All around, things were changing, especially in popular music. The BBC had started a televised version of Alan

Freeman's *Pick of the Pops* called *Top of the Pops* and it was dominated by guitar-playing boy-groups. On ITV a show called *Ready Steady Go!* was copying Jack Good's old formula of being chaotic and alive. This was the show that broke new acts – the Beatles, the Rolling Stones, the Yardbirds, the Fortunes, the Searchers, the Tremeloes, the Pretty Things, the Kinks, the Animals, Manfred Mann, Herman's Hermits, Gerry and the Pacemakers, Sandie Shaw, Cilla Black, Lulu and Dusty Springfield – the names were endless, all synonymous with the excitement that had swept Britain.

The younger generation's new lifestyle was fuelled by pop music and fashion. But there was one more ingredient that horrified their elders. Pills!

What triggered their mass popularity was the arrival of *the* pill. Whether the Beatles would have happened in the same way without it is questionable. Their success, and every one of their songs, became a celebration of the sexual freedom young people had been granted.

A pill that allowed everyone to indulge in sex without fear of a pregnant consequence was a 'pleasure' pill. Previously, the only legal pills were those that made you better when you weren't well. This pill made things better even when you were OK to start with. It not only gave sexual freedom to the women who took it, but to the men who fancied them too. From that moment on pills were given a new status in the eyes of young people. A pill that gave them freedom to indulge in sexual pleasure was the green light for all other pills that gave pleasure. The use of them, particularly amphetamines, spread swiftly through the urban teenage population. Suddenly young city-dwellers were highly energised and sexually free – and both the energy and the freedom were supplied by pills.

I used to go to an all-night café in Soho that served pick-me-up sandwiches sprinkled with pills like salt and pepper. Personally, I preferred a glass of whisky, but for those who wanted amphetamine the most popular pills were either purple hearts (legally made and lilac-coloured), or blues (home-made, or imported from France). The actual drug was Drinamyl, a mix of amphetamine and barbiturate. If you were overweight a doctor might prescribe you one a day to kill your appetite and boost your energy. Kids soon realised that the single tablet prescribed by the doctor wasn't nearly as much fun as a half-dozen or so. At four in the morning, when clubs and discos had closed, the café would still be crowded with a mixture of all of Soho – girls on the game, rent boys, pill-pushers, young entrepreneurs, musicians, record producers, managers, would-be artists and even some well-known ones – all of them speeding through the night.

With all these pills and not enough sleep, an artist's visit to his record company could be a disruptive occasion. Hugh Mendl at Decca told me about a visit they'd suffered from the drummer in one of their groups. 'He came towering into the office and went into a tirade ... Why hadn't the group's single gone straight into the charts? It was our fault it had flopped. We'd messed up their promotion, chosen the wrong song and colluded with their manager ... He swore at the secretaries, pulled gold records off the walls, kicked over wastepaper baskets, then got stuck in the lift. But the group's single wasn't due out for another two weeks.'

At the heart of the 'pill' scene were the mods.

Mods set out to dress themselves at least as impeccably as the Beatles. If there was money left over, they would buy a motor scooter, fit it with chrome gadgets and tie a racoon tail on top of an ultra-high radio aerial. But their main obsession was pills. Getting 'blocked' at the weekend was what separated 'them from us'. Lee Harris, a social worker at that time, remembers kids aged fifteen and sixteen with short hair and Parkas, out on the streets of Soho at two and three in the morning. 'They were all chewing gum with big dilated pupils and I started finding out about purple hearts. At sixpence each, some of these kids were taking eighty or ninety over a weekend and having amphetamine psychosis.'

There were three clubs at the centre of the speed scene, all of them known principally for their music.

The Marquee had a reputation for finding good new bands. Owner Harold Pendleton had infallible judgement – the performers he rebooked always seemed to be the ones who went on to subsequent success. Years later, he told me the truth. 'I was a jazz fan. I never understood rock bands. I used to ask the cloakroom girl.'

The Flamingo was run by Jeff Kruger whose father was an East End hairdresser. 'Luckily, one of my dad's customers was Jack Spot, the biggest mobster in London. My dad shaved him every morning. When I opened the Flamingo, Dad went to see Jack and explained that the Flamingo belonged to his son.'

The Flamingo had an all-night rhythm & blues session at weekends, the only one of its sort in London. Jeff had surprised everyone by getting permission to run it from the chief constable at the Savile Row police station. 'I told him, if you let me have an all-night licence, all the kids who hang around Soho in the early hours will go there and you'll know where they are. You can put any number of plain-clothes men inside the club, but you've got to promise only to arrest people outside, never inside. There'll be no alcohol, and we'll stay open till the tube starts running so the kids can get home again.'

The club became the haunt for young aspiring rhythm & blues musicians like Georgie Fame, Zoot Money, Geno Washington, Eric Burdon and Long John Baldry, but the key to the Flamingo's success wasn't just the music. Without any alcohol on sale, the kids who went there needed an alternative to keep them going through the night. The place was full of jazz musicians who liked to smoke dope, but smoking dope in a club packed with plain-clothes policemen was out. So the Flamingo became one of the best places in London to pick up speed. Every weekend it was full of American Air Force men on weekend passes who paid for their night out by selling Benzedrine tablets taken from their cockpit emergency kits, usually for sixpence each, though if you hadn't bought one by 2am you might find the price going up to a shilling.

The Scene was the epicentre of mod lifestyle. It was run by Ronan O'Rahilly who later pioneered pirate radio with Radio Caroline. The Scene was in a small yard opposite the Windmill Theatre which ran a twenty-four-hours-a-day strip show. Outside, the yard reverberated to the sound of mod scooters; inside, the sounds were all American. The DJ had the best collection of American records in town – r&b, soul and blues. And blues, in the form of Drinamyl, was also the most popular drug.

The conventional view of Swinging London was that it had been set in motion by the success of the Beatles. Drug historian Harry Shapiro thinks differently. 'It should have been called "Speeding London". The amphetamine-induced arrogance, edginess, narcissism and freneticism of mod culture was reflected right through the art, music and fashion of the period. London's pop art scene was like a giant Roy Lichtenstein painting – POW!! ZAP!!'

In 'Speeding London' the people with the greatest 'pow' and 'zap' were pop managers, and currently top of the tree was Brian Epstein.

Larry Parnes's technique of titillating his own sexual tastes by cleaning up working-class boys and sending them out to sing had become the template for all gay pop managers. Epstein had taken it to its ultimate heights. His beginnings were almost identical to that of Parnes. He was provincial, Jewish, middle-class, public school, homosexual, and earned his living by running a shop. He'd even started off with the same old hype. When he'd first met them in Liverpool, Epstein had taken an instant fancy to the four Beatles – then it became an obsession. He went endlessly up and down to London, playing their songs to people in the music business and being rejected.

'One day they'll be greater than Presley,' he'd told the collective heads of Decca.

'The boys won't go, Mr Epstein,' Dick Rowe, Decca's A&R man, had told him. 'We know these things. You have a good record business in Liverpool. Stick to that.'

Depressed and endlessly rejected, Epstein had tried here and there, searching for a way in, until he arrived at EMI where he finally secured a deal for the group with Parlophone Records. 'There was an atmosphere about the place that gave me tremendous hope.'

Perhaps it was his gay affinity with the company chairman.

Since they'd first taken him on as their manager, Paul McCartney, like the rest of the Beatles, had seen how this gay network could help them. 'We'd heard that Brian was queer … We didn't hold that against him … Pubs would stay open through Brian's influence, which was fine by us. It meant we could get a drink late at night, fantastic! … Then we got down to London and Brian had his contacts on the gay scene. People would say, "How are your boys, Brian?" "Well, they're doing rather well, they just had a hit." "Oh marvellous, do put them on my show!" So obviously that didn't hurt us.'

In November 1963 President Kennedy was assassinated. In London it had an enormous impact. Gloom pervaded the atmosphere and political pundits told us that world order might be undermined; some even thought it could lead to war.

At the time of the assassination, the Beatles were No. 1 in Britain with 'She Loves You'. When the following week's chart came out, they were still at the top and we all breathed a sigh of relief. World order had been maintained. Pop had overcome the political crisis.

It was obvious to people in Britain that the Beatles were just the sort of stabilising influence the world needed. Shortly afterwards, America got the message too. 'I Want To Hold Your Hand' went to No. 1 and four Beatles records moved simultaneously into the US Top Five. For Americans, Kennedy's death had created an emotional vacuum and the Beatles filled it. The British music industry was the benefactor and London swung harder than ever.

Clubbing was now an essential part of life in Swinging London. I was finding that it was in the small hours of the morning that schemes were hatched and deals were done. The nightly ebb and flow of projects and plans made the club-of-the-moment akin to a showbusiness stock exchange. Like everyone else, I was involved in countless different projects: editing movies, setting up TV specials, making documentary films and TV commercials, auditioning new pop groups – trying to make it big. And like everyone else, I went to the Ad Lib club.

The Ad Lib could only be entered by way of a lift from street level which took you right into the club. It had fur-lined walls, a tank full of piranha fish, great amplification, and a mirrored dance floor so dancers could check their movements and hairstyles. The Ad Lib featured good music – mainly black and American. At midnight the West Indian chef came out of the kitchen, banged a tambourine and made everyone dance the conga.

The Beatles took to it, so did the Stones and the Hollies and everyone else. From a picture-window pop stars, photographers, models, actors and film directors could look down on nighttime London and observe the world that had given them the money to be there. 'It was next to a nunnery,' George Melly reminded me, 'and they tried endlessly to shut it down because of the noise. You couldn't hear a word of conversation, but the whole point was the miniskirts, and the loucheness of the young men.'

At the Ad Lib, I became friends with Vicki Wickham, who booked the acts for *Ready Steady Go!*. We were trying to put together a 'special' for American TV – *Ready Steady Goes to Woburn*, Britain's most famous stately home. *Ready Steady Go!* had been started with almost no budget and the singers mimed. After a few months it was decided they should sing live. 'It was chaos,' Vicki told me, 'they gave us the sound engineer from *A Prayer Before Bedtime*. All he'd ever done was put a microphone in front of a vicar.'

It didn't matter. Chaos and bad sound were part of the programme's excitement. Each week, on the day before the show, the production staff scoured London clubs for trendy kids to fill the set. The regular comperes were Cathy McGowan and Michael Aldred, but once a month they were joined by Swinging London's only black pop star, Kenny Lynch. 'It was the most chaotic show I'd ever worked on. Cathy used to go on for ever introducing people. She'd say: "He's just come over from New York, and he's got a new record out, and he's so good-looking, and I went out to dinner with him last night, and ..." Her mouth would fall open. She'd forgotten his name.'

Vicki persuaded me it was time to try my hand at management. My first attempt was with Room Ten – three young actors who shared a dressing room in the musical *Flower Drum Song*. They wanted to record a song from the show so I booked the studio, produced it for them and paid the bill.

I made a deal with the group to manage them for 20 per cent commission, but I knew so little about percentages I also agreed to give them 20 per cent of the selling price of each record. I went to Decca where Dick Rowe agreed to release it, but the best deal I could get from him was 14 per cent, so every record was going to cost me 6 per cent.

Vicki then introduced me to Robert Stigwood. Stiggy was running an ever-enlarging organisation which included a record company, a management company, a booking agency, and *Disc Weekly*, a pop newspaper complete with its own weekly chart. We became great friends. Night after night we had dinner at the same restaurant in Hollywood Road. We talked and talked. Stiggy became my professor of the music business and my 'practical' was working with the group I'd signed. Their record got just one play, they got no TV shows and there was no chance of them ever playing live. It may sound as if there wasn't much for me to do, but with their recording career in such a pitiful state I concentrated on giving the group plenty of pep talks about their chances for the future. It was only when they suggested that I pay to make another record that I pulled out.

But by then I'd begun to understand the pluses and minuses of management. And I decided I liked it.

For the Beatles, the money to have been earned during this period should have been staggering, not so much from records as from every other ancillary product. But for some reason none of us could fathom, Brian Epstein gave away the Beatles' merchandising rights for 2 per cent and no advance.

One of the consortium of six young entrepreneurs who grabbed this prize was John Fenton. 'In New York we had the whole sixth floor of the Drake Hotel, and we each had the best apartments money could buy. We went through a fortune. We started with 13 authorised products and ended up with over 460 different pieces of merchandise. We were on 20 per cent of retail and the Beatles had accepted 2 per cent. It was Epstein's one big fuck-up.'

No one knows what made Epstein do such an insane deal. When asked, he didn't even know himself. John Fenton wasn't complaining. 'We were the kings of New York. We'd have breakfast for twenty every morning at the Four Seasons. In Japan alone we'd sold more than three million wigs.'

For Brian, what made things even worse was knowing he'd done an equally bad deal for the Beatles' recording rights. George Martin had signed the group to EMI for a penny per double-sided single. 'I gave them a four-year contract,' he recalls, 'increasing by a farthing each year if I decided to renew it.'

Merchandising could have been Brian Epstein's way of making up for what the Beatles were losing on record sales. When he went to New York to discuss things with the six young Englishmen who'd grabbed this prize from him, John Fenton met him outside the Plaza Hotel. 'I was in the biggest white Cadillac limousine in the country, which actually belonged to Liberace. Eppy walked round it, which took nearly a minute, then said, "This should have been mine."'

Epstein had made a bad deal, but he'd also set in motion the mega-industry of rock merchandising. Film director Derek Jarman was a student at the time. He bought a Beatles hat and wrote about it in his diary. 'My Beatles hat which cost me a fortune – £8 – in Herbert Johnson's has paid dividends, as everywhere I've travelled it's made me instantly recognisable as the most desirable of foreigners – an inhabitant of Swinging London.'

Girls bought objects that made them feel closer to the group. Boys who dreamt of becoming pop stars bought Beatles wigs and jackets to help them on their way to the top. Kids at business college were no longer studying to be bankers; they wanted to become pop managers. Epstein had done more than sell the world on the Beatles – he'd sold it on the entire music business.

Eventually John Fenton and his team got into financial difficulties. 'Altogether, we'd made over seven million dollars in six months. Compared with today that's like seventy. But we'd spent the lot in the same amount of time. We were stoned out of our minds the entire time.'

At last Brian Epstein made a clever move; he refused to authorise any new products. With no new money coming in, Fenton and his friends were unable to pay their enormous tax bill. 'We made a deal. The Beatles paid our tax liability, which stopped us going to jail, and we gave them back the rights.'

Increasingly, the Beatles were being photographed in excessive luxury – lounging in the back of limousines, drinking champagne for breakfast, living it up in hotel suites. People looked at them and thought, 'That could have been me' – as if a neighbour had just won the lottery.

Martin Lloyd-Elliott, a psychologist who specialises in the music business, thinks it was during this period that a certain jealousy began to creep into the relationship between the public and their pop stars. 'People were living out their fantasies through the lives of pop stars. It was the lifestyle they might have had if they hadn't had to study for A-levels, go to university, get married, or find a job. They didn't begrudge pop stars their excesses, but there was still a line to be drawn if they went too far – "Be careful," the public warned them. "Those are our fantasies you're playing with."'

In 1964 the Rolling Stones took the public's fantasies into unchartered waters.

CHAPTER SIX

GATHERING NO MOSS

The Rolling Stones were the first 'rock' band.

The Beatles never got beyond pop. They listened politely to their manager and copied his nice middle-class manners. On-stage, they wore suits, bowed to the audience and talked to them with exaggerated politeness, as if they were having afternoon tea with Auntie Eileen. Paul McCartney explained how they used to count their bow. 'One, two, three – and we'd do this big uniform bow all at once ... It was show business, we were just entering the whole magic realm.'

And the Beatles had won the jackpot. They toured the world in luxury, meeting people of power and influence. They were welcome guests wherever they went and became the honorary upper class of every society.

But the Rolling Stones were different. They didn't want to be patronised by the elite and welcomed like lottery winners. They removed themselves from normal society and lived in their own elitist bubble.

Andrew Oldham became their manager aged only nineteen. He'd been to public school, then worked as a window-dresser for Mary Quant and as a publicist for Brian Epstein. He was thin and pale and often wore make-up. He was obsessed with being dressed just right. Tony Hall remembers, 'He reminded me of the cool black guys on Blue Note record sleeves – all the latest fashions, the buttoned-down collars, everything that was ultra-hip.'

The Rolling Stones were part of a new surge of groups that were playing rhythm & blues. They'd got themselves a residency at the Crawdaddy Club in Richmond, jammed with kids hanging off the beams to hear them. They were the hottest unsigned band in town and Andrew Oldham got there first. 'I knew what I was looking at,' he told people. 'It was sex.'

The second ingredient for rock music was energy, or as Mick Jagger put it, 'energy and three chords'. Egged on by their new manager, the Stones also came up with a third ingredient: an underlying menace, a hint of mind-warp and degradation. Watched by the media at every step, the Rolling Stones searched for the worst inside themselves, and found it.

The Stones' music was the hypnotic beat of rhythm & blues, their vocals, mainly Jagger's, were slurred and southern, the words never easily understood. Mick offered an explanation. 'I remember when I was very young, I read an article by Fats Domino which really influenced me. He said: "You should never sing the lyrics out very clearly."'

Other factors also contributed. Producer Mike Hurst told me about going to Olympic Studios the morning after an all-night Rolling Stones session. 'All round the control room were left-over bits of hash cake – then we looked at the tape boxes and saw they'd done twenty-eight takes of whatever song it was they were doing. You knew at once the reason they'd done twenty-eight takes – it was because they were out of their skulls.'

Whatever the reasons, when the Rolling Stones were on TV parents couldn't decipher what they were singing. When they saw Mick Jagger's leering manner and swaying hips, they guessed the worst. John Lennon once said, 'You don't have to hear what Bob Dylan's saying, you just have to hear the way he says it,' and the same was true of Jagger. Playing it for all it was worth, he cursed and swore in interviews, and scowled menacingly at anyone who took an interest in him. But compared with what was to come later, the group's decadence was still at modest levels and still within the control of their young manager.

Before he'd started managing the Rolling Stones, Andrew Oldham had a chance encounter with American record producer Phil Spector. He gave Andrew a piece of advice that he took to heart, 'Never sign direct to a record company. Make the records yourself and lease them to the company.' As a result, when Andrew first signed the Stones, he raised a few hundred pounds and took the group to Olympic Studios where he proclaimed himself their 'record producer'. When the engineer suggested they start 'mixing', Andrew didn't even know what it meant. But just one year later he found himself being referred to as the producer of the 'greatest white rock album ever'.

It was around then that I decided to try and take my management career to the next level.

The success of the Beatles made many people dream of being a second Brian Epstein, but I never aspired to his role as an elegant background chaperone. It was Andrew Oldham's ability to manipulate that inspired me. To be clever was the principal attraction.

By now I was living in the multi-partnered manner of all swinging Londoners. One of the people I cared for was a pale young man called Nicky Scott whom I'd first noticed line dancing at a late-night coffee bar. Another was Diane Ferraz, a girl of West Indian descent who'd auditioned to sing a TV commercial for my film company. Their colour was different but their size was exactly the same – small and rather cute. Since they were both unsure about what they should be doing with themselves, I proposed they become a pop duo.

I stole 'Get Off Of My Cloud' by the Rolling Stones, rewrote it, produced it and leased it to EMI, getting a better percentage than I had with Room Ten plus an upfront advance to cover the recording costs. I'd turned the Stones' brilliant rhythm & blues riff into a daft love song – 'I love you girl, I love you boy' – that sort of thing. At that time there wasn't a single mixed-race group in the British charts. Even people with no overt racial prejudice thought it was daring to promote a mixed-race boy-girl image to the British teenage market. I had photos taken that emphasised Nicky's paleness, Diane's darkness, and their attraction to one another. There was no question about it, the best way to get publicity in the music business was with relationships that could be talked about.

One example was the way the sex lives of the Rolling Stones had quickly become the mainstay of every gossip column, even outdoing the Beatles. The Beatles had ordinary homely girlfriends, but the Stones attached themselves to supermodels and actresses. When they had rows with them, it was all fed to the public – like the time Brian Jones lost his girlfriend to Keith Richards after trying to force her into an orgy with two whores in Morocco. In comparison, Diane & Nicky were an unknown couple whose only claim to fame was to be black and white, but I reckoned it would work.

For a new act of this sort, the competition wasn't the Beatles or the Rolling Stones, it was the softer pop acts of the day – Cilla Black, Sandie Shaw, or Peter & Gordon – all of whom I considered to be promoted on paper-thin talent. Sandie's gimmick was to sing bare-footed. ('I was so shortsighted I couldn't see the edge of the stage without my glasses. So I took off my shoes. That way, while I was looking at the audience, I could feel the edge of the stage with my toes.') Peter & Gordon had shot to success on the back of a Beatles song given to them because Peter was the brother of Paul McCartney's girlfriend, Jane Asher. Cilla Black (who'd been the hatcheck girl at the Cavern when the Beatles played there) had a huge wailing voice with which she desecrated American hits made by Dionne Warwick, the subtlest singer in the whole of pop.

All these artists, and many more, owed their chart success to a new phenomenon – pirate radio. It had come about because of the BBC's failure to understand how to deal with the huge boom in pop music. For years, BBC executives had failed to recognise the demand for programmes of popular records. When they finally allocated a couple of hours a week to recorded pop music, the programmes were treated in the same way as drama or news. Johnny Beerling, later the controller of Radio One, was given one of them to produce. 'Everyone had to write a script beforehand. The DJ sat in a little box and announced the record. Outside, the studio manager played the record. And there was somebody else who produced the programme too. But the pirate stations changed all that. The DJs chose their own records and didn't have scripts.'

Pirate radio was revolutionary and the public loved it. It started with Radio Caroline, broadcast from a boat anchored in the North Sea outside British territorial waters. The idea came from an Irishman, Ronan O'Rahilly, who had previously run The Scene, London's number-one mod club. And the investment came from another Irishman, Phil Solomon, who had been the manager of Van Morrison. Soon, there were five stations broadcasting pop music non-stop, twenty-four hours a day, just like America. And the numbers were growing. Together they accomplished something no one had thought was possible – they brought commercial radio to Britain. But it was still against the law, so for the moment it had to be broadcast offshore.

Best-known of the pirate DJs was Tony Blackburn who loved the adventure of working on a ship. 'Naval ships kept coming and going to check we were more than three and a half miles out, and we never knew when we might be arrested. The most exciting moment was when we made our first pirate hit – "Have I The Right" by the Honeycombs. That was totally done by the pirates. We plugged it to death.'

For record companies, the beauty of Radio Caroline was its straightforwardness. When manager Don Arden called the station and asked how to get a single played, he was told the going rates. Don remembers, 'I haggled a bit, then sent them a cheque. And the record was played exactly as many times a day as they'd said it would be.'

At Radio London, the plays were acquired more subtly. The owners of the station formed 'Pall Mall Music', a publishing company run by music publisher Harold Shampan. To get their record played, the artist or his record company would call Harold and ensure that Pall Mall published their 'B' side.

When Diane & Nicky's record was ready for release, I sent it together with a photo to every TV producer in Britain with a music show. I called the TV producers and initially received the usual polite rejection – 'There are too many singles being released' ... 'not enough slots on the show' ... 'the song's not special enough'. But I'd not only been studying Andrew Oldham's ice-cold aggression, I'd been brought up in a household where any sort of racism was held as the greatest sin, so I had real moral indignation on my side. I accused each of the producers of pandering to the racist objections they knew their programme controllers would raise. And since most TV directors and producers were basically liberal people, I persuaded each of them to take a stand against such bureaucratic racism. The end result was that the duo was booked to appear on seven TV shows.

To play extra safe, I gave the 'B' side to Harold Shampan for Pall Mall Music, Radio London's publishing company. The next weekend, after a TV show in Manchester, I was driving back to London with Diane & Nicky on Sunday afternoon. We were listening to the BBC Top 30 and the song was nowhere. We listened to Radio Caroline's Top 50, and it was the same. Then at five o'clock came Radio London's chart. For the first week of release, I'd expected them to put Diane & Nicky between 40 and 30, but it wasn't there. When the chart got up to No. 10 and the record still hadn't been played, I stopped the car to phone Harold Shampan at home and complain. Just as he answered, the car radio blared out the intro ... 'Diane Ferraz and Nicky Scott, straight in at No. 5.'

It was enough to establish them as a working act and me as a proper manager. From then on there were pop shows to do all over the country. We were working with the elite.

One of the first shows we played was with Dusty Springfield.

Dusty stood out as having real quality; from the first note of any song, she was instantly identifiable. With Mike Hurst and her brother Tom, she'd previously been in the

Springfields, a folk group turned pop whose secret was to sing loud and fast. 'We were terribly cheerful,' Dusty explained. 'It was extremely important to be cheerful.' Mike Hurst explained in more detail. 'Our manager was Captain Emlyn Griffiths, the exclusive booking agent for Quaglino's, where we played endlessly. We recorded an Irish folk song called "Silver Threads And Golden Needles", and lo and behold, Mercury Records in the States put it out. Suddenly we were the first British vocal group ever to make the American Top Ten. We had to find a follow-up and Tom Springfield came up with "Island of Dreams". It was a brilliant bit of plagiarism – "Carry Me Back To Old Virginia" and "The Rose Of Tralee" put together.'

In 1963, Dusty had left the Springfields and had immediate success on her own. Fragile-voiced and panda-eyed with mascara, she was reclusive, lazy, petulant and totally charming. 'I was being called a star, but to me, I was still just me. To be the star they wanted, I had to hide behind a mask, and I chose mascara. And it was so difficult to get off, I sometimes left it three weeks or more, adding more as it was needed.'

Dusty was stubborn and principled. When she went to South Africa and found the audience was segregated, she refused to play. She was deported on the next plane and came home to great acclaim. It was the first time the public had seen a pop star becoming overtly involved in politics.

Politicians, on the other hand, were all too eager to benefit from involving themselves with pop. William Deedes, former editor of the *Daily Telegraph*, was the Conservative minister in charge of the government's information services. In a speech to the City of London Young Conservatives, he talked about the Beatles. 'The young are rejecting some of the sloppy standards of their elders ... they have discerned dimly that in a world of automation, declining craftsmanship and increased leisure, something of this kind is essential to restore the human instinct to excel ...'

Left-wing diehards took the opposite point of view and saw young fans as being exploited by the forces of capitalism. In 1964, Paul Johnson wrote about *Juke Box Jury* in the *New Statesman*:

While the music is performed, the cameras linger savagely over the faces of the audience. What a bottomless chasm of vacuity they reveal! The huge faces bloated with cheap confectionery and smeared with chain-store makeup, the open, sagging mouths and glazed eyes, the hands mindlessly drumming in time to the music, the broken stiletto heels, the shoddy, stereotyped, 'with-it' clothes: here, apparently, is a collective portrait of a generation enslaved by a commercial machine.

In fact, *Juke Box Jury* was a harmless enough programme. It had a compere and four panellists who voted new records a hit or a miss. On each show one artist was chosen to come and sit behind a curtain, unseen by the panellists as they voted. Then he had to come out and meet them. Some of the biggest artists went through this indignity.

David Jacobs, whom Jack Good described as 'smooth as liquid paraffin, and just as colourless', was the compere and chose all the records for the show. 'I had an innate sense of what would be a hit ... I was seldom wrong,' he would later boast.

Jacobs chose five records he thought would be hits and three that wouldn't. Record producer Ray Singer was once a guest behind the curtain. 'At that time I was a singer. On the panel were Laurence Harvey, the actor, and Maureen Cleave, who wrote feature interviews for the *Evening Standard*. I was voted a miss and had to come out from behind the curtain and shake hands with everyone, pretending I didn't care. Afterwards, in the Green Room, I remember Laurence Harvey being absolutely sweet, and so were all the others. But David Jacobs was horrible, completely horrible. There was me, a sixteen-year-old kid, feeling mortified because I'd been voted a miss, and he totally ignored me. Not a word – not even a glance towards me.'

David Jacobs was unashamed. 'Perhaps I'm being cruel but it was always more interesting if the record was slammed and the poor creature had to come round and shake hands with the panel.'

In October 1964, after thirteen years, the Tories finally lost an election to Labour. The new government promised equal opportunity for all but the British had become more interested in who was top of the charts than in who was running the country. Parents seemed as turned on to pop and fashion as their kids. Mums wore miniskirts and Vidal Sassoon bobs, and at the weekend, dads could be seen in C&A casual gear, which was little different from the clothes sold in Carnaby Street.

In no other country in the world were adults as fascinated by current pop stars and their chart placing as in the UK. The imagery of the pop business overwhelmed the media. Pirate radio blared from every boutique in every city. The Beatles and the Rolling Stones hit the front pages day after day, and the inside pages were full of all the other up-and-coming artists.

Keith Altham, a sports writer for IPC Magazines, saw what was happening and switched to pop. 'Sport was going down and pop was coming up – teenagers saw football as something to do with the older generation. When the sports magazine I wrote for folded, IPC gave me a job ghostwriting pop columns supposedly written by famous stars – Cliff Richard, Adam Faith, people like that. I realised pop was the thing to be involved with, so I left and joined *New Musical Express* as features editor. It was like being at the centre of the world. Pop seemed to be the most important thing in Britain.'

Adults and children alike were aware of the latest artists and even of their managers; like Billy J Kramer, whom Brian Epstein bought from his previous manager for £25, or Dave Clark, who refused to be managed and worked it all out for himself. Dave was twenty and had a dazzling smile. He was good-looking, clean-cut, and incredibly sharp. He was a film extra, but when he noticed what was going on in the music industry he formed a group and wrote some songs. He learned how the business worked, set up his own publishing company, published his songs, then made records and licensed them to EMI. His biggest hit was 'Bits And Pieces'. From it, he made 20 per cent of each record sold, with no deductions – twenty times what any individual Beatle was making.

Dave remained resolutely 'pop' and rejected the anti-social stance of rock. There wasn't much to his music, the secret to his success was his brain. If he'd chosen to do so, he could have taken over the whole British music industry. Instead, he just smiled his way around America and made himself a multimillionaire at twenty-one.

And he wasn't the only one. Peter Noone, a child actor turned pop star, did the same thing as Herman's Hermits, his gleaming teeth making American teenage girls fall in love with him the same way their elder sisters had fallen in love with the Beatles the year before.

Even prettier than Herman's smile was Jonathan King's voice. It was first heard on a record called 'Everyone's Gone To The Moon', but when Jonathan King appeared on *Top of the Pops* he turned out to be a bespectacled, round-faced student from Cambridge with an asymmetric nose. And he just couldn't stop talking. 'I deliberately wrote a song that rhymed moon and June in a way I hoped nobody would spot. Then I had the satisfaction of hearing Pete Murray say: "The song has meaningful lyrics and doesn't rhyme moon with June." Yet right in the middle of the song, it says "Sun coming out in the middle of June – Everyone's gone to the moon."'

Jonathan's physiology precluded him from becoming a real pop star, but he had a sharp eye for new talent. He spotted Scott Walker, a young American who had come to Britain with two friends to form the Walker Brothers. Scott was the singer, angst-ridden and unsure of himself. The group's first hit was 'Make It Easy On Yourself' which was the one thing Scott Walker never managed to do. He had a desperate inferiority complex and was terrified each time he had to walk out on stage. Sometimes he just couldn't do it and when that happened the only person who could persuade him to do so was Jonathan. 'I was quite often sent for when I was at my mum's, who lives in Surrey. I used to have to drive for about an hour and a half, go into the dressing room and say: "Stop being silly, go out there on stage." And he would finally concur.'

Belying Scott Walker's insecure character, the Walker Brothers' image was immensely strong – like pictures from Nazi youth recruitment films in the mid-thirties – three boys, naked from the waist up – blond, self-confident, and beautiful. The image was created almost by accident by Michael Lindsay-Hogg, the director of *Ready Steady Go!*. He shot the boys from below making them look like languid trees shaking in the wind as seen by someone lying on the grass. The image was half naturist, half erotic, and it sent teenage girls into raptures.

Lindsay-Hogg and *Ready Steady Go!* were responsible for the success of several other artists. Donovan Leitch started off as a one-man band. He hitchhiked from his home in Essex to the TV studios of *Ready Steady Go!*, got himself interviewed with a harmonica brace round his neck and a bass drum on his back, and then sang a few unaccompanied lines. His singing was an immediate joke – totally tuneless. But he set a standard for persistence that has been followed by aspiring pop stars ever since – Donovan just hung around and persuaded people he'd got something.

In April 1965, he had his first hit with 'Catch The Wind'. According to one journalist, he was 'as un-sexy as anyone could get and still be identifiably of one gender or another'. Donovan had a theory that he was tuned to F-sharp and could only get on with people who were tuned the same way. In July 1966 he gained the final accolade required by all top pop stars of the sixties – he was arrested on a drugs charge and fined £250. A Sunday paper reported 'a shocking scene of debauchery at a reefer-smoking party in his flat'. Presumably, with everyone tuned to F-sharp.

Donovan was signed to Pye, Britain's fourth biggest company. They were having a great run of success with the Searchers, the Kinks, Dave Clark, Petula Clark and Sandie Shaw. Pye were innovative. Their chairman, Louis Benjamin, had a natural understanding of pop music and how to market it. Way ahead of his time, he was the first person to have the idea of putting together compilation albums of his artists' greatest hits. He also produced EPs called 'Top Six', which were mini-versions of the same thing. More than that, Pye was the first UK company to release stereo records and to advertise on hoardings and TV.

But Louis Benjamin's far-sightedness in marketing pop was matched by his blindness for where the music itself was heading. Peter Prince, an A&R man at Pye, recalls, 'We signed a couple of groups, and like all groups they came to the record company for help to buy equipment for touring. Louis Benjamin had never heard of such a thing. He was incensed. He banged the table and screamed, 'NO AMPS!''

During 1965, I worked with Burt Bacharach, editing his score for the movie *What's New Pussycat*. The film was shot in Paris and while I was there I saw the Beatles play the Paris Olympia. It was the show that broke them in France, but the thing I remembered most was the group that played the first half – the Yardbirds.

The Yardbirds were definitely not a Pye group – the stage was stacked high with amps turned up as loud as they would go. On some songs the group had a musical quality that headed in a completely new direction – bluesy, but also sinister and heavy. They clearly had found the roots of something quite new – not pop, not blues, not rock 'n' roll. The group's image was studentish and ordinary, but their music had the same sinister overtones that Andrew Oldham was pushing into the Rolling Stones' image.

Andrew was now close behind Brian Epstein as the person with the greatest influence on youth culture. He was the first manager to turn *against* the music business establishment. He taught the Rolling Stones the importance of hating the record company. In doing so, he invented rock music.

Not only was Andrew sexually ambivalent, his whole personality was equally flexible. He would turn up at a restaurant with a fur stole, as camp and funny as Liberace, then he would play at being Al Capone and explode with violence. Ian McLagan of the Small Faces remembers once being with him in Amsterdam when he punched a journalist. 'It gave me the creeps, and I realised then that maybe he wasn't just the fun-loving, pot-smoking head he pretended to be.'

Most people assumed gay managers would want groups of cute boys to tease their erotic desires, as Epstein had done with the Beatles. But that wasn't always the case. None of us needed reminding that being gay was still against the law, but while the part of Andrew which was gay sometimes made him delightful fun, it sometimes filled him with rage at the position it put him in. He was a very angry young man. He wanted a group that would shout abuse at society. The Beatles looked like four boys set up by a sugar-daddy in a Mayfair penthouse. The Stones looked more like rough trade from the meat rack behind Piccadilly. Which was just what Andrew wanted.

In the beginning, Andrew and Mick Jagger were intimate conspirators. Mick borrowed Oldham's camp posturing and put it in his stage act. In the course of time, Andrew's violence got into the act too. There was no doubt about it, behind the charm, Andrew Oldham was volatile. He transferred this to the Stones and it made them what they were.

The Kinks were very different. They wrote satirical songs with social relevance and tongue-in-cheek humour. They were one of the few British groups who didn't really make it in the States. As a result they didn't turn into a rock group, but stayed British and pop, and delightfully quirky. Ray Davies wrote lyrics full of satire and frequently touched on the edge of politics, as when he commented on the plight of the aristocracy under the new Labour government. 'The taxman's taken all my dough and left me in my stately home.'

When Davies was asked whether he had a political viewpoint, he spoke for most pop and rock stars of the period when he backed away from the question. 'I don't know which side I'm on ... I'm a rock 'n' roll singer ... There's left, and there's right, and there's rock 'n' roll.' And if that was cowardly, there were many other things about which the Kinks were bold. The Kinks were the first group to bring overtly bisexual lyrics into their music. Ray was fascinated with the subject, all the more so because his brother Dave was openly bisexual. Later, the group had a hit with a song called 'Lola': 'Boys will be girls and girls will be boys.' It was based on an incident which had happened to Dave. 'It was a mixture of lots of things. It was a secret affair and also a true incident in a wonderful club in Paris called the Carousel. Robert Wace, one of our managers, was dancing with this beautiful black woman who was wearing this tight dress. Incredible. And I stole her. It was back to my place, and there was the stubble. I'm just not mad about stubble. It makes your face very red.'

Prime Minister Harold Wilson also had a red face. In an attempt to connect the government with the success of Swinging London, he'd decided to honour each of the Beatles with an MBE. But politics and swinging proved to be an impossible mix.

After collecting their medals, the Beatles let everyone know they'd smoked pot in the loo at Buckingham Palace. Harold Wilson's desire to join Swinging London stopped way short of condoning drugs. But as a result of the publicity surrounding their palace pot-smoking, his decision to give the Beatles the MBE had inadvertently given the campaign to legalise marijuana quite a boost.

The right-wing media suggested record companies were doing the same. By promoting artists who were known to take drugs, they were helping the 'Legalise Marijuana' campaign. The major record companies denied it. They all issued carefully worded press releases side-stepping the issue – they disapproved of drug-taking but believed in free speech, and that included an artist's right to say what he felt about drugs. Of course, they weren't defending free speech at all, they were defending their profits. And for the heads of these companies that could eventually mean knighthoods. So on this rather uncomfortable issue they stood cowering behind their artists even though they despised them for being working class.

George Martin hated this hypocrisy. 'It bothered me that record companies should behave as part of the establishment. They saw pop artists, and the young people who bought their music, as a source of profit and nothing else. Despite the success of the Beatles, there was still a lot of class snobbery.'

This was particularly apparent at Rediffusion, the company that produced *Ready Steady Go!*, probably the hottest show on TV. Their studios were run by a group of ex-naval officers and Vicki Wickham was one of many producers forced to organise her programme like the day-to-day running of a ship. 'The five floors of the building were referred to as "decks" – the times of day were called "bells". The notice-board read like a ship's bulletin ... 'Rehearsals for *Ready Steady Go!* will take place on the lower deck commencing at six bells".'

The greatest new success of 1965 was Tom Jones. His manager was Gordon Mills, the son of a Welsh army sergeant, born in India and brought up in Wales.

At fifteen Gordon left school to do National Service, worked as a bus conductor and became harmonica champion of Wales. Then he joined the Viscounts, a beat group managed by Larry Parnes, and wrote hit songs for both Johnny Kidd and Cliff Richard. Finally, he married a top model and set himself up in management. His first client was Tommy Scott, whose real name was Thomas Woodward Jones, and following in the tough business traditions of Larry Parnes, Gordon made Tommy accept a management contract that split all earnings 50-50.

In 1964, when *Tom Jones* became the hit movie of the year, Gordon told Tommy Scott to benefit from the film's publicity and go back to his original name. Gordon then took a demo of the rechristened Tom Jones to Dick Rowe at Decca. In those days the biggest compliment anyone could pay a singer was to say he sounded black, but after Dick Rowe had listened to the demo he said, 'He sounds a bit Welsh.'

Just then, Tony Hall, the DJ with the best soul programme on radio, wandered into the office and asked, 'Who's that? Is he black?'

Dick signed him at once.

Tom Jones's first record was 'It's Not Unusual', which shot up to No. 1. He then recorded the theme song for the film I was working on with Burt Bacharach, *What's New Pussycat*. My job on the film should simply have been to co-ordinate the recording of the music. I had to take the sections of the film that were to have music and run them on the screen in the recording studio while Burt conducted the orchestra. Then I would lay the resulting sections of music against the picture.

This was Burt's first film score and instead of creating an integrated piece of music that flowed throughout the film, he wrote a whole series of different, slightly disjointed musical sections. I laid the music tracks as he'd intended but Clive Donner and the producer, Charlie Feldman, didn't like the result. But by then Burt had gone back to America and they had a deadline to meet, so they gave the whole thing to me to sort out. I found myself playing a creative game on an unprecedented scale. The rules were simply that I had to make a score from the music Burt had provided; I could do whatever I liked to it. Had Burt known, I'm sure he would have been back on the next plane. But they never told him.

I took the backing track of Tom Jones's title song and replaced his voice with other instruments – a trombone, a flute, things like that. This gave me a basic theme to run throughout the film. In a similar way, I extended and augmented two of the other themes Burt had written, then edited all three themes together into a new score. I showed no respect for the score Burt had originally created, nor did I think about how he might feel about what I was doing to it – I was too young and full of myself for that. And I was having too much fun.

When the theme song from the film made Tom Jones into an international superstar, Tony Hall went to Detroit on behalf of Decca to meet with Berry Gordy, the president of Motown. 'I sold him on the idea of Tom doing an album with Motown musicians and songwriters. Berry Gordy thought it was a great idea,' Tony remembers, 'but Decca's general manager, Bill Townsley, said no.'

Later, Tony persuaded Motown to set up their own label in Britain. 'I persuaded Berry Gordy that Motown should do it through Decca. I proposed it to Sir Edward Lewis. He called in Townsley and asked him what he thought. Townsley said, "Mark my words, Sir Edward, this Motown stuff will *never* sell in England."'

Class distinction was still rife within major record companies and as far as Sir Edward Lewis was concerned 'black' music wasn't of the right class. Company bosses thought not only of profits but of endearing themselves to the establishment. Similarly, most of the young entrepreneurs who had moved into management also saw profit as less important than fun. Everyone agreed that music was a great business to be working in, but as an industry it was still unsure of itself. It had no organisation or society that brought the disparate parts together in a whole.

America, on the other hand, had long recognised music as a major industry. There were no class problems here, no effete gay clique. The industry was run by hard-nosed men who thought strictly in terms of profit. America was where the big money was and it had become the principal target for the British music industry. But if you were a manager or a record label boss trying to take on the States, you'd better watch out – this wasn't England!

In Britain, pop was pop – fun but trivial. In America it could bring you reward or critical disdain on an altogether different scale.

Newsweek magazine said of the Beatles:

Visually they are a nightmare: tight, dandified Edwardian beatnik suits and great pudding-bowls of hair. Musically they are a near disaster, guitars and drums slamming out a merciless beat that does away with secondary rhythms, harmony and melody. Their lyrics (punctuated by nutty shouts of yeah, yeah, yeah!) are a catastrophe, a preposterous farrago of Valentine-card romantic sentiments.

But despite the risks, success in the USA was no longer considered the icing on the cake – it had become the cake itself. The Brit who had the most success there was Mickie Most, the sharpest commercial British record producer of the sixties. He produced Herman's Hermits, the Animals, the Mindbenders and Donovan. The songs he used came mainly from America. 'From the Brill Building,' Mickie recalls. 'When you went into it, there was a buzz – "The British have arrived" – and they pulled out the stops.'

In New York's Brill Building there were countless publishing firms all of which employed songwriters on a full-time basis working nine to five. The ubiquitous Kenny Lynch was working there, the only British writer to do so. 'We worked in teams – me with Mort Shuman, Lieber with Stoller, Carole King with Gerry Goffin. Everbach signed me up after I had my first hit. They said, "You can be a songwriter." I said, "I can hardly sign my own name." But they gave me a seven year contract and my own company.'

Mickie Most remembers going there every second week to look for songs. 'Flight TWA 701 on Sunday. Monday to Friday I would speak with writers and publishers. Then I'd take the flight home on Friday night. Over the weekend I would be working out the arrangements and who was going to play on what songs ... Then, the next week, we'd be in the studios cutting them. The week after, I'd be back on the plane again.'

One week, Mickie decided to collect the gold records he had been awarded the previous year so he could hang them on his office wall in London. 'I called CBS and asked them when I should come. They said, "Whenever you want," so I said, "OK, Monday morning."'

Mickie flew to New York, hired himself a stretch limo and went to CBS. No one met him, so he introduced himself to the security guard, who took him down to a cellar full of cobwebs. Behind a boiler they found a stack of dusty gold records. 'It'll be amongst those,' the guard told Mickie, and left him to search through them.

How times had changed. Just six years earlier, British pop had been a sorry affair of cover versions and crooners. To have hits in America used to be an impossible dream. When the dream began to come true, gold records on the wall from America seemed almost as important as royalty cheques. But now, with everyone having so many hits, the Brits were becoming as blasé about them as the Americans.

In my case, my first gold record came via Dusty Springfield. She'd come back from the San Remo Festival with an Italian song she wanted to record in English and asked Vicki Wickham if she would like to write the lyrics for it. Vicki in turn asked me. One night after dinner we wrote them together without seriously considering that they might be recorded. The song was 'You Don't Have To Say You Love Me'. When we gave the lyrics to Dusty she wasn't too sure about them, but after she'd recorded them her producer called and said, 'I think Dusty's just made her first American hit.'

People thought of the British pop explosion as having started with the Beatles. In fact it had started as early as 1962. That year, *Billboard*, the American trade magazine for the music industry, published a chart which showed the best-selling artists in the world based on charts from thirty-four countries. Number one in the world was Cliff Richard, second was Elvis Presley, third were the Shadows, and fourth was a dreadful yodeller called Frank Ifield. All except Presley were EMI artists.

With Joe Lockwood's encouragement, EMI's general manager Len Wood had put together the best A&R team in the world. George Martin, Norman Newell, Norrie Paramor, Peter Sullivan, Walter Ridley and John Burgess were responsible for the production of virtually every record released. They were unbeatable. During 1963 and '64, EMI had the No. 1 record in the UK charts for an amazing seventy-six weeks, and all but one of the artists were British. Moreover, EMI was paying its artists next to nothing for each record sold. But despite this, Len Wood wasn't particularly popular with some of his team.

John Burgess eventually left EMI to join George Martin in setting up Air Music. 'Len Wood was credited with earning more money than anyone else in his time, but I felt it was as much luck as it was judgement. If he was as good as they said he was he wouldn't have lost his best A&R people. He would have paid us more money.'

Norman Newell was so frustrated by Len Wood's inflexibility that he left EMI and went to Hollywood for a while. 'But Joe Lockwood persuaded me to come back,' he recalls. 'He wanted to put me in charge, to make me number one above all the other producers. Joe and I got on well because we were both gay. I had a rapport with him that the other producers didn't have. I told Joe the others wouldn't accept me being in charge so I turned the offer down, but I came back anyway. As a result, I had enormous success, but I still found it difficult to put up with Len Wood.'

George Martin had signed the Beatles for a penny a record, but when he saw the money they were bringing to EMI he decided he should increase their royalty. 'At EMI, we were indoctrinated into giving artists poor deals. But when I saw their success, I thought, instead of waiting to the end of their contract, we should renew it straight away and double their royalty to two pence. I sent a memo to this effect to Len Wood. He asked me, "What do EMI get out of it? Make the group sign for another five years of options." I wanted nothing to do with that, so the royalties were not increased. After that, Len refused to let me discuss business with the Beatles again. He said I was on *their* side.'

As a result, the money kept streaming in. But it wasn't Len Wood who reaped the benefit of this penny-pinching, it was Joseph Lockwood. Since the fifties, EMI had become an enormously profitable company, the world centre of the record industry, and Lockwood had been knighted.

Ironically, the real instigator of this enormous boom was Dick Rowe at Decca. By turning down the Beatles, he'd made every A&R man in the industry frightened of repeating his mistake, so they all said yes to everything that came along. But George Martin feels Dick hadn't done anything particularly reprehensible. 'Dick Rowe got much maligned for turning down the Beatles, but so many other people turned them down too. And it was totally justified. What the Beatles were playing at that time was absolute rubbish.'

Over at Philips, Jack Baverstock was another person who'd turned down the Beatles. Philips were having a run of success with acts like Dusty Springfield, the Walker Brothers and the Spencer Davis Group, but corporately things were changing. They were now owned by PolyGram, a company jointly owned by Philips in Holland, and Siemens, a German company that made lightbulbs. Part of the agreement between these companies was that they would have a second record company in London, Polydor, which would run in competition to Philips and have a German managing director, Horst Schmolzi.

In Stratford Place, Horst set up offices for Polydor, which would be the fifth major record company. He tried to make them run with Germanic efficiency, but apart from installing top-class air conditioning from Siemens, the only German thing about the place was Horst himself.

In the Cromwellian club one night Bill Wyman asked me, 'Aren't you're the chap who stole "Get Off Of My Cloud"?'

I admitted the song I'd written for Diane & Nicky might have been influenced slightly by the Stones' hit, but Bill didn't seem too worried. 'We stole it too,' he told me.

For Diane & Nicky's next record I took the words from an old Crew Cuts hit, 'Sh-Boom'. This time I made the song too sickly sweet and it flopped, but since it didn't get a single radio play most people simply thought the duo hadn't yet made a follow-up. As a result, on the strength of the publicity I'd been getting for Diane & Nicky, I had a phone call from the Yardbirds. Vicki Wickham's secretary at *Ready Steady Go!* was the girlfriend of the group's bass player, Paul Samwell-Smith. She told Vicki the group were looking for a new manager and Vicki persuaded them I might be the person to talk to. I met Paul and we got on well.

'What percentage would you want?' he asked.

'Twenty per cent.'

'If it's not enough, we wouldn't mind paying twenty-five,' he told me. 'We don't want to be mean.'

'Not at all,' I insisted, 'twenty per cent will be fine.'

We were bending over backwards to be nice to each other, but when Paul went back to talk to the rest of the group I felt depressed. I was concerned that the opportunity to manage them might have slipped through my hands. The meeting had been too nice. There'd been none of the dark energy I'd felt in the Yardbirds' music. Surely meetings with rock groups were meant to be more confrontational than this.

The next day I read that CBS America had banned Andrew Oldham from entering their building in New York. That sounded more like the rock business.

Andrew could be all charm, but to people who were not his friends, he was sometimes arrogant and as cold as ice. Political incorrectness was his bible. He'd written sleeve notes for the Stones' second album which Decca refused to print. 'Cast deep in your pockets for loot to buy this disc ... If you don't have bread, see that blind man, knock him on the head, steal his wallet and lo and behold you have the loot ...' This was homage to Anthony Burgess's book *A Clockwork Orange*. The record was released but the public found the sleeve notes so offensive that it had to be recalled.

Andrew Oldham was setting new rules for both managers

and musicians. Those who ignored them stayed in the world of pop. Those who followed them entered the kingdom of 'rock'.

Mick Jagger, at that time his most faithful follower, later recalled, 'Rock was a completely new musical form ... At the beginning you felt like you were one of the chosen few, one of the only ones in the whole world who would get to play with this new toy.'

But that was just the musical part of it. Brian Jones, the Stones' guitarist, had started to degenerate into a hopeless junkie wreck. His drug dealer told people about it. 'He'd wake up in the morning, take leapers, cocaine, some morphine, a few tabs of acid and maybe some mandrax. Then he'd try to get dressed and end up with, like, a lizard-skin boot on one foot and a pink shoe on the other.' Somehow, even in that state Jones always made it onto the stage, and the show went on, hitting the headlines night after night. Like in Warsaw when Keith Richards screamed at children of the communist elite sitting in front of the stage, 'You fuckin' lot get out ...' Then waited while they moved sheepishly away.

This sort of thing started out as image-building, but it ended up setting the direction for all rock bands of the future – non-stop sex and drugs, and no respect for petty people. To turn rock music into a true art-form, Andrew Oldham decreed that it should also be anti-establishment, nihilistic, self-aggrandising, debauched and decadent.

He sent the Stones sliding rampantly down that path.

CHAPTER SEVEN

ALL THE WRONG PARTIES

By the beginning of 1966 I was managing the Yardbirds.

Although after my first meeting with Paul Samwell-Smith I'd felt the opportunity to manage them had passed me by, he had brought the others to meet me and they'd decided I was the right person.

Their biggest hit was 'For Your Love', a great pop song, but really the Yardbirds had never been pop. They'd started out playing blues.

Giorgio Gomelsky, who ran the Crawdaddy Club in Richmond, had planned to sign the Rolling Stones for management but at the last minute they were snatched from his grasp by Andrew Oldham. The Yardbirds were the next group to play at the club and Giorgio signed them straight away. He did well for them. Under his guidance they had a hit with 'For Your Love', and a second one with 'Heart Full Of Soul'. After that he suggested they mix Gregorian chant with blues and they had a third hit with 'Evil Hearted You'. Then they made a live album with American blues singer Sonny Boy Williamson. But from all this success the group had hardly earned anything.

Giorgio was extravagant in everything he did. He poured money into recording and promotion, and when the group went on tour he went with them, egging them on to eat at expensive restaurants when they would rather have had hamburgers. All this expenditure came out of their income. One time in New York, Giorgio needed some cash to take someone to dinner. He went to United Artists and offered them the publishing on the next Yardbirds single for the cost of the meal – $60.

Initially the Yardbirds had included Eric Clapton on guitar, but he was a gloomy, troubled person who told people he expected to die before he was thirty. He was far too dedicated to pure blues to follow the Yardbirds into pop, so he left to join John Mayall and the Yardbirds replaced him with Jeff Beck. Then they decided to change their management and chose me. At the time, the Yardbirds probably knew more about the music business than I did, but I grabbed the opportunity. I also treated it with respect – this wasn't like messing around with Diane & Nicky. The Yardbirds were one of the five most important rock groups in the world – the Beatles, the Stones, the Yardbirds, the Animals and the Who.

To start with I looked at what the managers of the other top rock acts were doing for their acts.

Kit Lambert and Chris Stamp had found the Who playing in a pub on a stage made of beer crates. The singer had crossed teeth. Kit and Chris offered the group twenty pounds a week, then, in the ensuing struggle to pay their wages, they sold both furniture and clothes. Eventually, to pay for the singer's teeth to be fixed, Kit pawned some cufflinks given to him by his father, the celebrated classical composer Constant Lambert.

Initially the Who's image was all pop – music, art and fashion. Their managers told them to watch mods in the audience as they danced then recreate their steps on-stage so the next audience would think the band had originated them. Pete Townshend insisted, 'The mod image was forced on us. It was dishonest.' Nevertheless, mods seemed to hang on his every word. When 'I Can't Explain' was released, they mobbed him, saying, 'You've managed to say something in the song that we've never managed to say for ourselves.' 'But I only said 'I can't explain'',' Pete responded. 'That's just it,' they told him. 'That's what we find so difficult to tell people ... We can't explain!'

The truth was, the only real connection between the Who and mod culture was the group's excessive use of amphetamine. Nevertheless, when Roger Daltrey sang 'My Generation' with the stutter of a pill freak, it made the Who the figureheads of the mod movement.

The Yardbirds were complaining of having nowhere to live. The best thing I could do for them was to get them a lump sum of money – say, £5,000 each. The only way to get that was from the record company. Their recording contract was with Giorgio Gomelsky, who leased their records to EMI. I decided that if the agreement for their management could be broken, so could their agreement for their recording. So I went to Len Wood, the general manager at EMI, and told him the group would want £25,000 to sign a new recording contract, and that EMI could have first option, but not for long.

From EMI, I went to Jack Baverstock at Philips who offered me £10,000, the most they'd ever paid for any artist. I called EMI and said Philips had offered the full £25,000 that we needed and within an hour EMI agreed to pay the same amount. They then had to negotiate with me over the royalties about which I was now becoming something of an expert. In the end, the Yardbirds got more than the Beatles were getting.

I took 20 per cent commission, and gave the group £4,000 cash each. In those days that could buy each one of them a house, or even two. But the next problem was even more daunting – EMI wanted a new single, and it had to be a hit. If the first single they made under their new manager wasn't up to the standards of their previous ones, I would have visibly failed. The group's previous records had been produced by Giorgio Gomelsky. The group's bass player, Paul Samwell-Smith, told me he'd been a co-producer and from here on would like a credit to that effect. I agreed he should have it and put myself in the position of the other co-producer.

Since each of the Yardbirds' hits to date had been distinctly different from the other, I thought their new single should contain elements of all of them. Moody, monk-like chanting, exhilarating lead guitar, bluesy riffs. But having once persuaded them of that, I was in the group's hands rather than they in mine. I'd never made a record with a rock group before and was surprised at their technique of first devising a backing track, then a song. Moreover, coming from a jazz background in which lush harmonic structures were everything, it seemed strange to have Paul continually telling the others to simplify the harmonies. In the end the entire first verse was played over one single chord. But this was rock music, and I was learning.

By the time the recording was finished, I'd contributed to both the words and the structure of the song, but I felt I'd learned more about production from working with Paul Samwell-Smith than he was likely to learn about management from working with me. The single was 'Over Under Sideways Down' and once it was a hit we went on to make an album, *Roger the Engineer*. Apart from making occasional musical suggestions, my primary function was to keep a working relationship between Jeff Beck, their brilliant guitarist, and the rest of the group. They were at loggerheads with him continually. Jeff was moody, brilliant and individualistic. The others thought he was insufficiently part of a team. I was too inexperienced to know which of them was right but brilliance was the more attractive quality, so I sided with Jeff.

If that was my first mistake, I soon made another one. Paul Samwell-Smith said he was tired of touring with the group and would soon want to quit. I didn't know that a manager's primary function was to keep the group together, so I told him to let me know when he was ready. But Paul was the primary musical influence in the group and in my opinion the only musician on a par with Jeff Beck. Letting him go would signal the eventual breakup of the group.

Meanwhile, the money I made from the group's live gigs compensated for putting up with the endless disputes between Jeff and the others. In the UK, the Yardbirds went out for about the same price as the Animals or the Who – £350 a night. This compared with £450 for the Stones, and around £1,000 for the Beatles. We were members of a cozy club of five or six top groups, and everyone did nicely – particularly the agents who took 10 per cent for nothing more than telling their secretaries to accept all offers and fill the group's diary.

On an equal level to the Yardbirds were the Animals. They came from Newcastle and had a singer called Eric Burdon. Eric was into sex with eggs and particularly liked egg orgies. John Lennon met him at one and shouted encouragement. 'Go on – go get it, Eggman ... I've been there already, it's nice.' Later, John used the phrase 'eggman' in 'I Am The Walrus'.

On tour with the Animals, Eric Burdon became fascinated by the differences between girls of one area and another. 'There is a certain kind of female that populates the Arizona area.

They are usually brown-skinned, blue-eyed blonde, healthy-looking girls, all apple pie and American flag. Excitable and very desirable, but when they are 15,000 strong and fifteen years of age, as the braces on their teeth flash, and wet knickers and jelly babies begin to fall on the stage, they can be a dangerous breed.'

Many of the healthy American girls Eric described became dedicated groupies. Gangs of them went hunting together – 'trophy fucking' – keeping a list of everyone they made out with. One gang grabbed British rock stars in hotel lobbies and whisked them upstairs to make plaster casts of their erect penises. Their leader was Cynthia Plaster Caster. 'I was horny, I was a virgin and I was very shy. I needed a way to get men's pants down.'

Touring America was what rock music was all about. Groups loved it, and so did the record companies – the group was away, they were busy, they were promoting record sales, and there was a constant supply of free tickets for the record company to give to DJs, radio programmers and TV producers, building up favours for the future. Everyone liked touring. The manager got 20 per cent, the agent took 10 per cent, the promoter took half the box office, and the publisher got a share of the performance money. Meanwhile, the artists got love from the audience, sex from the groupies and extrasensory experiences from drugs.

When I went to the States to set up a tour for the Yardbirds the first person I spoke to at the record company was a promotions man who told me, 'This ain't England, kid. In the States we got 7,000 radio stations to be bribed each time a record's released. That's a lotta cocaine!'

In America, there were other complications too. When an artist with an Italian name or background made it big, their management would be made an offer they couldn't refuse by one of the Mafia-controlled entertainment agencies. And though British artists were safe from such things, it was just as well to be aware of how the business worked. Thirty years later, Wall Street journalist Fredric Dannen would write:

There's corruption in just about every business, but I've never seen it anything like the level of the record business. I've covered the coal business, insurance, investment banking, the chemical industry, and trucking; and although they all have roguish elements, they're nothing like the record business, which to my way of thinking is no business at all. I don't know how to describe it except as some sort of cartel.

That was in the 1990s. In the sixties it was even worse. In America you had to step more carefully than in Britain. The man at the top of your record company might produce a ghastly blue-rinsed wife to whom he expected you to be nice. It was best not to offend her, because her husband would also be the friend of several Mafia bosses – in America no-one at the top of a major company could do his job properly if he was unable to deal with gangsters. Even so, every British artist wanted to make it there. First there was the prestige of taking popular music back to its roots, and secondly there were the groupies. American singer Joan Baez did a show with the Beatles and stayed at the same hotel. 'These poor little girls, just sitting downstairs waiting to see whether they were gonna be picked up by somebody. They don't talk ... They just sit there in these little outfits that they've worked on for months, waiting for this thing to happen.

And eventually a Beatle will come by and pick one of them, dragging her off to his lair.'

For British record companies, the size of the American market meant money on a scale impossible to contemplate in the UK. For artists, it offered more sex and more drugs. Most groups considered touring the USA to be the principal reason for being in the music business. And that went for most of their managers too.

Like other managers, I soon decided taxis were a thing of the past – only limos would do, and soon it became *stretch* limos. Then I discovered hotel suites, and from there it was only a small step to the *best* suites – the Presidential, the George Washington, the Suite on the Park – that sort of thing. After that, it was only a matter of getting used to dining at the Four Seasons and America had you hooked. Of course, this was all quite a drain on the budget which in turn meant the group had to stay there longer to earn enough to cover the costs. On top of this, groups had their drugs to pay for.

One Saturday morning I sat in the lobby of New York's Warwick Hotel with the manager of another British rock group. We watched as well-to-do parents arrived, one after another, with schoolgirl daughters. The girls would be given five minutes to go upstairs and get their idols' autographs. Five minutes would become an hour. Then they would reappear, jabbering with excitement, their faces aglow. The group's manager told me, 'They each get a joint to smoke, and some speed, that's why they come back so happy. It's like a conveyor belt up there – drugs and sex, drugs and sex. The parents haven't got a clue.'

'Don't you feel responsible?' I asked.

He shrugged. 'Groups don't hire managers to moralise about their private lives.'

It was no secret, most of the best managers were gay.

An upper middle-class public school background was still the principal key to success for the behind-the-scenes people in the music business, including managers. Record company executives were nearly all of that background and found difficulty in communicating with the new generation of young artists. However, young men in their early twenties with a public school education plus a modicum of unconventionality could cross the divide between the two cultures. And the most frequently found 'modicum of unconventionality' was a touch of homosexuality.

As well as Brian Epstein with the Beatles, there was Kit Lambert with the Who, Tony Stratton-Smith with the Nice, Ken Pitt with Crispian St Peters, Robert Stigwood with Cream, Vic Billings with Dusty Springfield, Ken Howard and Alan Blaikley with Dave Dee, Dozy, Beaky, Mick & Tich, me with the Yardbirds, and Andrew Oldham with the Rolling Stones (except on the days when he preferred to be straight, playing gangsters, threatening people with a beating from his tough-looking chauffeur, who of course was gay).

If being a popstar was going to be fun – if there was going to be sex and booze and pills and pot – perhaps these gay managers were the perfect choice. 'In London at the time,' noted Marianne Faithfull, 'there was a great honouring of the homosexual side of life ... It was just in the air everywhere.'

And so were drugs.

Although Larry Parnes had unwittingly presided over a stable of pot-smoking rock 'n' rollers, he himself had shown a puritan streak with regard to such substances. His successors showed no such inhibitions. If their sexuality was going to put these gay managers on the wrong side of the law, why shouldn't they go a stage further and indulge in recreational drugs as well? At the very least, they had no objections if their artists chose to do so.

Pete Townshend enjoyed having a gay manager. 'Gays were different. They didn't behave like other adults; they were scornful of conventional behaviour; they mixed more easily with young people, and seemed to understand them.'

It was gay managers, and their friends in fashion and media, who were chiefly responsible for creating the image of British youth culture that was being sold around the world. But as artists gained more power, they became increasingly more difficult. Managers found that their principal job had changed. It was no longer to build an artist's image, it was to mediate with the record company. Managers had become the link between self-centred, self-indulgent artists and insensitive, profit-driven corporations.

Personally, I found the job to be classically two-faced. The manager had to instigate promotion and touring plans that would gain the approval of both sides. I sometimes sat in record company meetings disagreeing only very moderately with their plans before heading back to the artist and pretending that what had been planned came mainly from my suggestions and had been pushed through despite record company opposition. To be a mediator required a certain subtlety of background. Gay managers seemed to be the best at it. Most of them had got used to playing a two-faced game between the straight world and their own. Jewish managers were also excellent, many of them having played the same double game since they were schoolkids.

In the sixties the media had not yet come to realise this. Instead, it saw managers as having immense power and sinister motives. For the managers, one of the delights of the job was to go along with that image and bask in the headlines, 'Machiavellis of the Media', 'Master Manipulators', 'Superstar Svengalis'. But the truth was, nine out of ten pop managers became successful simply by choosing a winning artist and persuading them to sign a management contract.

Robert Stigwood had done just this. He was now the manager of three superb musicians who were in the process of putting together a new group.

Eric Clapton, having left John Mayall, joined with drummer Ginger Baker and bass player Jack Bruce, both of whom had been with the Graham Bond Organisation. (Graham Bond was a twenty-stone keyboard player whose principal claim to fame was that every time he walked through customs at an airport, he would shout, 'If you want the drugs I've got them up my arse.')

The name of this new group was Cream, Britain's first 'supergroup'. They were supposed to be the masters of heavy blues, but Clapton later admitted, 'We rarely played as an ensemble; we were three virtuosi, all of us soloing all the time ... which wasn't the way to approach it at all. All we were doing was producing aggressive music.'

Cream's sound was louder than any other group before them. Instead of creating a hypnotic rhythm, like rock 'n' roll or rhythm & blues, the guitar and bass fought each other with soaring counterpoints while the drums thrashed wildly. The music was unmistakably heavy and the group did heavy drugs to go with it.

All three members plunged into heroin addiction and Eric Clapton wallowed in it as if it were the essential food of his music. At the time he said, 'To sing the blues your soul must be as empty as your stomach.' Later he told a journalist, 'There was definitely a heroic aspect to it. I was trying to prove I could do it and come out alive.'

When Robert Stigwood got on the wrong side of Don Arden, it was the manager rather than the group who nearly failed to come out alive.

Don managed the Small Faces. He wasn't gay and his management style involved neither mediation nor compromise. At the age of thirteen, he'd dropped out of school. After that he made money by being a stand-up comic, a singer and an organiser of Hebrew folk song contests. In his mid-thirties, he got the chance to compere a tour headlined by Gene Vincent who was alcoholic and mentally unstable. Arden became his manager. By the time he realised he couldn't cope with Vincent's problems he was hooked on management.

Like him or not, Don Arden did well. At one time or another he managed the Nashville Teens, the Small Faces, Amen Corner, the Move, ELO and Black Sabbath. But he always seemed to get into disputes.

Arden had his followers – like Peter Grant, whom he employed as a booking agent and who went on to become rock music's most influential manager – and rivals too, principally the Gunnells, two sharp brothers who managed acts and ran clubs. On one occasion the two rivals vowed to smash up each other's offices. Both sides phoned for demolition crews, but in London the demand for such specialist work was small – most of the available men worked for the same agency. Lenny the

Leaper (not his real name) told me of an occasion when he was heading for the Gunnells' office planning to do a little damage when he saw some of his friends heading for Don Arden's place. 'By the time we'd all 'ad a drink together at the Red Fox in Wardour Street, we couldn't be bothered any more.'

Ray Phillips of the Nashville Teens used to go and see Don in his office and barter for the money due to the group. 'If he owed us a grand he'd say, "Would you settle for six hundred?" Then he'd wait till the banks closed before he gave you the cheque.'

Once, when pianist John Hawken insisted on being given £120 he was owed, Arden went berserk and pinned him by the throat to the wall, screaming, 'I have the strength of ten men in these fingers.'

When the Who moved into the American rock scene, the Small Faces took over their crown as the mods' favourite pop band. The Faces became huge and played gigs up and down the country night after night. Rather than account to them in too much detail, Don Arden simply paid for them to live in grand style. The group shared a luxurious communal apartment and had charge accounts at every shop in Carnaby Street. They toured Britain in a chauffeur-driven Jaguar endlessly rolling and smoking joints. Keyboard player Ian McLagan was the master of their production. 'We'd take turns rolling spliffs and give ourselves points out of ten, the idea being to roll such an unsuss joint you'd be able to smoke it in broad daylight, passing a policeman in the street.'

The Small Faces' parents suspected that the group was being overworked and underpaid, and they worried that their beloved children seemed always to be tired. The parents asked for a meeting, but before they could speak Arden pre-empted them. 'They're not tired because they're doing gigs,' he said. 'They're tired because they're up all night with drugs.'

'It completely defused the complaints about money,' Arden told me, 'but the parents didn't like it, and nor did the boys. It turned them against me.'

When he heard they were dissatisfied with their current manager, Robert Stigwood invited the Small Faces to a meeting. Arden got to hear of it and paid him a visit. 'There was a large ashtray on the table. I picked it up and smashed it down with such force that the desk cracked. I pretended to go berserk. Two of my men lifted Stigwood from his chair, dragged him to the balcony and held him so he looked down to the pavement four floors below.'

Later Arden changed the story. 'It was only one floor,' he insisted.

Andrew Oldham had now moved beyond management and started Immediate Records. He decided to help Don Arden by buying the Small Faces from him. 'I just took a little of my Rolling Stones money and put it into the Small Faces.' In fact, it was £25,000 – a huge sum in those days – and Arden insisted that he deliver it in cash in a brown paper bag.

From the word go, Immediate Records declared war on the four major record companies. Not only did they have the Small Faces, they also got an instant hit by buying the rights to an American record, 'Hang On Sloopy' by the McCoys, which went straight to No. 1. Because they paid more for this record than it could possibly earn them, the music press accused Andrew Oldham of 'buying' success. Riled by their comments, he signed two British artists which he claimed he would develop – Cat Stevens and the Nice.

The Nice were managed by Tony Stratton-Smith, who soon began to feel his authority being undermined by Andrew Oldham's flair and showmanship. When the group played a concert at the Albert Hall, Oldham persuaded them to get publicity by burning an American flag during the show. Later, when they wanted to get visas to tour the States, they found it difficult. They then complained bitterly that Andrew was to blame. However, like all Immediate's artists, they could never complain about lack of chart success. Oldham was the master of chart fixing. 'There wasn't anything to stop you putting a load of girls in taxis, telling them which shops to go to, especially on Thursday and Friday. We'd send them back in on a Saturday to re-order when there was no stock there, so that you got big re-orders on the Monday morning.'

Tony Calder, his partner, also had another method. 'It was possible to identify key people in important chart shops and send them a regular weekly payment to list whichever records you wanted in the charts. It would cost around £500 a week, but it was reliable.' By this method, Tony once put an Immediate record in the chart when it shouldn't have been there. 'We had the Beach Boys' publishing, so we paid a certain person to put "Help Me Rhonda" into the chart. But we got the dates wrong. EMI called us up and said: "What's going on? The record's in the charts and we haven't even pressed any records yet."'

In May 1966, I sat and watched the NME Poll-winners' Concert at Wembley Arena. On the bill that day were the Kinks, the Who, the Yardbirds, the Rolling Stones and the Beatles – probably the best line-up of acts ever dreamed of, but these big concerts were not as good as people nowadays think they were. In fact, most of them were downright terrible.

There was insufficient amplification and far too much screaming. Groups were unable to hear themselves play.

There was no way of balancing the sound at live concerts the way it's done today, with a mixing desk. The size of the vocal amplifier was chosen according to the size of venue – medium for Hammersmith Odeon, large for Wembley Arena, gigantic for Shea Stadium. The amplification of the guitars and keyboards had to be built up to match it, so amps were piled one on top of the other in a towering stack. Then you couldn't hear the drums.

Kenny Lynch toured with the Beatles at the time they got their first hit. 'Nobody cared about bad sound because everyone was screaming. As soon as the audience heard the first chord of a hit record, in their minds they then heard the record. The screaming was deafening. There was no point doing a sound check because when the gig started no one could hear anyway. Besides, our voices were completely wrecked.'

On the same tour, DJ Jimmy Savile had the job of introducing the Beatles. 'The best work I ever had, because for fourteen days I never uttered a word ... All I did was stand by the various rostrums and imitate the guitar-playing action of the three Beatles and Ringo on drums. I whipped the audience into a fever without saying a word.'

Of all the top bands, the best live shows came from the Stones and the Who. The Stones had Mick Jagger's fantastic stage presence backed with hypnotic rhythm. The Who had their amazing instrument-wrecking climax.

Kit Lambert, one of the Who's two managers, was one of many people who claimed credit for this manic finale. His father, Constant Lambert, had been a famous composer who was hugely successful with a choral work at the age of twenty-three. He then struggled for twenty years to create something else as good. When it was finally performed at Covent Garden the critics blasted it, and within six weeks Kit's father had drunk himself to death.

Kit decided his father's death was a triumphant suicide – a slap in the face for the critics. In the Who's equipment-smashing finale he saw a theatrical representation of his father's death. The members of the group had other explanations. Roger Daltrey said it was because 'we were all pillheads'. Keith Moon thought it happened whenever the audience responded insufficiently. 'That's when your fucking instruments go, because – "You fucking bastards! We've worked our fucking balls off, and you've given us nothing back."'

Whatever the reason behind it, their instrument-smashing act was what moved the Who away from pop and into rock.

Around that time, Kit Lambert pulled off another coup. He persuaded *Ready Steady Go!* to devote a whole programme to the group and call it *Ready Steady Who*. One night over dinner Kit told me, 'We're going to bribe the right person with £10,000.' I persuaded him not to. 'If you give someone £10,000 he'll think what he's doing is really terrible. If you offer them less, he'll think it's not so bad.' So Kit offered £500 and got the show anyway.

Afterwards, the whole of Britain came to recognise the Who's trademark of swirling arms, swinging mikes and deafening destruction. Kit was constantly reminding the group, 'Never let the music get in the way of the act.'

For the Yardbirds, the very opposite was required, music had to come first. At their best they could play blues to match the

Rolling Stones, and more authentically too, particularly with Jeff Beck in the group.

In Paris one night, Paul Samwell-Smith settled on the date he would leave and we started looking for a replacement. To play bass, Jeff Beck proposed bringing in Jimmy Page, who was then a top session guitarist. I suspected that Page was too good a guitarist, and too ambitious, to settle for playing bass guitar. But Jeff insisted everything would go well, so Page came in. After just three or four gigs he persuaded Chris Dreja, the rhythm guitarist, to take over on bass. Jimmy Page became joint lead guitarist with Jeff Beck, which was the obvious thing to do. It should have made them the finest rock unit in the world, and for a few weeks it looked like they might be.

I booked the group to do a tour with the Rolling Stones. While it was in progress I had to produce their new single. Having laid down a basic backing track, I got them to fly to London each day from wherever they happened to be and add their part to the record. The record was 'Happenings Ten Years Time Ago'. On it, Jeff Beck used feedback – the first time anyone had done such a thing on a pop single – and we added bits of speech and sound effects, like a big stewpot of sound. None of this seemed to me to be particularly out of the ordinary in terms of inventiveness, but the critics picked up on it and called it revolutionary, so the Yardbirds were obviously still heading in the right direction. The problem was, with Jeff Beck and Jimmy Page together in the group they were also on the path to auto-destruct.

The Rolling Stones and the Yardbirds together made a great bill. The Yardbirds had the first hour, the Stones the second. Jimmy Page and Jeff Beck stood either side of the stage playing all Jeff's famous solos in stereo. For the first time, it gave the group a strong stage image, but tensions were rising within the group. For Jimmy the problem was that these solos were not his own creation. For Jeff the problem was that Jimmy was stealing half his applause.

There was a sinister potential in these two great guitarists standing each side of the stage. It should have been developed into some sort of contest – good versus evil, light versus dark, pop versus rock. It reminded me of exactly the kind of contest the press had created between the Rolling Stones and the Beatles.

For the media, the Rolling Stones epitomised the bad ways of this new rock music while the Beatles represented good clean pop. The public watched this struggle fascinated – clean living versus decadence and drugs.

Of course, it was never that straightforward. Behind the scenes the Beatles were not such good boys. Nor the Stones really so bad. It was Paul McCartney, for instance, who had first introduced Mick Jagger to pot. 'In my little music room at Cavendish Avenue, which is funny, because everyone would have thought it would be the other way round.'

Soon the opportunity to exploit the bubbling tension within the Yardbirds presented itself. Kit Lambert told me that the Italian film director Antonioni was in town. He was making a film with David Hemmings called *Blow-Up*. In it, a rock group went crazy on-stage and smashed their instruments. Antonioni had taken the idea from the Who, whom he intended to use in the movie.

Kit had met Antonioni and typically upset him by being rude in some way, so I went to Antonioni's suite at the Savoy and persuaded him the Yardbirds would be the better group for his film. There were two results. First, a few days later the group filmed the scene at Elstree Studios and became stars of the most famous movie of the decade. Secondly, in filming it, Jeff Beck was required to smash his guitar into his amp in the fashion of the Who. In doing so he triggered some previously unseen aggression inside himself and hungered for more.

A little later I arrived with the Yardbirds in New York on the first day of their American tour only to find a national airline strike. To do the tour we had to charter a plane. On the first night, Jeff smashed the neck of his guitar into the front of his amp, breaking both. His amp was a Marshall, made in England, and not readily available in the USA. The first time it happened we found a replacement quite easily, but a few days into the tour it was getting more difficult. Every night there was another amp to be found and another charter flight across America. For instance, when it happened in Montana, the only Marshall amp I could find was in Miami. For a week I was stuck in my suite at the Chicago Hilton waiting for phone calls, searching for amps, chartering planes, watching the money drain away, and by that I mean the group's money, for managers in those days were paid a percentage of the gross tour fees.

Three-quarters of the way through the tour, having given me a crash course in everything a manager should know, Jeff Beck quit the tour. The reasons he gave the press were: 'Inflamed brain, inflamed tonsils and an inflamed cock.'

In 1966, while the trend towards rock music continued, the more public face of the music business was still pop: 145 singles made the Top 20 and sold like never before. The prize for the most No. 1s went to Dave Dee, Dozy, Beaky, Mick & Tich who made hits that sounded like football chants. It was probably because the World Cup was on and everyone was football crazy – even so, after the World Cup was over Dave Dee, Dozy, Beaky, Mick & Tich still went on to have thirteen consecutive Top Five records.

World Cup year produced many classic singles, both pop and rock, and most of them had classic sales figures too. Selling more than half a million were 'Keep On Running' by the Spencer Davis Group, 'Groovy Kind Of Love' by the Mindbenders, 'The Sun Ain't Gonna Shine Anymore' by the Walker Brothers, 'Wild Thing' by the Troggs, 'Pied Piper' by Crispian St Peters, 'Sunny Afternoon' by the Kinks, 'You Don't Have To Say You Love Me' by Dusty Springfield, and 'Out Of Time' by Chris Farlowe.

Farlowe was a favourite mate of both the Stones and the Beatles, and to help him get a hit Paul McCartney wrote a song for him and went round to his house with a demo of it. The next day Chris called Eric Burdon and told him: 'I was out doing a show but me mum was in and he left her a demo disc for me to listen to ... I don't like it. It's too soft.'

'So what are you gonna do with the song?' Eric asked.

'Well, I sent it back, didn't I!'

The song turned out to be 'Yesterday'. Never mind. In the end Chris got a hit with 'Out Of Time', which included Mick Jagger on backing vocals.

Halfway through the year, the Beatles announced they were worn out by touring and were giving it up. I sympathised with them. Just organising a single tour for the difficult Yardbirds had been enough for me, whereas the Beatles had played shows all over the world for four years to an endless barrage of screaming. Noël Coward summed it up after seeing them perform for the first time. 'I am all for audiences going mad with enthusiasm *after* the performance, but not incessantly *during* the performance, so there ceases to be a performance.'

At the beginning of July, the Beatles had fled for their lives in Manila when a riot erupted at the airport as they were leaving, having apparently snubbed Imelda Marcos. At the end of the month, John Lennon did something that made their next tour even more difficult. Just before they set off for America, in an interview with Maureen Cleave, he said that, with today's mass communications, the Beatles were more famous among their generation than Jesus Christ had been among his.

In the Bible-thumping belt of the Southern USA, this was blasphemy. And that was where the Beatles were about to play. As they left London airport, fans screamed: 'John, please don't go, they'll kill you.' All four Beatles had the same fear, and Brian Epstein was forced to send a telegram to the press saying that John 'deeply and sincerely regrets any offence he might have caused'.

In the event, the concerts were packed and the organised protests were ill-attended. Nevertheless, outside the stadium, the Ku Klux Klan held a protest rally, which was something even the Rolling Stones had never managed to provoke. This, coupled with exhaustion from fighting the noise of 50,000 screaming fans every night, made the Beatles decide the time had come to stop touring. And they never played again together on-stage.

The Beatles never made it across the divide from pop to rock. Perhaps it was Brian Epstein's maternal style of management that held them back. He sent them memos like a nagging mother chivvying them with advice. One of his early ones said: 'You're playing Neston tonight, I'm looking for a re-booking, please wear the shirts and ties.'

At the beginning, Epstein's style of management had helped the Beatles but now it prevented them moving from pop to rock. It was the Rolling Stones who'd got it right, and the Who. 'Rock' not only meant playing guitar-based music that could be exported to America and played in stadiums, it meant projecting an image that rejected pop values – no compromise, no acceptance of the record company's authority, nor the manager's, unless he was as anarchic as the group themselves.

Both the Stones and the Who, having succeeded in making the transition, were now travelling the world in limousine luxury, staying in the best hotel suites and behaving like itinerant rock emperors, encouraged by their managers to excess in everything they did. Writer Nik Cohn described touring in America with the Who.

You sleep in sunlight and soak in brandy for breakfast, Bloody Marys for elevenses, tequila for lunch; swallow uppers by the handful, downers by the tub, smoke and suck and sniff on whatever comes to hand ... Thus the tour is littered with numberless corpses. Roadies fall down elevator shafts, groupies suffocate in the shower. Promoters go bankrupt, security guards run amok with their nightsticks, the warm-up group blow themselves up. Journalists, almost always, are shipped home under sedation.

The Who were the first rock band to realise the image potential of trashing hotel rooms, something the Stones had never thought of. Keith Moon travelled with an axe. 'If it's another bloody 'oliday Inn and I get bored, I just take out me 'atchet and chop the room to bits – the bed, the chairs, the floor, the wardrobe, the tele, the toilet.'

The Who were setting a trend that was being followed by others too – rock music was beginning to be connected with violence and antisocial behaviour, and the kids loved it. Journalist John Blake, still at school at the time, remembered how he worshipped the Stones and the other groups who were turning pop into rock. 'They represented everything we felt inside – resentment of the boring older generation who were still talking about the last war and eating grey roast beef. The violence the groups perpetrated was exciting, it was anarchy, it gave us hope that we could get out of our boring homes and do our own thing. My father was an ex-army man. He loathed these people. He saw rock groups as the enemy.'

Meanwhile, the Animals were still trapped in pop.

Eric Burdon complained bitterly about Mike Jeffery, their manager. 'He was doing all kinds of really small deals, like signing the group for a Wrigley's Spearmint chewing-gum commercial. And we had a No. 1 smash hit both sides of the Atlantic. I already felt uncomfortable when he forced us to wear shiny suits and clean up for the American tour ... Who needed cleaning up? And as for chewing-gum commercials, I knew who was going to be cleaning up and it wasn't going to be the band.'

Eric was right, chewing gum advertisements were not the right image, Mike had obviously missed the point of what rock music was about and where it was going. Yet when it came to making hits, all the other rock groups were just as poppy as the Animals. The only two groups that seemed able to move away from a pop sound when they made singles were the Spencer Davis Group and the Rolling Stones.

But while most groups still made their singles with a pop sound, in their lifestyles they mostly followed the Stones into drugs and self-indulgence. In the space of just a year it had suddenly become chic for groups to behave badly – to wreck hotel rooms, to wreak havoc wherever they could, to over-indulge in drugs. Even Brian Epstein, who'd started out as the epitome of well-behaved, nicely brought-up middle-class England, now admitted to journalists that he was taking acid. But that wasn't all. With the Beatles no longer touring, he felt left out of things.

Almost weekly he hospitalised himself for injections that gave him 48 hours' sleep to recover from the non-stop ups and downs of amphetamine and barbiturate. For the Beatles drug-taking was a part of youthful exuberance but for their manager it was a symptom of depression and loneliness.

In New York at the end of the year I had dinner with Andy Warhol and a bunch of his disciples. 'Brian Epstein was here last week,' Andy told me. 'He went to all the wrong parties.' He shook his head despairingly; it seemed such a put-down. Obviously nothing could have been worse and I hoped I wasn't about to make the same mistakes.

'He's doing the wrong drugs, too,' a disciple added. 'It's so important not to. Not in his position.'

CHAPTER EIGHT

THE ACID TRUTH

Lysergic acid diethylamide was first synthesised by Dr Albert Hofmann, a Swiss scientist working for Sandoz Pharmaceuticals. In the 1920s he began to synthesise a number of compounds derived from the fungus ergot, which comes from rye. The 25th in his series of distillations was LSD, but he had no idea what he'd discovered until in 1943 he accidentally ingested some of it.

'My visual field wavered and everything appeared deformed as if in a faulty mirror ... I thought I'd died. My ego seemed suspended somewhere in space from where I saw my dead body lying on a sofa ... Acoustic perceptions such as the noise of water gushing from a tap were transformed into optical illusions.'

In 1947 LSD was found to have calming effects on schizophrenics. It caused people to open up and communicate freely with one another, so the CIA ordered 100 grams a week, produced legally by Sandoz, and started testing it with a view to using it as an aid in the interrogation of prisoners. First they tested it in brothels with two-way mirrors. Members of the public were picked up by prostitutes, given LSD-spiked drinks, and observed by CIA agents as they attempted to perform the sex they'd come for.

Timothy Leary, the high priest of Psychedelia, was first turned on to LSD by an Englishman who turned up on his doorstep with a mayonnaise jar full of the stuff. The mind-changing view of the world it gave him caused Leary to become its greatest proponent, preaching its benefits to the rich and famous. Rumour had it that one of the women consorting with President Kennedy had turned him on to it shortly before he was assassinated. Time Inc. founder Henry Luce claimed it had given him a glimpse of God. Hollywood actor Cary Grant said that under its influence he had been born again. George Harrison said when he first took acid 'in ten minutes I lived a thousand years'.

In 1967, in a single year, acid infused British pop culture in a way that was unprecedented. It changed music, fashion, design, and the way young people thought.

I had my own hallucinogenic experience when I saw a group called the Silence. For some reason I thought I could make them world-beaters. From then on, instead of concentrating on the Yardbirds, I wasted my time on fantasy.

The fantasy was to create something of my own. On a short holiday to the South of France, I'd met the bass player with the Silence. When I got back I went to see his group play. They weren't strong musically but they had an energy and charm that was irresistible. From then on the Yardbirds got less attention than they should have done. As a long-term business move it was as foolish as Andrew Oldham preferring Immediate Records to the Rolling Stones.

I changed my new group's name to John's Children, John being the name of the bass player I'd first met and whom I rather fancied – a surefire recipe for disaster. I then made their first single with session musicians in Los Angeles and released it in the States through White Whale Records. In the States the track was called 'Smashed! Blocked!' which was considered pretty risqué since 'blocked' was a straight-up drug reference. But we actually got a hit. The introduction was long and jangling, with rambling speech from the singer – 'Where am I? My mind's spinning' etc. – but the verse that followed it was a straight copy of an eight-bar blues from an old Jimmy Hughes record, and the chorus was pinched from a German drinking song. Despite this, because of the stoned-sounding intro, an American reviewer called it 'psychedelic' which was one of the first occasions the word had been used about a record. As a result it was perceived to be extremely avant-garde and druggy.

By 1967 the mere sight of a pop star could cause people to presume there were drugs in the vicinity. But when the Rolling Stones released 'Mother's Little Helper' they reminded us that it wasn't only the younger generation who were taking them.

I'd taken on the job of writing the music score for the film *Here We Go Round the Mulberry Bush*, for which Stevie Winwood had written the title song. One night, after he'd been rehearsing for a week in the country with Traffic, Stevie turned up at the Cromwellian club with a good story. 'On Sunday morning we were playing in a field outside the cottage when a fox hunt passed by, all red jackets and tooting horns. A man galloped over and we thought he was coming to say we were frightening the foxes, but not a bit of it. "I say," he shouted, "any of you chaps got some speed?"'

The Cromwellian had taken over as the principal haunt of London's showbusiness set. It was in an elegant house in Cromwell Road. There were bars upstairs and down, some of them loud with music, all of them loud with gossip. But a lot of people seemed to have stopped talking – they just stared into space and said how beautiful everything looked. It was acid.

As usual I stuck to booze, but I thought acid might be worth finding out about. It was as well for a manager to know what his group was likely to be taking.

The Beatles said they'd been introduced to it by a dentist friend at a private dinner party. Without telling them what he was doing, their host had dosed John and George and their wives Cynthia and Patti. Then he told them: 'I advise you not to leave.' John and George thought he was trying to keep them for an orgy so they left and went to a nightclub. When the acid hit them they thought the club was on fire and their table seemed to elongate. Later, back at George's house, John imagined he was in a submarine floating eighteen feet above the ground.

In January, the *News of the World* had run a series, 'Pop Stars and Drugs: Facts That Will Shock You'. It revealed that Donovan and Pete Townshend were now taking LSD as well as the pills and pot they'd already admitted to.

By now, smoking pot was considered completely normal for anyone under thirty, but people caught doing it were still being given a six-month jail sentence. Prominent members of British society were planning to put an advertisement in *The Times* calling for a change in the law. But before the ad could be placed, the British police decided pop stars should be taught a lesson. They made two raids in quick succession.

At Brian Jones's house they found a lump of hash in a drawer. At Keith Richards' they discovered a party in progress. One of the guests was Mick Jagger with four amphetamine tablets in his pocket. Another guest was Marianne Faithfull, Mick's girlfriend, whom the tabloids reported as having been naked and abusing a Mars bar. Mick had purchased the amphetamine tablets legally in

Italy where they were sold as a preventative for air-sickness. He was charged with illegal possession. Keith was charged for allowing Mick into his house with them. After that the Stones went on holiday to Morocco.

My new group, John's Children, were keen on drugs of all sorts. While they sometimes smoked the odd joint with me, I was aware that their own preference was for amphetamines, especially the drummer who happily took them by the handful.

As the creative force behind this new group, I was taking the job very seriously. The Yardbirds had made me some money but hadn't rewarded me with much fun. From John's Children I was planning to get both money and fun. My idea was to be neither showbizzy, like the early Beatles, nor antisocial like the Stones. It was to create four instantly identifiable faces and make the group's image the relationship between them – good, bad, happy or argumentative – it wouldn't matter whether they were enjoying their music together or fighting over girlfriends. I wanted to create a living soap opera of four boys in a group.

The trouble was, in those days there was no chance of creating the thing as a real soap opera on TV, it could only be done through snippets of press and publicity. It was a grandiose idea and in the end its success would probably come down to nothing more or less than getting a hit record. Moreover, there was no way their story could ever compete with the real-life soap opera of the day – the Rolling Stones' drug trial.

During his trial, Mick Jagger was held for two days in the basement cells of Lewes prison. People asked was he really being treated this way for possessing four tablets bought legally in Italy; tablets that were also legal in Britain providing a doctor prescribed them? Barbara Hulanicki, the owner of Biba in Kings Road, remembered her mother taking them. 'It's quite funny to think how many middle-aged women in the sixties were unknowingly on amphetamines. Sometimes I pinched one of my mother's purple hearts, which the doctor prescribed for her to lift her spirits when she was feeling low.'

For being in possession of the same pills, Mick Jagger was sentenced to six months' imprisonment. For letting Mick into his house with them, Keith Richards was given a year. On appeal, the judges decided that by over-emphasising Marianne Faithfull's nakedness the prosecution had swayed the jury 'with prurience rather than legal consideration'. Keith's sentence was quashed and Mick received a conditional discharge.

The truth behind the party was only disclosed much later, when some of the people involved started to write autobiographies. Some time before, Keith and Brian had discovered acid and started taking it regularly. Because it changed the way they heard music, they wanted Mick to take it too. They invited him for the weekend intending to introduce him to it. In fact, he'd already been taking it with Marianne Faithfull.

In the aftermath of the case the Small Faces decided to spit in the face of the establishment. Even though they were now heavily into acid, they wrote 'Here Comes The Nice' – an anthem to pill-popping. With the Who spending more time in America, the Small Faces had become the new heroes of mod culture. As a sop to their pillhead fans they went on *Top of the*

Pops and sang, 'Here comes the nice – he knows what I need – he's always there when I need some speed.'

The drug squad were too preoccupied to notice.

In John's Children, I replaced the group's gangling guitarist with an elfin boy called Marc Bolan who turned up on my doorstep in search of a manager. He impressed me enough to record a first single with him, but it was turned down by every company. Nobody could accept the strange wavering sound of his singing, a sound he'd developed by listening to albums by Billy Eckstine and blues singer Bessie Smith speeded up to 45 rpm. So when it became clear that he wasn't going to get a deal, I suggested to Marc that he join John's Children who were now signed to Track Records, Kit Lambert's label.

Kit put the group on tour with the Who in Germany. I helped John's Children devise a suitably manic act in which they would appear to act out their frustrations with one another. A letter in *Melody Maker* from a British soldier based in Germany described it well. 'The lead singer ... rolled on-stage, had a fight with the bass guitarist, leapt into the audience several times and collapsed crying into the back of the stage. The lead guitarist kicked his equipment, beat the stage with a silver chain and sat in a trance between his speakers ... It was sickening.'

Working with Kit Lambert made me wonder what managers should really be aiming for. What were we supposed to be doing? Making money? Enjoying ourselves? Doing our best for the people we managed? Even if enjoying ourselves was the principal criterion, this would mean something different to each person. For one person it meant bucking the system, putting two fingers up at the world, getting the group to piss people off. For another it meant being stoned all day, and for another it might mean making loads of dosh and stashing it away in the bank. For me, as far as I can remember, it meant eating endless good meals, having sex with anyone pretty and making enough money to pay for it all. No wonder the acts we managed were sometimes upset with us. But then most of them had equally frivolous motives for wanting success.

Quite rightly, the Yardbirds became resentful at the time I spent on other things. I attempted to defuse their frustrations by encouraging each of them to do their own solo projects. Keith Relf, the singer, made a single on his own. So did Jeff Beck – 'Beck's Bolero' – on which Jimmy Page played second guitar and Keith Moon played drums. Nominally, I was the producer.

The producer's job is to get the best possible performance from the artists. With Jimmy Page, Jeff Beck and Keith Moon, it seemed that the best performances would be achieved by giving them time to work things out as they wanted. So I left them to it. It seemed like a good production technique, but while I was gone it led to more arguments.

Jeff Beck decided he wanted to leave the Yardbirds and Mickie Most agreed to produce a pop single with him. Mickie's partner, Peter Grant, said he would like to take over as manager of the Yardbirds which seemed like a good idea so I didn't contest it. Instead, I agreed to manage Jeff, who was forming a new group with Rod Stewart and Ronnie Wood.

The Beatles had a PR problem. All four of them were heavily into acid and Paul McCartney had inadvertently told a journalist from *Queen* magazine that he'd seen God while taking it. There was an immediate media backlash.

Just at that time, a pro-marijuana advertisement was about to appear in *The Times* endorsed by a list of famous people which included novelist Graham Greene, MPs Tom Driberg and Brian Walden, theatre critic Ken Tynan, artist David Hockney, and psychiatrist RD Laing. Stephen Abrams, the American behind *The Times* advertisement, persuaded the Beatles that by adding their names to the list they would deflect the public's attention away from their involvement with LSD. Brian Epstein was not only convinced by Abrams's argument, he also agreed that the Beatles would pay for the advertisement, and he sent a cheque to *The Times*.

Despite the number of famous names in the advertisement, it was the names of the Beatles and their manager that caught the public's attention. In one way, that was what they'd intended, but the result wasn't what they'd hoped for. The problem arose from them having paid for it. Derek Taylor, their press agent, explained, 'Although the ad was about marijuana, everyone knew the Beatles took all sorts of other drugs too. By financing it, they seemed to be endorsing all those other drugs as well – particularly acid.'

But really, who cared? Everyone else was endorsing it too. Marianne Faithfull said she watched Mick Jagger change for the better under its influence. 'He transcended all his pettiness, his guardedness.' She believed it was the act of taking acid together that bonded Mick and Keith so closely and allowed their relationship to last so long. John Lennon told friends about a trip to California with David Crosby and Peter Fonda, who kept whispering, 'I know what it's like to be dead.' Eric Clapton told friends that acid was 'conducive to exploring music', and after taking it he decided to quit playing pure blues. The Animals were totally lost in its haze. Eric Burdon tried to explain: 'The drug experience has taught us that to be deranged is not necessarily to be totally useless.' Deranged or not, under its influence Chas Chandler, the group's bass player, saw guitarist Jimi Hendrix playing in a New York blues club and immediately quit the group and took up management.

The previous November, 'Good Vibrations' by the Beach Boys had gone to No. 1 and been seen as the first 'acid' hit. Now the Beach Boys were coming to Britain and we all packed into the Hammersmith Odeon to see them. The main purpose of going to see them was to hear them sing 'Good Vibrations' which Brian Wilson called his 'masterwork'. But just before the show he announced they wouldn't be performing it because it was too difficult and had only been conceived as a record.

The support group for the first half of the show was led by Britain's most brilliant session singer, Adrian Baker. At the end of their set, just before the interval, they sang 'Good Vibrations' – perfectly – absolutely indistinguishable from the Beach Boys' single. After that, the Beach Boys played a grumpy, lacklustre set. It was Adrian Baker's evening.

Afterwards there was plenty of talk about the Beach Boys and their drug excesses. They lived in luxury mansions, breakfasted on hash-cake sundaes, and recorded their hits lying on the floor, too stoned to stand up. As children, whenever they misbehaved, their father had punished them by taking out his glass eye and forcing them to peer into the open socket. Like all other pop stars, the Beach Boys were now heavily into acid, which was probably why they'd never got round to working out how to perform 'Good Vibrations' on-stage.

Another singer none too firmly rooted to the ground was Donovan. His record 'Mellow Yellow' had promoted the benefits of marijuana from the No. 1 spot on both sides of the Atlantic and he'd become the idol of the drug crowd. On one occasion he was invited to meet his hero, Bob Dylan, on whom he modelled himself. Dylan politely asked him to play something so Donovan got out his guitar and sang a song that was plainly 'Mr Tambourine Man', but with different words. Eventually Dylan stopped him and said he knew the song already, thank you, it was his. Donovan was mortified. The tune had floated into his head one day, and even though he'd heard Dylan sing it a thousand times he'd failed to realise what it was. So he'd written lyrics to it and taken it as his own.

Now, having discovered LSD, Donovan was floating still further into unreality. He took to waffling to the press in the flower-power language so typical of pop stars on acid. 'I have big dreams ... beautiful things ... controlling the whole market ... all the art ... that's how we're gonna make it ... like Greece, like the Parthenon ...'

Meanwhile, actually heading for the Parthenon, was John Lennon. He'd gone on a holiday to Greece with his friend Magic Alex. But when they arrived at the hotel in Athens, Lennon realised he'd left his acid behind in a drawer at his London house. In a fit of temper, he screamed, 'What good's the bloody Parthenon without LSD!'

Groups who experimented with acid invariably changed their acts from violent rock to something gentler. The Move were from Birmingham. When they'd first arrived in London, they'd tried to take over from the Who as chief rabble-rousers. They smashed things on-stage – TV sets, furniture, pictures of Hitler. Their manager was Tony Secunda. If he saw a stroke to pull, he would pull it. When flower-power came along he told the Move to forget about violence and record a song called 'Flowers In The Rain'. To publicise it they concocted a picture of the Prime Minister naked in bed with his secretary. It got them a writ, but it also got them a hit.

My group John's Children had also experimented with acid and were now anxious to embrace flower-power too. Marc Bolan had decided to leave them and the remaining members opted for a peaceful image photographed naked except for a skimpy covering of flowers. The resulting picture was printed in sepia and postered all over London. Within days the posters had been stripped off the walls only to reappear in sitting rooms and bathrooms all over the city. The group's new record was a flop but their picture had been a smash.

Another picture making the news was Mick Jagger's bottom. Before their drug trial the Stones had gone to Marrakech. Staying at the same hotel was Cecil Beaton, friend and photographer of royalty. Beaton was fascinated with Mick and wrote in his diary, 'He is very gentle, and with perfect manners. He has much appreciation and his small, albino-fringed eyes notice everything ... we sat next to each other as he drank a Vodka Collins and smoked with pointed finger held high. His skin is chicken-breast white and of a fine quality ...'

Beaton persuaded Mick to walk with him in the woods. 'I took Mick through the trees to photograph him in the midday sun. I gave his face the shadows it needed. The lips were of a fantastic roundness, the body almost hairless and yet, surprisingly, I made him look like Tarzan by Piero di Cosimo.'

Mick then let Beaton take a picture of his naked bottom. Later, it was hung in an art gallery and sold for £2,000.

Acid, it seemed, had made Jagger gentler. His pill-fuelled menace seemed to have disappeared altogether. On another occasion, on a TV chat show, he argued with Britain's self-appointed preserver of 'traditional moral values', Mary Whitehouse. The audience sided with Mick and rounded on Mrs Whitehouse. Afterwards, as she was leaving the studio, he ran after her and apologised profusely for putting her in that position.

That summer, Tom Jones's manager, Gordon Mills, had a second consecutive triumph. He found a moody Anglo-Indian called Gerry Dorsey whom he renamed Engelbert Humperdinck. The song that launched him was even worse than his name. 'Release Me' was pure back-to-the-fifties slush, but it stayed at No. 1 for five weeks.

People were growing tired of endless groups and the energy of their music. Engelbert had dark good looks and was aiming not at the teen market, but at housewives in their twenties and thirties. His second record did even better. 'The Last Waltz' sold a million copies in the UK alone. Journalist Derek Jewell commented, 'Engelbert's success was extraordinary – after all the changes in the pop world, after the emergence of rock music, after young people everywhere had been turned onto drugs of all sorts – the biggest thing of the year turns out to be a throwback to the early fifties.'

Immediately after Engelbert's success with 'Release Me', Sandie Shaw won the Eurovision Song Contest with 'Puppet On A String'. It was clear that there was an enormous and growing division between rock and pop, although when it came to making singles, most rock bands reverted to a pop format.

Jeff Beck, for example, Britain's foremost blues guitarist, had now made an out-and-out pop record with Mickie Most – 'Hi Ho Silver Lining'. I thought by managing Jeff I couldn't fail. Eric Clapton and Jimmy Page may have had greater guitar technique but neither could match Jeff for sheer blues feeling. It must have driven Eric mad. There he was dosing himself to death with heroin, trying to reach the 'perfect vacuum' where he would play blues like a black man, but Jeff could play blues twice as well on a cup of tea.

When Jeff put together his new group I thought all I had to do was leave them to rehearse and I would be the manager of a supergroup. Of course it wasn't as simple as that. I set them up on a UK tour with the Small Faces and at the first gig they walked out on-stage as if they'd never played together. In the *Melody Maker*, Chris Welch said, 'They were obviously unrehearsed. They played badly and created a very poor impression.'

That was putting it mildly. They were utterly shambolic. Rod Stewart walked on-stage with his flies undone, the power failed after one number, and the curtain came down and knocked Ronnie Wood on the head, knocking him off balance.

Later, Rod said the Small Faces had pulled the plug because they thought Jeff Beck might steal the show. Whatever was behind the debacle, my inability to find an immediate solution to it left me without a group. A month later 'Hi Ho Silver Lining' came out and Jeff had a hit.

But I was no longer managing him.

In California, one weekend in June, a hundred thousand orchids were flown from Hawaii and scattered over crowds in a field in Monterey. They were there to see an incredible weekend of music. the Who played a stunning set, Eric Burdon played a less stunning one, and Jimi Hendrix was as brilliant as ever. Because the rumour was so strong anyway, it was announced that three of the Beatles were in the audience disguised as hippies. In fact they were in London, recording their greatest work to date.

Sgt. Pepper's Lonely Hearts Club Band was released in July 1967. It was rumoured that the Beatles had used acid to write it, but Paul McCartney insists they used mainly cocaine and grass. The public preferred the LSD story. They spotted 'Lucy In The Sky With Diamonds', with its talk of 'cellophane flowers' and 'kaleidoscope eyes'. In the *Sunday Times*, Derek Jewell said, '*Pepper* is a tremendous advance even in the increasingly adventurous progress of the Beatles.' Allen Ginsberg, the beat poet, said it was a 'towering modern opera'. In *Newsweek*, its finale was described as 'a growling, bone-grinding crescendo that drones up like a giant crippled turbine struggling to spin new life into a foundered civilisation'. By any account, it seemed a pretty good record.

Jimi Hendrix thought so too. When he played at the Saville Theatre on the Sunday after its release, he played the title track of *Sgt. Pepper* as his opening number. The audience that night was dazzling, and included everyone who was anyone in popular music. Graham Nash of the Hollies remembers,

'Hendrix came out in this flame-orange velvet suit playing "Sgt. Pepper" and we were just blown away.'

I was there too, but I can't remember the orange suit, just the charisma and showmanship. After the show, *Sunday Times* critic Nik Cohn wrote, 'He was mesmeric. He was ferocious and sexy. He was an ugly man and he had endless charm.'

'Incredible,' said Paul McCartney, and invited everyone to an after-show party.

Hendrix had learnt his showmanship playing guitar in Little Richard's rock 'n' roll band. He was brought to London by his new manager Chas Chandler, and Kit Lambert signed him to Track Records, the label he'd set up with Polydor. Hendrix then got two instant hits – 'Hey Joe' and 'Purple Haze', but apart from when he was on-stage, he wasn't a great communicator. Asked for tips on playing, he said, 'The best thing you can do, brother, is turn it up as loud as it'll go.'

When Eric Clapton first met him, he complained that Hendrix 'spent a lot of time combing his hair in the mirror'. But in no time at all, Clapton became obsessed with him. He told Pete Townshend, 'I stand on-stage now and pretend I am Jimi, and I play better.' John Entwistle, the Who's bass player, wasn't impressed. 'Certainly, he can play. But what he plays is an amalgam of every other guitarist he has seen.' Pete Townshend was also unsure of him. 'He came to London, saw a couple of Who shows, because he was on our label, and immediately started doing guitar pyrotechnic routines.' But when Pete met him again, Hendrix climbed onto a chair and played right into his face. 'Just Jimi, on a chair, playing at me ... like: "Don't fuck with me, you little shit."' After that,

Pete changed his mind and fell in love with him. 'He was a fucking genius. He could have stolen my wife and I would have been happy about it ... Compared to Hendrix, I'm a complete nonentity.'

It was probably acid that changed Pete's mind. That summer, everyone seemed to be in love with everyone else. It was true – people really were wearing flowers behind their ears.

In July, at Abbey Road Studios, the Beatles recorded 'All You Need Is Love' live on camera for national TV. They dressed in trippy silks and satins and were joined by famous friends, among them Mick Jagger playing tambourine in a purple toga with a ring of flowers in his hair. The Beatles and their friends truly believed in the message of love and peace that LSD had given them.

By the time they'd finished singing the song, the whole world believed it too.

When Marc Bolan left John's Children he'd planned to become the Elfin King of Rock. He wanted to form a new all-electric group, but he didn't have the discipline to rehearse them.

Marc told me he'd got himself a gig at the Rock Garden Club in Covent Garden and was putting an ad in the paper to find musicians. He ended up auditioning musicians on the day of the gig and set off to play it on a wing and a prayer. When it was a disaster, he decided to throw away electric instruments for ever and play by himself. He bought himself a rug on which to sit cross-legged playing acoustic guitar accompanied by a friend on bongos. This was Tyrannosaurus Rex. I went into the studio with this new group and we made an album in an hour. There were vocals, guitar, bongos and a gong. I said some of the songs might be better if they were resung. Marc disagreed. He thought it was magic.

Marc was playing gigs on a rug in student union halls for next to nothing. If I tried to act like a good manager and negotiate more money, he objected. 'Man, this business isn't about making money. The whole point of having a manager is to have a nice pad to drop into – somewhere I can listen to music, smoke a few joints and drop some acid.'

So I quit.

People who took acid drifted into a fantasy of coloured dreams. The imagery of being stoned under the effects of LSD started to crop up everywhere. First in magazine graphics, then in trendy ads, then in mainstream ones, like General Electric refrigerators. For most kids in Britain, while the idea of flower-power felt good, acid itself felt dangerous. Dave Ambrose, later to make his name as a bass player, and then as record-company executive, was then a student at art college. 'At first, for most of us, the easy way of connecting with the hippy scene was to smoke hash or grass. It didn't seem so dangerous.'

Journalist Charles Shaar Murray was also a student. 'People at the top of the creative tree were all doing acid. As a result, music and advertising graphics became psychedelised. This caused the kids to be psychedelised. Most kids weren't doing acid, they were getting the culture second-hand. They'd smoke pot because it fitted well with the same culture and was easier to get, and cheaper.'

So, as a result of flower-power and its acid imagery, there was a huge boom in marijuana usage. Both drugs had the same calming effect on the psyche. Young people in Britain had never been more easy-going.

At record companies, while the top executives remained aloof with their traditional middle-class values, a new generation of junior executives was about to replace them. These people had come up through A&R departments and were as well-versed in the new drugs as the groups they looked after. 'It was expected of them,' says Peter Jenner, who at that time was the manager of Pink Floyd. 'It was a part of being an A&R man that they had to join in with everything the group did. It was no secret, Pink Floyd were into acid like mad, so the group expected A&R people to get on the same wavelength.'

When the Beatles televised the recording of 'All You Need Is Love', it reinforced the all-pervading joyful atmosphere of that hot hippy summer. But it hadn't been a happy year for everyone. In February we'd heard about the demise of Joe Meek, the wonder producer of the early sixties. EMI had offered him a job as head of production, but Meek couldn't take it. He was being blackmailed. He was being sued for back royalties. His car had been stolen. He was behind with his rent. He'd been arrested for importuning in a toilet. Later, the dismembered body of a gay acquaintance was found in a hedgerow and the police questioned him. Afterwards, Joe Meek committed suicide.

Around that time, playwright Joe Orton was in talks with the Beatles to write their new movie. In his diaries, Orton reported meeting them over dinner at Brian Epstein's house.

We talked of the theatre ... We talked of drugs, of mushrooms that give hallucination – like LSD ... We talked of tattoos. And, after one or two veiled references, marijuana. I said I'd smoked it in Morocco. The atmosphere relaxed a little. There was a little scratching at the door ... someone got up to open it and about five very young and pretty boys trooped in. I rather hoped this was the evening's entertainment. It wasn't though. It was a pop group called the Easybeats.

Although Brian Epstein commissioned it, Orton never completed his script for the Beatles' new movie. At the beginning of August, just twelve days after the legalisation of homosexuality, Joe Orton's boyfriend murdered him. By the end of August, Brian Epstein's life seemed to be going equally wrong.

When the Beatles stopped playing live, Brian lost his sense of belonging. By taking acid, he also lost his sense of ego. He felt no need to prove himself, or to promote his other acts, or to run his business empire. Unknown to anyone at the time, for a derisory price, he'd agreed to sell Robert Stigwood half of NEMS, the company which controlled all the acts he managed. Robert told me, 'Brian wants to do something different with his life so he's asked me to become joint managing director. He'll still look after the Beatles but I'll be in charge of everything else. I've got a six-month share option. But then, if I pay him half a million pounds, the controlling shares will be transferred to me and I'll control the entire company *including* the Beatles.'

Of course, Robert jumped at it, and the minute he moved into NEMS, he started to change things. He poured the company's money into the promotion of his own new group, the Bee Gees. He had more money available to promote them than any other group in history. He sent them to America, gave parties on rented ocean liners and flew people in with helicopters. Then he plastered Britain with posters and paid Radio Caroline so much money for plugging their new record that they could barely find enough free slots to put them in.

Brian Epstein hated the Bee Gees. When Stiggy told him he'd bought 51 per cent of their publishing for a thousand pounds, Brian screamed petulantly, 'Well that's a thousand pounds out of the window.' When the Bee Gees went to No. 1 a week later, he was even more annoyed. What upset him was the thought of what was flowing between the Bee Gees and their manager, the person bringing them their success. The intimacy, the excitement, the affection. Epstein realised the acid truth. He'd lost it and Stigwood had found it.

Shortly afterwards the Beatles found themselves a new guru.

Maharishi Mahesh Yogi ran a course in North Wales offering fortune-cookie philosophy to anyone who could pay. One weekend in August, all four Beatles left London to go and worship at his feet. By Saturday evening, alone in his house in Belgravia, Brian was too depressed to count his sleeping pills.

He died of the resulting overdose and within weeks the Beatles were running their own independent company – Apple Corps.

CHAPTER NINE

BLACK VINYL, WHITE POWDER

'Remember! Art is for artists. Running a record company is all about shifting black vinyl.'

Maurice Oberstein barked this information at me like a bad-tempered Alsatian intent on scaring away the postman. Obie was head of marketing at CBS. He was American and he was gay, and his peculiar gruff voice was something of a defence, something he'd worked at because when he forgot himself and spoke normally his voice became rather high.

During the first six months of 1968 the biggest headlines had been the assassination of Bobby Kennedy and the US army's execution of innocent villagers at My Lai. But in July, when a pop group called Love Affair admitted they hadn't played a single note on their record, the British tabloids gave them even bigger headlines. Nobody really cared whether the group had played its instruments or not, but any publicity was good when you were plugging a record. Love Affair's song was catchy, the singer was pretty and the record soon went to No. 1. For record companies it was immaterial how a hit was created. All they wanted was to shift black vinyl, and that's what they were doing, as never before.

At CBS I got myself a record label.

Previously, I'd got myself into a tangle. I'd agreed to a contract that tied me exclusively to EMI for everything I produced without their having to pay towards the cost of my productions. When EMI refused to amend the agreement, I set up a label with CBS. To resolve the conflict with EMI, my name as producer was omitted from the credits. Instead, my initials were displayed as the name of the label – SNB.

I soon saw the truth in what Maurice Oberstein had told me. When a manager changed from looking after a group's interests to looking after his own record label, survival meant selling vinyl. For a while, I entered into it wholeheartedly. My objective was no longer to quell arguments among group members, it was to find songs and producers who could create hits that my label could sell in volume.

During 1968, the Top Ten contained an average of five new singles a week. Every artist who entered it could be relied upon to generate subsequent album sales. It was these that were creating altogether new amounts of money for the industry.

This had been triggered by acid. Acid changed hours into minutes and minutes into seconds. If someone was on it and you played them an album, when it was finished they were surprised it was over. Acid took people to another world. In an industry where everyone was doing it, acid helped change the perception of record company employees from singles to albums. Acid gave the industry its biggest boost in profits ever, yet the albums record companies pushed hardest were not the stoned sounds of the hippy generation, they were the ones they could sell most of – plain old-fashioned pop – Val Doonican, Tom Jones, Cilla Black, Engelbert Humperdinck, Des O'Connor, Herman's Hermits and Cliff Richard, who came second in Eurovision with 'Congratulations'.

Strangely enough, what kept the public's interest alive in all this pop music were stories about the same old groups – the Beatles and the Stones. Love Affair's admission that they hadn't played on their record was good for just one weekend's press. The pop story of the year was a love affair of a different kind, the story of John and Yoko and the slow death of the Beatles.

Earlier in the year, together with a couple of Beach Boys and Donovan, the Beatles had been to see their guru in India. On arrival, Magic Alex, John's best friend, saw the five-star living accommodation and the guru's private helicopter pad and realised at once that the Maharishi was taking everyone for a ride. 'An ashram with four-poster beds?' he said. 'Masseurs, and servants bringing water. Houses with facilities. And an accountant! I never saw a holy man with a book-keeper!'

While he was there, Donovan wrote one of his best songs, 'Jennifer Juniper', but the Beatles soon got tired of the place. Ringo was first to go, he said the food gave him the runs and Maureen couldn't stand the mosquitoes. John stuck it the longest, but when he caught the Maharashi seducing a girl he realised the man was normal after all and came home still looking for something to fill a hole in his life. Then he met Yoko Ono.

In May, when the Beatles got together to record at Abbey Road, they found an impostor in their midst. John had brought Yoko along. She stayed next to him all the time, stood when he stood, sat when he sat, moved when he moved. She even went into the studio with him when he overdubbed his guitar. This broke every one of the Beatles' rules. No one was allowed into the studio when they were recording. Even Eppy had always been encouraged to go and find something else to do.

Eventually the others started making nasty remarks about her and for John each one was like a knife in the back. Then Ringo went specially to his home in Weybridge to ask, 'Does Yoko have to be there all the time?' And of course, John told him 'yes'.

In July, John sponsored an art exhibition and dedicated it 'To Yoko, from John, with Love'. From then on the public hated her. The Beatles belonged to them. If the public couldn't get close to them, why should anyone else? Why couldn't Yoko keep out of sight like the other Beatles' girlfriends had always done? The public understood at once that Yoko had the potential to break up the Beatles and end the sixties dream.

John came up with two different explanations for his obsession with Yoko. First he said he wasn't happy with the way things were going. 'It happened bit by bit,' he told a journalist, 'gradually, until this complete craziness is surrounding you, and you're doing exactly what you don't want to do with people you can't stand – the people you hated when you were ten.' Then he explained to *Newsweek* how he'd needed someone to open his eyes to the way a star can become imprisoned by his own friends. 'What Yoko did for me was to show me what it was like to be Elvis Beatle, and be surrounded by sycophants and slaves who were only interested in keeping the situation as it was.'

Derek Taylor, the head of Apple, spoke for the whole of Britain when he said, 'It's not that we *hate* her. It's just that we don't *love* her.'

*

The media's obsession with the Beatles, and the group's continuing ability to sell records, confirmed a new marketing truth. The artist whose next record was going to sell as well as his last was likely to be an artist who'd made his life into an ongoing media saga in which the public could participate. To be 'heard of' had become just as important as 'being heard'.

The Stones' arrest and their trips to Morocco, the Beatles' escapades in India, their pronouncements on drugs, the publicity surrounding Eppy's death, these sorts of things were now seen by record companies as the essential tools of building of a major act. Because of this, record companies had started to encourage their acts to hit the headlines as often as possible whether it be drugs, sex, bust-ups, or scams. Keith Altham, the ex-features editor at *NME* who was now a publicist, found himself in the thick of it. 'I started with Amen Corner, who immediately had a No. 1 record. Then other major acts started calling me – the Stones, the Who – all the stars I'd done features for at *NME*. At the beginning, whenever things went wrong – like if Mick Jagger swore at a foreign politician or Pete Townshend smashed someone with his guitar at a concert or Keith Moon blew up a hotel room – record companies would call me in a panic and ask me to try and hush things up. But they soon found it helped sell records and I started working more subtly. Sometimes when journalists called me I pretended I was trying to cover things up, but often I was actually encouraging them to run the story. Record companies soon realised there was no such thing as bad publicity.'

In the wake of the Rolling Stones' trial it seemed to have become chic for rock groups to get themselves arrested whenever they could. The outstanding achiever in this area was Keith Moon.

In America, he'd driven a Lincoln Continental into a swimming pool at the Holiday Inn and spent a day in jail. On the *Smothers Brothers* TV show he caused more chaos. For 'My Generation', the producer planned a small gunpowder blast as the number finished but Keith found more gunpowder and packed his drums with it. The explosion, live on air, was so great that Keith was sent flying off the stage, his arm sliced open by a razor-edged cymbal, and Pete's hair caught fire.

A few years earlier, when drugs first became a part of rock imagery, record company executives raised few objections. Now, as rock stars began to make headlines with acts of mayhem, record companies again kept their eyes on sales figures and avoided condemning them. Horst Schmolzi at Polydor told me, 'Rock stars should behave the way they're meant to behave. When the Who smash up hotel rooms the fans like it, it's the image they want. It sells records, and so do all these stories about orgies and acid.'

He was right. For every pound that had been spent on records in the pre-acid era, three pounds were being spent afterwards, all due to the increase in album sales. Ron Wood, a senior manager at EMI, told me he'd commissioned a survey that showed sales of pop albums had increased from 25 million in 1966 to 50 million in 1968. As a result, already-rich record companies found themselves wallowing in cash.

In the midst of this boom, Immediate Records managed to go bankrupt. Andrew Oldham had lost the management of the Rolling Stones to Allen Klein, an American businessman.

So when Immediate, with their expensive promotion methods, missed out on a couple of hits, the money wasn't there to support them. But by then they'd led the way for all sorts of other independent companies to get off the ground.

Tony Stratton-Smith was the manager of the Nice, one of the groups who'd been signed to Immediate. To give them a new home, he started Charisma Records, which later went on to have several of the biggest rock acts of the seventies.

Some of these small companies only had a thin veneer of independence. Charisma, for instance, was financed by Polydor who had to rescue it several times when Tony's obsession with racehorses led him into financial problems. Only the choice of artists remained outside Polydor's influence; everything else was theirs. They took profits from distributing Charisma's records in the UK and from selling the overseas rights to other companies. The same applied to every other company Polydor financed.

The person most responsible for this new development was Roland Rennie, an ex-EMI executive who had left to work under Horst Schmolzi at Polydor. The German company was determined to break into the UK market in a big way and was spending on an unprecedented scale. They particularly encouraged managers and entrepreneurs to set up their own labels. Robert Stigwood had been one of the first with Reaction Records, to which he signed the Who and the Bee Gees. Then Kit Lambert, the Who's manager, got himself Track Records. There were lots of other smaller labels, like my one at CBS. But much more important was the one real independent company that was doing well for itself – Island Records. Just before Immediate had started up, Island had been launched by white Jamaican Chris

Blackwell with a hit by Millie Small – 'My Boy Lollipop'. Now it was building a reputation as a specialist label for West Indian music.

By this time, the big American companies had decided they couldn't afford to miss out on the action and were setting themselves up in London too.

MGM had been one of the first but had started disastrously. To run the company they hired Rex Oldfield, a department manager from EMI, but although they had American hits to sell, MGM lost a million pounds in the first year without getting a single chart success. Now they'd gone back to licensing out their product.

RCA had started out more cautiously and were now doing well, having hits with all their American artists – José Feliciano, the Monkees, Mama Cass, and Hugo Montenegro. But doing best of all was CBS, who'd invested in local product. They were now a genuine part of the British music industry with artists like Marmalade, the Tremeloes, Georgie Fame, and the group who didn't play their own instruments – Love Affair.

While the Americans were moving in, one of the British majors was on the way out.

Pye Records – the company which had failed to sign any of the major rock groups because of the 'No amps!' policy of its chairman Louis Benjamin – had originally been half-owned by Pye of Cambridge, a company which manufactured electronic hardware. When Pye of Cambridge sold their share in the record company to Associated Television, they limited the time for which it could continue to use the name 'Pye'. The rights would run out in 1980. They did, however, make an offer that would allow Pye Records to continue to use the name thereafter for a one-off payment of £2,000. In the chairman's office, 'No-Amps' Benjamin hit his fist on the table as he'd done once before. 'Two thousand pounds?' he shouted. 'No way!'

As a result, in due course, Pye would disappear altogether.

In Baker Street the Beatles opened offices for their new record company, Apple Corp.

With personal income tax often running as high as 96 per cent, the Beatles' accountants advised them to invest in everything they could. The group took this to mean 'spend, spend, spend' and poured money into Apple. They paid inventors to invent, designers to design, songwriters to write, producers to produce, accountants to sign cheques, and drug dealers to provide the staff with whatever was needed to make every day a holiday.

Derek Taylor – previously their publicist, and even more into acid than the Beatles themselves – was appointed managing director. He understood what they wanted to do and approved of it. But instead of pulling it together for them, he entered too wholeheartedly into the spirit of things. When someone turned up at Apple saying he was Adolf Hitler, Derek invited him in, opened a bottle of wine, and asked how Eva was.

Audition tapes for Apple Records arrived by the tens of thousands. Ron Kass, who was made head of the record division, said it would take five men five years to listen to them all. But still the general policy continued to be 'Sign 'em up!'

If John could sign someone, why couldn't Paul? If Ringo could, why not George? Or the head of A&R, or the head of publishing, or the office boy, or the doorman, or the chauffeur? From Britain, Apple signed Grapefruit, Jackie Lomax, the Iveys and the Black Dyke Mills Brass Band. From America, they took Doris Troy, Billy Preston and the Modern Jazz Quartet. An act called Bamboo arrived from Sweden. And from somewhere unidentified came Contact, a group who sang about flying saucers.

In the end Apple got a few hits but the company still ran at a loss. It was EMI who made the profit. They had the rights to the records and made money from pressing and distributing them. They never had to spend on promotion because the Beatles and Apple were doing it for them. All they had to do was to fund Apple from royalties due to the Beatles. Even so, they didn't like doing it.

Five years earlier, when George Martin had suggested to Len Wood that they should voluntarily increase the Beatles' royalties, he'd been right. The resulting good-will might have paid benefits. But by now goodwill was long gone. Brian Epstein, helped by publisher Dick James, had negotiated the Beatles' royalties to a higher rate than EMI had ever paid before. So although Apple was being run on Beatles' money, EMI somehow felt it should have been theirs.

Record producer John Burgess recalls, 'There was quite a sour feeling at EMI about the amount of royalties they had to pay the Beatles. People thought it had been handled all wrong.'

When Apple got a No. 1 with Mary Hopkin singing 'Those Were The Days', the excitement from the Apple office and the things the Beatles were doing permeated the whole business. Across the board, record sales continued to grow and so did the public's interest in all things pop. When they got into the charts with 'Baby Come Back', the Equals became Britain's first home-grown black group. Richard Harris, a Shakespearean actor, reached No. 1 with six minutes of 'MacArthur Park'. Fleetwood Mac had a hit with 'Albatross'. But the best news of the summer was when the Seekers, purveyors of 'Georgy Girl' and other cringe-making songs, finally split up.

There were also important new artists getting their first releases – Status Quo, Jethro Tull, Elton John and Tyrannosaurus Rex, now with a new manager. But the most important newcomer wasn't an artist, it was the Moog synthesiser.

The futuristic-sounding Moog had first started appearing in studios in 1967. By 1968 it was being heard on records. It then became a principal musical influence on the next three decades of pop. Keyboardist Keith Emerson first saw a picture of it on a semi-classical album called *Switched-On Bach*. He thought it looked like an early telephone exchange covered in a spaghetti junction of wires, knobs and switches. When he got hold of one and started using it at gigs he found it went out of tune if the surrounding temperature changed. 'Playing away with my right hand while tuning the Moog with my left was something I'd have to get used to during the next six years.'

That year, at the Reading Festival, Arthur Brown was lowered onto the stage from a helicopter with his hair aflame. He'd just released a record on Track called 'Fire' and this was a Kit Lambert publicity stunt. But Arthur jumped around too much and set the stage on fire. The gig was cancelled and there was no music, but the press coverage was good and the record got to No. 1.

More than anyone, it was managers and publicists creating stunts like this that fuelled the public's excitement for pop. Every week someone seemed to come up with a new publicity gimmick. John Fenton, the man behind the Beatles' merchandising, was now managing a band called Goldie & the Gingerbreads. He bribed someone at the London Zoo to release Goldie the golden eagle from its cage. 'I think it was twenty-five quid we paid. It was perfect. For two days, until it was caught, the word Goldie was all over the papers, just when we were pushing a record by Goldie & the Gingerbreads.'

Brian Sommerville, who'd been publicist for the Beatles when they first broke, was another master of scams. On tour with the Walker Brothers, he was checking them into a hotel in the north of England when he heard from the desk clerk that a local bank had been held up by three young men. From his room, Brian called the police and gave them an anonymous tip – he thought he'd seen the three men responsible for the robbery checking into a local hotel. Ten minutes later the police came to arrest the Walker Brothers and Brian was guaranteed a headline from every national newspaper the next morning.

These scams could never turn a bad record into a hit. But once a good record got moving, a few good headlines in the tabloids could help turn an artist's name into a household word.

Pink Floyd publicised themselves by announcing a psychedelic light show. Their manager at the time, Peter Jenner, explained how he made them some stage lights which in those days was a completely new concept. 'The group developed some Polaroid effects, putting a polariser and analyser in the projector and stretching condoms across it which gave good effects because they were very high-quality latex.' One evening Pink Floyd's van was stopped for a minor traffic offence. When the policeman peered inside he saw a young man cutting the tops off a pile of condoms. 'That's our roadie,' the group told him, 'he's crazy.'

Crazy was what people were beginning to call John Lennon. When journalists asked him how many times he'd taken acid he told them, 'A thousand. I used to just eat it all the time.'

People in record companies had begun to realise the degree to which acid destroyed their ability to focus on work. As an alternative, they'd started moving on to cocaine to get themselves fired up again. John Lennon too felt he'd had enough of acid. Having had his ego and his creative strength destroyed by LSD, he was now using a white powder far more serious than the coke the A&R crowd were taking. John and Yoko felt disowned by the other Beatles. They were hurt and needed a painkiller, so they spent the hottest summer in living memory lying together in their flat, stupefied with heroin.

Outside, the press were waiting. When Yoko emerged pregnant, the papers were full of it. When she had a miscarriage, there was even more. In photographs, John was always at her side with the other Beatles nowhere to be seen. To the public, it began to look as if the break-up of the group was inevitable.

As if to mock their problems, Joe Cocker had a hit with his version of 'With A Little Help From My Friends' which he sang with his feet rooted to the ground while the top of his body waved madly like a tree in a storm. It was something Yoko might have thought up for one of her art exhibitions – 'Mime of Pop Group Destructing'. Yoko was the intellectual, John the artist. Yoko would talk about her theories on art and John would turn them into music. They released an album that was intended to shock people – *Two Virgins* – with a picture sleeve of the two of them frontally naked. Then they appeared together in a white paper bag at the Albert Hall.

To the average coke-sniffing A&R man, this sort of thing looked silly. But if recording artists wanted hippy pictures or 'Save the World' slogans on their record sleeves, and it helped sell records, why not let them have it? On the back of a booming transatlantic drug culture, record company executives were now travelling endlessly backwards and forwards to America selling British rock artists. After Concorde was introduced, their lives got even faster. For those at the top, New York and back in a day became standard music-business behaviour.

And if any of them ever felt a pang of concern about the way the record business seemed to be turning into the 'records and drugs' business, a quick snort of white powder would blow away their worries in a second.

CHAPTER TEN

HEAVY METAL KIDS

John Entwistle once said, 'I'm only interested in heavy metal when it's me who's playing it. I suppose it's a bit like smelling your own fart.'

The Who's bass player couldn't have put it better. Heavy metal was never going to be satisfying to a musician except on that level. It had no groove, no enchanting harmonies, no intimacy. It was a sado-masochist test of the audience's ability to take punishment. Just as rape is about violence rather than sex, so heavy metal was about volume rather than music. But it was, everyone agreed, great showmanship.

The term 'heavy metal' first surfaced in a novel by William Burroughs, *The Soft Machine*. In it he wrote about Uranian Willy 'the Heavy Metal Kid'. Then music journalist Lester Bangs wrote a review of the Yardbirds in *Creem* magazine and used the term 'heavy metal' throughout.

It was the Jeff Beck-Jimmy Page axis that set the Yardbirds on the path to heavy metal, mainly by leading to the group's disintegration. That set Jimmy Page dreaming of a supergroup. He spent the summer of 1968 reforming the Yardbirds which he intended to call the New Yardbirds, a supergroup something like Cream.

As a session guitarist, Jimmy had played on most of the hits by Herman's Hermits together with bass player John Paul Jones. That was going to be the basis for a new band and they brought in drummer John Bonham and singer Robert Plant to complete the group.

They played the first few gigs under the name New

Yardbirds but before long they decided a new group needed a new name. Jimmy said the name they subsequently chose had been thought of during the session for 'Beck's Bolero'. Keith Moon had been asked if he would like to leave the Who and join the New Yardbirds but he'd replied, 'No – it'll probably go down with the public like a lead balloon.'

John Entwistle told people a different story. He said that he and Keith decided to go off and form a band with Richard Cole, who used to be their chauffeur. He was going to call the band Led Zeppelin and had designed a cover of an R/101 Zeppelin going down in flames. But when Richard Cole went to work for Jimmy Page, he took the artwork with him.

By the end of the year, the new group was ready. Peter Grant had become its manager and it was signed to Atlantic Records in America. Peter told the group, 'You do the music, and I'll take care of everything else ... Don't even think of anything else ... just take care of the music.' He never had a contract with them because he reckoned if they were fed up with each other they would each find somebody else.

Peter's most innovative idea was to refuse to do singles. He told me, 'Singles are like races, they're competitive, they hit or they fail. If you want to avoid failing, don't release them. Let the kids buy albums instead.'

Malcolm McLaren, a budding manager at the time, watched with admiration. 'Peter lived, breathed and slept beside the band ... and indulged in the same things they did.'

Musically Led Zeppelin were a development of Cream, the Yardbirds and the Who. But what gave them such a different and individual flavour was Jimmy Page's growing obsession with Aleister Crowley, a nineteenth-century world traveller and mountain climber. Crowley had been a heroin addict and was obsessed with Satanism, sexual ambiguity, and the occult. Page latched onto his writings and pursued the same philosophies, replacing mountain climbing with a climb to the pinnacle of success in the music industry.

Led Zeppelin later moved into America selling rock music as pagan religion, packing worshippers into stadiums that screeched with feedback and percussion. But in 1969, they were just four excited kids with an inexperienced manager.

Five years earlier, the first signs of a division had appeared between pop and rock. Now rock itself was fragmenting. Heavy metal was to become the property of Led Zeppelin and the Who, followed at a distance by Deep Purple. Classic rock belonged to the Rolling Stones, and traditional rock 'n' roll had been upgraded to stadium status by Status Quo. But there was another type of rock musician for whom personal lifestyle was more important than music.

Hawkwind slept rough or lived in communes. In thirty-six months they suffered sixty-eight drug busts. For an interview in *Melody Maker* they toned down their philosophy of living in a drug heaven and told their fans, 'We want people to get stoned on the show, not on acid.' But their manager revealed how they mixed acid, speed and tranquillisers to play gigs. 'Lemmy would be speeding out of his head and he'd think, "Can't take this any more", and the mandies would come out and they'd get slower and slower.'

Hawkwind were half hippy and half punk, using rock music to opt out of normal society. Others in the same mould were Technicolor Dream, the Pink Fairies, the Deviants, Third World War, and a group of itinerant musicians who went under the name of the White Panther Party.

Technicolor Dream stole a van and rammed the doors of the refectory at Essex University then distributed free ice cream to those inside. The Pink Fairies played free open-air gigs wherever it took their fancy – a car park, the back of a truck, or outside another band's gig. If they didn't like another group's attitude, they would barge into their gig and trash it, particularly if their music was pretentious. One of the shows they wrecked was by King Crimson whose album *In The Wake Of Poseidon* caused critic Richard Williams to say, 'If Wagner were alive today, he'd be working with King Crimson.'

The Moody Blues were even more pretentious. Their album titles said it all – *In Search Of The Lost Chord*, *On The Threshold Of A Dream*, *Days Of Future Passed*, and *To Our Children's Children*. And there were others too, like Yes, who insisted they were simply 'progressive', and Jethro Tull, who featured a manic flute player obsessed with tramps. It was hardly surprising that critics chose to label these groups 'pomp rock'.

While rock was moving into these new and rather dull areas, pop still lit up the charts. In 1969, January's best was 'Son Of A Preacher Man' by Dusty Springfield, February's was 'Albatross' by Fleetwood Mac, and in March there was 'Where Do You Go To My Lovely' by Peter Sarstedt.

For the Sarstedt song, arranger Ian Green had written a score for forty string players but producer Ray Singer tore it up. 'Ian had written the score for a huge bloody orchestra but I told all the musicians they could leave. I just kept two cellos and the accordion player. Ian was really upset. The bass player was Dave Holland who went on to play with Miles Davis, and I even made him leave too.'

Apart from an accordion in the introduction, Sarstedt sang the first three and a half minutes accompanied only by his own acoustic guitar. Then he was joined by two cellos for the last thirty seconds. The result was a record that stayed at No. 1 for five weeks. After that, Ray and I joined up to produce records.

A production team can have a moment when everyone wants to use them. Sometimes they'll get a lot of hits, sometimes only a few, but if they grab the moment and work hard when it comes, they can end up doing extraordinarily well financially. Ray and I travelled backwards and forwards to the States, making deals, picking up advances, and coming back to record albums, sometimes four at a time. Often, while Ray worked in one studio laying down bass and drums, I worked in another overdubbing strings and brass or mixing. We recorded a group called Fresh, another called Plus, then discovered Forever More (who were the Average White Band in an early incarnation).

We made albums with each of the Sarstedts – Peter; Robin, his younger brother; and their eldest brother Rick, who'd previously been Eden Kane, a rock 'n' roll heart-throb. Then we teamed up with the Scaffold whose members included Paul McCartney's brother Mike and poet Roger McGough. Ray and I went to Liverpool and sat in the McCartney family kitchen listening to stories about 'our kid' and discussing the meaning of the Scaffold's songs which were mostly a mixture of gimmicky pop and serious poetry. Roger McGough foolishly allowed me a free hand with the arrangements. Listening back now I'm amazed at what he let me do to his softly satirical words. My arrangements were way over the top – screeching strings and strident big band jazz. When Ray made a hit out of 'Where Do You Go To My Lovely' he did it by throwing away the band parts. It's a pity he didn't do the same with my arrangements for the Scaffold.

In June, it was announced that Brian Jones had been fired from the Rolling Stones. His pay-off was rumoured to be £100,000 on top of any royalties he might be due. In July, he died. Between the Stones and the Beatles, it was now a tie – one Brian each, both deceased.

Epstein died in his bed, full of drugs. Brian Jones did much the same thing in his swimming pool. Some people spread the rumour he'd been murdered, but whatever the final cause of his death, it had to be seen as some sort of suicide. Nobody could continuously take that many drugs unless they were searching for an exit from life. Now Brian Jones had found one.

The day after his death, the Stones released 'Honky Tonk Women' which went straight to No. 1. The day after that, a free concert was due to take place in Hyde Park and Mick chose not to cancel it. Questioned by journalists and caught off-guard, he said, although he was shocked by the news of Jones's death, 'the guy was unbearable'. But on-stage at the gig he dedicated the group's performance to Jones: 'I hope people will understand it's because of our love for him that we're still doing it.'

Most of the music business was there. We watched in baking sunshine along with a hundred thousand other people, most of them beaded and bangled, carrying joss sticks, trying to create a British Monterey. The concert started with Jagger reading two verses from Shelley's *Adonais*, then releasing thousands of white butterflies into the air. But the Stones played badly and Keith fluffed all his lead solos. Mick, dressed in a white trouser-dress by Michael Fish, tried to cover bad singing by strutting round the stage with his hand on hip. He even stripped off his dress and whipped the stage with his belt, but it didn't look good. It was as if he didn't really care about Brian, especially in contrast to his opening words of regret.

Phil May of the Pretty Things agreed. 'Much of Mick's speech clanged in my head ... If Jagger had confronted the reality and said about Brian, "Well, we fought like bastards, but we'll still miss him", more people in the know might have respected him, instead of expecting us to swallow all the bollocks he came out with.'

The truth was, a combination of drugs and incredible success had taken the Stones to a place where no group had been before. They were now living in a world of their own – out of touch with reality, usually stoned, always surrounded by a protective entourage. The nearest they came to normal life was when they mixed socially with other artists or had brief contact with groupies. It looked quite likely that the excessive use of drugs that had killed Brian would eventually do the same to the rest of the group.

In August, there was an open-air festival in the Isle of Wight, and in America 500,000 people attended a festival at Woodstock. These were billed as festivals of love and peace – but for the organisers they were festivals of profit.

In September, Jane Birkin and Serge Gainsbourg had a hit with French words and heavy breathing. 'Je T'aime ... Moi Non Plus' became the first ever foreign language record to top the charts and the first record of any sort to reach No. 1 without BBC radio play. Halfway up the charts Philips dropped the record. An independent label, Major Minor, picked it up and had the hit. In the UK, Philips put advertisements in the paper moralising about why they'd dropped it. In the USA they put equally big ads in the paper trying to sell it on the back of the notoriety they had created for it in the UK.

In October, 'Space Oddity' became a big hit for newcomer David Bowie. But with no follow-up, it looked like he was just a one-hit wonder.

In November, American bubblegum invaded Britain with the Archies singing 'Sugar Sugar' and the Hollies had a hit with their greatest song, 'He Ain't Heavy, He's My Brother'.

In December, at Altamont in America, a festival went terribly wrong ...

The Stones were now the world's greatest touring machine. They were the ultimate power in rock music. At Altamont there were half a million people with no barriers to protect anyone if they were pushed or fell. The security had been delegated to Hell's Angels and if people brushed against them, they were beaten up.

The Stones tried to hold the situation together by telling the crowd to keep cool, but with knives and guns and 500,000 out-of-control fans around them, they had little alternative but to keep playing. At the front of the crowd a young black kid was being teased by a Hell's Angel. The teasing turned to beating and the kid retaliated. Other Angels jumped in and the kid pulled a gun. He was stabbed, chased, stabbed again and beaten to death with a waste bin. 'I wasn't gonna shoot,' he managed to gasp. A helicopter whisked the Stones to safety.

Later, an eyewitness who'd picked up the dead man told the inquest what he'd seen. 'We rubbed his back up and down to get the blood off so we could see, and there was a big hole in his spine, and a big hole in the side of his head and a big hole in his temple. You could see all the way in. You could see inside.'

The Stones were condemned by the media, but it was difficult to see what they could have done to help the situation. People spoke as if, when the group originally set off down the road to rock decadence five years earlier, they should have seen for themselves where it was likely to end. Writer Albert Goldman described them as 'sado-homosexual-junkie-diabolic-nigger-evil, unprecedented in the annals of pop culture'.

Personally, I would have told him to watch his tongue.

CHAPTER ELEVEN
CURTAIN CALL

Some time in 1968, Kit Lambert let me in on a crazy idea he'd just had. The Who would write an opera.

When he first suggested it to the group they thought their oddball manager had finally gone mad. A rock group creating an opera and playing it at one of the world's greatest opera houses; it wasn't possible. Even Pete Townshend, Kit's greatest fan within the group, was seriously doubtful.

For Kit, the thought became an obsession and he pushed the group endlessly to get the songs written. The idea became his entire existence. He couldn't change the hurt he'd felt as a child when his father was mauled by the critics, but at least he would avenge it. As Pete Townshend said, 'Rock won't eliminate your problems. But it will let you sort of dance all over them.'

When it was performed at the New York Opera House, one of the first press reviews of *Tommy* called it 'sick and pretentious'. On the other hand, Leonard Bernstein said its 'sheer power, invention, and brilliance of performance outstrips anything that has ever come out of a recording studio'. On a TV chat show Townshend said he'd originally thought of something 'pompous, crazy, ridiculous – a deaf, dumb and blind boy who's given drugs by an acid queen, is raped by his own uncle, and becomes the Messiah. And I thought – "That'll make money."'

Although *Tommy* was conceived lightheartedly, its importance to the group grew as they developed it. When the critics praised it, the group became too serious about it.

Townshend said it was this seriousness that ultimately turned *Tommy* into light entertainment.

For the Who's manager, *Tommy* represented his ultimate achievement. Kit Lambert had instigated its creation, seen it performed at the New York Opera House, and heard it heaped with praise. He'd appeased the destruction of his father's life at the hands of the critics.

But with the success of *Tommy*, the focus had been removed from Kit's life. He couldn't cool down. He became incapable of properly managing the Who. He hired the *Queen Mary* for a promotion party and supplied a different drug on every deck. He holidayed for a month in Mexico and forgot the two stretch limos that were on twenty-four-hour call outside his hotel in New York. At Sardi's he set the lampshades on fire to attract the waiters' attention. He loved to walk into hustler bars with the tip of a thousand-dollar bill protruding from his half-zipped flies. Finally he bought himself a palace in Venice and renamed himself Il Baroni Lambert.

In New York, in June 1970, as the Who took their final curtain call at the Metropolitan Opera House, the curtain was also coming down on Kit Lambert's career as a manager. But in London a new manager was about to enter the stage with a huge new artist.

John Reid was from a tough district of Glasgow. When he left school he worked as a singer in the Locarno ballroom, then came to London and sold shirts at Austin Reed. After that he landed a job as a song-plugger at Ardmore & Beechwood, EMI's publishing company, where they liked him because he dressed in smart suits and ties accumulated from his time working at Austin Reed. John could hardly believe his luck. 'They gave me an office, a phone and a drinks cabinet. It seemed like I'd arrived at a gigantic party.'

It wasn't long before John came to the attention of Ken East, EMI's new general manager, whose wife Dolly had a reputation for enjoying the company of gays at her dinner parties. John fitted in well and Ken decided to give him a better job. At just nineteen years old, John found himself made label manager of Motown Records. There he met Elton John, an artist on the bottom rung, and the two of them started an affair. Later they moved in together and when Elton left EMI to sign with Dick James Music he asked John to manage him. Dick James was surprisingly tolerant of the set-up. 'Oh well,' he said. 'If he's living with his manager, at least he'll have someone to get him up in the morning.'

In April 1969 I had left England for tax reasons. For some years I'd idly boasted, 'I'll retire at thirty and go to live in Spain'. Then, when I reached thirty, I realised there was nothing I wanted less than to stop working in the music business in London. Unfortunately, among the people to whom I'd mentioned the idea was my accountant who not only thought it would be a good thing, he insisted on it. Income tax on earnings was running at 84 per cent. Making myself a foreign resident would mean staying out of the country for twelve months but it would enable me to put together a little nest egg. So for twelve months from April 1969 to April 1970, whenever Ray Singer and I made albums for the USA, my money was left outside Great Britain waiting for the day when I could go and collect it.

When the day finally arrived, Ray and I had tea at Fortnum & Mason and I set off for my new villa in the south of Spain.

It had a Roman swimming pool, an art gallery, a porticoed patio, but it was a thousand miles from London. There were no records to make and no artists to manage. The day I arrived it started raining and by the third day I couldn't stand it. I packed a suitcase, gave the keys to a sales agent and headed back to London on a first-class train.

When I arrived in Paris there was an hour between trains. It was five in the evening, late in April, getting dark, drizzling and cold, but I had the good sense to call my accountant and tell him I was coming back.

'No way!' he insisted. 'If you don't stay away for a year, every penny you've put away overseas will be taxed as unearned income at 96 per cent. You no longer have a flat in London, nor a company, nor a car. Why bother to come back? Go to a hotel, take the best suite, get drunk, think it over, call me again tomorrow.'

Surprisingly, I took his advice and woke up on a perfect spring day in a large suite in the Plaza Athene hotel with the sun streaming in through the window. I decided my accountant was right. To pass the time I would travel around the world doing whatever appealed to me. I flew to Japan to check out the cherry blossom, to the States to hang out with Kit Lambert, and to Australia to produce records. But every week I bought the British music papers and watched what was going on, waiting for my enforced year of absence to be over.

The first year of the new decade was a strange one. The sixties were dead but not yet buried. The seventies proper hadn't really started and the songs in the chart were more fragmented than ever. The first No. 1 of the year had been Rolf Harris with a ghastly song called 'Two Little Boys'. By the time I left England in April, Simon and Garfunkel had given us 'Bridge Over Troubled Water', and then in May came the first-ever football No. 1 by the English World Cup Squad. There was a high spot in June when Mungo Jerry went to No. 1 with 'In The Summertime' using the same quivering vocal style as Marc Bolan, but right behind them came Free with the best record of the year, the classic rock anthem 'All Right Now'.

There was now a growing body of pop literature. Sociologists were re-examining the sixties and discovering cultural happenings that no one had been aware of at the time. And in the same way that they categorised popular music as pop or rock, they were now talking of drugs as being soft or hard. Soft drugs were the ones you took to make life more fun, to have a happy moment or to boost the party – marijuana, amphetamines and coke. Hard drugs were for running away from life, for altering your mind or searching your soul – heroin, morphine and barbiturates. Acid lay somewhere between soft and hard.

The same sort of psychological concepts were now being attached to 'pop' and 'rock'. Pop groups targeted their audience with instantly commercial records – a quick buzz, like a soft drug. Rock groups created their music with no compromises and waited for the public to discover it. For some reason rock musicians were more prone to depression and angst than pop musicians and the easiest escape was heroin. The list of people who were into it grew daily and would eventually include at least one member of nearly all the groups who'd gone on to America to become rock superstars.

Just as acid lay in between hard and soft drugs, so too between rock and pop there was sometimes blurring at the edges. Rock groups, having once been discovered by the public, often compromised with pop and began targeting the charts more deliberately. Pop groups tended to push themselves in the other direction. To gain credibility among their peers they would toughen their image and present themselves as rock bands. Unsurprisingly, the principal reason for both these directional shifts was money. If you could straddle the gap – if you could make pop records for the British charts and play rock to college audiences in American stadiums – the world was yours. And at rock festivals and stadiums, there was now the potential to play for more than 100,000 fans.

The Stones had been the first of the mid-sixties pop groups to get themselves redefined as rock. And with 'Brown Sugar', which compared the taste of unrefined heroin to a black dancer's pussy, they let the public know they had jumped the divide between soft and hard drugs.

Towards the end of 1970, the Who, having shaken off their original pop-art image, and with *Tommy* behind them, also completed their move to pure rock. Once again drugs were the chief agent of transition with Pete Townshend checking out heroin and Keith Moon taking any drug within reach. His drug use had been legendary since the mid-sixties. Kit Lambert told me, 'When the group recorded "Substitute", Keith was so out of it he couldn't remember playing. Later, he heard the record and presumed someone else must have been on drums. For weeks he was worried about being replaced.' With neuroses like these it wasn't surprising that Keith found it hard to sleep, so when he went on tour he took his axe to help pass sleepless nights. His work on ceilings and bathroom fittings was considered the best in the business.

Outdoing even the Who were Led Zeppelin. By now, Peter Grant had moulded them into the supreme travelling rock machine; they were publicised as the ultimate in decadence, indulging themselves in an endless smack-addicted orgy of hotel-wrecking, groupie-fucking, kneecap-smashing, and self-degradation. In her book *Rock Bottom*, Zeppelin's favourite groupie Pamela Des Barres tells a story of drugs, sexual perversion, coprophilia and violence. Jimmy Page wearing Nazi uniform, messing around in toilets with drag queens doing drugs; John Bonham urinating on first-class airplane seats and humiliating groupies by shitting in their shoes and handbags; manager Peter Grant facing assault charges in city after city.

Record companies were now eager participants in the imagery of rock and the debaucheries expected of their artists. Not only did it sell records, it helped the record companies gain street credibility. For young record-buyers this was important. Rick Sky remembers starting out in 1970 as a young journalist. 'Back in the sixties, record companies were horrified when their artists threw TV sets out of hotel windows and drove cars into swimming pools, but by the time I came into the business they'd found out that for rock stars there was no such thing as the wrong type of publicity. The whole ethos of rock was based on rebellion and scandal. Record companies began to realise that a full-page story about Rod Stewart trashing his hotel room was better than a full-page ad, and much cheaper too. I had record company press officers pushing stories at me that any normal person would try to keep the lid on.'

Allen Klein, the American businessman who'd taken over the Stones' management by ousting Andrew Oldham, was intent on representing the Beatles as well. He'd been chasing them for years and since Epstein's death he'd become unstoppable. Now at last he succeeded. Three of the Beatles agreed he should represent them. Only Paul refused.

Having finished his affair with actress Jane Asher, Paul had fallen under the spell of an American girl, Linda Eastman. Her father, Lee Eastman, a showbusiness lawyer, insisted that Klein was bad news. So Paul refused to sign with him, but seeing how good he was, Paul raised no objections to Klein negotiating the Beatles' new deal with EMI. That way it seemed he would get the benefit of the new deal without losing 20 per cent commission to the man who negotiated it.

As a business move it was shrewd, but it put Paul into conflict with the other Beatles and with the public. They wanted to see the Beatles continue and saw Paul's intransigence as a factor in their breaking up.

Then Dick James sold his shares in Northern Songs, the Beatles' publishing company. This meant the Beatles no longer had control over it, or rather, that they'd never had control over it in the first place. If they had done, Dick wouldn't have been able to sell the shares.

And there was worse to follow. When the shares were investigated it turned out Paul had more than the other three – he'd been buying them on the stock market. To Paul it had just been the obvious thing to do but the other Beatles were incensed.

Meanwhile, Allen Klein moved into Apple and started firing all the layabouts, which meant pretty well everyone including some long-time Beatle friends. Very soon there was little left to pretend about – the Beatles were heading for a break-up. Yoko's relationship with John Lennon had created a gap in their close relationship and what was perceived as sharp business practice by Paul McCartney had widened it.

When stories in the press said the Beatles were on the verge of splitting, Mick Jagger was asked if the Stones would ever break up. 'If we did,' he said, 'we wouldn't be so bitchy about it.'

In Australia, the weather was good but I felt out of the swing of things. To make me feel better my accountant phoned me frequently to tell me how sensible I was being. To pass the time, in Sydney I made a Top Five album with a girl called Alison McCallum and discovered a singer who became a worldwide star – actually 'discovered' is an exaggeration, it was an exercise in pure laziness.

While making the album with Alison McCallum, I'd gone looking for songs and among the ones I found was one called 'Pasadena' by Harry Vanda and George Young of the Easybeats. It was for a man's voice and wasn't right for what I wanted, but I was sure I could make it into a hit. Ted Albert, the owner of the company that published it, agreed to give me a healthy recording budget if I could find the right singer. He booked the best studio in Melbourne, paid me to make the musical arrangements and bought three air tickets to Melbourne for the following week – for him, for me and for the singer. But two days before the recording, not only had I not yet found a singer, I hadn't even started looking for one. With the beach beckoning, it was increasingly obvious to me that music was becoming more work than fun.

The evening before we were due to record the song, I looked in the local paper to see if any bands were playing. It was Wednesday, the worst day of the week for gigs, and the only one I could find was at a pub in Newcastle, an hour by train from the city. Hoping to find a decent group, I went there with the spare air ticket and a demo cassette of the song, but all the bands were dreadful and the pub smelt of vomit. I went outside and stood on the balcony where an attractive young guy was smoking a cigarette.

'Can you sing?' I asked him.

'I don't really know,' he replied.

I gave him the air ticket and the demo, and said, 'If you learn this and come to Melbourne tomorrow afternoon you might end up a star.'

In the morning I flew to Melbourne with Ted Albert and recorded the backing track. I was afraid the kid wouldn't show up but I told Ted, 'You'll love him – he's a superstar.' When Ted asked me his name I couldn't tell him. I'd forgotten to ask.

At 3pm he arrived and sang the song in one take. His name was John Paul Young and three weeks later he was No. 1 in Australia. Later, he was No. 1 all over the world with a song called 'Love Is In The Air'. In interviews he's always been generous enough to credit me with being something of a talent spotter.

Increasingly wrapped up as they were in self-indulgence and getting rich, very few pop stars felt comfortable about politics.

In the States, the Who had played a gig at a US airforce base and been asked 'to do a little something' on the radio before the show. What they did was to record a radio commercial urging listeners to join the US forces, the airforce in Pete's case, and the navy in Keith's. Pete now feels thoroughly ashamed: 'Young Americans were concerned about being blown to bits in Vietnam and I, a naive English twit, came prancing over hot on the heels of the Beatles and Herman's Hermits to make my fortune and bring it back to Britain. And I really didn't give a fuck about what was happening to the American young men. I really didn't!'

In 1970, American students protesting against the Vietnam War were shot and killed on the campus of Kent State University. Opposition to the war was causing some pop and rock stars to become increasingly vocal, even in Britain.

Pete started off being non-political, Mick Jagger went the other way. In 1968 Mick attended a protest against the Vietnam War but afterwards he never made such an overt political statement again.

Of the sixties stars, only Lennon was firmly political, first in a general way with Yoko and the love-ins, then with 'Give Peace A Chance' which was used by the anti-Vietnam movement in America where half a million people sang along with it at the Washington Memorial on Vietnam Moratorium Day in 1969. After that, John rushed headlong into every protest campaign going. He paid fines for demonstrators who'd objected to the presence in Britain of a South African rugby team. He publicly telephoned his support to a CND demonstration, and he helped to raise money for the British Black Power leader, Michael X. He paid defence costs for the editors of *Oz* when they were sued for obscenity and sent £1,000 to striking Clyde shipbuilders. Then he joined a fast for Biafra and put up posters around the world saying 'War Is Over (if you want it)'.

'Peace,' John Lennon explained, 'is only got by peaceful methods. To fight the establishment with their own weapons is no good because they always win. They know how to play the game of violence. But they don't know how to handle humour, and peaceful humour.'

John and Yoko got married. Announcing that a happening was to take place in their bedroom, they moved into the Amsterdam Hilton for their honeymoon. The press jumped to the inevitable conclusion and were disappointed. They found John and Yoko wearing white pyjamas and talking about peace.

John and Yoko wanted to go from the Amsterdam Hilton to the USA but the American government refused to give them bed-in facilities. Then Prime Minister Trudeau of Canada invited them to set up shop at the Hilton in Montreal. It was hard to see how lying in bed was going to help the war in Vietnam, but Yoko tried to explain. 'If I was a Jewish girl in Hitler's day, I would become his girlfriend. After ten days in bed he would come to my way of thinking.' While she was spouting this nonsense to the press, John got out his guitar and wrote 'Give Peace A Chance'.

When they came back to London, John and Yoko were arrested by forty policemen who arrived at their house with press photographers waiting. The drug squad was scalp-hunting and the media had been tipped off. At the time, John was on heroin, but one of the journalists warned him and he managed to get the house cleaned out in advance. Afterwards, John and Yoko went to live in America and involved themselves in politics. They wandered round New York making friends of the locals, but Lennon was being bugged. He'd been denounced to President Nixon by none other than Elvis Presley himself.

Presley was a multiple drug addict, but because his doctor prescribed the drugs for him, and because his addictions didn't include heroin, he considered himself purer than pure. He'd written to the President complaining about 'Drug Culture, the Hippy Elements, and the Black Panthers'. Nixon, who'd been planning a heavy anti-drug campaign to deflect public attention from Vietnam, welcomed Presley to the White House. Presley told the President that the Beatles were a force for 'the anti-American spirit', they'd come to the US to make money to use back home for the promotion of anti-Americanism.

When the sixties ended, the show lingered on. Many of the characters stayed on into the first year of the seventies waiting for their final curtain call.

At EMI, Sir Joseph Lockwood took his final bow when the board pushed him aside in favour of a new chief executive, John Read, who had previously worked for Ford. Another person to leave the stage in 1970 was Jimi Hendrix whose favourite saying had been 'once you are dead you are made for life'. When he died he proved himself right. His sudden exit left him permanently at the top.

By the end of 1970 many social changes too had taken place. For one, it was now essential for anyone connected with the music industry to side with the liberal point of view on everything. The age of majority had been reduced to eighteen, racism was not tolerated, the Gay Liberation Front had held its first demonstration, minor cannabis offences were no longer being prosecuted.

The Labour government was gone and the incoming Conservatives banned free concerts in Hyde Park. They disapproved of them, not because they were rock music, but because no one made any money out of them. They failed to understand why 250,000 people should be allowed to listen free, so they put the concerts out to tender.

Perhaps they were right: rock had become big business. What had previously been underground had become mainstream – what had previously been fun for many of us had now become nothing more than work. For pop stars and their managers the accent had changed from expanding their minds to expanding their bank balances. To underline the change, the Beatles' final disagreements turned out not to be about songs or drugs or girlfriends, but about money. The curtain fell on them too.

On 31 December 1970 Paul McCartney instituted High Court proceedings to wind up the Beatles' affairs.

PART TWO

PART
ONE

CHAPTER TWELVE
MAINMAN GLAM

Cocaine hydrochloride is an odourless white crystalline powder with a bitter numbing taste. It's derived from the leaf of the coca plant. The leaf itself, gently sucked between gum and cheek, nourishes the South American Indians who grow it and provides them with all the daily vitamins they need plus a little physical stimulation. In the late nineteenth century, John Pemberton, a druggist in Atlanta, invented Coca-Cola, a syrup-based cola laced with cocaine. It was sold as 'a valuable brain tonic and cure for all nervous afflictions'.

For most of this century Coca-Cola has been coke-free, which is more than can be said of the music industry.

To take it, cocaine is chopped finely with a razor blade and drawn into lines on a flat surface. It's then sniffed up one nostril through a rolled-up bank note, the plastic casing of a ballpoint pen, or something more elegant in gold or silver. The result is a powerful short-lasting stimulus to the central nervous system. 'Straight up your nose and into your brain' is how Marc Bolan once described it to me. 'A sexual, mental, physical blast-off.'

And that's what happened to his music.

In 1967 I'd put Steve Peregrin Took and Marc Bolan together to form Tyrannosaurus Rex, an acoustic duo who sat on a rug surrounded by joss sticks. When Steve first met him, Marc had just left John's Children and was still thinking of playing 'electric'. Steve told me, 'To change himself into hippy mode, for three years Marc did acid and smoked endless joints. But his real personality was coke. When he finally got into it, there was no way he could stay on that rug any longer.'

It was Kit Lambert who claimed credit for getting Marc back into electric mode. Marc had signed to Track along with John's Children in the mid-sixties. When Marc moved to Fly Records, Kit kept a piece of the action and wanted to see him make it big. At the time, Kit told me, 'Marc's always wanted to be a rock 'n' roll star but after his experiences with John's Children he's afraid of failure. That's why he sits on a rug playing acoustic music. But I know he really wants to play electric, and so does Tony.'

Tony Visconti was Marc's producer. He tried persuading Marc to turn T Rex into an electric group by playing him endless rock 'n' roll records. Kit was less subtle. 'I sat up all night doing coke with him. The next thing I knew he was having electric guitar lessons from Jimmy Page.'

Tired of his rug and his joss sticks, Marc suddenly realised he wanted to be on-stage surrounded by floodlights. Egged on by Kit Lambert and Tony Visconti, and encouraged by his wife June, he threw away his acid tabs, plugged in an electric guitar, and revved himself up on cocaine. The result was 'Hot Love', which Marc described as 'a two-minute thirty-second, funky, snappy foot-tapper'. It had a bluesy groove with singalong choruses delivered in Marc's daft little vibrating voice. 'It was done as a happy record,' he told journalists. 'I wanted to make a twelve-bar record a hit, which hasn't been done since "Hi-Heel Sneakers".'

In April 1971 it got to No. 1. In his hippy days Bolan's lyrics would have been filled with wizards and witches, now it was cool dudes and hot women. Tony Visconti said the sound was a matter of the right people meeting at the right time. 'A unique drummer, a jazz keyboard player, and Marc ... as if the hobbit had learned to play electric guitar ... It was pure Kismet – like winning the pools.'

This was urban pop created in the jazz tradition of jamming at three in the morning in a haze of coke and cognac.

Just as important as his music was Marc's new image, created from women's clothes bought from second-hand clothes shops by his publicist Chelita. She put silver on his eyelids, added mascara, gave him a velvet jacket and flung an ostrich feather round his neck. Between the thumping, grooving music and the androgynous image, Marc thought he'd found the message for the seventies: 'People are works of art. If you have a nice face you might as well play with it.'

What he really meant was 'Paint it!' And he did. When 'Hot Love' got to No. 1, he threw glitter on his cheeks for *Top of the Pops*. The next day make-up counters across Britain sold out. Marc Bolan was the new idol of the freshly pubescent, all of them glittering madly. After a concert at the Empire Pool, Wembley, Charles Shaar Murray reported in *Creem*, 'I've never seen so many beautiful fourteen-year-old girls in my life.'

'The pop scene was waiting for an explosion,' Marc said modestly. 'And I was the perfect person to provide it.'

It was a double explosion.

Following right behind was David Bowie, even sharper than Bolan when it came to egging on the press. After a false start in 1969 with 'Space Oddity', Bowie found himself waiting three years for his next big hit. In 1970, to keep things on the boil he announced he was bisexual and in future would be playing concerts wearing a dress.

'Why aren't you wearing your girl's dress today?' asked a journalist.

'Oh dear,' Bowie replied. 'You must understand. It's not a woman's dress – it's a man's dress.'

Bowie was fascinated by the world of Andy Warhol. It first started in the mid-sixties when his manager, Ken Pitt, came back from America with a Velvet Underground album. 'I'd been in New York with Crispian St Peters. I'd met Andy Warhol and the people from the factory and I knew everything about them would appeal to David, so I brought their album back for him. He was living in my flat at the time. He put it on, listened to part of it, turned round and said, 'I'm going to pinch that.''

Bowie had a friend, the transsexual rockstar Jayne County, previously Wayne. Jayne persuaded David to shave his eyebrows and paint his nails. Shortly afterwards he met some of Andy Warhol's Factory friends who reported to their boss that David was 'flirtatious and coy ... in his Lauren Bacall phase, with his Veronica Lake hairdo and eye-shadow.'

When Bowie changed his record label to RCA he recorded a new album, *Hunky Dory*, and got one step nearer to superstardom. But in the end it was his obsession with American rock star Iggy Pop that pointed the true way. Iggy termed himself 'Detroit trash'. He performed on-stage half naked. While he sang he would flagellate himself, shoot up with heroin, roll on the floor and cut his arms with razor blades. Jim Kerr of Simple Minds remembers seeing one of Iggy's shows. 'At the end of the show, of course, he pulled out his penis. He'd been singing about it the whole night and I was just thinking 'Let's see it.' And there it was.'

'Thirteen inches long,' claimed Iggy's ex-manager, Danny Sugerman, 'and his proudest possession.'

As much as he admired Iggy, Bowie found himself unable to attempt a similar role. So he invented a substititute – a glamorous science-fiction stage version – Ziggy Stardust – a 'polysexual space invader with a carrot-coloured puffball muffler, snow-white tan and skin-tight PVC jumpsuit that helped exaggerate his ectomorphic physique'. It shot him up to Bolan's top rung. Far from objecting to it, Bolan seemed pleased. He and Bowie became great friends, teased each other and competed in outraging the press.

Bolan and Bowie were the indisputable megaczars of glam rock. On-stage, Bolan would strut around covered in black peacock feathers. Bowie would mime fellatio with the neck of Mick Ronson's guitar. It wasn't long before teenage Britain was copying.

Glam flirted openly with decadence. Sixties children had been brought up in a period steeped in the influence of gay pop managers. They'd been subjected to flower-power, hippy lifestyle, pot-smoking and acid. From all these ingredients, they concocted their own style of music – glam rock – androgynous, theatrical and outrageous. It tempted boys to experiment with eyeliner, seven-inch platform boots, and to tease their girlfriends by mimicking fellatio with anything long and hard. Before anyone had time to consider whether this might contain an underlying moral subversion, glam rock had seduced the nation.

In 1970 David Bowie had changed his manager from Ken Pitt to Tony Defries. Defries set up a company especially for his management and called it MainMan (from a line in a Marc Bolan song). Bowie was given a document to sign from which he mistakenly concluded that he owned half of the company.

He did not. What he'd done was to sign an agreement that said half his future earnings would go into the company. In other words, he would be paying 50% management commission and not 20%.

Defries flew to New York and persuaded RCA to commit huge money to the promotion of Ziggy Stardust in the States. He set up offices in New York, then in order to give the impression that success had already been achieved, he instructed everyone to spend to the hilt. To give the offices a feeling of success he hired the entire cast of *Pork*, a recently closed Broadway show, and told them to act as secretaries and personal assistants.

For his first tour of the States, Bowie travelled to New York with his wife in a first-class stateroom on the *QE2*. He was given a suite at the Plaza and an open charge account with both the hotel *and* the local coke dealer. Angie Bowie said, 'It felt as if our party would just go on getting bigger, richer, sweeter and wilder for ever.'

Back in London, every other act in town was copying what Bolan and Bowie had started. Slade, for example, looked like construction workers who'd stolen their girlfriends' clothes to have a drunken laugh on a Saturday night. They wore make-up as if it was a joke, and high-heel clogs. Their guitarist had the word 'SuperYob' emblazoned across his guitar. They made pub music with a rock 'n' roll beat. It was working-class yobbism with mock glam imagery. Their fans were fifteen-year-old boys who left school with no O-levels, held beer-drinking competitions and were mad about soccer. Slade's music was an explosion of energy for young males to jump up and down to. Their song titles were filled with bad spelling, like 'Cum On Feel The Noize'.

'One thing about Slade,' claimed manager Chas Chandler, 'no one could ever mistake them for gay.'

The Sweet were the opposite. They had a golden-blond singer and a pouting bass player, but manager Laurence Myers later said, 'I've never seen a more heterosexual group than the Sweet ... The thing that bound all those artists together was the camping it up ... It was done in spite of the reservations, and even to the horror of managers and record companies. So then all the kids would go around wearing make-up, and it was fine; it was healthy and it was terrific.'

Suzi Quatro was glam in reverse – twice as butch as the male stars of the era. Like Iggy Pop, she came from Detroit where she'd played in her sister's garage band, the Pleasure Seekers. Mickie Most spotted her and brought her to London. 'I left her in a small hotel for a few weeks to give her a feel for what was going on.'

Mickie asked Nicky Chinn and Michael Chapman to write songs for her, but in the end he decided they should produce her too. ' I knew they were going to do it just right. There was no need for me to be involved. With Suzi's first hit, 'Can The Can', my only contribution was when they phoned me in New York from the studio in London and played me the tape. I said, 'It's a bit slow." And I suggested they varispeed it up a bit.'

Chinn and Chapman said the sound of her record had been carefully designed. 'It had to be right – we were very conscious of giving pop back to the kids, giving them something to smile about and hop to and generally get off on.'

Suzi's trademark was her black-leather catsuit, which she occasionally swapped for a gold one. 'I feel funny in dresses and skirts,' she said.

'Suzi thinks she's the new Gene Vincent,' Marc Bolan told me, 'but to everyone else she's just pure camp.'

Equally camp, but doing it more deliberately, was Gary Glitter.

Paul Raven went all the way back to the days of skiffle and Hamburg. Well over thirty, he bumped into an old friend, record producer Mike Leander, who thought Paul should become the Liberace of rock 'n' roll. 'I wanted him to be a send-up of the whole glam rock scene. I told him to call himself Gary Glitter and we made a record called 'Rock And Roll".'

Laurence Myers agreed to take him on for management. 'Mike had made this record with Gary called 'Rock And Roll", and me being cheap, instead of recording a new B-side we left the voice track out, whacked on a bit of guitar and called it 'Rock And Roll Part 2".'

No sooner was the record released than a DJ turned it over and played the side with no vocals. It became a hit and Gary Glitter had to appear on *Top of the Pops* with nothing to sing. According to Mike Leander, it didn't really matter. 'Glam rock was all about putting on a spectacle. The records were constructed to be seen ... The glam audience became part of the show. They dressed up and it was like a party.'

The most unlikely candidates for glam rock success were Mott the Hoople. They were rural rockers – West Country farm boys. David Bowie took a shine to them and gave them a song called 'All The Young Dudes'. Across the country teenagers sang along with it in unison, like football supporters with their club song. It was the ultimate glam rock propaganda, 'We're young and fast and glittering. We may be gay but we kick like mules.'

The kick might have come from cocaine, but as with all the other glam stars, it was the kick they needed to get them up the ladder to success. Six months earlier most kids in London would have called the group country yokels. But that was beside the point. In the world of glam rock, you had to push yourself into the limelight. Marc Bolan had laid down the law for success, 'Flaunt it if you've got it, fake it if you haven't.' Privately, Mott the Hoople were a bit doubtful about all this. They sometimes referred to Bowie and Bolan's music as 'fag rock', but success seduced them. So they slapped on their make-up and went to work.

Sometimes a glam star's make-up could prove a liability.

At the height of Marc Bolan's success, Kit Lambert received a letter from him challenging Track Record's continuing right to a small percentage in his recordings. Kit called me and asked if I had any old recordings with Marc. In fact, the very first night Marc had knocked on my door seven years earlier, he'd arrived with an acoustic guitar. When he started to play his songs I was so impressed I phoned and booked a studio to which we went at once in a taxi. I recorded twenty or so of his songs and the tape had been in various cupboards ever since.

I agreed to lease them to Track Records and Kit proposed putting them out as an album under the title *The Beginning of Doves*. Marc contested their release. He'd just signed a new megadeal with EMI in which he'd guaranteed there were no old tapes hanging around in cupboards which could be released in competition with his new recordings.

Kit insisted on going ahead with the release and Track were served with a writ. Kit and I planned a special strategy. We found the most outrageous of all Marc's glam pictures – his face covered in glitter, his lips glowing red with glossy lipstick – and had it blown up in colour, three foot by four.

Marc didn't attend the court case but his counsel painted a picture of him as a serious young musician who after years of disciplined practice and hard work was in danger of having his career destroyed by the release of our album. Kit had instructed his counsel, at some stage of the proceedings, to provoke the judge into asking, 'But what does this Marc Bolan chap look like?'

On the third day the judge finally said it. In a flash our gaudy colour picture was held aloft for all to see. 'Inadmissible evidence,' insisted Marc's counsel.

In the end we compromised with Marc in exchange for him taking us to dinner at the Savoy Grill.

In the States, the attendance on Bowie's first tour was patchy – sold out in some cities, empty in others – and there were big gaps between dates. Bills mounted, but RCA was subsidising it, hotels and travelling were on account. If a gig was sold out and there was cash to pick up it was quickly spent on cocaine – everything else could be signed for.

Defries was determined to keep up the appearance of success. 'We were encouraged to drink champagne and eat huge dinners and sign everything,' reported Leee Black Childers, one of the advance road crew.

The tour finished in LA where Defries persuaded RCA

to let the entire touring party stay at the Beverly Hills Hotel. There were forty-six people – the band, the management, the road crew, a few groupies, and Bowie's star guest, Iggy Pop. Bowie and his manager had private bungalows, everyone else had suites; on one side of Bowie's bungalow was Perry Como, on the other, Elton John. By now every last bit of cash had been used up and everything had to go on the tab, even cigarettes. And since there was no cash left, eating cheaply outside of the hotel wasn't possible. All forty-six people ate expensively in the hotel restaurant and charged it to RCA.

By the time the tour ended Bowie had played twenty-one concerts in seventy-one days. He'd run up a debt to RCA of $400,000, which in today's figures would probably be $4 million. Defries wasn't the slightest bit concerned. He told RCA, 'The first tour was just a rehearsal for the next.'

By this time Elton John had broken in America, but in Britain he was still without a first chart record. Twenty-five and never good-looking, he thought he'd passed his peak. He felt too old to compete with British glam rockers but he became friendly with Marc Bolan and began seeing him regularly. With his glittery clothes and simple approach to making hits, Marc influenced Elton. They had a running joke that they both loved themselves too much. For his birthday, Elton had a picture of Marc blown up twelve foot high, covered it in tinsel and delivered it as a birthday card in an articulated truck.

Elton suddenly got a hit with a joke rock 'n' roll track – 'Crocodile Rock'. Not only was it his first British hit but it happened just at the time when dressing outrageously was a requirement for British pop stars. To Elton, this was a dream come true and he decided to export the image of glam rock to America. For a concert at the Hollywood Bowl his stage set consisted of a spangled staircase leading down to five grand pianos. Porn star Linda Lovelace came on-stage and introduced 'the Queen of England'. At the top of the staircase a royal lookalike appeared and descended. She was followed by Batman, Robin, Groucho Marx, Frankenstein, the four Beatles, and finally, Elton, in white pants, white top, white feathers and five-inch platform boots. As he reached the stage 400 white doves were released and the five piano lids opened to reveal a silver letter in each, 'E-L-T-O-N'.

Thereafter, as he toured America, Elton's live performances got even wilder. Music critic Derek Jewell remembered seeing him change his outfits song by song. 'From Marie Antoinette to a gold lamé cowboy – from a hooker in pink tights to a multi-sequined prima donna.'

There was another rock star using glam imagery to project himself into superstar orbit.

In 1969, when singer Steve Marriott left the Small Faces, the remaining three went looking for a replacement and came up with Rod Stewart. Rod had been on the London blues scene since 1965. To most people he'd become something of a has-been but his voice perfectly fitted the music of the three remaining Small Faces so he joined the group together with Ronnie Wood and they renamed themselves the Faces. They found a new manager, Billy Gaff, previously the tour manager for Cream.

From the beginning, Rod let people know he was a fancy dresser. He swapped his jeans for spangle-pants, cut his hair to look like a giant feather, and like Elton, sold glam to America.

When success went to his head, his haircut got featherier and his trousers silkier. Mick Jagger told a journalist, 'Rod seems to be wearing the pyjamas I threw out last year.'

Despite Mick's bitchy comment, the Rolling Stones too were enjoying borrowing from glam rock's imagery. They went back to their androgynous sixties image, as reported by American journalist Stanley Booth when he toured with them. 'We all got faggier by the day. You never saw a more limp-wristed bunch of sissies.'

In the sixties, the big break for artists was to be able to write their own material. Now, it was the freedom to explore their own sexuality in public.

Lou Reed, an ex-member of Warhol's Velvet Underground, came to live in London and Bowie produced his new album, *Transformer*, an ode to sexual decadence. Lou Reed was gay, and under his aura Bowie decided to tell everyone that he too was 'gay, and always had been'. It wasn't really true. Bowie was irrepressibly bisexual – all over London, his one-night stands, male and female, could vouch for it, particularly his new wife Angie.

'David is a stud,' she said at the time.

David countered by telling the press, 'When we first met we were both laying the same bloke.'

On their second night together Angie had thrown herself headfirst downstairs because David insisted on going to a rehearsal. But when it came to sexual infidelities she wasn't bothered, especially with men. The point was: in 1972 it was cool to be gay. Tom Hedley wrote later in *Esquire*, 'Homosexuality was chic ... They were the most stylish people in town, they ran the galleries, they had the best clubs, they had the best dinners.' In his book *Glam*, Barney Hoskyns refers to London in 1972 as 'the year of the transsexual tramp'. Writer Albert Goldman compared it with Paris a hundred years earlier, 'a degenerate, opium-dream existence'.

John Lennon once told David Bowie, 'Glam rock is just rock 'n' roll with lipstick.' But glam was more than that. It was the degeneracy of *rock* marketed through the imagery of *pop*. It was rock *plus* pop. And in finding ways of combining the two, Bolan, Bowie and Elton had hit the jackpot.

Glam was the first musical style to flow directly from the use of cocaine. Seventies pop publicist Tony Brainsby summed it up perfectly. 'Coke was the "fuck-you" drug. You didn't give a damn what other people thought. You put on your spangled costume, slapped up your face, threw back your shoulders, shoved some more coke up your nose and strutted on to the stage ... You could see that cocaine arrogance in all of them – Bowie, Bolan, Elton...'

David Bowie's second tour of the States was when he really made it.

As before, manager Tony Defries poured money in all directions to make sure it happened. And why not? The money Tony was throwing around wasn't his. When Bowie finally made it and went into profit with RCA, all the money spent on touring would be charged against David's 50 per cent of the royalties.

When the second tour opened at Radio City Music Hall, it was clear that Bowie had cracked the States. Amongst the celebrities in the audience were Salvador Dali, Allen Ginsberg and Andy Warhol. From thereon the money rolled in, but only to MainMan. Bowie was kept happy with hotel suites and cocaine.

In New York, MainMan moved to larger premises. The exactors and actresses of *Pork* were each given their own office and told to decorate it as they pleased. In the centre of this extravagance was Defries, smoking a Havana cigar, talking about one day buying out RCA, and maybe Sony too.

As general manager, Defries appointed Tony Zanetta, an ex-member of Warhol's Factory, who was told to throw as much money around as possible. 'Defries encouraged everyone to spend recklessly to create the illusion that MainMan was a company of great wealth. One secretary had an operation to lift her breasts and charged this down to expenses; others had their teeth capped.'

MainMan had buildings of its own all over New York – the MainMan apartment at the Sherry-Netherland Hotel – the MainMan penthouse on Upper East Side – the MainMan duplex on East 58th Street – the MainMan country estate in Greenwich, Connecticut – and there were MainMan offices in Tokyo, Hollywood and London. Defries was convinced, like many managers before and many more to come, that he was responsible not only for Bowie's success, but for his entire existence. To prove his ability to be God, he launched other acts. Mick Ronson, Bowie's guitarist, was launched as a solo artist with the biggest billboard ever in Times Square, but his album failed to sell. Singer Dana Gillespie got the same sort of treatment and suffered the same lack of success. There was to be a film based on the life of Jayne County, the transvestite rock star who'd first taught Bowie to do make-up. A Broadway play based on the life of Marilyn Monroe closed on the first night. But no one at MainMan seemed to care.

When David Bowie met Mick Jagger, David was amazed to find that Mick had cash in his pocket. David, of course, had nothing but cocaine.

CHAPTER THIRTEEN

RAINBOW ROOM

In 1972, I got the idea of managing an artist in Spain.

Over two million Britons a year were travelling to Spain for their summer holidays. Sooner or later a Spanish pop star with a hit during the summer would find British tourists carrying his popularity back home with them. To try and forecast who it might be, I flew to Madrid. There were three male singing stars who seemed suitable, I went to meet them all. The first was Camilo Sesto who didn't speak any English. The second was Julio Iglesias who sang with a strange Spanish warble that I thought would never be acceptable in Britain. The third one was called Junior and had been the lead singer of the sixties group Los Brincos, the Spanish equivalent of the Beatles. He spoke perfect English and seemed perfect for what I had in mind. We hit it off at once and started writing songs together. Four months later we had a No. 1 in Spain and right across South America.

When we started travelling together I discovered Junior was extraordinarily mean. During a week in Rio de Janeiro, he constantly avoided changing his Spanish pesetas for Brazilian cruzados. Whenever we ate lunch he would roll his eyes apologetically, put his hand over his pocket and say, 'Oh dear, I still haven't remembered to change any money.' One afternoon when we went to look at the flea market Junior said he wanted an ice-cream. I told him I'd left my money at the hotel. He was quite unperturbed, 'Call the record company and tell them to come at once. They can pay for it.'

'I don't have any change. How can I make the phone call?'

'Reverse the charges. Tell them to send someone at once to pay for an ice-cream.'

So I did. And we waited an hour until someone arrived with some cash. Then we both had cornets with chocolate stuck in the top.

Although trips to Mexico or Rio de Janeiro could be fun, London was still the best place to be. Helping it stay that way was Biba, a monument to glam rock.

Biba was a department store like no other. Since the mid-sixties, Barbara Hulanicki had owned and run a small fashion shop in the Kings Road. It had become the place where every pop star shopped. Now, like a dream, she'd acquired the finance to open a department store in Kensington as big as any in the world. This wasn't a copy of Tiffany's or Harrods, it was an art deco palace, a social centre for stars.

Commerce wasn't in Barbara's thinking. At the mere sight of a celebrity she gushed with superlatives. 'The doors slid open and the lovely fresh-faced Liberace sailed into the Rainbow Room. He looked magnificent in his white mink double-breasted coat fastened by rows of real diamond buttons.'

Photographer Mick Rock used the store's roof garden to shoot pop stars. 'The wonderful thing about Biba was that they were never concerned about making money. It was one of the first stores where they actively encouraged you to hang out, and if you didn't buy anything no one was gonna bother you.'

The top floor of the building was turned into the Rainbow Room, a restaurant where the cost of the black lacquered china alone guaranteed there would be no profit made. It seated 400 people; its art deco ceiling moved with endless permutations of coloured lights. It was open day and night. It was a film set.

We all loved Biba. If you went there for dinner, you might find yourself dining next to Barbra Streisand or being entertained by the Pointer Sisters. If you popped in around midnight for some caviar among the pink marbled splendour, there might well be a party going on that included Andy Warhol or Elizabeth Taylor, Lord Snowdon or Princess Margaret, or the *real* aristocracy – David Bowie, Marc Bolan or Gary Glitter (whom Bowie described as 'obviously a charlatan').

All three of these stars were shortly to be eclipsed by an act whose name they didn't yet know.

Queen! It was such a brilliant name. People tried to pretend it had other connotations but Freddie Mercury was, and wanted to be, everything the name suggested. That's what made him so good.

Freddie was really Farrokh Bulsara, a Parsee – an Indian of Persian origin – born in Zanzibar and brought up in India. He should have become known as the first Asian to make it big in the British music business but he was as shy of his Indian heritage as the Indian community was of his being gay. However, by persuading the other members of the group to accept the name Queen, he was able to come out without ever mentioning it.

On-stage, his poise, his projection and his expressive hands all conveyed the reality of his own personality. And although Queen's music stayed in the rock genre, Freddie's voice owed more to the power and theatricality of Judy Garland and Patti LaBelle than to previous rock stars.

Freddie used his Parsee background to the full. The arrogant confidence of his body movements conveyed the strutting male chauvinism of the Middle East. The shiny silk trousers and the flowing robes were the costumes of the male hero in Indian movies. The twisting lower abdomen and endlessly moving hands contained a noticeable resemblance to a Persian belly dance. One gay music critic at the time wrote, 'He knocks spots off the other half-assed, half-committed rock queens like Bowie and Jagger.'

To begin with, Freddie had tried a solo record under the name Larry Lurex. When it failed, his girlfriend, a Biba floor manageress, persuaded him to cultivate a camper look, to use black nail polish and backcomb his hair. Not that this sort of dressing-up was new to him. In 1969, he and Roger Taylor had taken over a stall in Kensington Market. 'Roger and I go poncing about and ultrablagging just about everywhere,' he'd written to a friend. 'Lately we're being termed as a couple of queens.'

Delighted with what people were calling them, they decided to form a group and take the name for themselves. 'It's ever so regal,' said Freddie.

At that time, I was not only travelling backwards and forwards to Spain and South America, I was also producing records in Australia, Indonesia and the USA. London had become the hub of the world's music industry, as close to Asia as it was to Los Angeles. For British artists and managers, flying back to London from Sydney or Rio felt as ordinary as driving back down the motorway had been a decade earlier. Casual jet-set travel had become an everyday part of the British music scene.

One night in Tokyo I watched backstage as David Bowie performed. Then I flew on to do business in America – then France. As I checked into the George V hotel in Paris, David walked in having just arrived back from Japan by Trans-Siberian Express. A few days later I flew to London to see *Mad Dog*, a new play at the Hampstead Theatre featuring Marianne Faithfull. There was David again, sitting in the next seat.

But while David and other new stars had been selling glam rock around the world, British rock groups from the sixties had been securing their places on the American stadium circuit. Led Zeppelin, the Who, Yes, ELP, Elton John and Paul McCartney with Wings – all were cleaning up. Though for the moment, at the top of the money tree were two groups playing 'progressive rock' – Yes and ELP.

On the surface, Yes were almost as pompous as the Moody Blues. But underneath their seriousness there must have been some element of fun – their line-up included keyboardist Rick Wakeman who'd played boogie piano on Marc Bolan's 'Get It On'.

ELP also displayed no humour as they ploughed through their stage act, yet it was often a hilarious circus. ELP were Emerson, Lake & Palmer, three virtuoso musicians. They played much like Cream in the sixties, a three-way on-stage musical fight, vying to outdo each other. At one point in the show they each took a fifteen-minute solo. Emerson would play at breakneck speed on a Hammond organ, stabbing it with knives. Greg Lake would play his bass through a thousand arpeggios before strangling it with his bow. Carl Palmer would thrash his drums to extinction. Each of them paid the bill for extra theatrical effects to highlight their individual efforts. One would let off rockets, another would introduce weird lighting effects.

At an outdoor festival in Rome one summer's day, Palmer decided to outdo even Elton John's show at the Hollywood Bowl. He ordered a thousand white doves to be released at the climax of his drum thrash. But it was the hottest day of the year and for four hours the doves had to be cooped up in their cages at the side of the stage. When the electronically operated doors flew open not a single bird flew skywards. They just flopped out – a thousand dazed pigeons – hot and tired, blinking in the lights, staring bemusedly at the audience. Shitting.

When a new single by my Spanish artist sold two million copies in Mexico, and then sold a further two million in Argentina and Brazil, I decided it was time to bring him to London. I persuaded RCA to launch him in the UK. He fitted easily into the glam scene and spent most of his time at Biba stocking up with suitable clothes. But when it came to paying his way he was as mean as ever. At dinner with his record producer and musical arranger he counted how many glasses of wine each person had drunk before working out his share of the bill. I tried to be tolerant – maybe in England he was missing the feeling of being a superstar, perhaps it made him feel broke. When he left, I booked a Rolls-Royce at my expense to take him to the airport. I went with him and as we arrived at Heathrow he did his old trick of rolling his eyes and patting the outside of his pockets. 'Can you lend me ninety pence?'

'Why?' I asked.

'I want to buy a copy of *Playboy* and I don't want to break into a pound.'

In London, Iggy Pop turned up.

Flattered by David Bowie's theatrical representation of

him as Ziggy Stardust, Iggy decided to change himself to match. He covered himself in make-up and went clubbing in long dresses. For a while he stopped using heroin but made himself even worse with too many tranquillisers. Journalist Nick Kent watched him at a disco 'stoned, looking at himself in the mirrored walls for hours on end – it was pretty sad'. Kid Congo Powers, guitarist in the Gun Club, saw him 'in the street outside the disco, pulling his dress up and exposing himself'.

Iggy's worship of Bowie was strange, for it was Bowie's worship of Iggy that had created the Ziggy Stardust character. It arose from David's desperation to escape the mental instability that ran in his family. 'I felt very puny as a human. I thought, "Fuck that, I want to be Superman."'

But it worked the other way round. When David Bowie became Ziggy Stardust he lost touch with his own personality and later admitted he'd come close to losing his mind. 'Everyone was convincing me that I was a Messiah.'

Then, as his success in the role of Ziggy receded, he fell into serious drug dependency. 'I used to try a new drug every time one came on to the market.'

Over-exposure to drugs and Los Angeles pushed him towards cult religions and strange mythologies. He was going downhill.

So was Marc Bolan.

Marc's peak had been in 1972 when 'Telegram Sam' and 'Metal Guru' had both been at No. 1. He'd also had a top-selling album and Ringo Starr had produced a film about him. But by the end of 1973 he was feeling serious competition from the other artists that he and David Bowie had inspired.

In an interview with journalist Michael Wale, Marc sounded much less on-top-of-the-world than he had previously. 'I have to find £500 a week before we even do anything, you know, it's been going on a long time, I mean I don't make money. I'm not skint, you know, but it's all taxed. I've got a Rolls-Royce but I don't have a big house. I didn't buy my mum a house. If things continue the way they are now, perhaps in five years' time I might be a wealthy young elf, but I don't know. It depends. I spend more than I earn anyway – on records mainly – clothes, guitars, stuff, people.'

'Stuff', of course, meant cocaine. And while it was true that a regular backing group could sometimes drain the coffers, drummer Bill Legend and bassist Steve Currie were only on £50 per week. Bolan's career was slipping and he was looking for someone to blame. One day he announced, 'My next thing won't be glam rock. I'm telling you that, babe. I don't want to be involved in any of that. I wore gold suits and that sort of shit for a while, but it was a flash.'

Despite Marc's disillusionment with it, glam still showed no signs of dying out. The only new artist to have ignored it completely was Gilbert O'Sullivan, Gordon Mills's new protégé. Gilbert dressed himself scruffily, like a Dickensian street urchin, almost identical to the image Marc Bolan had first used in 1966. But he sang wonderful self-written songs, like 'Alone Again Naturally', whose meandering melody line was almost as long as that of 'Hey Jude'.

At the end of 1973, while Marc Bolan was feeling the strain, new glam groups were still coming onto the scene. In December, Roxy Music emerged with *Street Life* – glam rock for adults. Singer Bryan Ferry brought brains to the scene and used glam as the packaging for intelligent avant-garde music.

Even so, fashion was still the major attraction for the group's followers. When *Melody Maker*'s Richard Williams saw Roxy play a gig at London's 100 Club, he described their fans as a 'ready-made audience of girls in pill-box hats and tight skirts'.

The No. 1 record at the end of the year was 'Merry Xmas Everybody' by Slade. Chas Chandler excitedly told me how the record had been made in the middle of a summer heatwave. 'It was in New York in June. We wanted to capture that incredible silence that follows after a heavy snowfall – no echoes, no footsteps, no traffic. We just couldn't get the sound right. Then John Lennon turned up with a harmonium he was about to use in the studio next door. It was just the sound we wanted.' And six months later 'Merry Christmas Everybody' went to No. 1.

Such a glamorous, jet-setting year was topped off for everybody by news of a shambolic New Year's Eve party at Biba. The hostess, Barbara Hulanicki, remembers how it was beset by accidents. 'As the bells sounded we released the net full of balloons. Somehow we had not got it quite right; the balloons came down all right, but when the waiters in charge tried to raise the net several customers had become attached to it and were dangling above the heads of the crowd, who grandly ignored them. We released the net and let the hanging guests crash back into the crowd.' Among those treated this way were the painter Patrick Hughes, Janet Street-Porter, Tony Elliot the publisher of *Time Out*, and Michael Roberts of the *Sunday Times*, dressed as Diana Ross.

Despite its manic glamour, Biba was starting to burn out. From the day it first opened its fortunes had somehow seemed linked with the glam scene. Fittingly, it was Biba that provided the transitional moment between glam rock and what came next. The occasion was when the New York Dolls came to play at the Rainbow Room, the most sought-after ticket in town.

Before the show there was a packed press conference at which singer David Johansen announced, 'We have come to England to redeem the social outcasts.'

The band was heavily into drugs. The previous year one of their members had died of an overdose. Johansen sidestepped the issue by giving journalists his first impression of London. 'Everyone here seems to be ... homosexual.'

In *Melody Maker*, Michael Watts wrote that the Dolls are 'a great kick in the ass to the corpus of rock 'n' roll ... crude musicality and exaggerated posturing ... the new children of pop, mimicking their elders and blowing rude noises'.

Glam producers Nicky Chinn and Michael Chapman were also in the audience. 'We loved the New York Dolls. We thought they were absolutely superb. They were everything we were doing, but much darker.'

Darker still was the new album by David Bowie, *Diamond Dogs*.

In *Rolling Stone*, Eric Emerson wrote: 'Most of the songs are obscure tangles of perversion, degradation, fear and self-pity. Are they masturbatory fantasies, guilt-ridden projections, terrified premonitions, or is it all Alice Cooper exploitation?'

The album provided the basis for a world tour using the biggest stage show ever mounted in rock history – a $250,000 set weighing six tons and depicting 'Hunger City', in which the album was set. Halfway through the US tour, Bowie decided to scrap the whole set and start again. After a break, he re-emerged in a tight-cut jacket and baggy trousers looking like a camp waiter in a 1920s cocktail bar.

Fame apart, Bowie's other obsessions were catching up on him – drugs and sex. In 1970 he'd announced he was gay. In 1973 he suddenly recanted. 'Absurd! No positively not! I've never done a bisexual act in my life.' But in 1976 he got back on track. 'It's true. I'm bisexual ... I can't deny that I've used the fact very well.' He even admitted that there'd been a 'pretty boy in class in some school or other that I took home and neatly fucked on my bed upstairs'.

Then he owned up to drugs. 'I'd done a lot of pills ever since I was a kid – thirteen or fourteen.' He said he'd also done coke at the same age but didn't try grass until John Paul Jones turned him on to it when he was seventeen. What he failed to tell the journalists was that he was now hooked on heroin.

None of this helped the reviews for *Diamond Dogs*. Rock critic Charles Shaar Murray called it 'the final nightmare of the glitter apocalypse'. But Bowie's real 'glitter apocalypse' wasn't his descent into drugs, it was his slow realisation that he'd been the subject of one of the music industry's biggest ever rip-offs.

Still without cash of his own, and with his manager's business empire devouring his royalties, he finally took legal action.

Marc Bolan disappeared to Monte Carlo, coked to the eyeballs, hanging out with Ringo Starr, gambling every night, getting fatter, his career disappearing up his nose. Before he left he told a journalist, 'Glam rock is dead. It was a great thing, but now ... what those guys are doing is circus and comedy.' He had a valid point.

Mud was fronted by a pub-contest Elvis Presley who dressed in fifties teddy-boy clothes. 'Mutton dressed up as glam,' said Nicky Chinn, writer of 'Tiger Feet', Mud's biggest hit.

The Electric Light Orchestra combined rock rhythms with classical instrumentation but singer Roy Wood was addicted to fancy dress, particularly gorilla outfits.

Leo Sayer dressed in a Pierrot's outfit and painted his face white, but the most interesting thing about him was his manager, sixties rock 'n' roll singer Adam Faith.

There was a group of pretty boys called Kenny who were in danger of breaking the BBC's advertising rules by wearing white T-shirts emblazoned with a large red 'K' similar to the one on packets of Kellogs cornflakes.

But most dreadful of all were the Wombles who dressed in furry costumes like animal Teletubbies.

Glam had turned into vaudeville. Only Gary Glitter limped on, unchanged.

During the period of glam rock's supremacy there'd been yet another rise in record sales. This, together with the success of British rock groups in America, had fed the music industry with too much money for it to be thrown haphazardly back into unproven artists. Moreover, in 1972 a company called K-Tel had discovered there was money to be made in repackaging old hits and selling them by means of TV advertising. They were closely followed by a second company, Arcade, and by the mid-seventies the resulting compilation albums were accounting for 30 per cent of all albums sold in the UK.

For the major companies it was time to take stock and reorganise. They needed to form an organisation that would give them negotiating power with retailers and suppliers of raw materials. They came together to form the BPI, the British Phonograph Industry. The initial members were Decca, Polydor, Phonogram, EMI, Pye, WEA, RCA, A&M, United Artists and DJM (a tiny British record company belonging to Dick James) – and to begin with CBS Records stayed out.

The formation of the BPI soon led to a more co-ordinated record industry and a more professional approach. Breaking a new artist began to be talked about more in terms of marketing rather than music. And it wasn't just record companies who started looking at the sale of records as a marketing exercise, artists too were beginning to understand the mechanics of the industry. They could now be seen attending marketing meetings and referring to their own record sales as 'units sold', previously the exclusive language of record company executives.

The *Melody Maker* summed it up when they said, 'At the heart of the Rock Dream is a cash register.'

Malcolm McLaren was the owner of Sex, a rubberwear shop in Kings Road where the cash register was empty. In 1974 Malcolm went to America in search of his Rock Dream. He visited the New York Dolls and warned them of the impending demise of glam rock. He said they should get into communism and to help them he bought several pairs of red trousers. Soon he was claiming to be their manager, but the group denied it. David Johansen said, 'He was like our haberdasher for a while.'

Meanwhile, dressed in white satin, the members of Queen drew a final line under glam rock. Their video of 'Bohemian Rhapsody' was both a requiem mass for its passing and a hallelujah chorus for the group's entry into American stadium rock.

Earlier, when the group had finished making it, they'd taken the record to EMI who said it couldn't be released because it was too long. The band then gave an acetate to DJ Kenny Everett who played it on Capital Radio fourteen times over one weekend.

Record producer Jeff Jarratt remembers waking up one morning with it blaring from his alarm clock radio. 'I just lay there absolutely spellbound ... I don't remember where I was when Kennedy was shot, but I will always remember the first time I heard 'Bohemian Rhapsody".'

EMI capitulated and released it – a six-minute, million-selling glam rock finale.

CHAPTER FOURTEEN

PURE SCAM, PURE SHAM

Biba had gone bust and glam fans had removed their earrings.

In October 1974, after the miners' strike had put Britain on a three-day week, the Conservative government were replaced by Labour. People thought the new government would make things better, but they made things even worse. Britain looked increasingly gloomy. The unemployment figures were the worst since the war.

In the music business, although glam had gone, nothing had arrived to replace it and the singles chart lacked new trends. To pass time, the industry trifled with the Bay City Rollers. There was no glam androgyny here, just pretty young Scottish boys with a homosexual manager. Briefly, they were screamed at by sub-teen girls. On one occasion the lead singer fired a gun at fans camped outside his house and a girl was shot in the head. The group's manager defended him to the press. 'He's not a bad kid. None of them are. The pressure's just built up and they're all on cloud nine.'

Cloud nine, of course, consisted of drugs and booze – the normal things that destroy pop groups too immature to cope with the benefits of fame.

Meanwhile, the pound was falling, inflation was rising and financial analysts talked of Britain going bankrupt. A grey mood pervaded people's thinking and all over London every A&R man you met was nervous and wary.

Dave Ambrose had been a bass player with Shotgun Express, now he'd got himself a job at EMI music publishing. 'I was only in a junior position but what surprised me was that the company didn't seem to be finding anything new. Glam rock was over and the people in A&R seemed to be paralysed, just hoping for something new to come along.'

Artists looking for deals were too diverse in their musical styles. When glam had been the rage, it had been easy, everyone knew what they were looking for. But with no particular trend dominating the market, committing money to an artist meant making a subjective judgement. For an A&R man with a mortgage to pay and a coke habit to feed, that was a high-risk strategy. So they hung on to their budgets and waited.

When glam took off, cocaine had become the favoured buzz for the in-crowd, but for ordinary kids coke had always been too expensive. They relied on poppers, small glass capsules of amyl nitrate. Now a new drug appeared, as speedy as cocaine but much cheaper, and it revitalised the music business.

Amphetamine sulphate came as pinkish-white crystals that had to be chopped fine enough not to scrape the nose when they were sniffed through the plastic casing of a ballpoint pen. It was a drug of pure aggression, the high came quickly and made you want to charge like a bull, but it was also disgusting, even the people who used it said so. As an *NME* journalist, Charles Shaar Murray couldn't afford cocaine, so like everyone around him he took sulphate instead. 'It was like sniffing powdered razor blades off a toilet floor. It got you speeding, but for two hours you'd have a post-nasal drip of foul-tasting mucous flowing down the back of your throat. It was disgusting, but it did the trick. It was the Embassy cover-version equivalent of cocaine.'

To complement its foulness, sulphate users needed to find a new type of music as rough-edged and disgusting as the drug itself. What they came up with was punk rock – simple, fast and angry. Leftover acid-heads were still telling us to love the world. Newly amphetamised punks demanded that we trash it. The names of the new groups seemed endless – Stinky Toys, Siouxsie & the Banshees, the Slits, the Vibrators, the Damned, the Clash, the Buzzcocks – all driven by buckets full of foul speed sniffed through unpleasant little tubes. The best known, of course, were the Sex Pistols.

Their singer was Johnny Rotten. The *NME* described him as 'Spikey, dyed red hair, death-white visage, metal hanging from lobes, skinny leg strides. He looks like an amphetamine corpse from a Sunday gutter-press wet dream.'

Neil Tennant was working for the *NME* at the time. After watching the group get into a fight during a gig at the Nashville in West Kensington he wrote, 'So how do the Pistols create their atmosphere when the music has failed? By beating up a member of the audience. How else?'

'Actually, we're not into music,' Johnny Rotten told a reporter. 'We're into chaos.'

The truth was even simpler. They were into amphetamine sulphate, like everyone else.

After he'd failed with the New York Dolls, Malcolm McLaren had retreated to Sex, his kinky clothes shop in the Kings Road. He was obsessed with the way Larry Parnes had turned working-class boys into rock 'n' roll heroes and he was in love with the myth of the barely articulate rock star. Then one day John Lydon came shopping.

Malcolm grabbed him and made him the centre point for a new group. John Lydon, in the classic Parnes tradition, became Johnny Rotten. The fashion concept came from

Television, an American group whose singer wore ripped T-shirts held together with safety pins. From his time as haberdasher to the New York Dolls, Malcolm borrowed the musical idea – the same riffs, speeded up, overlaid with Johnny Rotten's threatening snarl. And the fuel which got the whole thing moving was amphetamine sulphate.

'I loved the stuff,' says Johnny Rotten. 'I'm normally a very slow person and it made me more intense. I'm naturally paranoid, and it made me feel better.'

In their song 'New Amphetamine Shriek', the Fugs described it even more succinctly.

I don't have a bedtime, I don't need to come
For I have become an amphetamine bum
If you don't like sleeping, and don't want a screw
Then you should take lots of amphetamine too

Throughout the glam period McLaren had been watching the growing number of disenfranchised teenagers who called themselves skinheads. They shaved their heads and bashed up Pakistanis. Their lives were empty and negative, which was what made them so attractive to McLaren. By presenting his new group as anti-social monsters he would grab the respect of these disenfranchised kids and turn them into a captive audience.

He started the Sex Pistols off with a gig at the 100 Club, advertising it all over town with strikingly stylish fly posters. On the night of the gig, Dave Ambrose got a phone call from someone urging him to go and look. 'There was hardly anyone in the club but they were brilliant. Johnny Rotten kept arguing with the others, then he walked out of the club for a while. Malcolm had to run after him and bring him back to finish the set. There was something riveting about them; they looked so dangerous. Then a few days later, Malcolm McLaren turned up at EMI with all these demos and things and tried to get a meeting. I rushed to find Terry Slater who was my boss and told him – "You *must* sign this group. I saw them the other night, they're fantastic." So he signed them to a publishing deal.'

Shortly afterwards, EMI's record division signed the group to a recording deal. The group had turned into a tight musical unit with well-constructed songs and lyrics that sounded like political slogans. They played with good tension and timing, and even some sensitivity, albeit an angry one. But instead of focusing on their musical ability, McLaren continued to urge them to behave as badly as possible. 'Cultivate hatred,' he told them, 'it is your greatest asset.' He encouraged them to spit and vomit in public, but to begin with they were often surprisingly pleasant.

At the time of their first record the group had to do an interview with Annie Nightingale, a journalist who lived in Brighton. On the way down in the train McLaren rehearsed his four protégés. 'Put your feet on the coffee-table and swear a lot – and for heaven's sake don't say please or thank you.'

When they arrived Annie offered them tea. 'Do you take sugar?'

'Yes please,' said Johnny Rotten.

When Annie left the room Malcolm flung his arms above his head in a fury. 'Dammit,' he yelled. 'How many times have I told you – *don't say please!*'

Johnny was apologetic. 'Sorry, Malc, I forgot.'

McLaren howled in despair. 'For Christ's sake. You can't say *sorry* either.'

Later, of course, the group got the hang of it.

As amphetamine sulphate and punk philosophy spread across Britain, punk groups got the blame. 'Terrifying the Bourgeois' claimed the *Observer*, which was just what Malcolm McLaren intended. As far as record companies were concerned, they were just grateful to see the music business buzzing again.

The Sex Pistols' first single was 'Anarchy In The UK'. The group promoted it by vomiting at airport lounges and touring Britain, spitting and swearing their way round the country with the media in full pursuit. EMI's directors met to discuss the situation.

Sir John Read was chairman of a board split between the record division and hi-tech electronics. Geoffrey Howe, the Shadow Chancellor, was one of the traditional corporate members who had recently voted to invest tens of millions in electronic medical equipment. The A&R division tried hard to explain the money-making rationale behind the Sex Pistols' bad behaviour. In a memo to the board they compared it to the early days of the Rolling Stones and advised that the group be retained.

They were – until they went on Bill Grundy's early evening TV show and said 'fuck'. In their lead story, the *Daily Mirror* reflected Britain's horror. 'A pop group shocked millions of viewers last night with the filthiest language ever heard on British television.'

It was too much for the stuffy board of EMI directors. They ordered the Sex Pistols to be dropped. Malcolm McLaren responded by telling the press that he wanted to find Sir John Read and 'puke all over his face'. In EMI's offices, secretaries and A&R staff quickly removed the safety pins from their shirts and sweaters. Publicly, however, the company acted with good grace. They presented the group with a cheque for £50,000 and put out a press statement wishing them 'luck in the future'.

Shortly afterwards, Dave Ambrose was at an EMI staff party when the DJ accidentally put on 'Anarchy In The UK'. 'I was dancing like mad and suddenly looked round and saw everyone else had left the dance floor. I'd just blown my chances of promotion.'

Punk rock had originally started in America. The first DJ to play it on British radio was John Peel who disliked music that was too slick or pretentious. For him glam rock had been popular music's lowest ebb. He hated people who overdressed and his love of punk started when he received from America an album full of 'short, sharp energy-bursts' by a group called the Ramones. From the photo on the sleeve he could see that 'at least the Ramones were not velvet-clad ninnies'.

After he'd played the album on his programme, John heard from bands all over Britain trying to do the same thing. Since there were still no British punk records available, he offered free studio time to groups he could subsequently play on air. His favourite, he said, was a girl group called the Slits. 'Their inability to play coupled with their determination to play – the conflict between these two things was magnificent.'

Another programme sympathetic to punk was *So It Goes*, a TV show from Manchester, the first to use the Sex Pistols.

Producer Tony Wilson loved punk not just for its anarchy but for the actual sound of its music. 'When punks picked up their first guitars and tried to play a chord they learnt just one – the 'F' shape. Then, rather than learn other chords, they simply moved their 'F' shape up and down the fret board. The result was the distinctive sound of punk, featuring overtones and harmonics only previously heard in Shostakovich.'

The saga of the Sex Pistols continued when they were offered another cheque, this time for £75,000 from A&M. Previous to the celebratory signing, managing director Derek Green had avoided meeting the group in case they put him off. They arrived drunk – fighting, bleeding, vomiting, swearing and belligerent. A few days later they beat up a TV presenter at the Speakeasy, the music industry's lush late-night meeting place. Green told them to take their cheque and leave.

McLaren warned the industry, 'The Sex Pistols are like some contagious disease.' But really, the Pistols weren't the only group behaving badly, the Damned were easily their equals.

The Damned had punk's best-named drummer, Rat Scabies, and a singer called Captain Sensible, who explained 'We thought up crazy names so we could keep signing on at the DHSS. Mine came on the way to a festival in France. I'd bought a second-hand shirt with epaulettes and I was pretending to be a pilot. I shouted out, "Everything's under control. We're on autopilot." Someone said, "Oh, it's Captain Sensible." Now I'm forty-six, and I'm still stuck with the same name.'

The Damned were signed to Stiff Records, Britain's newest independent label. Stiff thrived on punk, not so much because they loved the music, but because its amateurishness suited their budget. They relied on eye-catching graphics and great slogans. 'Today's Sound Today' and 'Lo-Fi Production' were two of them. And they gave out stickers for schoolkids to stick on their satchels: 'If it ain't Stiff, it ain't worth a fuck.'

At the festival in France, the Damned got out of their heads on speed and ran around the hotel all night climbing out of the windows and bashing on people's doors until the concierge went crazy and called the police. At eight in the morning they finally got to sleep, but at eleven they had to be on-stage. 'We had a huge argument,' says Sensible, 'we said it was impossible, we just wanted to sleep. But in the end we took loads more speed and played in a muddy field for 150 people.'

A couple of months later Malcolm McLaren organised an all-punk festival at the 100 Club. There were three groups the first night and four the next with the Damned headlining. Captain Sensible thought the whole thing was just another McLaren scam. 'The word "festival" made it look like punk was taking off but the 100 Club didn't have any more people in it than that field in France.'

The music industry is a strange place. If you're in it and read *Music Week* and *NME*; if you listen to Radio One when you're in the car, and a bit of John Peel in the evenings, you can feel as up-to-date as anyone about what's going on. Yet, at the end of the first year of punk, there were probably more people in the music business who'd never seen a punk band play than people who had. Because I'd been travelling round the world too much in the previous few years, I was one of them. So I went one night to a punk club in Soho to see what I'd been missing.

When the group came on-stage they stiffened their bodies and bounced up and down as if they were on pogo sticks.

The audience threw beer at them and spat, and the group spat back. It was ritual rather than war, and not having seen it before I was impressed. What surprised me most was that the band was good musically. Thirty minutes later I was backstage offering a management contract with an advance of £10,000.

The band called themselves London. The next morning I called Derek Everett at CBS and described what I'd seen. 'So what?' he asked. 'Is there anything special about them?'

'They jump up and down as if they're on pogo sticks and spit at the audience.'

'So do a thousand other bands in England,' he told me.

In the end I got lucky. MCA were just starting up in Britain and were eager to sign new acts. Like me, managing director Roy Featherstone had never seen a punk band perform. When I took him to see London he signed them at once. Then I had to start working with them.

As was to be expected from a punk group, they were vile, bad-mannered, foul-mouthed and dirty. They deliberately trod in dog shit before coming upstairs to lounge around in my plush pad in South Audley Street. I presumed they didn't have an O-level between them. If I hadn't watched them sign their names on my management contract I wouldn't have believed they could write. I began to appreciate why EMI and A&M had dropped the Sex Pistols.

Rumour had it, the Pistols were getting desperate. During their brief stay at A&M, they'd recorded their new song 'God Save The Queen'. A&M had thrown them out in March but the group wanted the record released in time for the Queen's Silver Jubilee celebrations in June. Malcolm suddenly realised for the first time that the games had to stop. The group were in dire need of a company that would actually release their records.

The answer was Richard Branson, bearded and young with the image of an easygoing hippy. People thought he was a soft touch, but those who knew him knew otherwise. He was a ruthlessly determined businessman who had succeeded in records through an extraordinary stroke of luck. When he'd first started Virgin Records he'd been offered *Tubular Bells* by Mike Oldfield. Initially he'd turned it down but when nothing better turned up he released it. By chance a clip from the record was used as background music for *The Exorcist*. When the film took off, *Tubular Bells* became the best-selling album in the world.

In the pop business, Virgin had gained little credibility from this success. Branson was now looking for something that would put his company firmly in touch with youth culture. McLaren headed on over.

Branson signed the Sex Pistols and climbed on board McLaren's publicity bandwagon. The first single was 'God Save The Queen' which included a sleeve with a safety pin piercing the Queen's nose.

Britain had been given a holiday for the Silver Jubilee and nothing was going to spoil it. But when the world's press arrived to watch Britain party, there was a big black blot in the middle of the celebrations – 'God Save The Queen' by the Sex Pistols.

Virgin's marketing skills and McLaren's provocational expertise joined hands. The front and back of every London bus was splashed with punk ads. McLaren's dream of recruiting Britain's disenfranchised youth as the captive audience for his group had at last materialised. He didn't care about the 54 million Britons who were celebrating the Queen's Silver Jubilee, he was interested in the half million who hated it. That would be enough to get the record to No. 1.

But 'God Save The Queen' stuck at No.2.

The No. 1 record was by Rod Stewart, who like the Sex Pistols was distributed by CBS. McLaren says CBS told him the Pistols were outselling Stewart two to one.

The establishment elements in the music industry disapproved of the Sex Pistols. Richard Branson, who'd been keen to see them reach No. 1, thought the charts might have been manipulated against them. Mick Brown, his official biographer, says, 'Branson's suspicion that the chart had been fixed was lent weight by an anonymous phone call alleging that, in the week that the Sex Pistols might have been expected to reach number one, the BPI had issued an extraordinary secret directive to the BMRB [the organisation that compiled the charts], that all chart-return shops connected with record companies be dropped from the weekly census of best-selling records. Virgin, the store where most Sex Pistols records were being sold, was struck off the list. A week later, the decision was reversed.'

At the time this was alleged to have happened, the chairman of the BPI was John Fruin who was also managing director of WEA Records. Later, in 1981, Fruin lost his job after irregularities were uncovered about the chart placings of several WEA acts.

In September 1977, Marc Bolan died in a car crash. He'd been attempting a comeback. Granada had given him a TV show in which he sang and interviewed guests. The show's producer was Muriel Young who vividly remembers the week before he died: 'We'd filmed with David Bowie, Marc's bosom pal, and they'd been fantastic together. David had really wanted to help make the show good for him.'

Bolan had emerged from a long self-indulgent period during which he'd fattened himself up like a Christmas turkey. For the TV show he got rid of the fat and almost managed to look as he had done at the height of glam. Then he died.

Muriel Young had spent the day with him filming the first half of the show. 'We did the shows over two days. At the end of the first day Marc's girlfriend Gloria was coming in from America, so he went back to London to meet her – picked her up at the airport and went out to dinner. At three in the morning she drove him home and they crashed. Afterwards we finished the show without him. His folks insisted that we did it. It was a terrible feeling, we kept expecting him to come on-stage.'

Shortly afterwards, on a quite different TV programme, there was the possibility of a Sunday afternoon slot for London, the punk group I was managing. In case it came up I needed to know where each of them would be on Saturday evening. The drummer had just been thrown out of his bedsit. He told me, 'I s'pose I'll be stayin' wiv me bleedin' mum and dad.'

The TV show materialised, so on Saturday I called them. At the number the drummer had given me the phone was answered by a charming woman, refined and polite. I said, 'I must have a wrong number. I was looking for John.'

She called upstairs in sweet motherly tones. 'John, darling!'

I'd discovered the truth. 'John' lived in a big house in Hampstead, the son of a millionaire tycoon. His name was actually Jon Moss and later he joined Culture Club and even turned out to be gay. As for the others, the biggest trickster of all was the all-swearing, all-spitting singer. He called himself Riff Regan, but his real name was Miles Tredinnick. His father was a vice-marshal in the Royal Air Force.

It was typical of the period. Punk wasn't really anarchy, it was a sham. To most kids, so was the adult world. They were playing it at its own game.

The Sex Pistols had now become role models for artists like the Mopeds, Smak and Dee Generate, most of them more interested in mayhem than music. But the Pistols also inspired a few groups with real musical talent.

When Paul Weller first formed the Jam, they were a halfhearted glam group with long hair and flared trousers. Then he became obsessed with sixties mod culture. He cut his hair like the Small Faces, bought a Lambretta scooter, a Rickenbacker guitar and the Who's first album. What attracted him about the Who was the pent-up fury that flowed from four musicians in conflict with one another. From himself alone, Paul Weller found enough anger to match the lot of them. He called himself 'a very, very moody bastard'.

In 1976 he'd heard about the Sex Pistols and had gone to see them play an 'all-nighter' at the Lyceum. That evening the band's act came together as never before with Johnny Rotten doing an 'Iggy Pop act', stubbing out cigarettes on the back of his hand. Weller remembers watching in admiration. 'They were the last band on, six in the morning or something – and we were all speeding out of our heads – French blues.'

For Weller and his band it was a seminal experience. It resulted in the aggressive sound for which the Jam became famous – a speed-blues combination with angry teenage lyrics, many of them lifted from Paul's favourite record, the Who's first album. 'I plagiarised the whole album,' he admitted. 'I just changed the titles.' Polydor, who were looking for a punk group with musical ability, signed them for a stingy £6,000.

One of Paul's punk rivals, Captain Sensible, disapproved of punk groups signing to majors. 'I met Paul Weller, and he was a reasonable bloke if you like po-faced bastards. But Paul was all about believing he was marvellous which was the entire opposite of what punk was about. It was about "No heroes".'

From then on, Weller grew increasingly political, but his politics were simplistic. He loved the Queen, wanted Britain to be great and wrote lyrics expressing his dislike of the Labour government. ('Whatever happened to the great empire – you bastards have turned it into manure.') Captain Sensible remembers seeing him outside Woking station. 'He was dressed in a Union Jack suit telling people to vote Conservative.'

Poor Paul. He came in for a massive media backlash and journalist Rick Sky suggested he'd had 'a Damascus vision on the way to Woking'. Weller's reason for making political statements was the very reverse of the Sex Pistols. If the Pistols touched on politics it was because they'd been fed lines by their manager, eager to provoke the public. Paul Weller was sincere. When he was laughed at, his music got even angrier.

At CBS, there'd been another punk signing. Managing director Maurice Oberstein had given the Clash an advance of £100,000, sixteen times what Polydor paid for the Jam, and he allowed them to go into the studio without an A&R man or a producer. 'All I did in the beginning,' said Obie, 'was to take a gamble that they had a sound and a noise that they wanted to make.'

Critic Jon Savage said the Clash had simply 'speeded up the heavily chorded, stuttering sound of the Who and the Kinks', but there was something more important about them – singer Joe Strummer was articulate and political, which hardly tied in with being a punk.

Punks were not only meant to be angry, they had to be nihilistic. The trouble was, learning to play a musical instrument could lead to satisfaction, and this defused their anger. When they realised what they were doing to themselves, it often made them even angrier than before, but by then it was too late. They'd ceased to be punks and started to become reasonable people. As such, they had to redirect their anger at something specific, and this could sometimes involve politics. Thus for most musicians, punk proved to be a transitory stage.

Elvis Costello began as a furious young poet, then exchanged aggression for melancholic humour. 'I got tired of it. You become a bit pathetic after a while if you're still ranting on.'

The Stranglers were quite happy to use angry punk music as a transit camp on their way to becoming a conventional rock group. So were the Pretenders, whose singer Chrissie Hynde offered practical advice to all girls who wanted to be rock stars. 'Don't think that sticking your boobs out and trying to look fuckable will help. Remember you're in a rock band. It's not 'fuck me!' it's 'fuck you!''

Poly Styrene wrote 'Oh Bondage Up Yours'. The idea, she explained, was: 'Look, this is what you have done to me, turned me into a piece of styrofoam, I am your product.' For Poly too, punk proved to be a transitory stage. After releasing one album she saw a vision outside a hotel window and joined the Hare Krishna movement.

Tom Robinson also passed through a punk rock stage on his way somewhere else. Tom preferred to call his group a rock band, but either way, with his song 'Glad To Be Gay', he plunged himself into sexual politics. 'I'd been to a Quaker co-educational boarding school, where homos were so hated that I'd tried to kill myself when I was sixteen. When I moved to London and came to terms with being gay, that was the thing that goaded me up and made me become a ranting gay liberationist.' But having ranted for a while, Tom followed the transitory nature of musicians of the period and went off and got married and had a child.

The Police, too, used punk as a staging post. To begin with Sting even spoke like a punk. 'I come from a family of losers. I've rejected my family ...' But the Police moved away from punk when Andy Summers joined them and started playing reggae guitar.

Mostly, punk was just a useful label for guitar groups with little technique but loads of attitude. When they started out, Siouxsie & the Banshees had no idea how to play their instruments, they just banged on them. At their first gig at the 100 Club, Siouxsie told the audience, 'We may not have anarchy in the streets, but at least we can have it in our little club.' Unrehearsed, they played twenty minutes of 'The Lord's Prayer' interspersed with 'Twist and Shout', 'Rebel Rebel', and 'Knocking On Heaven's Door'. Pop manager Tom Watkins thinks Siouxsie's band should never have been termed punk. 'It was pure crap,' he insists. 'She proffered nothing in the way of any kind of anarchical statements. It was a nonsense.'

But Tom is being tough on her. Performing on energy alone for twenty minutes with no knowledge of how to play an instrument is as good a form of anarchy as any other. If the yardstick for punk bands was to be the quality of their anarchy, then the Sex Pistols weren't punk at all. In his book *Is That It?*, Bob Geldof made the same point. 'For all the anarchy in the UK, the Pistols still signed contracts, attended rehearsals, and wrote songs; whatever the rhetoric, in the end being in a band was about hard work and demanded discipline. But saying that about the Pistols in those days was like attacking Marx in a Soviet politburo meeting.'

In the beginning, Malcolm McLaren had looked like the logical successor to Andrew Oldham and Kit Lambert. Like the other two, he believed chaos and disruption were good for an industry that is normally far too self-satisfied, and he saw anarchy as art. For all three of them the problem was when to turn it on and when to turn it off.

By 1978 Kit had given up running the day-to-day business of the Who, but remembering their beginnings and the way he'd promoted them through outrageous scams, he considered himself to be the forefather of punk. When punk emerged as a musical force, Kit felt jealous of those who were in the middle of things. He returned to London from his decadent palace in Venice, trying to get back into the business. Arriving unexpectedly at Polydor Records he insisted on taking Horst Schmolzi to lunch. Horst was busy and waved at a pile of papers. 'I can't go now. Look at all that correspondence.'

'That's easily dealt with,' Kit said, and flung it out of the window.

Malcolm McLaren could get away with things like that because he had the group to go with it. All Kit had was memories. Though his philosophy was punk to the core, he'd missed out on punk's moment of triumph.

One day Kit called me out of the blue. 'I need your help. I'm in Mexico. You'll have to come at once.'

I told him: 'I'm sorry Kit, I've got a leaking bank account, a nagging accountant, and a group to manage.' But in the end I went anyway.

Over dinner at Fouquet, in Mexico City, he told me: 'I'm in an awful fucking mess. My friends want me to declare myself insane.'

I was shocked. Kit was a model of sanity. He sometimes acted a trifle crazy but that was because he was bored, or lonely, or because life was too dull, or maybe just too long. 'It's the money,' he explained. 'It's been flowing out like the spring tide. On drugs and boys and lovers. On villas and penthouses and chauffeurs and cars. On Chateau Lafitte and jars of beluga. My friends say I'm incapable of running my own affairs. They say I should make myself a ward of the court, and to be honest, I don't have the self-control to look after my own money. So I've decided they're right.'

I tried to protest but he lifted the edge of the tablecloth and stuck his head underneath it. I thought, 'Maybe his friends are right, maybe he *is* mad.' But then he burst out from behind the tablecloth laughing uproariously with white dust round his nostrils. 'Let's forget coffee. It's too boring. Waiter! Check please!'

He whirled us out of the restaurant and into a limo. We shot across town to a bar where a drag queen was introducing a show. 'The big cock contest. El Pollo Grande!' Kit went to the toilet and came bubbling back with more powder round his nose. Then he whisked me off to another club, then another.

By the fourth one he'd gone out of control. We were thrown out and Kit fell in a heap on the sidewalk. The limo driver slung him in the back of the car and took him back to the hotel. The next time I saw him he was a ward of court.

From having lived the life of a rock emperor, Kit Lambert was reduced to begging in a government office for his own money. Well-meaning civil servants sold everything he owned – his palace in Venice, the furniture, the paintings – all at knock-down prices. They were now paying for him to stay in a seedy hotel in South Kensington. Every Monday he went by Underground to a government office in Holborn where he collected £200 of his own money, which instantly went on drugs.

There was a part of him that enjoyed it. It was nihilistic. It was punk. He'd been the first great master of rock scam, the forerunner of Malcolm McLaren. Now he was giving his life story a suitable ending.

The Sex Pistols' story was also heading to an end.

'God Save The Queen' had been the high spot of the group's career. It was followed by recrimination and aggression from the media. A headline in the *Daily Mirror* urged people to 'Punish The Punks', and punished they were. On several occasions they were threatened with violence but the worst punishment was self-inflicted. Bad business management was wrecking the group's progress and amphetamine sulphate was wrecking their minds, but while tension grew within the group, Malcolm continued to court outrageous publicity. 'He's hopeless at dealing with people,' said Johnny Rotten. 'He couldn't care less about you. "Hello, I'm having a nervous breakdown." "Go away, I'm busy scandalising you in the press."'

Slowly, all the big plans turned sour – the album, America, the movie.

The album had a great title – *Never Mind the Bollocks* – but when it finally came out it contained nothing intrinsically new.

America was a disaster, the gig in Texas being typical. Johnny Rotten walked on-stage wearing a T-shirt that said 'You cowboys are all a bunch of fucking faggots'. The lights went out, the gig ended in a riot and Malcolm claimed, 'It was just what I wanted.'

Then there was the movie – *The Great Rock 'n' Roll Swindle*. Quite simply, it was the group's obituary.

The biggest guitar group to emerge during the punk era had nothing at all to do with punk either musically or philosophically. Ed Bicknell, a booking agent at NEMS, was called by Phonogram and asked if he would book a new band called Dire Straits. He said he didn't think so because the name was too awful, but he agreed to see them play a gig at Dingwalls. 'I arrived to find the whole music business trying to sign them. I pushed my way into the dressing room and knocked over Mark's Stratocaster. It wasn't a good start but I persuaded them to come and see me at NEMS.'

Ed decided it was time to move on from being an agent to becoming a manager. At NEMS, he shared an office with another agent whom he persuaded to move out for the afternoon, desk and all. Ed replaced it with a chaise longue, hung the gold records from reception in his own office, and told the receptionist, 'Keep calling me. Make out I'm busy.'

Dire Straits sat studying the gold records on his wall while Ed shouted fake million-dollar deals down the phone.

The next day he became their manager. He had no illusions about what was required of him. 'I guess everyone knows the truth. Managing a rock group is just a matter of knowing how to bullshit.'

Malcolm McLaren could hardly disagree. It was his bullshit that had led people to think of this as the era of punk. In the Kings Road on a Saturday afternoon the kids all wore the punk uniform – ragged black waistcoats, platform shoes, purple hair, fishnet stockings, rubber mini-skirts, sew-on patches of Hitler and Marx. But the boutiques where they bought these clothes mostly played reggae or blues or current pop songs.

During the era of the Sex Pistols, genuine punk music hardly appeared in the charts at all. In their inimitable rock-boogie style, Status Quo had more chart records than any punk band could ever dream of. Other big-selling British artists were Rod Stewart, Showaddywaddy, Hot Chocolate, Kate Bush, and the Wurzels. The biggest songs were: 'Save Your Kisses for Me', 'Sailing', 'Don't Cry For Me Argentina', 'Mull Of Kintyre', 'Wuthering Heights' and 'I Am A Cider Drinker'. Moreover, from 1977 onwards, the world was being swept with disco mania.

So where was punk?

Sociologists have written books about the period, the influence of punk groups and the way they swayed musical taste, but the charts belie their claims. From 1963 to 1966 the Beatles had nine No. 1 records and every other record in the charts echoed their sound and style. From 1976 to 1979, the peak years of punk, the Sex Pistols only made the Top Ten on four occasions and throughout the period the sound of current pop had little to do with them.

*

By 1979, true punks were sinking in a flood of cheap heroin from the Middle East. Sid Vicious, treble-dosed on smack, had stabbed his girlfriend to death and later killed himself with an even larger overdose. The Sex Pistols were finished but punk lingered on, although mainly in the form of sanitised fashion tips – columnists in teenage magazines explaining how to put safety pins through your skin without endangering your health, mass-produced punk clothing from C&A, mohican hairpieces for weekend parties.

Tony Wilson, the first TV producer to give the Sex Pistols a break, thinks they could have been a genuinely great band. 'Malcolm's dream as an anarchist was to create the "Bay City Rollers of outrage". He wanted his band to be the biggest band in Britain because they were so disgusting. But he failed, 'cos for three years the Pistols were the biggest band in Britain because they were so fantastic.'

When EMI Records dropped the Sex Pistols the company entered the worst five-year period in its history. The A&R staff lost confidence in signing anything new or out of the ordinary and in the second half of 1978 EMI's record division lost £14.6 million.

All this came about because of Malcolm McLaren's obsession with publicity. He spent three years creating media mayhem but failed to spot the moment when the hype had to stop and the music begin.

Malcolm revelled in creating social tension and made the Sex Pistols fill their songs with provocative political imagery. But it was the provocation that interested him not the politics. He preferred the title to the content, the question to the answer, the surface to the hidden depths. That was his legacy. Pure scam! Pure sham!

CHAPTER FIFTEEN

FOUR-TO-THE-FLOOR

In the fifties, long before anyone danced to flashing lights, I was a teenage jazz fan on holiday in Paris. I found a bar near the Boulevard St Germain which was a cross between a gentleman's club and a library. Around the walls, instead of books, were jazz records, 78s in those days. The barman doubled as a DJ. He found the records the customers requested and played them while they listened over a glass of wine. The club was called La Discothèque.

The next time I heard that word again was in London in the early sixties. The place that defined what discotheques were to become was the Ad Lib club – dark and sexy, with mirrors round the dance floor.

Later, when the Ad Lib burned down, the showbusiness crowd moved on to the Scotch of St James, the Cromwellian, Maunkberry's, Tramp and the Speakeasy. Although loosely termed discotheques, these clubs had small dance areas which were secondary to the club's social purpose of providing a meeting place for 'in' people. They were important, not because of the numbers of people dancing, but because the people who danced there were those who controlled the record business. These discos had their equivalents in other capitals, like Arthur in New York, run by Richard Burton's ex-wife, Sybil.

At Arthur, only the showbusiness elite could get in. The week Dusty Springfield's version of 'You Don't Have To Say You Love Me' went to No. 3 in the US charts, I was in New York negotiating a publishing deal. My friend, film director

Clive Donner, was also there, promoting his new movie *What's New Pussycat* which had just hit the No. 1 spot in the US box-office charts. We decided to go to Arthur together, but despite our up-to-the-minute showbusiness credentials we were not allowed in because we were 'two men together'. Only couples were allowed in – one guy, one girl. For ten minutes we stood arguing with the doorman, then made him fetch Sybil Burton. Finally we were told we could go to the bar but not the dance area. Clive, who was recovering from a bout of hepatitis, had been told by the doctor to drink milk. When he ordered some it proved to be the last straw. 'Two men coming in here together is bad enough,' shouted the manager. 'Letting them drink milk is out of the question.' So we were ejected.

The history of modern dance music in Britain and America is intimately tied to the social and financial expansion of four urban minority groups – Hispanics, blacks, gays and teenagers.

Teenagers are the biggest of minority groups and the largest customer for dance music. When they reach the right age, they change almost overnight from children to adolescents and instantly turn to club culture. Then, five or six years later, they drop out of it again. As a result, they have little influence in developing and shaping that culture, they simply accept what is currently on offer. The club culture they enter is not really theirs, it's a commercial imitation of the more serious club cultures that exist parallel to it. In America this has traditionally meant the club cultures of Hispanics, blacks and gays – in Britain, mostly of gays.

Gay culture is hedonistic. Gays don't get married, don't breed, don't take on family responsibilities. They are lifetime subversives to normal society. They have more spare money, live in the city rather than the suburbs, have better cars and greater freedom. When it comes to dancing, they're less inhibited than straights. Gathered together in exclusively gay places, the mere acceptance of their sexual nature becomes an uninhibiting factor. They stuff themselves with recreational drugs and dance with abandon from sixteen to sixty. As a result, they dominate Britain's dance culture. Broadly speaking, straights only dance from fifteen to twenty-five. During that period they enter a copycat version of current gay dance culture.

In post-war Britain dancing was strictly straight and mainly the province of eighteen- to twenty-five-year-old university and college students. And it meant jiving to trad jazz.

The 100 Club in London was typical – jammed to the gills with young people in simple clothes, only drinking soft drinks and coffee but flowing with excitement. The dance was the jive, invented in America in the days of swing and designed to be erotic. The man swung the girl round in circles. If she was dressed properly her skirt flew up around her waist and everyone could admire her underwear. It was energetic, but it was good clean fun.

When rock 'n' roll arrived, young people jumped on the dance floor and freaked out. It wasn't so much dancing as energy release. Rock 'n' roll freed them from inhibition and they went berserk. But by the end of the fifties, rock 'n' roll had diluted into mainstream pop. With nothing left to freak out to, young men no longer threw themselves onto the dance floor. Dancing with enthusiasm all but died out. The coolest dude was now the stillest. He stood rooted to the floor, twitched his thighs, snapped the fingers of his left hand

and offered his right hand as a stabilising point for the girl to spin around him, entertaining his mates with the colour of her underwear.

Then, with the help of a hit record from Chubby Checker, the Twist whirled out of Harlem and hit downtown New York. The city went wild for it. Just off Times Square was the Peppermint Lounge where all the faces of the day came to try it out – Judy Garland, Tennessee Williams, Richard Burton, Elizabeth Taylor, even Noël Coward – all of them on the dance floor copying Chubby Checker's instructions to pretend 'you're towelling your back'.

Within weeks, the Twist had crossed the Atlantic to Britain and become a national fad. Girls were no longer tied to sullen, undemonstrative guys – they could twist alone, or with girlfriends. Blokes no longer had to suffer the embarrassment of asking girls to dance – they could twist together, hanging onto their pints of beer, puffing on cigarettes, losing none of their masculine reference points. Little did they realise they were dancing the way the queers did in Harlem. And black queers at that!

Before the Twist, men weren't allowed to dance together. If you went to a club, even a gay one, you had to stand and twitch to the music on the sidelines. If you got on the dance floor, you had to be with a girl. If plain clothes police entered a gay club and found two men dancing together, it was considered indecent fondling. You could be arrested; and the club could be closed.

The Twist was a dance of provocation, two people dancing slightly apart, twisting their bodies together, teasing not touching. Its roots were in the Caribbean where people had danced that way for years. Since they didn't have to touch in order to do it, the Twist allowed gay men to dance together while staying just on the right side of the law. And the beauty of the Twist was that it was the act of *not* touching each other that made it so erotic. The trick was to writhe snake-like between each other's limbs, legs between legs, arms between arms, lips a teasing centimetre apart, crotches even closer.

The Twist freed gays on both sides of the Atlantic from the prying eyes of policemen checking for signs of men dancing cheek to cheek. And when the Beatles arrived, a second way of dancing was added. You stood rooted to the spot, like Paul and George singing falsetto 'ooohs', waving your arms to the rhythm and shaking your head madly. Dancing in gay clubs boomed, and so did gay culture.

In the sixties, due to Britain's archaic licensing laws, drinking in pubs and dance halls stopped at 10.30pm. Young Londoners danced at the old venues like the Hammersmith Palais or the Streatham Locarno, which had been given a new lease of life by teenage spending power. The music was pop, sometimes current, sometimes backdated.

To dance after these public places closed it was necessary to go to a restaurant with an entertainment licence or to a private club. Private clubs were mostly found in the basements of coffee shops where only soft drinks were served. Many of these were dark, crowded rooms, good for groping but not much use for dancing. But in Soho there were two late-night clubs where dancing was a principal part of the action – The Scene, which was large and straight, and Le Duce, which was small and gay – both of them packed with young mods.

The Scene had once been the 'Cy Laurie club', the first club to start Sunday afternoon record sessions. Around the walls there were cushions on the floor and drugs were sold all over the place. The music was British pop mixed with American soul.

Le Duce was a members-only club down a staircase. There was a huge fish tank in the middle of it and the club had a restaurant, which meant as long as you ate something you could drink till 1am, but most people were too full of pills to care. The music was 100 per cent Motown.

Motown records were mostly made with an even rhythm of four equally emphasised beats to the bar. They weren't too fast and they were never syncopated. They perfectly suited the dancing style adapted by gays, which was a development of what the Twist had been, separate but erotic. These records were made as pop, but they provided a wonderful solid base for dancing. Gays latched onto them and they became the standard fare for gay dance clubs. With Motown music and a few purple hearts the average British gay could feel he was dancing the night away like a black New Yorker.

Gerry Collins, a DJ and a partner in Marquee recording studios, used to go to the Catacombs, a coffee cellar in Earls Court. 'Everybody was stacked up on pills and the DJ was Gordon Frewin who worked for Motown. He used to bring in all the latest product plus a lot of imports, things you could never hear except in a gay disco. He was known as Pamela Motown.'

Clubs like the Catacombs were too stark and grubby for the showbusiness set. They stuck to showbusiness places – small, exclusive, and expensive – which allowed people to drink till two or three in the morning. Coffee cellars were fun places for regular kids or gays on the make but because they couldn't serve alcohol there was little profit for the owner and even less glamour for the clients. But then someone figured how to bend the rules and serve alcohol after hours.

A cellar under the Sombrero restaurant in Kensington High Street would let anyone in for a couple of shillings and serve them drinks till 2am. Everyone was given a paper plate with a dollop of coleslaw and a slither of pork pie, which legally constituted a meal. The place became predominantly gay and renamed itself Yours or Mine?

Gerry Collins went to the opening night. 'I think it must have been about 1969. On the door was a guy called Amadeo. Liberace was there, I remember him well, with all that hair. It was dark, and there was a raised area of tables overlooking the small dance floor which could be reserved by anyone ordering champagne. The rest of the room was a free-for-all.'

Many of the showbusiness crowd preferred the Sombrero to the more exclusive showbusiness clubs, certainly those who were gay did. Far from being something to be shy about, to be seen at the Sombrero came to be considered rather smart. Soon we were all going there filling it with pop stars and music business people, from lawyers to managers – Bowie was there almost every night, blues singer John Baldry was a regular, as was Dusty Springfield. So were several well-known pop managers. Billy Gaff who managed Rod Stewart, and John Reid who handled Elton John, would dine regularly at Mr Chou's in Knightsbridge then breeze in with their entourage for after-midnight champagne.

More important than the social aspect was the fact that this place set the trend in dance music. New music from the States, or even new tracks by British acts, were often first heard at the Sombrero played off acetates (specially cut records good for just a few plays).

The Sombrero was soon matched by another club which took the idea a stage further. At the Masquerade in Earls Court the raised area for champagne drinkers became a glassed-in restaurant. Outside the glass, gay teenagers, young dykes and funky hustlers consumed their drugs and grooved to the music. Inside the restaurant, the fun half of the music industry wined and dined in luxury till three in the morning and observed the spectacle outside. In the grubby outside area, young hustlers who aspired to pop stardom were equally observant of the diners within. Occasionally, the head of a record company, a manager, or a pop star, would pluck one of these young hopefuls from the dance floor and request his pleasure for the night. Sometimes, they even tried to turn one of these young hopefuls into a presentable face for *Top of the Pops*. One of them who made it was David Garrick. He even had a hit. But then he blabbered to the press about his beginnings and was never heard of again.

Like the Sombrero, the most important thing about this sleazy little club was the influence its DJs had on the key people in the music industry who were its customers. The Masquerade set trends in dance music. One of the regulars was Pamela Rooke, known as Jordan, the manager of Malcolm McLaren's outrageous clothes shop, Sex. 'I went to the Masquerade ... I liked good dance music ... the only places you could get that were those gay clubs.'

As the seventies moved along, what really excited everyone were the great black hits that began to emerge from America. Barry White's were the first – 'You're The First, The Last, My

Everything' and 'Love's Theme'. Then Kenny Gamble and Leon Huff appeared with the Philadelphia sound, which had an even more solid groove. And there was music from Florida too, like 'That's The Way I Like It' from KC & the Sunshine Band, and 'Rock Your Baby' by George McCrae.

These became the songs everyone in the clubs danced to, but they weren't recorded with that intention. Mike Collier was the British publisher for Gamble and Huff and knew them well. 'Songs like "Love Train" by the O'Jays, or "When Will I See You Again" by the Three Degrees, were thought of in Britain as dance music. But they weren't made with that in mind. They were just Kenny and Leon's idea of pop.'

As dance music, these tracks were fine for the uninhibited, but they still weren't simplistic enough for lumbering Europeans, especially adolescent males afraid of looking foolish. The records that were easiest to dance to were old Motown songs with the weight of the rhythm spread equally across four even beats in the bar. The Philadelphia sound was often syncopated and more sophisticated. It required the whole body to flow with a gentle pulse, something which white Europeans were incapable of doing.

Gay clubs everywhere stuck to Motown records, preferably ones made in the sixties style of a steady four to the bar. The followers of Northern Soul also appreciated the same thing. Northern Soul was a strange subculture that sprung up among working-class teenagers in the north of England at the tail end of the sixties. For more than ten years, it dominated dance halls across the north of the country. Obsessive DJs would scour America unearthing thousands of unknown black pop records in the style of Motown which they would then play at special all-night pill-fuelled sessions in northern dance-halls like the Casino in Wigan or the Twisted Wheel in Manchester. The dancers would stuff themselves with speed and jerk their bodies at a thousand miles an hour, disguising their lack of rhythm by moving faster than the eye could see.

Around this time, in a gay club in New York, something began to happen that would change the future of dance music.

The club was the Sanctuary, a converted church, which rapidly became home to the most decadent scene in New York's history – the first totally uninhibited homosexual discotheque in America. The club only lasted a couple of years, but during that time its resident DJ invented a new form of dance music. He was Francis Grasso. Writer Albert Goldman claimed that 'Grasso invented the technique used by every DJ ever since of holding the record he was about to play at the precise point he wanted it to start playing, while a felt mat underneath it revolved on the turntable. Then letting it go, to make a seamless connecting point between two pieces of music.'

Grasso's other speciality was to play two tracks at the same time, mixing the raunchy heavy drums of British rock music with the soaring voices of American soul. Led Zeppelin's thumping solid drum breaks would throb like an amphetamised heartbeat under the delicate vocals of Gladys Knight or Aretha Franklin. According to Albert Goldman, Francis Grasso didn't just play records, he 'reinvented them out of their composite parts, the top end vocals and the bottom end rhythm. His method of mixing the different parts of different records to make altogether new music was fifteen years ahead of its time.'

While Grasso did this, 1,500 gays, liberated with every drug in the book, freaked out on the dance floor. Crammed together with a sound system that sent the bass throbbing through their genitals they indulged in a nightly orgy of dance. Goldman called Grasso 'an energy mirror, catching the vibes off the floor and shooting them back again, recharged by the powerful sounds of his big horns'.

The club's popularity caused massive queues outside and while they waited gays often had sex openly in the street. As a result, its closure was inevitable, but by then it had been copied by similar clubs in other north-eastern cities of the USA – Chicago, Detroit, Philadelphia. But for some semblance of this erotic partying to sweep the straight world, something musically simpler was needed. Francis Grasso's DJ-ing was like the clothes at a Versace fashion show – just *too* exquisite, and at out-of-this-world prices. What was required was a high-street equivalent – ready made, ready mixed, ready-to-dance-to Grasso-type sounds, with a great thumping rock 'n' roll bass drum pounding through them.

One day in the early seventies, German music publisher Peter Meisel had to attend a wedding near Munich. As he drove there, he was pondering on the very same subject – how could he get German kids dancing the way American kids did? Or could it really be that Germans just did not have rhythm in their bodies?

When he reached the wedding party he was confronted with square middle-aged guests dancing easily to the Bavarian band with a marching drum banging hard on each beat of the bar. Meisel realised, if German kids were going to dance, this was the sort of music they needed. And there were precedents. New Orleans jazz had always been played to a four-to-the-bar bass-drum beat, and that was what British teenagers had jived to in the fifties. And although Motown music used a bass drum only on the first and third beats, it had always been based around an absolutely steady four-to-the-bar feel, usually coming from the guitar which played four-to-the-bar chords like the old-fashioned banjo players in trad jazz bands. Moreover, four-to-the-bar bass drum had occasionally made appearances in British pop. Billy Hatton of the Fourmost said when he first heard the Beatles' original drummer, Pete Best, 'His bass drum technique was four-to-the-bar – bom, bom, bom, bom – which initially gave them that thumping sound, but when they started doing stuff that required more sophisticated drumming techniques they needed a better drummer.'

Punk groups too had used four-to-the-bar bass drum to hold together short songs played at breakneck speed. And in the sixties, the football terrace songs of Dave Dee, Dozy, Beaky, Mick and Tich had been underpinned with four solid beats from the bass drum. Dave Dee's producer was Steve Rowland. 'I shared a flat with a guy called Jericho Brown who was six foot six and got laid four times an hour. Because he was so tall he'd loosened the headboard on his bed. All over the weekend, when he was screwing these girls, I'd sit and listen to it banging on the wall. I used to come home with the songs in my head that I'd have to produce with Dave Dee on the Monday. I'd try to work out how to do them, but all I could hear was boom-boom-boom from upstairs. So in the end, that's how I did them. I took a piece of the headboard into the studio and banged it on the floor to make my bass-drum sound.'

But the songs Steve Rowlands had recorded with Dave Dee had been pub singalongs. Peter Meisel worried that German teenagers in the seventies might think a bass drum plonking down on every beat was too uncool, too reminiscent of Bavarian weddings.

He decided to make his new records more credible by using black singers.

In Munich, at Music Life Studios, a bunch of European producers were working together and exchanging ideas. Meisel went there and talked with some of them. One of them, Giorgio Moroder, liked his idea of four-to-the-bar bass drum so he and Meisel went looking for black faces. But while they were away, back at Music Life Studios, producer Michael Kunze went ahead and cut a track with the bass drum playing four beats to the bar.

That year, Pete Waterman, a DJ from the Midlands, went to the Midem Music Festival in Cannes. 'While I was talking at a record company stand, I heard a record playing from the next one. It sounded like Barry White meets the Three Degrees, with a bass drum played on every beat of the bar. It was like the old Motown sound except they'd replaced the snare with the bass drum. I immediately bought the rights to the record, took it back to London and remixed it. We changed the song around and made it into more of a pop song. The track was called 'Save Me" and it was released under the name Silver Convention. That record became the catalyst for every four-to-the-floor dance record that ever followed, which means almost every dance or dance-pop record made since.'

While Waterman was doing this, Giorgio Moroder and Peter Meisel found the black face they wanted – LaDonna

Gaines – an American girl who'd gone to Germany to sing in a production of *Hair*. She'd married a German actor called Somer, but Meisel and Moroder renamed her Donna Summer. Then Moroder got her to moan orgasmically over a four-to-the-bar bass drum and called the resulting track 'Love To Love You Baby'.

Meisel's wife, Trudi, took it to Casablanca Records in America. Neil Bogart at Casablanca loved the track. Realising it had been made specially for dancing he felt there was one more thing to be done.

In America, club DJs had lately started to use two copies of each record so they could mix them from one turntable to another, extending their length to ten or fifteen minutes. Kraftwerk, the technologically advanced German avant-garde group, had made a track that ran for one full side of their album *Autobahn*. Innovative DJs loved the crisp, sparse rhythms and the sheer length of the track and it was receiving play in underground dance clubs in Detroit and Chicago. Bogart told Giorgio Moroder to go back to Germany and make an equally long version of the four-to-the-floor 'Love To Love You Baby'. He did. And it was a smash.

From then on long versions of records were made especially for dance clubs, nearly all of them with a solid four-to-the-bar bass-drum beat. Back in Germany Peter Meisel got together with another producer, Frank Farian, and put together a four-piece black group with an English lead singer – Liz Mitchell. This was Boney M and it repeated the same formula – four-to-the-bar simplicity fronted with black faces. Meisel knew at once he had a winner. 'The bass drum thumping relentlessly to the floor was like a heartbeat, square maybe, but exciting. The black faces gave the whole thing credibility. That deep voice on the records was the German producer, but the singer who mimed it was black. When you saw his face it changed the sound from a joke to something sinister and slightly voodoo.'

The end result was a group which sold more albums than the Beatles. Meisel had struck gold.

All over the world kids suddenly found they could dance better than ever before. One, two, three, four – boom, boom, boom, boom – who in the world was unable to move to that?

The rest of Europe followed suit – Baccara from Spain, Amanda Lear from France, Raffaella Carrà from Italy, and even Abba from Sweden getting in on the act with 'Dancing Queen'. But it was when the Bee Gees used four-to-the-bar in their songs for *Saturday Night Fever* that disco really swept the world.

The Bee Gees finally became as big as manager Robert Stigwood had always predicted. In the sixties their success had been largely due to Stigwood being able to use Epstein's money to hype them to the top. In the early seventies they flopped and broke up. Five years later, when they got together again, they were seen as an oldies act. They were rescued by Atlantic producer Arif Mardin who got them to write songs like 'Jive Talkin'' and 'Nights On Broadway' and recorded them with soul musicians. In doing this they discovered Barry Gibb's extraordinary falsetto, a voice aligned to neither sex. As a result, the lyrics entered everybody's mind without sexual prejudgement – was it a man, a woman, or the listener's own inner conscience?

Stiggy bought the rights to the movie *Saturday Night Fever* and became its producer. He then commissioned the Bee Gees to write five songs for it. When Barry Gibb's falsetto singing combined with Giorgio Moroder's four-to-the-bar bass-drum throb, the resulting sound took off as nothing had done before. Love it or hate it, the strange falsetto voice of the Bee Gees wormed its way insidiously into the world's subconscious. The soundtrack album broke sales records worldwide – over 30 million. And it topped the US album chart for 24 weeks with three No. 1 singles – 'How Deep Is Your Love', 'Stayin' Alive' and 'Night Fever'.

For three years, from 1977 to 1980, disco ate the world. Even heavy rock artists got in on the act. First Rod Stewart allowed a disco remix of 'Do Ya Think I'm Sexy' and it became his biggest hit ever – then other British rock acts followed. The Rolling Stones, Fleetwood Mac, Pink Floyd, Queen, Elton John – all of them made disco singles with a four-to-the-floor bass drum. But it was a Frenchman, Jacques Morali, who remembered the original gay decadence of the Sanctuary Club, and finally captured it on a single record.

The four-to-the-floor rhythm of the Village People's records was plodding, but the bravado of the music made you leap to your feet. 'YMCA' was as rousing as a religious anthem, as stirring as a military march, as outrageous as a night at the Sanctuary Club. It preached outright homosexuality. 'Go to the Y, find a young man, get him into the shower, and fuck him.'

Gays went mad for it. They shovelled speed into their mouths and obeyed the order to dance, leaping up and down four times a bar, 120 times a minute. Within weeks, still without a clue what the song was about, the whole of America was copying. Every small-town club, every bar, every church hall could be heard thumping out a mini-version of the decadence that had once been found only at the Sanctuary in New York.

It was extraordinary. It was unbelievable. Gays the world over laughed openly at America's blindness. The American military even tried to secure the rights to another song by the Village People – 'In The Navy'. They wanted to use it as a jingle for a recruitment film.

When America realised the truth, it never forgave the gay dance scene for making it look so foolish. The American music industry has ignored dance music ever since and relegated it to gay clubs and underground urban society.

But everywhere else in the world, dance music has ruled supreme from that time onwards.

From the beginning, disco was truly international. Its four-to-the-floor bass drum was derived from traditional European marching bands; its soulfulness was black America but its camp falsetto tinsel had come from Britain's Bee Gees. And it had taken a Frenchman to reveal its gay sexuality to the public.

Like all truly international brews, America wasn't the place for disco to develop to the full. The USA was never a centre for fashion, and disco was as much about fashion as it was about music. So with Americans relegating dance music to second-class status, Britain took over as the dance centre of the world.

More than anything else, there was a definite feeling at the time that it was the power of dance music that integrated gay and straight in Britain and broke down the barriers of prejudice among young people. In 1976 the first large gay disco opened in London. With a capacity of 2,000, as big as any regular teenage dance-hall anywhere in the country, to step inside was liberating and exciting. Gerry Collins, who'd missed out on the lease for the Sombrero club, had now gone to work for Top Rank. 'I got transferred to the Sundowner in Charing Cross Road. I asked the acting manager if I could do a gay night on Mondays, which was their worst night. He said OK and charged me £100 for the rental. It went from strength to strength to strength.'

Jack Barrie, manager of the Marquee club, came in with him. 'We went to the police at West End Central and said we wanted to run a gay disco called Bang. Because they knew the Marquee's reputation for running an orderly house, they agreed.'

The Sundowner's owner, Top Rank, had been founded by J. Arthur Rank, a zealous Methodist. It was now Britain's biggest leisure company, partly owned by EMI. DJ Norman Scott tells how the club ran into trouble when it booked him to play at Bang one Monday night. 'The *Daily Express* said I was the same Norman Scott who'd claimed to have had an affair with Jeremy Thorpe, the disgraced Liberal Party leader. The William Hickey column wanted to know if Lord Rank, the well-known Methodist, was aware that his "£300 million empire was sheltering a successful discotheque for homosexuals".'

Jack Barrie heard they were about to be closed down, so he alerted influential members of London's gay network. 'I called John Reid, Elton John's manager, and he agreed to call "someone of influence on the board of EMI".'

The Monday after the story in the William Hickey column the press came down to the club in force. Gerry Collins was on-stage DJing. 'Suddenly I saw the head of Rank Leisure's Dance Hall division, John Lesley, pushing his way towards me through the crowds on the dance floor, which included a load of journalists. He walked straight up to me and said: "Give me a kiss." So I did, and all around there was flash, flash, flash! He said, 'I just want you to know that you have the full blessing of the Rank Organisation.'"

As pop music became more and more dance-oriented pop, British record companies at last came to see the importance of having a dance department. It had taken them fifteen years to realise that dancing was an industry worthy of special music, and it had taken the Germans to show them how to do it. Now, with four throbs to the bar, they learned something else new. Whether or not a particular record was suitable for dancing was dictated by the type of drugs being used in the place where it was being played – different drugs required different tempos.

I got my hands on a report by H.E. Scamell of Yale University that seemed to confirm this. He claimed that at 120 beats per minute continuous dancing by African tribes (or in his case, teenagers in Connecticut) led to mood changes resulting from the release of endorphins into the blood. This arousal was activated by 'a subconscious regression to the womb where once we were surrounded by the throb of our mother's heartbeat at almost the same tempo'.

In *Rock and the Pop Narcotic* Joe Carducci accused modern dance music of being 'processed and designed for dancing, stirring up hormone levels and introducing a background of sexual intent'. Scamell agreed, and in regard to faster tempos asked: 'When we were in the womb, and our mother had sex, did her heart rate rise to 140 beats per minute? When we dance at *that* tempo, are we recreating the vicarious sexual excitement we felt as a foetus? As a foetus, were we sharing her endorphins?'

The A&R men I spoke to at the record companies were not as interested in Professor Scamell's findings as they were in their own. The young men they hired to run their dance departments soon realised that people who smoked grass preferred their womb regressions at slower tempos – 116 beats per minute, or even 110 – while those using amphetamine needed the tempo raised to 130 beats per minute or more. The connection between tempos and drugs was self-evident and clearly here to stay. 'Beats Per Minute' became standard record company talk accurately conveying the prevalent drug-taking habits in any particular dance establishment. Britain had the most sophisticated drug scene, and that meant the most sophisticated club scene. Record companies could now target records at every one of them.

Gay clubs set the trends and straights went to them because the music was better. Young gays and straights learned to mix together in these clubs with little inhibition, and gay taste in dance music flowed directly into the mainstream pop market.

By the end of the seventies, with the bass drum throbbing firmly on every beat of the bar, the dance market was already boom-boom-booming.

CHAPTER SIXTEEN

'SIGN HERE KID, I'LL MAKE YOU A STAR'

David Batt cruised down Wigmore Street with an ultra-cool saunter. He had a torn shirt, tight threadbare jeans, orange-blond hair down to his waist and an acoustic guitar slung casually over his back, the neck knocking gently across the curve of his buttocks. He was sixties Jagger crossed with teenage Bardot; young Elvis with adolescent Fonda; instantly provocative, pouting and sultry. He wasn't camp, nor even slightly effeminate, he was a self-creation, an obviously unique species created from months of hard work in front of a bedroom mirror.

In the audition room he sat down and played his guitar without wasting time on tuning (being cool was more important). And although he sang with apparent indifference to my reaction, I knew I was under scrutiny, as if it were me being auditioned, not him. Anxious to pass I listened carefully.

His voice was as much self-created as his look – Bowie out of Bolan, a flirtation with Jagger and sometimes a rasping Rod Stewart. The songs weren't constructed with the crisp technique of a pop craftsman, they rambled, but each one had a haunting quality, with lyrics of startling imagery. There was a fondness for good-sounding words regardless of meaning or narrative, and here and there a truly odd phrase leapt out and grabbed my attention: 'She keeps her love in a carrier bag.' He sang the words arrogantly, with a defiantly cold stare into my inquisitive eyes.

For anyone with a feeling for chic or style or star quality, for anyone in the music business, for anyone who reacted to provocation, sexuality, good-looking boys or good-looking girls, he was a natural – irresistibly stamped with instant success.

In true music-business style, I grabbed him greedily. 'Sign here, kid. I'll make you a star!'

On drums was Dave's brother, Steve, only sixteen and a dead ringer for young Elvis. The bass player was Mick, their best friend, with hair that matched David's – orange-blond and down to the waist. On keyboards there was Richard, thicker-set and slower-thinking than the other three, but like the others, from the same school in Lewisham. Lastly, there was Rob from North London, a guitarist acquired by way of a *Melody Maker* ad.

I put the group into a recording studio and got some good examples of their best songs, then I sent them off to a photo session. When I had the perfect picture, I put together a smart-looking package and sent it to every A&R man in London. It wasn't the first time my enthusiasm had blinded me to the realities of the music business. In the sixties I'd got much the same reaction when I first sent tapes of Marc Bolan round the industry. I should have remembered that A&R men immediately turn down anything that doesn't sound exactly the same as the current best-selling artist – they have no understanding of being prepared for the next change in style or the next development. Among the stack of depressing rejection letters were two which stood out. One was from Alan Sizer at RCA: 'If you change the group's bass player and find someone who knows how to play, I might be prepared to listen again.' (Mick Karn's unusual playing of the fretless bass eventually made him one of the most influential bass players of the seventies.) The other was from Robin Blanchflower, someone CBS had seen fit to employ. 'This group has potential. Unfortunately, we are not in the potential business.'

This was 1977 and punk was the prevailing fashion. I already had my punk group, London, and I'd picked up Japan because I'd mistakenly thought they might buck the prevailing trend and take off in a flash. Now I had to reconsider. While I did so, I bought them a van and some amps and sent them off to do gigs.

The band looked too out of touch with what was going on and the audience reaction was predictably cool. The group's image was 'New York Dolls' but their music was neither that nor punk nor pop. They only played their own material which, for a first-time audience, was unfamiliar and difficult to follow. I took them out for a drink and asked them how a group so young could be so hopelessly out of touch with current trends? 'We don't care about current trends,' David explained. 'We only became a group as a way to stay together when we left school.'

(Before they'd had the idea of forming a group, Mick and David had got themselves a job in the post room of a large company where, instead of sticking stamps on parcels, they dumped the parcels in a cupboard and used a thousand pounds worth of stamps to make a mural on one of the walls.)

I asked if they would be prepared to put together a set of forty-five minutes with every second song being a well-known one? That way they could play six of their own songs and seven that the audience knew. If they agreed, I would continue to finance them. Surprisingly, they did.

Four weeks later they were ready with their new set. The songs were classics – 'I Shot The Sheriff', 'This Old Heart Of Mine', 'The Freak' – arranged in the group's own peculiar style and accompanied by David's inimitable voice. The songs had never sounded better; I was on the way to a fortune or bankruptcy.

For a new band, obtaining gigs was never easy. In the mid-seventies it cost at least £50 to play a gig and the group usually earned less than £10. Three of these a week for a year might build some minimal recognition for the group in pubs around the country but it would also add another £10,000 to what I'd already spent.

Just then, a large poster appeared all over town which looked at first glance like an ad for Woolworths or British Home Stores. It featured a girl on a motorbike dressed in that hopelessly over-smart unfashionable way that Germans dress themselves when they're on holiday in Ibiza or Marbella. This unattractive advertisement did indeed turn out to be German. It had been put up by a record company from Berlin called Hansa who planned to come to England and find acts to promote. The poster was so amazingly non-credible that I felt embarrassed even to have noticed it, but I sent a tape anyway. Three weeks later Hansa called to say that from 5,000 tapes they'd been sent, they'd chosen twenty to audition and one of them was Japan. Two weeks later the group had a recording contract.

Hansa was run by Peter Meisel, the man behind all those European disco records. After his success with Donna Summer and Boney M he decided to move to England and run Hansa from London. He arrived with his wife, Trudi, who was rather noisy.

Peter was charming, hugely successful and wildly eccentric. Every Monday he had the top ten records from every European country delivered to his office where he stacked them in piles on his desk. He stopped all his incoming calls and sat for the next ten hours analysing every nuance of every record – the key, the tempo, the bars of the verse, the bars of the chorus, whether the solos were played on sax or guitar. By Tuesday morning he would have worked out the overall average – for instance, the key might be C sharp, the tempo 117 beats per minute, the intro six bars, the bridge four, and a solo would occur one minute and fifty-eight seconds into the song. In Germany, using these and other methods, Peter's company had produced hit after hit – Boney M, Donna Summer, Amii Stewart, Revolution. In London Peter's golden touch was not so much in evidence. British producers were less willing to listen to his strange ideas. But his unstoppable enthusiasm and Trudi's loud voice still drove Hansa to considerable success.

To produce Japan's first album for Hansa I recruited my old friend Ray Singer. When recording was almost complete Trudi called me to say that Victor Records in Japan liked the group's image so much that they'd signed a licensing agreement without even hearing anything. Since the album consisted mostly of the group's own songs, with no sign of a hit among them, the Japanese market seemed like a straw worth clutching at. I decided to go to Japan and meet the record company.

At JVC in Tokyo I met a cabinet of people quite unlike anyone at a British or American record company. They were serious and considered. They told me they'd analysed the look of the group, done market research and were convinced they could turn them into stars.

'What about the music?' I asked hopefully. 'Do you like it?'

'We have now heard some rough mixes of the album and we think they are very unsuitable.'

I corrected their bad English as politely as I could. 'You mean "suitable", don't you?'

'No! We mean *unsuitable*!' they reiterated. 'But we have great faith in the group and we think one day they will record music which will be *suitable* for our market, consequently we are going to get behind them.'

I'd never heard of such a thing. A record company who made long-term judgements. A record company which would invest in a group's potential even when the music gave no indication that there was one. 'How are you going to overcome this problem?' I asked.

'We won't release the album for six months but we'll start publicity immediately. We'll send press photographers and journalists to England. We'll do pictures and interviews and start a fan club.'

In Japan at that time, young girls were fascinated by the West but frightened of the tough imagery of rock groups. They liked young men who looked polite and gentle, like Cliff Richard, or the American group Cheap Trick. But these artists made records that were out-and-out pop – Japan made music which was esoteric even by the standards of progressive rock.

The people at Victor Records didn't seem to mind at all. 'Normally,' they explained, 'thirteen-year-old girls who buy records by these soft-looking Western stars grow tired of them a couple of years later. With Japan, they will stay with the group because the music is more challenging. Through photographs and publicity we can build a fan club for your group of 30,000 members without releasing the album – then, when we release it, these young people will rush to buy it. Once they've bought it, they'll learn to like it. So you see – your group has great potential.'

I was flabbergasted. This was a different music industry from any that I'd previously encountered.

Back in England I decided, if the record company in Japan could be so far-sighted, perhaps I should be too. For the next six months I got up at six o'clock every day and drove to the Anglo-Japanese Foundation in Beaconsfield to study Japanese language and culture for four hours before going to the office. At Hansa, plans were afoot for the release of Japan's album in England. The songs were pleasant but bizarre, original but rambling, and David's extraordinary voice made most of the lyrics indecipherable. While Peter and Trudi Meisel were considering what to do with it, David Batt arrived at my house to announce he and his brother had decided to change their names. In the future he would be known as David Sylvian and his brother as Steve Jansen. Trudi Meisel took massive exception to this and ranted for days. On the other hand, Peter only objected to it because it made Trudi so noisy round the office.

David then announced that their album would be called by the title of one of his songs, *Adolescent Sex*. Hansa commissioned a small avant-garde advertising agency to design a series of ads and promotional tools to tie in with the title of the album. One of them consisted of a cardboard cut-out of a samurai sword with *Japan are up and coming* written on the blade. When it was turned over, the other side turned out to be a stiffly erect penis coloured rosy pink. Surprisingly, Trudi's only complaint was that the penis was unnaturally straight.

One day David turned up in full make-up.

Despite his long hair and gentle manner, David had never seemed an effeminate person but wearing make-up changed that in a flash. I presumed he'd done it because he simply couldn't wait any longer to be a star. Wearing make-up on the train from Lewisham to London caused him to be watched – it was exciting – it put him immediately on-stage.

Before long, on David's instructions, Mick and Steve followed suit, and more reluctantly, Richard too. Only Rob managed to stay aloof from the group's new fashion.

At first the make-up was slapped on roughly, dollops of lipstick and mascara that made the group look like a gang of cheap whores. But when their girl hangers-on started to help them, the make-up became more sophisticated and they began to look like supermodels swinging down a Paris catwalk. Only Richard continued to look like a whore, slashing his lips clumsily with thick magenta, then compensating by slouching around like a truck driver.

Meanwhile, in Japan, after six months of promotion, the album was released and sold 30,000 copies exactly as Victor Records had said it would. In the UK, interviews with Japanese journalists and photographers were now a daily occurrence. A telex from Tokyo offered the group a major tour starting with two days at the Budokan, Tokyo's most prestigious rock venue. In England, the group's pub gigs had begun to have a following of Japanese students who were studying in London. Three days before the group left for their first Japanese date, they played their biggest gig ever – the Red Lion, Hammersmith, with around a hundred people. The next gig they played was at the Budokan, stuffed to capacity with 11,000 screaming teenagers.

Two sell-out nights in Tokyo were followed by two groupie-filled weeks of limousines and bullet trains. Then – after fine dining, sake and sex – Japan came back to London to face reality. They were unknown and unwanted.

Although their first album had sold miserably, Peter Meisel agreed to pay tour support for the group to open for Blue Oyster Cult. It was a strange choice but it was the only tour available. The first night at Bristol was disastrous. Blue Oyster Cult arrived late and by the time they'd sound-checked, the audience couldn't be kept outside any longer. In front of 2,000 people, Japan had to help their two roadies carry the equipment on-stage and set it up. They struggled through it, facing up to Blue Oyster Cult's belligerent audience as if they were undertaking some sort of college initiation ceremony.

As the tour progressed northwards the audiences got rowdier and became more impatient with a support group they saw as a bunch of sissies. Glasgow was going to be murder, it was the toughest audience in Britain. The night before it, David completely lost control of a barracking audience and asked to pull out of the tour. But I came up with an idea. 'Play as much of the set as you can before the audience get totally out of hand. Then – just when you're on the edge of losing it – announce that you're going to sing the next song *a cappella*. For a heavy metal audience that will be the ultimate provocation. Then start singing. Whatever reaction you get, whatever noise they make, it will be *you* who've caused it, not them. That way it becomes *you* who's in charge.'

I wasn't sure my philosophy was sound but David took hold of it magnificently. In the middle of Japan's set, at the same point where he'd lost his nerve on the previous night, David walked to the front of the stage and waited quietly while 3,000 heavy metal thugs booed and catcalled. David stood silently, waiting for a hint of a lull. Then he started singing, completely unaccompanied.

The audience was taken aback. They let him get surprisingly far before the catcalls started again, but when they began they were phenomenal. I'd never heard such an incredible volume of hatred from an audience – shrieks, whistles, boos, wails, handclaps and footstomping – it was even louder than the welcome they gave to their own group.

When the cacophony seemed to be reaching its absolute peak, David stopped singing. He stood calmly at the front of the stage and turned his head slightly upwards towards the vortex of the noise somewhere near the middle of the balcony. As he did so an enormous smile spread slowly across his face. Distinctly happy, noticeably relaxed, he stood gazing at the manic wailing audience. Within seconds they'd quietened down. They'd been sent up and they knew it.

Japan got through the rest of the set with little more than the odd boo. David's *a cappella* singing was one of the most remarkable performances I'd ever seen and he was never again fazed by anything an audience did to him.

CHAPTER SEVENTEEN

DOLLARS AND DECADENCE

The following rock stars have something in common – Paul McCartney, John Lennon, Rod Stewart, Elton John, David Bowie, Jimmy Page, Joe Cocker, Eric Clapton, Gary Glitter, Johnny Rotten, Mick Jagger, Keith Richards, Keith Moon, George Michael.

They have all been arrested by the police.

Among the elite of one single profession, frequency of arrest on this scale is unheard of, except for unlicensed street traders, burglars, drug smugglers and prostitutes.

Why?

Rock keeps a tough timetable. Record companies and booking agents often fail to realize that just because the airline schedule says you can do it, it doesn't mean you actually can.

A group might record all night in LA, keeping themselves awake with coke and speed. At ten in the morning they get on a plane for New York, whacked out but still buzzing from drugs. To get to sleep they take valium and quick glasses of liquor. The time difference is against them – after just two hours' sleep they wake up in New York to find it's six in the evening.

They try to ditch their hangovers with more coke as they rush by limousine to a stadium in Connecticut. They arrive at eight, too late to sound check. They're on at ten, they can't sleep, they can't stay awake, they do more coke, more speed, and finally get on-stage at 10.30.

This is their sole purpose for touring – the gig – the audience – the music and the applause. There's a crowd of

100,000, they play for ninety minutes and come off-stage surging with adrenalin. They're whisked out of the stadium, back to New York and into a hotel. At midnight they're exhausted but still high from the gig – and hungry. The restaurant's closed so they order room service with wine, and take more drugs. Some of them choose to go up, some to come down, either way they're giving themselves a problem – at 6am they'll be leaving for Rio to headline that evening in a rock festival. Then they have to fly to London to do *Top of the Pops* before coming straight back to the States to get on with their US tour.

In between there'll be a bit of bad behaviour. Tiredness or drugs or booze or boredom will cause something to happen within the touring party that might not be tolerated if it were to happen in normal society – there'll be a gang-bang with a less than willing groupie, or a hotel room will be wrecked, or someone will be so zonked out that they fall asleep on the plane and piss in their seat, or an air hostess will have her bottom pinched and the long-suffering tour manager will have to spend the rest of the flight placating her.

It's like living as an outlaw, like being Bonnie and Clyde. And in the cosseted environment of a supergroup's touring party, group members are supreme. Their behaviour, however bad it is, will be tolerated – their wishes are commands for their road crew of hired slaves.

But when superstars cross the line and enter the outside world they have to watch out – especially when the line is blurred by drugs or tiredness or bad temper.

A step too far, and they can easily find themselves under arrest.

*

For most people, the seventies meant glam, punk and disco. But that was only half the story. While new artists hit the British charts, others had completed their apprenticeship and were now superstars, making it very big indeed in America.

The seventies were the great years of rock. At its best, rock was not heavy metal, nor was it progressive or pompous, it was a driving beat with great riffs and melodies. The response to it from rock audiences was a lack of inhibition usually identified only with drugs and discos, yet more often than not their only stimulant was the music itself, plus a little grass or beer.

Of course, there were plenty of American groups, but the greatest rock seemed to come from Britain – Queen, the Rolling Stones, Genesis, Black Sabbath, Pink Floyd, Dire Straits, the Police, Status Quo, the Who, ELP, Yes, Rod Stewart's band, Elton John's band, and in a category of their own, Led Zeppelin. Some of these groups could exist for ages without a hit single yet they could still pack stadiums throughout America and sell albums whenever they found the time to produce one.

To people in Britain, some of these artists had almost disappeared from sight, but in the USA they were cleaning up, playing to hundreds of thousands of people a week – trekking from stadium to stadium in limousine luxury, losing track of place and time, screwing their way through hordes of nameless groupies, living on room-service hamburgers, booze and more often than not cocaine.

When the public first became aware of rock stars using drugs, they were tolerant.

By the late seventies, tolerance had changed to total acceptance. Drug-taking, it was clear, was a necessary part of rock stardom. But one thing wasn't clear – did rock stars take drugs to help them make music, or did they make music to gain access to drugs?

Either way, having experienced the thrill of standing on-stage and being sent sky-high by the intense release of adrenalin it produces, rock performers found they simply couldn't come down after performing. The periods between shows become an intolerable vacuum.

Elton John described his relationship with the audience as like having sex, 'so emotional and so physical you don't ever want to do anything else.'

Jimi Hendrix said: 'I can't express myself in any conversation. But when I'm on-stage, it's all the world. It's my whole life.'

For all rock artists, the problem was the same – when the audience was not present, the emptiness was all-consuming. Usually there was just one answer.

Drugs! And one drug in particular.

Heroin comes from the opium poppy, *Papaver somniferum*.

The pod of the poppy produces opium, a milky juice containing a variety of alkaloids one of which is morphine.

Morphine, boiled with equal quantities of acetic anhydride, produces heroin.

Heroin, ingested into the body, produces a warm, dreamy self-sufficiency. It can be sniffed, smoked or injected.

The ritual of injection often hooks addicts as much as the drug itself. Powdered heroin is prepared by placing it in a small amount of water in a spoon which is warmed underneath with a flame to dissolve the particles. The liquid is then sucked into a syringe and injected.

For 'skin-popping' the target of the needle is the fatty tissue under the skin of the forearms, thighs or buttocks. For 'mainlining' it's shot straight into the main vein that runs the length of the inner arm. For smoking, heroin is placed on tin foil with a flame underneath. It heats up, turns black, wriggles like a snake and the rising fumes are sucked through a tube into the nostrils. For sniffing, finely chopped heroin is snorted like cocaine up one nostril at a time, but the drug's intense bitterness deters most people from this method.

Eric Clapton said of heroin, it was 'like being wrapped in a large cotton wool ball which totally protected and insulated you from the world'.

In Victorian times doctors usually treated symptoms rather than attempt diagnosis. Since pain was the most common symptom, painkilling became the doctor's principal work, and opium, from which heroin is derived, was medicine's greatest painkiller.

By the end of the seventies we'd got used to hearing rock artists talk about the 'pain of fame'. But was it really the pain of fame? Or was it the pain of the dead periods between on-stage highs?

When heroin was first invented doctors thought it was a non-addictive variety of opium. They prescribed it for so many ailments that a recent government committee researching into the expansion of drug use in Victorian times concluded that a list of ailments for which it wasn't used would be shorter than a list of those for which it was. Similarly, it seems that a list of rock stars who never took heroin would be shorter than a list of rock stars who did, which includes David Bowie, John Lennon, Joe Cocker, Pete Townshend, Jimmy Page, John Bonham, Keith Richards, even gentle, home-loving Charlie Watts.

Journalist Nick Kent described the Rolling Stones on tour. 'Jagger, Wood, and Richards were all going off and doing vast amounts of drugs. By that time the heroin abuse had got so bad even the roadies would come in and score. I mean, it was really just incredible, it was heroin city.'

Mick Jagger refers to it more casually. 'It wasn't really anything special. It was just a bit of a bore really. Everyone took drugs the whole time, and you were out of it the whole time. It wasn't a special event.'

The pleasant-mannered Jagger of the sixties, who'd apologised to Mary Whitehouse and allowed Cecil Beaton to photograph his naked bottom, had now disappeared almost completely. Nick Kent described him at an after-gig feast when a falling candelabra had burnt two girls who were dancing naked for him. Jagger 'continued to watch with cold dead eyes ... just sat there radiating this numb, burned-out cool, this "you can never reach me" sense of otherness. Not a pretty sight.'

Journalist Robert Greenfield toured with the Stones and says they often used drugs to stay one step ahead of hangers-on. 'Drugs were an elitist, chic commodity.' Hangers-on came backstage with piles of drugs like 'the three Kings off to see Jesus in his stable'.

At that time, rather than travel with the band Keith Richards travelled with his own entourage. Every time they crossed an international border they were bound to be searched, but because scoring heroin in the brief time they had in each city was nearly impossible given their international fame, Keith had to take a hands-on approach to the problem. He had a fountain pen with a secret compartment which operated normally and was unnoticeable unless it was taken apart. It could carry two grams, and there was also a shaving cream container. Even so, promoters often had the job of locating smack while the audience was kept waiting, often for an hour or more.

From the mid-sixties onwards, British groups, who at home smoked grass and popped a few pills, increasingly came back from America hooked on cocaine and barbiturates, and often with the seeds of heroin addiction planted. For many of them, as soon as they stopped touring, the slow pace of life quickly became unbearable. Keith Richards felt unable to survive without being on the road. 'Every minute spent off the road ... I either turn into an alcoholic or a junkie.'

Elvis Costello claimed, in the world of rock, 'if you drank all the drinks and took all the drugs you were offered, you would die. Simple as that.'

And a lot of rock stars did.

In the sixties, the British music business lost Brian Jones to excessive drug indulgence, and at the beginning of the seventies, Jimi Hendrix, who by then was honorary British. In 1974, Robbie McIntosh of the Average White Band attended a welcome party in the States at which he chose the wrong saucer from which to take a generous sniff of cocaine – it contained heroin. He turned blue and died.

Wings' guitarist, frail Jimmy McCulloch, hidden permanently behind his dark glasses, also died of a heroin overdose. And in the eighties, Led Zeppelin's drummer John Bonham drank enough vodka in an afternoon for the press to say he'd died of drink even though the heroin he'd also taken was the more likely cause of his death.

Ozzy Osbourne's band and road crew had a reputation for fearsomely insane behaviour. On the road from Nashville to Florida the bus stopped for gas near an airfield. The tour driver, who had a flying licence, spotted a light aircraft for hire and suggested he give the crew members a spin round the airfield. Jake Duncan, the tour manager, was the first to volunteer. 'I went up with him, and he was flying pretty crazily. But it was exhilarating – stalled turns, that sort of thing. He brought me back and took up a couple of other people. As he came in to land he did a turn that put the plane almost vertical to the landing strip, but he was too low and the edge of the wing clipped the tour bus where people were resting. The bus was wrecked and the plane ended up exploding into the garage at the end of the runway. Ozzy Osbourne lost a guitarist and two crew members who'd been on the bus.'

Later, an autopsy showed traces of cocaine in the tour-driver's blood.

Disasters seemed to feed the public's need for more and more shocking rock imagery. In 1979 a disaster in Cincinnati did nothing to dampen the public's desire to see the Who. Eleven people were crushed to death, their bodies only discovered at the end of the show when everyone else had left. They'd been squashed into the floor, stomped on and danced over for two hours.

Pete Townshend dealt with it by using what he called 'tour armour' – blotting out all sensitivity, thus allowing a more abandoned tougher exterior. 'It was – "Fuck, we're not gonna let a thing like this stop us."'

But underneath Pete's 'tour armour' he was cracking up.

What was happening to the Who was almost exactly what had happened to the Stones. 'The band was killing people in Cincinnati, killing off its own members, killing its manager. We were making big money, and anyone who got in the way, or had a problem, we dropped.'

Not surprisingly Pete used all sorts of drugs to survive. So did everyone else in the group. And in every other group too.

In the days when the biggest venues were concert halls for 3,000 people, singer Tony Bennett was an American superstar. Tony isn't surprised at what happens to young rock stars confronted with modern superstardom. 'Fifty thousand people at worship in a stadium. People aged twenty-six aren't equipped for that. That's like Hitler.'

A rock singer on-stage is like a sponge soaking up the reaction of the audience. An audience of 80,000 can fire a burst of energy at the stage like a strike of lightning. When the energy's good, it wraps the performers in love and appreciation. When it's bad, things can go horribly wrong.

Marianne Faithfull was on tour with the Stones when there was a bad show with riots and people trampled. 'Mick came straight from the concert to the hotel. I was waiting for him in my negligee in bed. The minute he walked in he was a different person, it was as if he were someone I didn't know. He was possessed, as if he'd brought in with him whatever disruptive energy was going on at that concert ... He didn't say hello, he didn't even acknowledge me, he just walked over to the bed and began slapping me across the face. Not a word was spoken. I was terrified and fled ... Nothing brought it on. It just erupted out of some inner turmoil, as if a demonic force had come over him.'

Usually the audience lifts an artist to a gigantic high. But as with Mick Jagger that night, a bad reaction from the audience can bring an artist down to a frightening low. A normal person suffering these extreme emotions would seek help from a psychiatrist and be given drugs. Rock stars just leave out the middle-man. They keep the drugs waiting and ready, backstage.

From the mid-seventies onwards, the public were becoming increasingly aware of this. The stories they heard of drug indulgence were endless.

Ozzy Osbourne was arrested for trying to murder his wife. He explained, 'There's two sides to every coin ... it's a long story. But this one morning I'd been on a booze and drugs binge that had left me going temporarily fucking nuts.'

The bleating Bee Gees slanged each other in a drug-induced family feud. Maurice accused brother Barry of being a pot-head and brother Robin of being a pill-head. Meanwhile younger brother Andy celebrated the success of his solo career with regular overdoses of heroin, of which he later died.

Freddie Mercury's drug dealer told of arriving with supplies at his hotel suite to find young men crouched on dishes waiting to be 'served up' to Freddie in his bath. 'More sperm than water' was how the dealer described it.

A touch too much heroin can kill outright – too much cocaine kills in a more insidious way. One star told me, 'I had a twenty-year-old heroin habit that I was managing quite well. Once I started on cocaine, it all fell apart in six months.'

Little Richard was one of the first rock 'n' roll stars to get a bad cocaine habit. 'Every time I blew my nose there was flesh and blood on my handkerchief where it had eaten out my membranes.'

Cocaine not only eats away the membranes, it eats away an artist's creativity, his income and his savings. Nevertheless, it seems everyone uses it, especially in combination with sex. Ozzy's philosophy for touring was 'a gram of coke, a stiff drink, a joint and a cute female messing around with my private parts'.

Elton John too mixed coke with sex. He admits: 'I did cocaine basically for sex. My sexual fantasies were all played out while I was on cocaine.'

At the height of his addiction to coke, Elton admitted he was doing a line every four minutes. 'I felt like the top of my head was going right round. Terrifying ... and still ten minutes later, I'd put coke up my nose. That's how bad it was ... You get up in the morning and you're surrounded by empty bottles and the mirror's covered in smears of cocaine and the first thing you do is lick the mirror.'

By the mid-seventies, Eric Clapton was spending a thousand pounds a week on his heroin addiction. Over three years, he'd converted virtually all his money into the deadly white powder. 'I wanted to make a journey through the dark, on my own, to find out what it's like in there. And then come out the other end.'

He became known as 'Eric Claptout'. Today he admits, 'I told one of the roadies to sell the guitars for whatever price he could get. I couldn't get cash from anywhere.'

Eventually, broke, unhappy, yet feeling that he 'didn't want to die', he clawed his way back with a five-week acupuncture cure.

When rock stars talk of 'kicking the habit', it never means giving up drugs or alcohol, it simply means giving up heroin, which can be replaced by something else. When Clapton kicked heroin, he turned to alcohol and became an alcoholic. He took to 'streaking' whenever he was drunk, which was virtually every day. He was jailed in Tulsa on a drinks charge and finally ended up in hospital with a perforated ulcer.

In the late eighties, Pete Townshend was another person to kick his heroin habit, but he never considered giving up drugs altogether, and certainly not alcohol. 'I always felt that drinking and work were tied together in a totally appropriate way – in the tradition of Fitzgerald or Hemingway.'

Because he was far too careless with his habit of smoking marijuana, Paul McCartney got busted over and over again. But it did him no harm. The McCartney legend just grew bigger.

Rock psychologist Martin Lloyd-Elliot sees it like a bullfight. 'The real fight is not between the bull and the bullfighter, it is between the bullfighter's pride and his fear. In rock music, the public has begun to realise that the real spectacle is not the artist on-stage, it is the excitement of watching the artist's frailty when confronted with the opportunity to indulge in excesses of every available type. They watch his downfall with the morbid excitement that passing motorists watch a car-crash.'

On tour in America in the seventies, Joe Cocker's drinking went out of control. Keyboard player Mick Weaver described it as 'a drunk watch'. 'Will Joe fall off the stage tonight? A lot of Joe's crowd used to go to see him stumbling about. He'd managed to get a reputation for it. There was one line in the song he used to do ... "Guilty" – "Got some whiskey from the barman, got some cocaine from a friend." And every time he got to the cocaine bit the whole place used to erupt. I think if he'd stood there and had a snort on-stage that would have brought the house down. Just about every night he'd try making the high notes, and he'd gag. Then he'd throw up, and we'd pack in. Then carry on. I got the feeling people were coming just to see if he'd get through the concert.'

One widely reported debacle occurred in early June '74 at the Roxy Theatre on Hollywood's Sunset Strip, when an invited audience of journalists and music business people – Diana Ross, Cher and Marc Bolan among them – gathered to see Joe preview the material from his new album. Record company boss Jerry Moss remembered having lunch with him the week before the show. 'He'd been fishing for a couple of days ... he looked fantastic ... his eyes were clear ... he was wearing a white suit ... I'll never forget this. He was so charming at lunch, he said, "Man, we're gonna do it. It's gonna be great. Don't worry about it."'

But when Joe showed up for the gig he was too drunk to perform and Jerry Moss told them to pull the curtain.

'Jim Price had put together a band that was just extraordinary... Jimmy Webb on piano ... but Joe couldn't remember any words. He was stumbling around the stage ... had that sort of naughty boy look in his eye, like he was pulling one out on everybody. I remember looking down at Diana Ross, who just had these tears streaming down her cheeks. Everybody knew what he was going through – it was just terribly sad. By the third song he was lying on the stage in the foetal position.'

Martin Lloyd-Elliott thinks that scenes like this are part of a rock star's attraction. 'The public's fascination with an artist includes knowing how they will cope when they are offered everything in the world on a plate. And it's important to us that our favourite artists come unstuck now and again, and make a hash of it. It gives us a reason to be able to believe we made the right choice in sticking to our own more conventional lives.'

Syd Barrett was the power behind Pink Floyd when they emerged in the sixties. But Syd had soon gone bananas, gobbling buckets of pure LSD.

On tour, he unravelled. He got a bad perm and his hair frizzed out from his head like a fright wig, the blazing bright colours of his clothes giving his face a dreadful green glow. In San Francisco he bought a pink Cadillac and gave it away to a stranger the next day. On-stage he sometimes played a different song from the rest of the band, or he didn't play at all, sitting cross-legged, staring blankly at the audience, or he just played the same chord endlessly.

Syd Barrett's most famous gig was when he appeared on-stage with his hair slicked down by a jarful of Brylcreem mixed with a bottle of crushed Mandrax tablets. Under the hot lights, the Brylcreem melted and the mixture slid down over his face feeding his lips with an endless drip of downers which he happily licked throughout the show.

Since the sixties, managers and record companies alike have persuaded their stars to shock and titillate the media by any means they can think of. Usually these are no more than the come-ons the industry intends. Sometimes, like children who draw attention to themselves, or neurotics who attempt suicide but fail, the resulting behaviour of the artists is a cry for help.

Keith Moon took excessive drugs and behaved madly. He seemed to be saying, 'I am a crazy whacky rock star and I can do anything.' Pete Townshend knew differently. 'It was really a cry for help and he never got it.' Today Pete sees this all too clearly. 'Unfortunately, rock 'n' roll is one of those professions that accommodates insanity.'

If the basis of an artist's creativity is a mental abnormality – if he lives in a fantasy world, or is dependent on drugs, or perverted sex – the music industry will never interfere. This is unlike any other profession. Not even film stars get treated in this way.

The music industry doesn't censure its artists. The record company view is that an artist's abnormality is likely to be the source of his creativity. It has to be nurtured and protected. So the industry supplies them with whatever they need to keep going – fame, flattery, drugs, sex, royalty cheques, doctors or clinics. The idea is not to cure them but to keep them creative and profitable.

Pete Townshend watched as the music industry gradually killed Keith Moon. 'I'm talking about an industry that feeds on the frustration, the insecurity, and desolation of the young. They don't care whether the stuff they sell is wholesome, whether it's true, helpful or whether it has a function. All they care is if it sells. And there's no mechanism to help artists ... I used to look at Keith and think "This guy is gonna die" and I was afraid for him ... What he got was his disease fed and fed until he finally died.'

Keith Moon was found dead from an overdose of a drug prescribed to help him kick alcoholism which he washed down with a bottle of champagne laced with cocaine.

Wiping oneself out with drugs was never just a British trait. American rock stars fell just as thick and fast.

Elvis Presley's death was a lesson to those who thought they could stay clear of drugs. He connected drug addiction only with illicit drugs. He was so against heroin he tried to hire a hit man to annihilate a local dealer. Meanwhile, surrounded by sycophants and slaves who were only interested in keeping the situation as it was, Elvis consumed an average of twenty-three pills a day. On the day he died he took delivery of 150 painkillers, 262 tranquillisers, and 278 amphetamine tablets – just one month's supply, all legally prescribed by his doctor.

Almost unbelievably, some artists seemed to get away it.

Keith Richards thoroughly enjoyed a life of massive drug abuse. 'I never had any trouble with drugs – only with the police... I'm a Sagittarius man – half horse, half man – with a licence to shit in the street.'

Sometimes though Keith did lose out by taking drugs. Ian McLagan, the keyboard player with the Faces, was due to play on a new song Keith had written. Before the session, Keith decided to introduce Ian to Iranian opium. 'He cut off a chunk of the opium, cooked it on the gas ring and inhaled the smoke through the cardboard tube of a toilet roll and passed it on.'

In the process of doing this, Keith dropped an ice-pick through his foot.

After they'd recorded the backing track, Keith's foot began to throb badly. He took painkillers and tried to sing sitting down, but as soon as he was propped up in front of the mike the painkillers put him to sleep. When he woke up the song had gone out of his mind.

By the end of the seventies, one group was outdoing all others in stories of drugs and degradation. Led Zeppelin's addiction to heroin, violence, power and cash had become legendary.

The group's manager, Peter Grant, was consistently portrayed as a satanic, itinerant gangster chief. He enjoyed the image and always portrayed himself as a man who did things his own way. Lawyer Irving David once had to negotiate a deal with him. 'He came into the office and lay flat on his back in the middle of it with his huge mountain of a tummy rising up towards the ceiling and his tummy button like a volcanic crater in the middle of it. He stayed like that throughout the meeting, but his negotiating was as tough and sharp as I've ever come across.'

Grant was credited with changing the way promoters did business. He refused to make deals on the traditional 50-50 basis and got the group 90 per cent of the takings.

Grant claimed to have been a fairground wrestler, taking on anyone who wanted to bet ten shillings on the outcome. Ahmet Ertegun, boss of Atlantic Records, admitted to watching him break a bootlegger's arm by squeezing it. John Bettie, one of his personal assistants, recalls, 'He sort of perfected the technique of slapping you, and he could slap you quite hard round the head. I've seen it happen a few times to people that he didn't get on with.'

Punk manager Malcolm McLaren considered Peter Grant to be a mythic character which no British record company could even come near to dealing with. 'They were like Noddy people in Toyland in comparison to where Peter stood in the eyes of the USA.'

But Don Arden, manager of the Small Faces, ELO and Black Sabbath, saw Grant from a different viewpoint. 'Peter was hugely overweight. I knew him when he was twenty-one or twenty-two, he wasn't able to walk any great distance, and nobody ever knew this. There was always something wrong with him from the day I met him. It's so easy to tell the world you're a mean killer, but if you ever saw him without a shirt, I mean, Jesus Christ ... Once or twice when we travelled together there was a confrontation, and he backed down immediately. He took everyone in, you know, because he never was a bloody wrestler. I knew him once to smack somebody ... he slapped this little guy across the face who wasn't capable of smacking a newborn babe. I was surprised when one or two people talked about the good he'd done for the business. I still don't think he was the first guy who got 90/10 from promoters. There were always artists who more or less did their own business, who said, 'I don't need a promoter, but if you want to book the theatre you can have 10 per cent.'"

Whether Peter Grant's reputation for personal violence was justified or not, his ability to manage wasn't questioned. Nor was Led Zeppelin's manic lifestyle. They had their own Boeing jet – the Starship – equipped with beds, chefs, booze, broads and a chemist shop of narcotic substances. While on tour in the States they would centre themselves on one city, New York, for instance. From there, every night the group and their entourage would jump into a fleet of a dozen black stretch limos and drive to Newark airport where the Starship was waiting for them.

Endless snippets of rock information would filter through the industry grapevine ...

John Bonham and Peter Grant had pummelled a security man in San Francisco and were charged with assault.

Bonham, waking from a deep sleep on the Starship, had attacked a stewardess, unzipped himself, and tried to take her from behind. On another flight, he yanked a journalist's glasses off his face, broke them into smithereens and squashed them into the carpet.

Robert Plant recalled amusing himself one night on tour by 'shoving a plastercast of Jimi Hendrix's penis up one of the girl's assholes at some hotel in Detroit'.

Dire Straits manager Ed Bicknell remembers checking into the Hyatt House on Sunset Strip. 'As I was going up in the elevator, the bellman pressed the wrong button and we stopped on a particular floor and the doors automatically opened. The door had been boarded up with bits of wood. I said to him, "Good heavens, have you had an earthquake?" He said, "No! Led Zep were here last week."'

Pamela Des Barres, Zeppelin's favourite groupie, described Jimmy Page dressed in Nazi uniform touring transvestite clubs in each city they went to, picking up drag-queens and doing drugs with them in the toilet. If he got too riotous, tour manager Richard Cole, himself a junkie, would padlock Jimmy to the toilet in his hotel room where he would sit, obediently jailed, until the tour manager thought he was ready for release.

Des Barres describes turning up early one evening when Jimmy had been padlocked to a groupie in the toilet for over two hours. 'I'm really over this,' Jimmy told Richard Cole forlornly. So Richard agreed to unlock him. 'Right,' said Jimmy promptly, 'where are we going to dinner?'

John Bonham enjoyed shitting in girls' shoes. Once in Japan, a girl whom Jimmy Page had picked up and who was now travelling with the group on a bullet train, opened her purse to find one of Bonham's little presents. When she screamed horrifically, Bonham leant over to the tour manager and said joyfully: 'It looks like the shit hit the purse.'

If the early sixties were Ancient Greece – the first great flowering of rock culture, then the early seventies were like the

Roman Empire – initially confident and brash but descending into total degeneracy as rock's superstars left for America to exchange their talent for dollars and decadence.

Throughout the seventies, rock of all sorts had flourished. The punk movement promised great things but was ultimately rock's last gasp. As a genre, rock was coming to an end. Its freshness was long gone, its participants decayed, many missing, lost in action.

By the end of the decade, the death and destruction associated with the music industry was unprecedented. Many musicians, managers and record company execs became almost anaesthetised to the pain and anguish around them. That things would turn out like this had never occurred to any of us when we'd embarked down the road of pop music twenty years earlier. Andrew Oldham, Robert Stigwood, Chas Chandler and I all had a dead rock star on the books. It was very sad indeed.

In December 1980, exactly ten years after the Beatles had dissolved their partnership, a degenerate decade of rock was brought to an end with the assassination of John Lennon.

In the same year two other household names in the British music industry also disappeared. Decca Records went out of business, sold to PolyGram after the death of Sir Edward Lewis, the company's founder and owner. And Pye Records finally lost its name, Louis Benjamin having refused ten years earlier to pay a mere £2,000 for the right to continue to use it.

But more than anything, it was the first death of a Beatle that drew a line under all that had gone before.

The age of rock was over.

It was time for the Renaissance.

PART THREE

PART
THREE

CHAPTER EIGHTEEN

RENAISSANCE

Adam Ant first turned up as a punk. He had bad skin, terrible hair and a fetish for rubber. After a suicide attempt he went to a mental hospital where a manic girl came into his room one night and pissed on the floor. After that Adam decided to put his brain back in order and make himself into a star. He got a new band which performed in bondage gear while Adam wore a rapist's hood. When Derek Jarman featured the band in his movie, *Jubilee*, Adam felt he was on his way. For final instructions he paid Malcolm McLaren a thousand pounds. 'Get an "Apache" look,' said Malcolm, then stole Adam's musicians to back a fifteen-year-old Burmese girl with whom he intended to sell 'porn for underage kids'.

Unperturbed, Adam found himself another band and followed Malcolm's suggestion. He dressed himself in a cobalt-blue kilt and decorated his face with Apache war paint. One night at an out-of-town gig he jumped too high on a small stage and crashed his head on a low beam. Blood flowed everywhere. At the end of the gig the road crew rushed him to the local hospital and carried him to the doctor, almost unconscious, wearing a blue kilt, his face covered with congealing blood and war paint.

'Don't tell me,' the doctor said, 'the Martians have landed. What's his name?'

'Mr Ant!' the road crew told him.

Finally, CBS gave Adam the recording deal he'd been looking for. He fixed up his skin, restyled his hair and became the first pop idol of the eighties, setting the style for all those who followed.

During the days of punk, political ideology had been important. Adam quickly let everyone know where he stood on such things. 'I find politics the single most uninspiring, unemotional, insensitive activity on this planet.'

His attitude upset Paul Weller, who told *Record Mirror*, 'This showbusiness crap, like Adam Ant wants to bring back. He just makes me puke ...'

Punks had avoided anything erotic, but Adam wanted to bring back sex appeal. He tattooed the words 'pure sex' on his arm and dressed himself like Prince Charming. His music leant heavily on African drumming so he waffled to journalists about 'tribalism' and the 'warrior ideal'. It showed what good value he'd got from Malcolm McLaren for his thousand pounds. Not that Adam denied it. 'None of the ideas are mine,' he admitted with refreshing honesty.

Punks had despised and ignored the business side of music, but in his new reincarnation Adam was obsessed with it. When he built his image around Prince Charming, it was Adam not his management who insisted that the image be registered and that every T-shirt, badge, poster and sticker must earn him money. He was also obsessed with controlling the creative side of his career. He not only wrote his own songs and designed his own record sleeves, he conceived and directed his own videos. In doing so he changed the industry's perception of what videos should be. Thereafter they were no longer filmed performances of an artist's song, they became three-minute epic movies.

My group Japan watched the disintegration of punk culture with some hope for the future; it seemed possible that at last their day of attrition was near. Peter Meisel typically suggested they should make a disco record. But not just any disco record. It should be produced by the most successful disco producer in the world, Giorgio Moroder. And since Peter was the person behind his original success, Giorgio quickly agreed.

I flew to Los Angeles with David Sylvian. He was so solidly committed to his own material and style that I felt sure the meeting would come to nothing, especially when, two minutes into it, Moroder said he would only agree to produce a record if it was one of his own songs. David asked to hear them and several were great. He chose one that was outstandingly awful. Outside, I asked in amazement why he'd picked that song. 'Because,' he said, 'it's so bad that I'm sure Giorgio won't mind if I change it. That way I can turn it into something suitable for our style.'

He was right. David rewrote the song and Giorgio hardly turned a hair. In fact, when it was being recorded he hardly even turned up. At the beginning, when the all-important drum sound was being worked on, Giorgio came into the studio and told the engineer to go for the 'Munich Sound'. Six hours later, when the backing track had been laid down, he came back and raised an eyebrow when he heard how different the song was from the original. When he heard David sing it he raised the other one. After that he went back to lobbying Hollywood, trying to get himself an Oscar for his film score to *Midnight Express*.

David had done brilliantly. He'd got all the benefits of a Moroder production – the clarity of sound, the superb engineering, the uncluttered mix – without actually compromising the artistic integrity of his group. No other Moroder record had ever sounded so off-the-wall, both melodically and vocally – it was unmistakably *Moroder*, yet unmistakably *Japan* – but when it was released in Britain it failed to go anywhere near the Top 30. Amid the acrimony Peter Meisel said the group could leave Hansa and the next day I took them to Virgin where we signed a new deal.

A few days later David turned up with a new hairstyle. After four years of knowing him with hair down to his waist it was a shock – it barely reached the base of his neck and it was no longer orange-blonde, it was platinum in front and squirrel red at the back. Connie, the group's publicist, loved it and went to work at once.

Two weeks later in the *News of the World* there was a photo of David with the caption: 'The Most Beautiful Man In The World!' David loathed it. 'I don't want to make my name with cheap publicity stunts. You mustn't do things like this with Japan, we're a serious group.' Connie lied as only she could. 'But darling, it wasn't me who did it, it was the Japanese press. As soon as they saw the new hairstyle, they voted you the most beautiful man in the world.'

David left the office dissatisfied. As soon as he'd gone, Connie was immediately on the phone to Japan. 'Have you heard? The *News of the World* in London has voted David Sylvian "The Most Beautiful Man In The World". I'll send you a photocopy.'

A week later it was in all the Japanese teen magazines and soon after that it was in the British monthlies. Then copycat hairstyles began to be seen around London's trendy clubs, like Blitz.

Blitz had gestated from Billy's, in Soho. There, it was 'Bowie Night' on Tuesdays, and as the punk boom receded a couple of hundred kids started recreating the style and excitement of the glam era. All of them were fashion crazy; many of them were gay. When their numbers grew they moved on to the Blitz club.

During the glam era these kids had been under twelve. Now they were on the verge of becoming fashion designers and pop stars. They hated what punk had become, and favoured fancy dress with elaborate hairdos. At the Blitz club, Rusty Egan was at the turntables, Boy George looked after the cloakroom and Steve Strange was on the door.

'Steve was a bit of a fashion nancy,' says Midge Ure of Ultravox. 'He would just stop anyone who didn't look right from coming in.'

Steve says it was just that he 'wouldn't let people in just to gawp at the people already there'.

The club had special evenings like the 'Come As Your Favourite Blonde' night. And at Blitz, it wasn't enough just to dress well, you had to look immaculate right through to three in the morning. Getting drunk and falling over were out. A pill to keep yourself alert was a safer bet.

These people chose their music as carefully as their clothes. To begin with, it was strictly Bowie, but it gradually changed to anything stylish – Dietrich, sixties soul, early black funk and Kraftwerk. Instead of playing just a succession of dance tracks, Rusty Egan put together a co-ordinated evening of electronic music. Steve Dagger, who later managed Spandau Ballet, said it was 'so well chosen and conceived that it almost felt it had been recorded as one three-hour piece of music.'

Because of changes in print technology, colour pictures were now appearing in daily newspapers. While punk had been the perfect imagery for the days of black and white, editors were now looking for colour. When the media discovered the Blitz kids, they had a field-day. Imitation Greta Garbos were photographed next to lookalike Frank Sinatras. Fake Oscar Wildes were snapped flirting with replica James Deans (perhaps with a touch more make-up than the real thing). The Blitz kids became the focus for a new era of fashion – the eighties – glamorous and hedonistic. The media named them the *New Romantics*.

The first New Romantics to make it big were the people behind Blitz, Steve Strange and Rusty Egan. They called their group Visage and had a hit with 'Fade To Grey'. Journalist Robert Elms commented, 'Steve Strange was the best doorman you'd ever seen, but he wasn't the best singer.' The group did well, but their keyboard player, Billy Currie, did even better. He left to join Ultravox who'd had a huge success with 'Vienna'. These two hits opened the floodgates for a new era of pop.

When Margaret Thatcher had become Prime Minister, she'd promised we would 'escape from the drab seventies and enter a vibrant new decade'. Prince Charles and Diana were the first to set the escapist tone with a Hollywood-style romance and a royal wedding. Then the Walkman came on the market, allowing people to escape their surroundings even while remaining within them. But the greatest escapism was the music of the New Romantics. All of a sudden, almost out of nowhere, there were young, colourful, fashion-conscious pop groups, promoted with videos as glossy as TV commercials – Visage, Ultravox, the Human League, ABC, Soft Cell, the Thompson Twins, the Eurythmics, Culture Club, Classix Nouveaux, Modern Romance, A Flock of

Seagulls, Tears for Fears, Kajagoogoo, Heaven 17, Spandau Ballet, and Duran Duran.

I'd known about Duran for some time. They were dedicated Japan fans and had been hanging round the office begging me to persuade David Sylvian to produce them. If he had done, Duran Duran probably wouldn't have happened, but because he refused they hit on something much more commercial. The end result was a tribute to marketing – a triumph of packaging over substance. There were five of them, all with copycat versions of David's haircut and strangely shaped trousers.

Dave Ambrose, who'd instigated the signing of the Sex Pistols to EMI's publishing company, was now working for EMI Records. Like many other A&R people, the commercial failure of punk had left him feeling directionless for a period. When he heard demos of Duran Duran and went to see them at a gig in Birmingham he thought he'd hit the jackpot again. 'I honestly thought Simon Le Bon was the new Elvis Presley. I came back to London and begged my boss, Terry Slater, to sign them. There was competition from Roger Ames at London Records so I decided to go on tour with the group in their Winnebago. When discussions between their management and EMI went well they were friendly and chatted with me. But when talks with PolyGram were going well, they moved to the back of the bus and ignored me. Eventually though, it paid off and they signed to EMI.'

Musically, Duran were always trying to find something they didn't have – originality. The nearer they got to it, the more roads led them away in other directions – like trying to reach the centre of Birmingham, the city from which they came. Serious philosophy wasn't a part of their style. When asked about his views on ecology, singer Simon Le Bon said, 'Who wants to save the bloody world?'

Most New Romantic groups emphasised style over content, but at least it was their own style. Duran looked for other people to do the styling. Having copied David Sylvian's hairstyle, they'd chosen a producer who gave their music a four-to-the-bar disco beat. Duran's recorded sound was immaculately finished, as were the visuals to their albums. The designer of their album sleeves said, 'My job is to make it all look as if it's coming from them.'

Their first big hit was a four-to-the-floor disco track called 'Girls On Film'. To make a video for it they went to Godley and Creme, once members of the seventies group 10cc. Realising that videos were now being played in dance clubs, they had the idea of making a specially edited porn version that would never be shown on TV. The directors added sections featuring naked girls with ice cubes cooling the parts that normal pop videos never reached. It worked. Duran's video was played in dance clubs non-stop. To follow this up the group turned to Russell Mulcahy, another rising star in video direction. First he flew them to Sri Lanka where he copied the imagery of James Bond movies, then to the Caribbean where he filmed the group singing on a fast-moving yacht.

It became clear that in future pop and rock stars would have to see music as only a part of what they were selling, the other part would be lifestyle. The video would take these two components and homogenise them, like supermarket milk. Artists could call themselves 'rock', 'pop', 'techno' or 'punk', but it would make no real difference. In reality, it would all be pop, and it would be sold through video imagery.

The stars of glam rock were children of the sixties making it late. New Romantics were babies of the seventies making it early. In the fifties, teenage boys were picked up by businessmen and groomed for stardom. In the eighties, learning from thirty years of pop packaging the boys finally realised they could do it for themselves. They created their own image, wrote their own songs, even worked out their own public relations line. For the record industry it was a blessing. Just when things had been at their lowest ebb, along came a bunch of musicians with commercial savvy.

Spandau Ballet's founder was Gary Kemp. 'We wanted to do something different, not just be another pop group.'

Lead singer Tony Hadley remembers it differently. 'We wanted fame.'

Spandau were working-class teenagers from Islington who became classy Blitz kids. Steve Dagger, their manager, got them off the ground with a clever idea – he would only book them to play at parties. When people had a good time at the party, Spandau would be connected with it. And because parties were private things the group would build an exclusive buzz. But then Steve had an even better idea, he made Spandau Ballet the resident band at the Blitz club and very soon they were huge.

Spandau announced their public manifesto, a hangover from the days of punk when every group had to state their principles. The philosophy of punk had been self-destruction; Spandau's philosophy was self-love. They were full of smooth talk and spoke endlessly of style rather than music. Gary Kemp told a journalist, 'My flat's got character ... if you take all the furniture out of it, it's got a style all its own.'

Their speciality was intellectual bullshit. Bolan and Bowie had both done it better, and at least they'd always laughed at themselves, but that was something Spandau were incapable of. Their debut album was released in a pure white sleeve with a perfect Aryan torso. The sleeve notes spoke about the 'soaring joy of immaculate rhythms' and 'the sublime glow of music for heroes'. The press accused the group of 'toying with Nazi chic'. Their column inches grew. It was just what Spandau wanted.

The Thompson Twins were even more full of bullshit.

The Thompsons had been signed by Hansa at the same time as Japan but had been passed on to Ariola from whom Peter and Trudi Meisel now took an override. The press release for the group's first album said: 'We wanted to touch what is "human" and common to all people, regardless of age, sex or race. Rhythm was our starting point because it has that driving heartbeat. Everyone has a heart.' Inside the album sleeve was an order form for merchandise. Everyone, regardless of age, race or sex, was offered a choice of T-shirts, button badges, out-of-date tour programmes, baseball caps, colour postcards, or a ten-inch by two-foot nylon flag with an inverted 'V'. Orders were payable by cheque or postal order, cashed, presumably, by someone with a heart.

Despite the success of all these groups, Japan's progress to the top was still painfully slow, but at least their first album with Virgin was a step forward. To go with his new haircut, David had invented a new voice. Whereas the old one had been Jagger mixed with Rod Stewart and Bolan, the new one was based on the languid tones of Bryan Ferry mixed with the musical dissonance of the modern classical composer Erik Satie. The result was a sort of atonal moan.

The new album was produced by John Punter, who had produced Roxy Music. He made huge, copious notes of every note, phrase or handclap that was recorded on any track of any song then went home and pored over them, planning the final mix like the chairman of a select committee planning his final report. To compensate for his over-intellectual approach he brought his seventy-year-old father to the studio who told him when things didn't sound right.

The front cover of the new Japan album was a picture of David's new hairstyle with David underneath it wearing a red leather jacket. It seemed we'd tried everything. The music, the voice, the producer – all had been changed, polished and repackaged. But Japan still didn't click with the public.

We made a long-term plan. We booked a fortnightly gig on Wednesdays at Camden Palace, persuaded Virgin to subsidise it, then rented sound and lights from Pink Floyd together with their best sound engineer. Each weekend flyers were given out in King's Road offering free entry, thousands of them. Wednesday night was the worst night of the week for gigs – if it was free anyone would go anywhere. Over six months the audience slowly grew from two hundred to overflowing. But since everyone was getting in free, it was difficult to know what degree of popularity had been achieved, so we booked a weekend gig at the Lyceum for which everyone would have to pay. Its capacity was 2,500 and three days before the gig we received conflicting reports on how it was going. The promoter told us 'not a ticket's been sold', but the box office insisted 'it's a sell-out'.

David wanted to pull out of it. I forsook rational argument, yelled at him, shook him and refused to cancel the gig. Three days later the Lyceum was packed beyond capacity with over 4,000 people. Two weeks after that Japan played two sell-out gigs at Hammersmith Odeon and David agreed that the group would make a single of a well-known song – 'I Second That Emotion'. The version they made of it was extraordinary – hypnotically slow and out of tune – but it was a hit. After five long years, Japan had arrived at last.

Japan were often compared with Depeche Mode, but whereas Japan had struggled for over five years to get their first British hit, Depeche Mode had long passed that stage and moved on to making it in America. The brains behind the group was their principal songwriter, Martin Gore, who moved to Berlin where he absorbed the cool futuristic influences of Kraftwerk. When the group moved in on the States and made it big, the bitchy British music press hated them for it. 'America's Favourite Euroweenies' was just one of the many putdown comments. But little by little their presence in America led Depeche Mode to become one of the two most influential groups of the decade.

The other was New Order. Formerly a punk band called Joy Division from Manchester, they had reorganised themselves as a synth-based group after their singer Ian Curtis had killed himself. Together with Depeche Mode, New Order provided a direct link between punk and the flood of dance music that was to erupt from America at the end of the eighties.

*

When Japan first signed to Virgin, both the group and the record company thought it would be just a matter of weeks before they topped the charts. What Japan didn't know was that they were Virgin's last desperate fling. While EMI had lost direction and money by refusing to be involved with punk, Virgin had lost money by embracing it. The Sex Pistols had failed to live up to financial expectations and throughout the period the company had been losing money badly. The four houses they inhabited in Vernon Yard, a mews off Portobello Road, had been reduced to two. When Japan's album failed to become a hit, the staff started planning how to cram themselves into the last house, but they were rescued by the Human League.

The Human League had started out as a four-piece boy band until two of them left to form Heaven 17. The remaining two boys thought that replacing them with girls would be more fun. Singer Phil Oakey had just read a trashy story in a magazine about a guy who picked up a waitress and made her into a star. The two boys followed it to the letter. They found two girls in a cocktail bar, turned the story into a song and the song into a video.

When 'Don't You Want Me' went to No. 1, the Human League became the biggest group in the country. Virgin rushed out an album, licensed it round the world and refinanced themselves.

Throughout the early eighties, pop culture swamped the media with floods of magazines, books, television chit-chat and TV commercials. But it was videos that identified the era.

Without one, it was no longer possible to have a hit. And even though they were basically just advertisements, they became an accepted form of entertainment at dance clubs, pubs, shops and shopping malls.

During the punk period, the 'also-rans' had been groups who never had hits. During the New Romantic period, the also-rans were artists who had hits then died away, like Kajagoogoo, Howard Jones, Classix Nouveaux, Toyah, Modern Romance, Bow Wow Wow, A Flock of Seagulls, Tears for Fears, the Associates, Heaven 17 and Marilyn. It seemed to be the advent of videos that was causing such a huge turnover in acts. There were just too many sparklingly cinematic groups for any one of them to stay at the top for long. The amount of competition made video costs spiral alarmingly.

Videos were basically a three-and-a-half-minute advertisement for a single. A regular TV advertisement might cost the advertiser up to £100,000 for thirty seconds. But videos were shown for free, all three and a half minutes of them. Because of this, record companies were prepared to spend an enormous amount on their production.

The videos that advertised the best four tracks on an album could often cost more than the album itself. Because major record companies had more cash in the bank, it gave them the edge over independent companies. Besides, they didn't really care what the video cost, they just took it back from the artist's royalties.

Although they were free advertisements for records, the companies that formed the British Phonograph Industry campaigned hard for TV stations to pay them each time a video was shown. This seemed extraordinarily unreasonable, but Maurice Oberstein, by then the Chairman of BPI, explained their reasoning to me. 'If TV stations don't pay us for the right to show videos, where will we find the money to bribe them to show the videos in the first place?'

More than anything, the New Romantics owed their rise to colour. Colour TV was in every home, colour pictures appeared in daily newspapers, colour magazines could now go to print just a few days ahead of their press date instead of the previous six weeks. Media people everywhere wanted to use the new technology and magazines proliferated. *ID* and *The Face* were aimed at young thinkers, *My Guy* and *Smash Hits* at non-thinkers. But for thinkers and non-thinkers alike, if pop stars were going to get press coverage, they needed to be dressed in every colour of the rainbow. Faces, too, benefited from a little additional colour, so gender-bending came firmly back into fashion. The colourful make-up of pop androgyny fitted perfectly with the new print technology.

Soft Cell were the most blatant. They were a synth-pop duo whose singer, Marc Almond, went on *Top of the Pops* as a boy siren. He attracted straight guys with his delicate manner and they hated him for making them feel that way. He sang Soft Cell's second hit in drag, which was probably less provocative than appearing as himself.

Soft Cell had a weird manager called Stevo who'd made his name compiling the first chart of 'electronic music' hits. He showed his contempt for record companies by not turning up to meetings. Instead he would send a teddy bear together with a cassette that 'spoke' his demands. Stevo worked hard at being controversial: he announced, 'Companies are there to be used. The people in these companies are sycophantic parasites.' When CBS wanted to sign one of his acts, Stevo made Maurice Oberstein meet him at midnight and sign the contract in Trafalgar Square sitting on one of the lions in the pouring rain.

Stevo liked to help Soft Cell get their mixes just right. 'I remember walking into this little East End studio at 10.30am. I was drunk. It was Daniel Miller's birthday and he'd been up all night, so I said "Happy Birthday, Daniel" and spewed all over the floor. It stank. I still reckon that's what gave the record its raw edge. Have you ever tried mixing a record in those conditions? You just want to get out of there.'

Stevo's brashness, and Soft Cell's cool style, were just camouflage for a bubbling new drugs scene. Several of the New Romantics had been to New York and encountered a new drug. Marc Almond was among the first. 'We can take a pill and shut our eyes and let our love materialise.'

The drug was ecstasy, and Soft Cell had a girl singer whom Marc named Cindy Ecstasy. 'She supplied us, so we thought, well, let's put her in the group, then we'll have her with us all the time. She was basically our dealer and she was singing on the record – the singing dealer.'

But Soft Cell faded quickly, leaving Marc Almond confused and without direction. At the time he said, 'Five minutes of stardom means another sixty-five years of emptiness.'

Having compromised to get his first hit with a cover version of 'I Second That Emotion', David Sylvian certainly wasn't going to do it again. He was determined to make amends to the God of creativity by dressing in horsehair and taking a shot at the charts with the most uncommercial track he could find. It was 'Ghosts', a torrid, dark-sounding moan above an atonal track lifted from Erik Satie's music, probably the least commercial single ever to enter the British Top Ten. But by now Japan's fashionability overcame all commercial obstacles. They achieved the impossible and had a hit with it. From there on they were flying. Their next album was *Tin Drum*, a brilliant series of images of Communist China in the mid-eighties. The critics agreed it was a classic album and even sourpuss music journalist Paul Morley managed to pay it an oblique compliment by saying, 'Japan were crap for the first three albums.' The public agreed too. They sent it to the top of the album chart.

I'd been to Communist China several times; I'd seen it and David hadn't; yet he captured it perfectly, both in writing and production. I asked him how.

'My girlfriend gave me a book of photographs.'

I asked him what the follow-up album would be about.

'Politics. Next week I'll buy a copy of *The Times*.'

Before the New Romantics, pop had always implied a different set of values from rock. While rock musicians liked to think of themselves as uncompromising, pop, with its need to be instantly pleasing, had to be carefully 'manufactured' with its artists becoming mere puppets. But from the eighties onwards, whether they chose to call themselves pop or rock, it was the artists themselves who were doing the manufacturing. New acts no longer found success from playing arduous tours of pubs and clubs. They planned a strategy for success, then found a record company to finance it.

Martin Fry got himself a degree in English Literature from Sheffield University then started a magazine called *Modern Drugs*. He met two musicians from a local group called Vice Versa and the three of them decided to form a new group under the name ABC. 'We liked listening to Earth, Wind & Fire, the Clash and Elvis Costello – and we wanted to glue it all together. We wanted to use a lot of different influences, from Noël Coward to Sammy Cahn lyrics.'

Sax player Steve Singleton explained, 'Instead of writing about tower blocks and pylons, we wanted to use a lot of different influences ... We wanted this kind of grandiose epic.'

Producer Trevor Horn remembers how impressed he was when he first met them. 'When they brought "The Look Of Love" in they had it incredibly well worked out which, believe me, doesn't happen too often with groups.'

But like many groups before them, the one thing ABC hadn't been able to work out in advance was how success would affect them. It made Martin Fry so shy he could hardly continue. 'I had absolutely no way of knowing how to cope with it all. I just curled my brain up into a ball, and hid everything inside from everybody.'

Once again, the solution was to hide behind video imagery. ABC's videos were the stars of the piece, not the group, nor its music. In them they used Charlie Chaplin lookalikes, Busby Berkeley dancing girls, gold lamé jackets and leather belts hung with dildos.

Videos had taken over from album sleeves in presenting a group's imagery to its fans. But sometimes, just as with album sleeves, the razzmatazz of the video presentation could drown the real personality of the individual group members. Many groups made stunning videos yet failed to build strong personal images of themselves.

To remind them how to do it, David Bowie stepped back onto the scene with 'Let's Dance', his biggest transatlantic hit ever, and during 1983 he had ten albums in the Top 100 albums chart.

In the seventies, Bowie had been the first major star to realise the power of the pop video, now he had to compete with the money and imagination of dozens of new young stars. But with 'Let's Dance', he outdid them all. He shot it simply and starkly – a minimalist piece of film in a bleak Australian pub.

The ability of new groups to plan their own image and marketing set several people in the business thinking again about how the industry should be run. In the seventies, Dick Leahy, the head of Bell Records, had led the record business into market research. 'We don't go picking up products just for the sake of it,' he explains. 'We always ask first, "Who's going to buy it?" If we can't answer that question we don't release the record.'

At that time, Dick seemed to be as wrong as he could get. The general consensus in the industry was that the choice of artist and material had to come from instinct. People with good instinct became the industry's backroom heroes, people without it sunk. Most people thought that using market research would be like keeping afloat with water wings – you weren't going to win any races. If you researched people with regard to what they wanted, their answer would be 'more of what we already know and like'. The public depended on the imagination of artists to widen their vision.

With the New Romantics movement, artists devised their own imagery and worked out how to market themselves. It made record company executives realise how little they themselves knew about conventional marketing techniques.

Some companies began to hire outside marketing men but all too often these outsiders lacked an understanding of the music industry. So record companies turned to their own marketing people and sent them away to be re-educated.

Tony Powell was head of marketing at Polydor. 'I knew all there was to know about marketing from a music industry point of view, but to real marketing men what we did seemed to be a joke. I'd been thinking about the way the big fashion houses dreamt up new perfumes and set about creating it and marketing them. I was interested to try their techniques with pop so I went to my managing director and said, 'Look, I know I'm head of marketing but to be honest I know next to nothing about it." So he agreed to send me to college so I could study modern marketing techniques and brand management.'

At about the same time, Paul Russell, managing director of CBS, was also wondering if more intensive marketing could push the sale of albums by British artists beyond the accepted maximum of 300,000, which was a platinum record. He tried doubling his marketing budget on a few major acts – re-promoting their records when sales reached a point at which most companies would have happily taken the proceeds and called it a day. The first two artists to benefit from his new marketing ploy were Paul Young and Alison Moyet. Paul Young's records had a good gimmick – Paul's fine bluesy voice singing good melodic pop songs (like the cover version of Hall and Oates' 'Every Time You Go Away'), coupled with the distinctive sound of a slurring fretless bass, already the trademark of Japan's bass player, Mick Karn. When his initial success was harnessed to CBS's new high-budget marketing, the sale of Paul's albums broke the normally accepted British barrier of 300,000 and soared to an unprecedented 450,000.

Alison Moyet was Paul Russell's other instant success. She was a big girl with a big voice – half Howlin' Wolf, half Billie Holiday – with an album called *Alf*. When it was re-promoted with CBS's newly increased marketing budget, her album became a coffee-table necessity. Suddenly 'marketing' was the new word on every executive's tongue.

'Marketing' wasn't a word often heard on *The Old Grey Whistle Test*, a TV show where music was treated so seriously it hurt. It had been running since the early seventies and presented popular music starkly, strictly on musical merit only. It was the TV equivalent of John Peel's radio show, but with a significant difference – listening to John Peel's dry voice, one imagined he sometimes laughed. Bob Harris, the compere of *The Old Grey Whistle Test*, didn't appear to laugh at all.

Seven years earlier, Bob had been recruited to the programme from the Marquee club where he'd played dance records on a Saturday night and had sometimes been seen to smile. Now he'd grown very serious indeed. *The Old Grey Whistle Test* ignored pop unless the music had a pseudo-intellectual tinge, like Roxy Music or the Jam or the Clash. But with the coming of the New Romantics the programme's musical policy was forced into becoming more liberal. New Romantic groups were self-created and part of a fashion movement. Even though their product was pop they had to be taken seriously. For many of the New Romantics, wrapped up with style and serious artistic philosophies, *The Old Grey Whistle Test* gave them a chance to prove they were capable musicians. The viewers didn't necessarily agree. It was often pitiful to watch these commercial pop groups standing unattractively in a bleak studio playing without humour, subjecting themselves to a musical inquisition.

Fortunately, in 1982, *The Old Grey Whistle Test* was almost obliterated by a new, more light-hearted show. *The Tube* was on Friday nights. Like *Ready Steady Go!* in the sixties, it made getting home early a must for kids. They turned on the telly at half past five and the weekend started there. The man behind the programme was Malcolm Gerrie. 'We proposed a new pop show for Channel 4 – eight episodes of half an hour each. Jeremy Isaacs, the new boss, came back to us and commissioned twenty-five shows of one and a half hours.'

The show was broadcast from Newcastle, which Malcolm thought was good for the insular people in record companies who hardly ever travelled outside of London. 'To begin with, anyone who did the show had to drive back 300 miles or stay the night. Many was the time you'd walk into the pub and saw amazing combinations of people, like Annie Lennox getting pissed with Tina Turner, or Bono with Olga of the Toy Dolls.'

Later, to allow performers to get home, British Airways agreed to change the time of the last flight to London from 6.50pm to 7.30pm, but the show continued to be famous for its ability to be different. The Jam used it to announce they were disbanding. The Clash refused to do any other TV show. And when Tina Turner first did the show she had neither a record deal nor a manager. After the show she played for another hour just for the TV crew and the studio audience.

Being from Newcastle himself, Malcolm Gerrie was keen to help provincial groups. 'We deliberately featured groups who had a hard time getting started because they weren't London based. It was something we understood all too well.' One of the groups they helped in particular was U2, from Ireland. Their first attempt at breaking into the British music industry had been a trip to London to play a gig at the Hope

& Anchor, a pub in Hammersmith. Only nine people turned up so they tried again in 1980. This time they got a record deal and their first album was made by old-time rock producer Steve Lillywhite.

From the beginning, U2 had a tendency to be defiantly political. Singer Bono complained, 'I could go on-stage, unzip my pants, and hang my dick out and people would think it was some statement or something.' But the truth was, he loved making statements. He was a proselytising Christian who liked to meddle in other people's moral affairs. Despite this, or perhaps because of it, U2 took off in America where Bono performed the group's tuneless songs like a trendy vicar introducing rock music at the evening service. Fortunately, there were plenty of people around ready to deflate his ego, like Meat Loaf's record producer, Jim Steinman. 'Do you know who the most boring group in the world is? Fucking U2. Give me Barry Manilow any time.'

Japan's album *Tin Drum* was one of the great album successes of the year and it set the group up for the long haul into America. But things went wrong. Mick had a Japanese girlfriend to whom he was devoted. He was learning Japanese and had settled down domestically, but one day he came home to find she'd left him for David.

The group came to me and said they were breaking up. It was instantly apparent there was no point trying to persuade them otherwise, but I told them, 'For the future of your own solo careers, don't announce it. I'll tell the press you're working on your next album. That way you'll continue to have the status of being part of a top group while you each sort out what you want to do with yourselves.'

I was playing for time and, in truth, hoped to keep them together. After four months I persuaded them to play a final tour starting in a further four months' time. The tickets were put on sale at once and sold out in three days. It was a long wait, but on the first night I held my breath – going on tour again, being on-stage, receiving rapturous applause – surely it would bring them back together.

The answer was 'No!' On the first night I went into the dressing room and there was David with Mick's ex-girlfriend billing and cooing together. Mick had moved to another dressing room further along the passage.

From there on, despite a finale of ten consecutive nights at Hammersmith Odeon, it was all downhill.

In America, MTV loved the New Romantics and their classy videos, and it led to a new British invasion of the US charts. But some people said it owed more to the British film industry than to the British music industry. For some strange reason, moving pictures of young men dressed in silks and satins, their faces covered in make-up, was just the thing that MTV wanted. But a woman dressed in trousers proved to be too much for them.

In 1983, the Eurythmics topped both the British and the American charts with 'Sweet Dreams Are Made Of This'. They were a duo – Annie Lennox and Dave Stewart – and the mainstay of their image was Annie's masculine hairdo. But when MTV executives saw what Annie looked like they got themselves into a tizz. They refused to play the group's video until a birth certificate had been sent from England proving that Annie wasn't an unusually dressed male.

The basis of the group's existence was Annie's relationship with guitarist Dave Stewart. When they'd first met, Dave had been taking LSD for a year and had almost given up on music. 'She was really the turning point because she was someone I wanted to be "all right" for. When I met Annie I was about as far off as you could be into orbit. She was my saving grace.'

This excess of acid had turned Dave into the coolest man in the world. One night in America, Annie came off-stage furious with the audience after a bad gig and grabbed a pot of mustard from the hospitality table. She slung it at the wall just as Dave appeared in the doorway. The jar exploded and mustard flew all over his white suit. 'Go easy on the mustard, Annie,' he suggested.

Mostly she did. And by 1984 the Eurythmics had made it to the cover of *Newsweek*, sharing it with Boy George.

Boy George was far and away the biggest star to emerge from New Romantic culture. Although he came last, he'd been around since the beginning. He perfectly combined all the ingredients of New Romanticism – colour, style, endless smooth talk and masterful gender-bending.

To George, flamboyance came naturally – he'd been practising it ever since childhood. To make himself noticeable, he'd always gone against the flow. In the Blitz sub-culture, he'd developed his technique of ostentation into an art form. As his success grew so did his ideas for self-marketing.

'The most abnormal thing in the world is to want to look like everyone else,' he told the *Daily Express*. 'I feel sorry for those who laugh at me. I am only being an individual.' And to a public speculating wildly about his sexual habits, he declared, 'I'd rather have a good cup of tea.'

Boy George always knew exactly what he was doing. The lyrics of 'Do You Really Want To Hurt Me?' anticipated the hostility his appearance would create. As soon as he was seen on *Top of the Pops*, he became an object of instant debate. The *Sun* dubbed him 'Wally of the Week'.

Some people agreed and some disagreed, but they were all fascinated. Most fascinated of all was the group's drummer, Jon Moss, previously the foul-mouthed drummer of my punk group London. Jon admitted quite openly, 'I fell in love with him.'

And Boy George's gay persona was no turn-off for sub-teen girls either. At gigs, they dressed in pretty frocks and screeched as other sub-teens had once done for Marc Bolan. But even at that young age they understood that George wasn't a potential sex object – none of them threw their pre-pubescent panties onto the stage.

When 'Do You Really Want To Hurt Me?' became the biggest British single in the US since the Beatles, George was openly amazed. He told a journalist, 'I couldn't believe that I'd got away with it,' but he had. By the end of 1983 he was as recognisable as Princess Di and treated with much the same reverence. Arriving for tea at Claridge's without a jacket and tie, he wasn't ejected like anyone else, he was found a private room.

But while the world was discovering Boy George, Boy George was discovering a world of his own. In New York, starting with cocaine and moving ever onwards, he tried drugs one after the other until he came to ecstasy.

'I'd opened Pandora's pillbox,' he said, 'and found the meaning of life.'

CHAPTER NINETEEN

WHAMAGEMENT

Mark Dean left school and got a job at PolyGram. There he was given credit for discovering two hit acts – Soft Cell and ABC. He became an industry whizz kid and was offered jobs left, right and centre. Instead, he decided to set up his own record company, Innervision.

The twenty-one-year-old Dean was tough-talking and flash. One of the first artists he signed to his new company was Wham! – George Michael and Andrew Ridgeley, two young men from his own home town of Bushey. Wham! had been trying for a long time to get a record deal and had been turned down everywhere. George's father had given him six months to get a record contract; after that he would have to find a 'proper job'. The six months were just about up when Mark Dean offered his deal. So George and Andrew grabbed it. Although their lawyer had told them the contract Mark was offering was not too good, Mark wanted them to sign it at once. They did – at a coffee shop round the corner.

With Wham!, Mark Dean knew he had something really big, but he wasn't sure how to go about breaking them. He gave their tape to Bryan Morrison, someone with whom he'd previously worked.

Bryan Morrison had been an agent in the sixties, and then the manager of the Pretty Things. Currently, he was a music publisher, having gone into business with Dick Leahy.

Dick Leahy had been at Philips Records in the sixties. Ken

Howard, who managed Dave Dee, Dozy, Beaky, Mitch and Tich called him 'a real livewire – the person at Philips who was most on top of what was new and happening.' After Philips, Dick made his name running Bell Records, then GTO, which throughout the glam rock period was the most successful independent record company. When he sold GTO to CBS, Dick was prevented from running another record company for five years, so he started a publishing company with Bryan Morrison.

Dick was quietly spoken and liked to sit in a darkened room listening to tapes sent in for consideration. Bryan preferred a big bright room in which he enjoyed speaking loudly on the phone in a rough London accent. Both men liked sharp suits and large Havana cigars.

When he heard their demo tape, Dick knew at once that Wham! were special. He told me, 'There was such a breadth of material – it was so unusual to hear something so good from someone so young.'

So, in April 1982, the same month that Margaret Thatcher had her mini-war with Argentina over the Falkland Islands, Wham! signed a publishing agreement with Bryan Morrison and Dick Leahy.

That summer, Innervision released the group's first single 'Wham Rap!'. It got nowhere, but in November, their second release, 'Young Guns', made it to the bottom of the Top Ten. At the top of the charts, stealing their glory, was Boy George and Culture Club with 'Do You Really Want To Hurt Me?'

Innervision then re-released 'Wham Rap!' which got to No. 8, followed by 'Bad Boys', which might have got to No. 1 had it not been for the Police with 'Every Breath You Take'.

At the very moment that 'Bad Boys' hit No. 2, Margaret Thatcher was re-elected Prime Minister, promising prosperity for everyone, but George and Andrew seemed to be missing out. After a third hit, they were still travelling on public transport and had no more money in their pockets than when they'd been on the dole. They went to see Mark Dean to persuade him the contract needed amending, but they got nowhere with him. So they went looking for a manager.

Jazz Summers had been the manager of folk singer Richard Digance, and then of Blue Zoo, a group that had one big hit and one small one. He'd heard tapes of Wham! and wanted to manage them. Dick Leahy and Bryan Morrison thought he might be capable of it but said Wham! would want someone with a more substantial reputation. Neil Warnock, the booking agent who'd worked with me on Japan, told Jazz it might be worth meeting me.

Jazz called me and we had dinner together. His idea was for me to do nothing – he would do all the work and I just had to provide the necessary credibility. As nice as the idea sounded, I knew that once the act was signed it would be impossible not to feel responsible for them and to work just as hard as he did. But his enthusiasm was catching and it wasn't long before I'd said yes.

I'd seen Wham! on *Top of the Pops* and been hugely impressed.

Top of the Pops had endured for over twenty years. During that time the quality of the show had varied greatly, and for a while in the seventies it came close to being an industry joke. But somehow it had survived and by the mid-eighties was recognised as the most important piece of promotion any record could receive in Britain. An appearance on the show would turn a record creeping into the bottom of the charts into a good-size hit.

Top of the Pops was a programme on which the director never directed the artist. He left them to perform as they wished and simply directed his own TV crew. When Wham! came on to do 'Young Guns' they completely changed the way the programme looked. It was as if they'd rehearsed with the TV crew for a couple of days beforehand. Together with the two girls with whom they always performed, George and Andrew danced their way through the song with more vibrancy and exuberance than I'd ever seen from first-time performers on the show. And there seemed to be an extraordinary intimacy between them.

For over fifty years Hollywood's favourite fallback story has been the one about two young men – cops, cowboys or crooks – who were the greatest friends. Throughout the movie they could go womanising or money-making, but at the end they would throw it all away to get back together again, heading off into the unknown. Starsky and Hutch had been a perfect example, as had Butch Cassidy and the Sundance Kid.

In pop, an image or relationship cannot be faked as it can be in movies. It has to be real. When an artist leaves his house each day, he is immediately on-stage. To perform a lie for a movie is to act. For a pop star, to act out a false persona on a permanent basis is too big a lie to maintain. It usually means ending up in psychiatric treatment. Consequently, Hollywood's favourite image of the two great friends had never been done in pop simply because it had never happened for real. There'd been the Everly Brothers, but because they were brothers it wasn't quite the same. Then there was the

Righteous Brothers (who acted like brothers even though they weren't), Sam and Dave (who fought tooth and nail), Simon and Garfunkel (who came across completely asexual), and Hall and Oates (who never managed to convey the homo-erotic intimacy that was such an important part of the required image).

The Beatles, of course, had done it perfectly, but there were four of them which was hardly what Hollywood intended.

Now, at last, Wham! had done it according to the script.

Jazz Summers and I decided to approach Wham! and persuade them we were the right managers to take them from *Top of the Pops* to American stadium tours. Jazz called them and fixed a meeting to which they failed to show up. Jazz then left an abrasive message on George's answerphone which seemed likely to put an end to the whole thing. Instead, George called back and we finally got to meet them in my apartment in Bryanston Square. George arrived with suspicious eyes and probing questions. He finally seemed won over by the combination of Jazz's drive and my experience. Andrew seemed less concerned with the details of our plans; he was more influenced by a book I'd written about the sixties in which I was permanently drunk or sexually compromised. He took a copy away with him then called two days later to say I sounded like the right man for the job.

Our first proper management meeting with them was at the Bombay Brasserie. George and Andrew said they wanted to be the biggest group in the world, which would also mean being the biggest group in America. But George added, 'We don't want to tour America for months on end or do endless radio interviews and photo sessions.'

Jazz and I explained that in the USA there were no national newspapers that could be manipulated through publicity stunts into making the whole nation aware of a pop group's name in a single day. When new artists had hits, what entered the public's mind was the song, not the artist's name. At that time MTV was still in its early days. A couple of hit records could spread the word to youngsters in New York and Los Angeles but couldn't produce real fame. Notoriety in America only came as a result of endless touring around a circuit of some thirty cities for three or four years.

George and Andrew didn't want to do all that touring, and they couldn't wait three years either. Somehow, over the third bottle of wine, Jazz and I came up with an idea that might work. 'Maybe you could be the first group ever to play in Communist China. That would get you into every headline and TV news programme in the world.'

It was trite and simple, easily thought of and easily said, and George seemed to like it. In his inimitable manner he nailed us to it. 'Good! You're our managers. Go ahead and fix it!'

Then, as if that wasn't enough, there was something else they both wanted.

'Get us out of our record deal!'

Before they'd signed their contract with the newly created Innervision Records, Wham!'s lawyer had already warned George and Andrew that the deal was no good. But they'd been turned down by too many other companies to care. They were right of course. At the beginning of a record career the most important thing is to get into a contract, get a record out, have a hit – then you can set about improving things. This contract certainly needed some improving.

The deal CBS had given Innervision was tight. The advance was insufficient to set Mark Dean up as he would have wanted, and the royalties were low. So with his eye on a good profit, Mark had to knock down the royalties even further when he made deals with artists.

The royalties he paid Wham! were less than half the industry norm for a new artist. The advance was only £500 and the group could be tied up for as many as eight albums. Moreover, 12in singles, the mainstay of the pop dance market in the mid-eighties, would be royalty-free.

Andrew and George had met at Bushey Meads School seven years earlier and remained best friends ever since. At school George had found himself something of an outsider – a podgy boy with glasses and curly hair. In his first term he found himself sitting next to Andrew, the boy everybody wanted to know – good-looking, brainy, athletic and funny. To George's amazement Andrew befriended him and became his best mate. Probably it arose from something they had in common. Despite the difference in their looks, they both had immigrant fathers. George's was from Cyprus, Andrew's from Egypt.

George rose to the challenge of being Andrew's best friend. He bought hair straighteners, took the curls out of his hair, put in contact lenses, threw away his glasses and lost weight. Soon Andrew and George looked almost like twins.

People often asked me what Andrew contributed to Wham!. They thought of him as a non-singer, non-musician and non-writer. But in a group, the thing of greatest importance is the image. Backing singers and musicians can be paid by the hour, professional songwriters can be brought in to provide the songs, producers can be hired. Only the image has to be real, and Andrew provided it.

When I first saw Wham! I thought they couldn't fail. A real relationship between two people is the world's greatest publicity image. If they argued it was just as good as getting on together – it would still create publicity. The best-known example of this had been Elizabeth Taylor and Richard Burton. Fighting or making up, the daily lives of Burton and Taylor had created endless publicity for over a decade. George and Andrew's relationship was different, but just as real. They were two bosom pals living out a teenage dream – they were going to beat up the world and make millions.

'Young Guns' and 'Wham Rap!' were their first two hits, followed by 'Bad Boys', the last of a trilogy of songs that celebrated two rampantly straight kids having a fast time round London. Critics in the pop papers called their music vital, youthful, naïve and exhilarating. Older, wiser, more embittered critics hated it. Especially Paul Morley who wrote for the *NME* and *Blitz* magazine.

'You're banal,' he told George.

'Yeah, I'm banal,' George responded, 'but life is banal ... It's just the way people are, people are banal, their lives are boring, and they just try to get through life as enjoyably and as simply as possible.' So Morley wrote:

> *Through their sour passion for enjoyment and their rejection of irony and curiosity they do not demonstrate strength but simple obstinacy ... Just because the feeble ego-*

*blast of their music is enjoyed by thousands doesn't mean
that the thinking ones amongst us shouldn't mock its lack
of excitement and invention ... You can tell by their faces
that their minds are made up: life is for simplifying,
down to the last trickle of vanity and vacancy.*

Jazz and I thought they were brilliant.

We became their managers just as their fourth single was
coming out – 'Club Tropicana'. People who had thought
Wham!'s songs were about social dissent were about to be
disappointed. The group's image changed from raunchy
leather jackets and London discos to sun-drenched
cocktails and sub-tropical swimming pools. In fact, it was
less of a change than many people realised. George and
Andrew used to go to a run-down disco in Greek Street
called the Beat Route. For two years, every time George
had passed through the door into that damp, sweating,
mildewed interior, he'd pretended he was entering paradise
– 'Club Tropicana'.

George decided to shoot the video in Ibiza, a holiday
destination to which ordinary teenagers could aspire. In those
days Ibiza wasn't the drug-ridden pleasure-hole it was to
become. It was an island of two cities – San Antonio, where
cheap package tourists drank lager in imitation British pubs
– and Ibiza Town, full of expensive restaurants and popular
with gays who took recreational drugs and danced all night.

The video would cost over £30,000. Innervision couldn't
afford that much and CBS refused to help them. Eventually,
Jazz and I found the money from other sources, including
Wham!'s publishers.

*

CBS's refusal to help with the cost of the video let us know there would be no easy way out of the group's contractual problem with Innervision. Now that Wham! were a major act it would have been reasonable for CBS to increase their funding to Innervision and allow the company to improve its deal with the group. But they didn't.

Perhaps it was part of a far-sighted plan by CBS to remove Wham! from Innervision and get them for themselves. Or maybe there was just bad communication between Mark Dean, Innervision's uppity young boss, and Maurice Oberstein, CBS's crotchety managing director. Either way, it became increasingly obvious to everyone in the Wham! camp that the only solution would be litigation. But first, to give them the power to win, Wham! had to become as big an act as possible.

With 'Club Tropicana' safely up the charts, Wham!'s album had to be released. Success with that would be the biggest possible weapon with which to fight Innvervision – or CBS – whichever one it might be. So we held back from firing the starting shots in the litigation battle, pretended we were all friends and co-operated with Innervision in the release of the album. In the meantime, it was decided to record 'Careless Whisper'.

Everyone was convinced that 'Careless Whisper' would one day become Wham!'s biggest hit. It was the song that had persuaded publisher Dick Leahy to sign the group in the first place, a song that George and Andrew had written together some years earlier.

At my suggestion, we asked the great Atlantic Records producer Jerry Wexler if he would do the production. He heard the demo and agreed at once. It was to be done at Muscle Shoals, that strange small-town recording centre two hours from Nashville. I flew there with George.

We were staggered at the great musicians that Jerry had booked for us. A list of all the soulful American hits they had played on would fill this book. The track they made for the song was impeccable – the tempo was perfect, the playing, the notation, the quality of recorded sound. But it didn't have the one thing that we'd flown to Muscle Shoals to find – soul. It was as stiff as a wooden spoon, yet it was impossible to fault it except by simply saying 'we don't like it', which neither George nor I had the nerve to do. It wasn't easy to tell someone of Jerry Wexler's stature that we were disappointed. It seemed impossible to imagine that the great Jerry Wexler, working in Muscle Shoals, could have produced anything other than the perfect recording of the song. But there was something too tidy about it.

In September 1983, Jazz and I attended the CBS conference at Bournemouth with George and Andrew. The point was to build goodwill with the sales force. After dinner there was speech-making. As CBS's most important new artists of the year, George and Andrew were asked to speak. George was brief and courteous and thanked the army of CBS salesmen for their hard work in helping create Wham!'s success. Andrew was less tactful. He stood up and asked: 'What I want to know is, when are you going to give us our first bloody number one?'

It should have been enough to wreck the group's future with the sales force, but Maurice Oberstein, the shrewdest of managing directors, started his speech by thanking Andrew for saving him from having to ask his sales force the same question.

Three weeks later, Wham!'s album came out. *Fantastic* went straight to No. 1.

*

It was almost time to start litigation. But first – to secure money with which to pay costs and to further boost Wham!'s image – a national tour was arranged. Jazz and I wined and dined the editors of every tabloid newspaper and arranged exclusive competitions in return for guaranteed double centre-page spreads and front-page headlines. If all the deals worked out right, teenage Britain would be in the grip of Wham!-mania one week into the tour.

Just before the tour started, we launched the court case.

A twenty-four-page letter was sent to Innervision by Russells, Wham!'s lawyers. It claimed that their contract was unfair and unreasonable, that they'd signed it under duress, and that they'd signed it without proper legal representation, their signatures having been obtained by fraudulent misrepresentation. By return delivery came an injunction from Innervision restraining Wham! from leaving the company. A court hearing to resolve the case was set for November.

Meanwhile, the tour started and Wham!-mania hit the headlines as planned. And then – just as it was getting under way, and before we'd even got the contract sorted out – George let his bombshell drop. 'I don't want to go on with Wham!,' he told Jazz and me. 'After this tour I want to go solo.'

It seemed to be only five minutes since we'd started on our task of making Wham! the biggest group in the world. Now we'd been given another problem, the classic manager's task with which I was now so familiar – keeping the group together.

I'd learnt a lot about management since the days of Diane & Nicky. I'd come to realise, before starting to work with any new group a manager first had to talk with them and obtain a reasonably coordinated brief of what their objectives were. This became the manager's employment instructions.

From time to time group members are inclined to change their mind about things. It can be the result of insecurity, stage fright, financial difficulties or a nagging girlfriend. Sometimes it's a rationally thought-out shift in direction arising from experience they have acquired to date. Sometimes it's a sudden whim.

Mostly, if new instructions run counter to the original ones, they're best ignored. The method the manager chooses for ignoring them is up to him. Usually the best way is simply to do nothing. With luck, the group will forget what it was they wanted changed.

George never explained why he wanted to leave Wham!; he simply said he couldn't go on with it. He was probably uncomfortable being a fake Andrew rather than being himself. Yet it had only been by turning himself into a replica of Andrew that he'd found the bravado to get up on-stage and be a star. Now, having found he could do it, he couldn't wait to move on to the next stage and be a star on his own.

His impatience was understandable. It wasn't simply a matter of ego; he felt he was wasting his creativity on something false. He was still unsure of his real nature, but to go solo and write for himself was the best way of finding out about it. Breaking up Wham! and becoming George Michael wasn't a petulant whim, it was almost certainly a necessity for his mental well-being.

For Jazz and me it was disheartening, so for the time being we brushed it aside. George knew we had enough on our plates with the tour and the court case so he let it drop. But later, when everything was steaming along nicely, he told us, 'I was serious, you know. Don't think I've let the matter drop.'

*

The court case with Innervision was never something we were likely to win outright.

CBS had two options. The first was to give Innervision sufficient funds to fight the court case and keep it going until they won. This could take so long that Wham!'s career would fade away, from which no one would benefit. The second was for CBS to pull the financial rug from under Innervision's feet. With Innervision unable to pay their court costs, and Wham! about to win their case, CBS would then offer the group an out-of-court settlement and sign them directly. From the outset we banked on CBS taking this course of action.

As we'd forecast, CBS played a typically tough corporate game. Having set Innervision up in business and backed them to sign artists, they now refused to assist them with sufficient legal fees to hold on to those artists.

When Innervision were on the verge of collapse, CBS made Wham! the offer of an out-of-court settlement. The group would sign to CBS and receive a substantial advance. Innervision would receive a relatively low pay-off.

All this had taken nearly six months. Despite the huge publicity from their tour and a No. 1 album, Wham! were in danger of fading from the public eye. But George had made a magnificent comeback record, 'Wake Me Up Before You Go Go', which again went straight to No. 1.

Jazz and I headed for the States to sort out the next stage.

In America, Wham! were on Epic. The label was run by Al Teller, who did things his own way.

Al didn't want a couple of English managers turning up and dictating what he should and shouldn't do. He'd already decided that Wham! were just a flash in the pan – the sort of peculiarly British phenomenon that never did well in the USA. To make his point he herded all his executive staff into the conference room so that when we arrived we would feel overwhelmed – thirteen to two.

We started by telling him we wanted a major US campaign. Al said, 'No way!'

We pointed out that 'Wake Me Up Before You Go Go' had gone straight to No. 1 in the UK.

Al said the record was just a 'novelty song'. Records like that only got into the charts in Europe.

We told him that was a disgusting attitude. CBS was an American company and had a duty to the artists it signed in other countries of the world. CBS should give any artist who had a hit in their own country a fair shot at the American market. If Al didn't want to do that, he should release the group from their contract here and now and we would take them straight to Clive Davis at Arista who was crying out to get his hands on them.

(In fact, four weeks earlier, on another trip to New York, I'd dropped in on Clive and played him an acetate of 'Wake Me Up Before You Go Go'. He too had called it a 'novelty song' and said it would never happen in the States.)

Al was slow in responding to what we said and his staff were not in a rush to take our side. So we went a bit further ...

We told him that for an American company to set up in the UK, to sign UK artists and then to deny them access to the American market was to give a misleading impression. British artists chose to sign with CBS specifically because it held out the promise of better access to the US market. I told Al how sad it was that a major record company seemed to be incapable of understanding the aspirations and dreams of the artists on whose talent the corporation was built.

We could see that Al was becoming angry. He was shaking slightly, and his staff noticed it too. Jazz and I caught each other's eye. In for a penny, in for a pound.

I told Al CBS had already shown a lack of morality in not standing behind Innervision during their court case with Wham!, now they were again showing a lack of morality by refusing to stand behind the group they'd fought so hard to get hold of.

I was going to say more, but surprisingly it was enough. In front of all his staff Al's temper exploded embarrassingly. He shouted, he shook, he banged his fists on the table.

Jazz and I remained silent and let him simmer down.

When he could talk again, Al asked, almost despairingly, 'Look – what do you two guys want?'

'We've already got it,' I told him. 'We just wanted your attention.'

'We'll do whatever you want,' he said suddenly. 'Just tell us what you want us to do.'

'We don't want to tell you what to do,' Jazz told him. 'We just want you to give Wham! the promotion they ought to be given. It's best left to you to decide how to do it. You're the experts. We just wanted to make sure we'd drawn your attention to the matter.'

Al calmed down fast. The meeting was over and he even managed a wry smile. Half an hour later he was charm itself, and within a week we'd become good friends. The deal we made was that, providing the group finished a new album for release by the end of the summer, Al would throw everything into their promotion.

And he certainly kept his word. In the autumn the album was delivered and 'Wake Me Up Before You Go Go' went to No. 1 in the States.

*

While this was happening, George had been re-recording 'Careless Whisper'. What came out of the studio was one of the great all-time pop classics. It was the backing track that made it so special – the flow and groove.

Hugh Burns played guitar on the track and remembers George making them play through it over and over again. 'When it reached the end we would just play on and on – busking. About the fourth or fifth time we went on for seven or eight minutes and got into a real solid groove. George suddenly stopped us and said, "That's it. That's the groove I want. Now start again and keep that groove right through." We did, and the next take was the backing track we used.'

Jerry Wexler felt bad. 'It really hurt. It only ever happened once before that a record I'd made was rejected, and that was with Linda Ronstadt. I'm sure my version of "Careless Whisper" would have been just as big. I decided the whole thing had been a ploy – something to do with Wham!'s legal fight with their record company – my version had never been intended for release.'

But that definitely wasn't the case. Everyone involved had hoped for Jerry's version to be perfect.

In the UK, 'Careless Whisper' was released as being by George Michael. In the States, as 'Wham! *featuring* George Michael'. In both countries, it went to No. 1.

From that moment on, it was hard work persuading George to keep Wham! together a minute longer.

CHAPTER TWENTY
POP AND POLITICS

In 1968 Enoch Powell made a speech for which he was sacked from the shadow cabinet. 'Like the Romans,' he said, 'I seem to see the River Tiber foaming with much blood.' He was proposing that black immigrants be sent back to the West Indies.

In 1976, at the beginning of the punk era, Eric Clapton played a concert at the Birmingham Odeon. In the middle of it, he stopped and said, 'Enoch is right – I think we should send them all back.' After he'd played another song, Clapton repeated his comments and said he wanted to 'keep Britain white'.

Clapton's entire existence revolved around the blues, the blackest of all black music. When Jimi Hendrix died he'd been inconsolable. 'I went out in the garden and cried all day because he'd left me behind.' And Clapton admitted to being even closer to Muddy Waters. 'I felt so much love for him. I felt he was my father and I was his adopted son.'

More recently, Clapton had been asked what debt he owed to black music and black musicians. Surprisingly he'd replied, 'Nothing ... We're all in the same boat.'

Eric was always a strange person. 'I've got this death wish,' he once told a journalist, 'I don't like life'. Whatever went wrong inside his brain that evening in Birmingham, the most shocking thing was that no one booed and no one walked out. The audience, nearly all of whom disagreed with him, and some of whom were black, failed to make their feelings known. Perhaps because it was so unexpected, and coming from Clapton, so unbelievable too, the audience were too stunned to respond.

1976 was a bad year for race relations. The National Front was at its strongest and most vociferous. Their slogans included 'Two million immigrants, two million unemployed'. Other things too were helping stir up racial controversy. David Bowie had arrived back in Britain by rail. At Victoria station, he descended from the train and gave a Nazi salute. Then he climbed into a black Mercedes flanked by blond outriders and told the press, 'Britain would benefit from a period of fascism.' Later he made it sound more like a joke. 'I think I might have been a bloody good Hitler. I'd be an excellent dictator. Very eccentric and quite mad.' Unfortunately, this sort of talk fed racism.

Early punks too had toyed with Nazi imagery. The idea was to shock and it did. But it wasn't long before the message became confused. On the King's Road, very few of the teenagers who bought swastika patches to sew on their jackets were racist – most were just fashion-conscious kids who enjoyed taunting their elders. But inadvertently they were spreading a message of intolerance.

A few days after Eric Clapton made his remarks there was racial violence at the Notting Hill Carnival. There was also a letter in the *Melody Maker* from several musicians which finished, 'So who shot the sheriff, Eric? It sure as hell wasn't you!' It was signed 'Rock Against Racism'.

Within days, *Melody Maker* was inundated with hundreds of letters asking, 'What is Rock Against Racism? Where can we join?'

Tom Robinson became one of the founding members. 'This wasn't something that came from artists, this was from the gut, a grassroots thing – people just wanted to do something to help, to counter the damage done by Clapton's remarks and Bowie's Nazi salutes.'

Rock Against Racism's plan to fight racist attitudes wasn't particularly successful, but at least it made people commit themselves. Despite their swastikas and swearing, even the Sex Pistols had to own up that anarchy didn't extend to race hatred. Johnny Rotten did an interview for RAR's magazine and made it clear he loathed the National Front and very much admired reggae and other black music.

'Were the Sex Pistols political?' I asked John Lydon on a chat show.

'Of course not,' he insisted. 'That was just Malcolm. We were never anarchists – we were just wallies.'

Later I asked Malcolm McLaren, had *he* been an anarchist?

'Only as a fantasy,' he told me. 'I was never really committed to it. I just liked causing trouble – like getting £50,000 from EMI for a group they were afraid to sign but equally afraid to miss out on – then causing so much trouble that they had to drop them, then getting the money all over again from another company. That's the sort of anarchy I loved.'

While the Pistols weren't really committed to politics, by pretending to be, they influenced the groups who followed them. The Clash, the Jam, Sham 69 – all expressed political opinions and committed themselves to Rock Against Racism. Even the Stranglers, who'd refused to join it, rushed onto the stage at a gig to defend reggae group Steel Pulse from National Front elements in the audience. The fact that many punk groups lent their support proved that punk wasn't the nihilist philosophy it was supposed to be. Rock Against Racism brought punk and rock bands together with anomalies arising all over the place. The Tom Robinson Band was pop rock with a little gay preaching thrown in but they found themselves playing a gig with Sham 69 who had a predominantly National Front audience. Tom thought it would end up as a disaster, but the gig went surprisingly well. 'Sham 69 weren't really punk, they were more like early seventies skinheads. Jimmy Pursey, Sham's singer, was a left-wing idealist, and their manager was Jewish. Yet there they were attracting the National Front. The bizarre thing was, they played a gig at London Polytechnic with a black band supporting them – the Southall Rastas Misty in Roots. The fans from both bands came to the gig and mixed together, and there was no violence.'

By 1979, something else had arrived on the scene that was doing far more to undermine racism than RAR. It was the cult of '2-Tone' groups.

First were the Specials with a debut album produced by Elvis Costello. They started their own label, also called 2-Tone, and not long after race riots in Brixton and Liverpool in 1981 they had a No. 1 with 'Ghost Town'. Through records like this they were more successful in combining political statement and commercial success than any other group before them, but their most important statement was made simply by being a large gang of both black and white musicians.

Others followed – the Beat, the Selector, the Belle Stars. The mere existence of these groups was full of contradictions. 2-Tone's musical inspiration was Jamaican ska and bluebeat. In the early part of the seventies, this music had been popular with pre-punk, working-class skinheads. The skinheads, with their violent, uncompromising image, were easy pickings for the neo-Nazi National Front party. Many teenage skinheads found themselves persuaded to support neo-Nazi ideology and demanded that blacks be deported to the West Indies. But they still liked West Indian music.

As if to sum up the craziness of the situation, the biggest 2-Tone group of them all was called Madness. Racially, Madness was strictly a 1-tone band – all white – but their music was 2-Tone, combining ska, punk and catchy pop melodies. This imbued their existence with a political spirit. By the middle of 1982, Madness had clocked up their tenth hit single. They said they wanted to be the people's band and their lyrics were full of indiscreet references to laddish fantasies and fears – stealing ladies' underwear, life in prison, or on the football terrace. Madness became masters of video vaudeville. Where Duran Duran had spoofed James Bond movies, Madness spoofed the *Carry On* series, as in 'Night Boat To Cairo' where they dressed as Egyptian explorers in pith helmets and khaki shorts.

Despite their love of fun, the members of Madness found themselves thrown into serious racial politics. At their concerts they, and the other 2-Tone groups, could see confused white skinheads dancing to what was essentially black music with their black mates – and wearing National Front badges. The National Front often used 2-Tone concerts to cause trouble. And because Madness was the biggest group, they saw the most trouble. The media demanded they take a stance against Nazism. Suggs, the group's good-looking singer, was always well-dressed and softly spoken. He projected an image of easy-going tolerance, but now he found himself in the middle of something he hadn't wanted to be involved with. 'We had a non-involvement stance,' he explains. 'And that meant things became misunderstood.' Grudgingly, Suggs let it be known that the group were in favour of Rock Against Racism, Greenpeace, and CND. Thankfully, unlike Paul Weller, Madness never expressed their political viewpoints in song, only in interviews.

As a punk, Paul Weller had been inarticulate and arrogant. He was disliked in the television world because he had a habit of spitting at presenters. When the Jam split up in 1982, Weller formed a new group, the Style Council, which had Motown and jazz as its musical roots. With age Paul had become a little more articulate, but he was no less unreasonable.

Tom Robinson once said, 'There's a fine line between an angry young man and an angry young bore.' It seemed that Paul Weller found it hard to stay on the right side of this line. He had a chip on his shoulder at every turn. With his new band, the old angry lyrics sounded distinctly odd. 'You don't have to take this crap,' he sang sarkily to a funky beat. And the backing girls chirped back prettily, 'Doopee doop doo'. It was difficult to make out whether this was satire or some sort of musical dyslexia. And because the music was pretty, people didn't get the message. This made Weller furious. He just couldn't believe his music was unable to make people change the way things were.

Meanwhile the New Romantics actually were changing things, not through politics, but like the 2-Tone groups, simply by their existence. By creating themselves in their own image, and through controlling their own destiny with apparent success, they dealt with the class system by ignoring it altogether. By 1984 the UK was heading towards being middle-class only, but Paul Weller was still very much caught up in socialism. He sneered at the New Romantic movement. 'Their attitude is that they'd like to go out with Princess Di or shag her sister or something. They wish *they* were aristocracy. They wish they had the aristocracy's sophistication, which doesn't interest me because I *hate* the fucking aristocracy.'

But of course, to all intents and purposes pop stars *are* aristocracy. They surround themselves with chauffeurs, limousines, villas and servants. They buy islands and aeroplanes, and build private recording studios.

In the early seventies, Pete Brown, the lyric writer for Cream, wrote a song called 'Ministry of Bag'. 'It's a series of very nasty images of whoever is at the helm at the time. A sort of microcosm; an allegory of the government – "the government" being the same as the pop industry.'

Among young people, there will always be a chip-on-the-shoulder brigade, and in the early eighties Paul Weller volunteered himself as their leader. He announced, 'We are socialists, and try to lead by our actions', then he looked around for a cause. What he found was miners having a tough time under the Thatcher government and about to go on strike.

John Taylor of Duran Duran made it known that he disapproved of Weller's interest in such causes. 'Bands like the Jam and the Clash,' he complained, 'seem to encourage these sorts of tribal movements, this gang mentality – and I don't like it.'

But surprisingly, when the strike started, the miners got support from musicians everywhere – not just the chip-on-the-shoulder brigade.

The miners' strike wasn't just a strike, it was a bloody great brawl with picketing and rioting. It appealed to the young.

To them, the miners were behaving like teenagers standing up for their rights at school – a sort of St Trinian's done seriously. But in this case jobs and entire communities were at threat. Even gays sided with the miners, perhaps because they were reminded of the beginnings of gay activism in New York a few years earlier. Journalist John Blake feels that gay groups developed political skills from their involvement with the miners. 'They learnt how to recruit people to their cause by finding a common enemy.' Jonathan King thinks their attraction to the cause was more likely to have been triggered by Arthur Scargill's hairstyle. 'Pulled up on one side, dragged across the top of his head and fixed with lacquer on the other side. It was simply the campest thing anyone had ever seen.'

The miners' strike became a catalyst in persuading many young musicians to take a more political attitude. One concert to raise money for the miners included the unlikely mix of New Order, Aztec Camera, and Wham! Afterwards, George Michael said he didn't like Scargill. 'I think he's the worst thing the miners could have. He's enjoying the whole thing. That's what's so awful.'

When a group called the Flying Pickets offered miners the use of their house in London, the miners found themselves alongside women with pink Mohican haircuts who accused them of being sexist. It began to change their working-class attitudes, and later after a gay band had played a benefit concert for them, the miners even sent a delegation to the Gay Pride march, 'in solidarity'.

The middle-class press saw miners as working-class hoodlums and they regarded gays and music business personalities as decadent. They found it extraordinary that such diverse sides of society could find common ground with each other. Singer Billy

Bragg pounced on it and told the miners, 'We must thank Mrs Thatcher for bringing people like you and us together.'

But as the miners made a last hopeless stand for socialism, the pop world was about to embark on a capitalist scam the like of which even Malcolm McLaren could only have dreamed about.

The rise to fame of Frankie Goes to Hollywood was planned and executed perfectly. Malcolm McLaren would never have had the cool skill to pull it off. Besides, he had no understanding of gay culture. The people who planned and executed this scam were producer Trevor Horn and journalist Paul Morley, and they set up their own independent record label to release the record – ZTT.

Morley was famous for being ridiculously over-intellectual and outrageously rude to the stars he interviewed. 'As a perfectionist, you surely reject the type of superficiality and vacuity that you seem to celebrate,' he said to drag pop star Marilyn by way of a question. And hoping to get Meat Loaf talking, he prompted him with, 'American rock 'n' roll is exertion, safety, religion, dread handling, absent wishes, escape.' Then, for Phil Collins, he started off, 'Just who the hell do you think you are?'

Morley teamed up with Trevor Horn, once a singer in the pomp-rock group Yes and now the producer of ABC and other New Romantic groups. The plan was to record a song written by Frankie Goes to Hollywood, a five-piece group from Liverpool fronted by two gay guys – Paul Rutherford and Holly Johnson. The group wanted success at any cost and they were happy to let Trevor Horn and Paul Morley take them over. Morley hyped the press and Horn did the production.

With a thumping four-to-the-floor bass drum and power-chords from the guitar, their first single was sexual rather than sexy. It was all aggression and masculinity, except that the chorus contained the lyrics: 'Relax, don't do it, when you want to suck it, chew it. Relax, don't do it, when you want to come.'

It took off and took hold of the nation's imagination. Half-amused, half-shocked, Britain was subjected to endless repetitions of the song's keyword. There was no heavy breathing and no beating about the bush. This record had got right to the point. 'Come!' it said, and 'come' it clearly meant.

Paul and Holly were not the limp-wristed jolly-boys the British public so loved, like Larry Grayson or Kenneth Williams. They were aggressively queer and out to scare you. They looked 'hard', had crewcuts and dressed themselves in T-shirts and leather. After years of gay giggling, Britain was now getting outright promiscuous homosexuality.

Holly Johnson was the lead singer and could be provocative. He told *Him Monthly*, 'Although Boy George and Bowie are gorgeous boys if you like that sort of thing, they're working in a grey area, they're playing with androgyny. But we're black and white. There's no pussy-footing with us. We are into PLEASURE and we think that what has been regarded as a sexual perversion should be brought into the open.'

Paul Morley took credit for the entire concept. 'We wanted to create a teenybop dream that belonged in an eighties context. When you look back, you'll know what the eighties were all about.' But the truth was, the band had not only written the song themselves, they'd performed it on television before they even met Morley, which was why Holly Johnson became increasingly agitated about the way Morley spoke of the group as puppets. 'Paul Morley had such an ego he wanted to make out he'd created us. But when he first met us we were already called Frankie Goes to Hollywood, and we'd done the songs on a John Peel radio session. The words were exactly the same, the bass line, the beat, the groove were all exactly the same. We had this outrageous stage act which all the record labels thought was too hot to handle. Then Paul and Trevor got this idea to do something with a gay group.'

When 'Relax' was already the biggest climber of the week, Radio One DJ Mike Read suddenly refused to play it, calling it 'overtly obscene'. His outburst led to the song being banned by the BBC. It was absurd. When the song first came out the BBC had played it, yet when the public started to take to it they refused to play it any more. But outrage and controversy in the media was just what Paul Morley wanted. A week later the record went to No. 1 and stayed there for five weeks.

'Relax' was followed up by 'Two Tribes' with a video featuring a fist fight between Reagan and Chernenko. It was a satire of the Cold War and the sleeve notes contained obscure facts and figures about alcoholism in Russia, homosexuality in the American armed forces and a list of which countries were aiming missiles at which others.

Money, glamour, outrage and downright devilry – Frankie Goes to Hollywood tied it up just the way McLaren had failed to do. And Morley, in his own way, was just as outrageous as McLaren. 'I always thought the teenybop bands of the eighties would be horrific, 'cos kids in the eighties would have so much stimuli, so much lust. That's what we've noticed in all the letters written to Frankie Goes to Hollywood from fourteen-year-old-girls; they all want to fuck the band, every single one. They want little bags of sperm.'

At the time it was released, the remix of 'Relax' was the most successful 12in club record ever, and 'Two Tribes' stayed at No. 1 for *nine* weeks. But success brought differences of opinion. Holly Johnson was particularly irate. 'Paul's contribution was good – it added to the thing. But he shouldn't claim he created us. I don't think any marketing division in any record company ever stood up and said, "We created the Beatles." They just said, "We marketed them".'

But who cared? Frankie's sound was the sound of cash. Paul Morley had intended the group to be a send-up of the consumer society and it was. With cash in their hands the group spent to the hilt, exchanging leather and studs for designer suits and expensive sweaters. But with their new well-dressed image, the threatening fetishism of gay conspiracy faded away and so did the group's success. Consumed by consumerism.

In 1982, when Margaret Thatcher attacked the Falklands with all the gusto of a Wembley Cup Final, she caused a lot of pop musicians to offer vocal opposition to her. But when she provoked the miners to strike, she achieved something that had once seemed impossible, she caused pop musicians not just to support a cause, but to support an actual political party – the Labour opposition.

Paul Weller was the ringleader and quickly got together with Billy Bragg, another political activist. They started working for the re-election of the Labour party. Bragg wasn't only hostile to Mrs Thatcher and her attack on the Falklands, he was also upset by record companies' profits. He had a message printed on his album that the record should sell for no more than £2.99, and record stores were furious. 'If someone wrote a song saying "shoot the Queen", nobody would mind,' commented Bragg, 'but if you hit their profits, they worry.'

Tom Robinson, who also joined them, had yet another point of view. 'For me personally, the main thing was still my hatred of racism. I felt Labour were the party most likely to work for racial equality. Frankly, if a Conservative organisation had proposed concerts against racism, I'd have been there playing for them just the same.'

Despite their mixed purposes, Paul Weller said they were all united. 'If you ask us all questions, you'll get different answers, but we all want to get rid of the Tories.'

In 1984, I too had an idea that concerned politics – Chinese politics – Wham!'s proposed trip to China.

Shortly after Wham! had settled their court case with Innervision, I made the first of thirteen trips to China, trying to set up a concert for them in Beijing. I had to persuade the Chinese that to invite a British pop group to play in Beijing would prove to the outside world that they were serious about opening up to the West, which would lead to more international investment. If they felt it was dangerous for their own youth to be subjected to such music, they could keep a lid on the local press. All they had to do was to let the international media attend the concert and relay it to the world.

I went backwards and forwards to China every six weeks for the best part of two years. During that time, Wham! became the biggest group in Britain and 'Careless Whisper' the most played song on both sides of the Atlantic. Moreover, when George Michael received the prestigious Ivor Novello award for songwriters, he became the youngest person ever to do so.

Apart from their single appearance at a miners' charity, Wham! had shown no interest in political involvement. The older, more intellectual critics loathed them for it, particularly Paul Morley who interviewed them with a degree of aggression unusual even for him. 'Wham! are just a little too belligerent in wanting you to believe that they haven't a care in the world nor a thought for it. They might yet realise how thick they are. Isn't that so, Andrew?'

But Wham!'s philosophy of having fun and enjoying life had obviously hit the right nerve with young people. And that's exactly what made them saleable to China.

The method I used in dealing with the Chinese was to create a situation where there was never a question to which they could answer 'yes' or 'no'. That way the door was always kept open for further negotiation. Instead of saying, 'Could Wham! come and play in China?' I started off with, 'It would be really nice if, one day, a British pop group were able to come and play here.'

Slipped into a dinner with a government minister, that would be enough for one visit. The next time I was in China I would say, 'You know I said how nice it would be if one day a British pop group could come and play in China – well, it would be really nice if it could be Wham!' Then I slipped in a little background about the group – their cheerful uncomplicated music, the absence of any hint of anarchy or teenage aggression.

Two years later, after thirteen trips to China, it seemed I'd finally persuaded them. I felt confident enough to say, 'If Wham! were to come and play in China one day, it would be really nice if it was on April 7th, at the Workers' Stadium.'

The government official with whom I was talking seemed

to digest this thought as easily as he'd digested the dinner I'd just bought him. So I decided I was home and dry.

I flew from Beijing to Singapore, checked into the Shangri-La hotel and took a gamble. I called Jazz Summers in London and told him, 'We've done it. We're going to play at the Workers' Stadium in Beijing on April 7th.'

Jazz wasted no time announcing it to the press. When I woke up the next morning the news was on the front page of the *Straits Times*.

I gambled that after all the talking and travelling the Chinese government must be serious about Wham! playing in Beijing. My suggestion that 7 April 1985 would be a nice date had not been rejected. Now it was in the headlines of newspapers all over the world. Surely the Chinese government would never dare pull out of it; if they did, they would suffer a huge loss of confidence from the world business community; all those mega-million joint-venture deals with multinational companies would be put in jeopardy.

I flew back to England and every newspaper was full of it. At the airport, the *New Musical Express* pounced on me for an interview and were scathingly sceptical. Why should the Chinese invite Wham!, a group that approved of Margaret Thatcher's England, rather than Billy Bragg or a leftward-leaning Liverpool group? Why didn't they invite a pro-Communist group?

NME couldn't understand that subversion is subversion. The anti is always anti. Wham! were a group who approved of the status quo in the country where they lived. The Chinese wanted a group that conveyed political acceptance to their youth, or to be honest they didn't want anything conveyed at all. They hoped to contain the concert in one concert hall of 20,000 'safe' young communists and keep news of the event out of the Chinese newspapers. It was for outside eyes only. The Chinese government wanted the rest of the world to think they were opening up, but opening up was the last thing they really wanted to do.

Back in London I went at once to CBS Records. Wham! had to borrow money from them. This was no ordinary tour support, it was a huge amount of money for one gig, and all the expenses would have to be paid by the group.

Wham! had to pay for the hire of the concert hall, pay to print the tickets, pay to sell them, and then had to donate the income to a Chinese charity. There would be diplomatic banquets to welcome them and facilities would be provided for the world's press. The Chinese would decide how much to spend on all these things but it was Wham! who would have to foot the bill. And all this was on top of the normal expenses of taking a major rock group and its equipment to a country the other side of the world where nothing could be hired locally.

Jazz and I reckoned up the cost and it came to half a million dollars. Could CBS really be convinced this one event was worth subsidising to that extent? Paul Russell, head of Epic in London, told me if CBS were to consider it, there would have to be a full-length movie of the event. It meant half a dozen cameramen, a major director and three months of editing. And it doubled the cost. Now we needed a million and the gig was in two weeks' time. We had to have the money from CBS within twenty-four hours. What record company in the world would come up with that amount of tour support for one single gig in a country where they couldn't sell records?

I thought the chances were nil, but at ten the next morning, Paul Russell called to say I could collect a cheque. Suddenly Jazz Summers and I were setting up a million-dollar trip to China – chartering a 747 for freight, hiring cameramen and road crew, contracting a top movie director – and I still had no official invitation to play this gig at all.

I needed to know in a hurry if my gamble was really going to come off so I played one last game of 'Never ask Yes or No'. I telexed Beijing and asked for a plan of the Workers' Stadium with the seating laid out as it would be on 7 April.

Two days later the plan was couriered to me. It showed the stadium set up for a concert rather than a basketball game. And on the stage area was written the word WHAM!

While all this was going on, I became aware that Bob Geldof was attempting something of infinitely more value. He was using the music industry to bypass political obstacles and raise money to feed starving people in Africa.

Two months earlier, in November 1984, I'd been approached by Bob who'd asked if George might agree to sing on a record to support Ethiopia. I said I didn't see why he wouldn't, and I was right. George agreed instantly.

Live Aid was Bob's equivalent of what I'd done in China, only with a lot more practical use. Once the idea had grabbed him it wouldn't go away, and then the implications and possibilities grew and grew. Instead of paying a million dollars for the right to play a gig, as I'd done, Bob was going to earn a million dollars and give it to charity. The people who were to receive it could thank the fickleness of British rock audiences. Part of what triggered Bob was the disastrous failure of his group the Boomtown Rats. In his book *Is That It?* he explains:

The tax scheme had fallen through when it was discovered it wasn't legitimate and now we were all being stung for back taxes. We had no money and yet we were employing a manager, a fan club organiser, press officers, a tour manager, a sound guy, a lights guy, the backline man for the road crew – all these were on a salary or a retainer. We owed money to our English lawyer, our American lawyer, our accountant, our agents, the pluggers, even to the road crew.

With little chance of resurrecting his group's fortunes, Bob channelled his energies into something much more worthwhile. It was interesting watching his idea grow at just the same time that I was running around fixing Wham! in China. We played in Beijing on 7 April – on 13 July Live Aid took place.

'Wham! in China' had been organised by the group's management entirely for promotional purposes. It involved no investment by the record company since the money CBS paid us to fund it was only an advance against Wham!'s future royalties. Geldof's ideas were different, and they set record companies worrying.

Geldof's Live Aid record, 'Feed The World', was made in the face of all the odds. It seemed a high point in pop music's involvement in politics and social affairs, but record company executives took it uneasily: they felt there should be a limit to what record companies were expected to donate. They didn't mind their artists making charity records but they didn't much like the idea of pressing and distributing them free. If Geldof's ideas caught on, there was no way of knowing how many times a year record companies might be asked to give up their profits to help some cause or other.

*

On 4 April, Wham! set off for Hong Kong. On the plane with us were twenty-eight reporters, one from every British daily and Sunday newspaper, plus the Wham! party – the group, the management, the road crew, the film crew, lawyers, publishers, friends and relatives – altogether 180 people.

The economics of the trip were horrendous. Wham! would pay for everything – the hire of the stadium, the printing of the tickets, the salaries of the people who worked at the box office, and the cost of the buses to bring the approved ticket-buyers to the concert.

We asked the Chinese for twenty people to help unload the trucks, but we were given a hundred. Tour manager Jake Duncan was in charge. 'Government officials insisted we use fifty local crew to unload the trucks, but access was so cramped we could only unload one truck at a time. There were fifty overly eager Chinese trying to lay their hands on any piece of equipment. Then twelve hours later another shift of fifty stagehands turned up.'

Wham! also had to pay for their food – three meals a day – and judging by the bills, the stagehands were eating just as well as the government officials.

To round things off, Jake Duncan was informed Wham! would have to pay for five extra hotel rooms, complete with food allowance. He says, 'I've yet to meet our five mystery hotel residents. Only the substantial room accounts bore any witness to their presence.'

And that was just the beginning. The Chinese respected great artists, so there had to be an official reception for Wham! with a thousand people in the grand banqueting hall of the Ministry of

Culture. And there were other lesser meals and banquets – 200 people at a special Beijing duck restaurant; 150 at a special dinner before the show; and so on, all paid for by Wham!.

But when the gig finally happened, it was definitely worthwhile.

One thing that worried us was that the people attending the concert were only doing so because they'd been told to by the co-operatives they worked for. As it was at Wham!'s expense that tickets were being printed and sold to them, we decided to include a cassette with each ticket. That way they could listen to the songs and get to know them before the concert. In the event, we went even further. We recorded all Wham!'s songs in Chinese using a reasonably well-known Mandarin singer. We then made one side of the tape Chinese, and the other English. That way, the audience would even know what the songs were about. And then we had another thought, purely subversive, we would give away two cassettes with each ticket. The second cassette would surely end up being sold on to someone else. And we were right. A week before the show took place, the cassettes were being sold on the Beijing black market, and pirated too. So now Wham! actually were building a name in the country, or at least its capital city.

Once I'd been sure it was all going to happen, I'd flown back to Beijing and been to see the ambassador, Sir Richard Evans. I explained that this was the first cultural exchange between the two countries since Margaret Thatcher had made her agreement to return Hong Kong to the Chinese. Since the Chinese were obviously making an effort to show they were opening up, wouldn't it be appropriate for the British ambassador to attend the event? Sir Richard agreed, so I went straight to my Chinese political contacts and said, since the British ambassador would be coming, shouldn't there also be someone from the Chinese cabinet? Suddenly, for the Chinese, the event was being forced beyond a secret pop concert only meant for the eyes of the outside world. It was becoming a diplomatic event.

When the Beijing concert took place, it was one of the largest turnouts ever by the world's press in China, and it was broadcast to nearly every country in the world. In America, for a week Wham! featured in all the daily news bulletins of CBS, ABC and RCA television.

The week before the gig I'd flown into Los Angeles and been asked by immigration what I did. I said I was a pop manager and they asked who I managed. When I said Wham!, they hadn't heard of them. When I hummed them 'Careless Whisper' they knew the song at once. But they still didn't know the name of the group.

The week after the Beijing concert I flew back to the States. This time when I said I managed Wham! the immigration officials rushed to ask for free records and autographed photographs.

'Wham! in China' had worked as it was meant to, but back in London I watched Bob Geldof slaving to get Live Aid together and felt somewhat ashamed. Geldof was doing something *really* worthwhile.

George Michael put it better.

Outside the Great Wall Hotel where we stayed in Beijing there was a stone dragon. One evening as we returned to the hotel we saw that someone had forced a Coke can into the dragon's mouth. George pointed to it. 'That just about sums up our trip to China!'

*

In setting up Live Aid Bob Geldof was enormously persuasive. Among other triumphs he managed to get the Who to come together again for an appearance after they'd sworn they never would. But he didn't just go for big stars, he went for big white stars. Two years after the event, there were still black British musicians who felt insulted at the lack of representation they'd had at Wembley.

Bob hit back, saying he just wanted to raise money and was obviously no racist. But the inclusion of Billy Ocean or Hot Chocolate might have balanced Wembley's almost all-white image. On the other hand, all Bob was trying to do was pick acts that were big in the USA. On that score, Madness were also left out, despite having had nineteen British hit singles. So they made their own benefit single, 'Tam Tam Pour L'Ethiopie'. Sadly, by then Radio One DJs were bored with Ethiopia. 'Too ethnic,' one of them said, which was just the type of arrogance that caused Africa's problems in the first place.

Some artists who complained about being left out were accused by the press of being more concerned about being on the bill than about helping the starving in Ethiopia. *Daily Mail* journalist John Blake disagreed. 'There was a lot of egomania – one artist wanting more attention than the next – that sort of thing. But there was also a feeling of genuine altruism. After all, just because someone's an egomaniac it doesn't mean they don't want to save the world too.'

Strangely, for an event which was all about feeding people, the only people who refused to give their services for nothing were the Wembley caterers. Geldof begged them to give their profits for the day to Live Aid but they refused, so he put flyers on the posters telling people to bring their own food.

The biggest criticisms of the event came from people who observed the backstage indulgences of the musicians. Writing in the *Melody Maker* Chris Maud said, 'If most of those groups at Live Aid had donated their cocaine bills for the year, it would have saved as many lives.'

In an interview with *Q Magazine*, Francis Rossi of Status Quo confirmed his feelings. 'We were the first band on and we were already as high as kites by midday. After we finished we spent most of the time doing cocaine in the toilets. We didn't spend much time thinking about the starving in Ethiopia.'

The Live Aid record sold more than three million copies and the Live Aid concerts eventually raised more than £140,000,000 but as with all charities the majority of people donated mainly to keep the problem at bay, like paying a mobster protection money not to smash up your shop. Bob Geldof, on the other hand, threw himself into Live Aid with total emotional commitment. 'I never once stopped to consider what happened next. I acted intuitively all the time. I played it by ear, as they say.'

Live Aid could never have happened in the sixties or seventies, it was a result of the growing power of artists in the industry. It was artists who instigated it, and it was artists who pressurised the record companies into cooperating. It was almost as if the roles had been reversed. Record companies had now become the irresponsible teenagers, interested only in their own self-centred desires. Pop stars it seemed had grown up and were now lecturing them on human rights and personal freedoms.

Of course, many artists remained sceptical of the close link between Live Aid and politics. But Geldof insisted, 'Famine is above politics.' And whatever the motives of those who took part, it was impossible to disagree with him.

As for what I'd achieved with Wham! in China – one month after they'd become the first Western rock group to perform there, I was back in Beijing negotiating another deal (in New York I'd sold Walter Yetnikoff the idea of CBS setting up in China). On the way into town we passed the arena where a few weeks earlier Wham! had played to 15,000 Chinese.

'What's going on there this week?' I asked.

'There's a show trial,' my Chinese friend told me. 'Do you want to watch?'

Ten minutes later I was sitting in the same stadium where I'd watched Wham! perform to the world's media. Now, in front of an audience of 10,000 specially chosen 'ordinary people', a shifty bunch of Chinese officials sat on a podium passing judgement on a succession of hang-dog petty criminals – adulterers, pick-pockets, black-marketeers. Most of them received the death penalty. They were then taken outside to a field near the river and given a bullet in the back of the head.

Shortly after the Live Aid concerts, the Labour party teamed up with a bunch of pop stars, actors and actresses to form Red Wedge. On the terrace of the House of Commons they held a launch party. Hot punch was served to a crowd of 200, including Paul Weller, Billy Bragg, Jimmy Somerville of the Communards, and Tom Robinson. Their aim was to change young people's voting habits and win the youth vote for Labour.

Journalist Rick Sky wasn't sure their motives were altogether genuine. 'Most stars are very cynical. They may have a good heart, but at the same time they're very aware of what is advantageous to them.'

It wasn't only journalists who had doubts about Red Wedge. Politically committed rock stars found little support from the poppier end of the music business. Barry Gibb was one of those who sneered at what was going on. 'Politicians have no idea how to save the world, so why should pop stars?'

Red Wedge's terrace party at the House of Commons wasn't Parliament's first pop party. In 1980, the Members' Dining Room had been used by Norman St John-Stevas, the Conservative Arts Minister, to host a party to launch a pop book. The party was invaded by the Village People dressed as Red Indians. Compared with that, the Red Wedge party was a lot less enjoyable. Most of the MPs and union officials looked thoroughly miserable.

'Cheer up,' Billy Bragg told them, 'socialism is supposed to be fun.'

To make it more so, he recruited another group – the Smiths – best-known for throwing gladioli into the audience and the celibacy of Morrissey, their singer. American critic Henry Rollins loathed him. 'Get that grease outta your hair, get a girlfriend, get a James Brown CD, get some vitamin C, get some fucking clean air and some sunlight, go for a walk – get over it.'

But Morrissey couldn't. He was angst-ridden and publicity-seeking. He told journalists, 'The only thing that could possibly save British politics would be Margaret Thatcher's assassination.'

And about Bob Geldof and his Live Aid record, he said, 'One can have great concern for the people of Ethiopia, but it's another thing to inflict daily torture on the people of England. It was an awful record.'

With a chip on both shoulders, Morrissey was a perfect new recruit for the Red Wedge brigade. Many people were looking forward to him making a fool of himself on-stage, but he didn't. Tom Robinson, who previously had not been a Smiths fan, remembers their performance at Newcastle City Hall. 'They borrowed equipment, walked on-stage with other people's guitars and drum kit and blew everyone away. It was their presence, their commitment, and their music – just by being on-stage they were being political without actually saying it. They were telling everyone – "This is what it's meant to be about."'

Despite the efforts of the Red Wedgers, at the next election the Conservatives were re-elected. A few days afterwards, U2 performed at Wembley with Bono singing an angry rendition of 'C'mon Everybody' including the new line 'Screw the Election'. Later he seemed to calm down. 'I'm not in a position to be seen as a spokesman of the generation. I mean, how can you be spokesman of a generation if you've nothing to say other than "Help!"?'

Red Wedge may not have got the result they wanted, but they'd certainly been an influence on young people. The biggest swing to the left had been among eighteen- to twenty-four-year-olds. Even so, Billy Bragg admitted, 'The disappointment was incredible and we went away thinking we'd failed. But what is pop music capable of? Is it capable of winning elections? I don't think it is.'

Miles Copeland, the Police's manager, was much more succinct. 'Pop stars should just stick to things they know about, like drugs.'

CHAPTER TWENTY-ONE
LIFE PLUS SEVENTY

In 1990, at the Grosvenor House ballroom, I watched Mike Stock, Matt Aitken and Pete Waterman receive the Ivor Novello award for 'Songwriter of the Year'. The Ivor Novello awards are Britain's most highly regarded awards for songwriters and the most coveted of all is the award for 'Songwriter of the Year'.

What made this occasion more special than usual was that this was the third year in succession that the same three writers had won it – a feat not even achieved by Lennon and McCartney. When Stock, Aitken and Waterman walked on-stage, they were booed. They'd found the formula for success and people throughout the industry were seething with jealousy.

The greatest pop and rock writers have been those who gave us clever lyrics but simple tunes. Our brains enjoy complexity in words, but not in melody. Our taste in lyrics requires them to reflect current speech and social attitudes, but our taste in musical phrases doesn't change. But this shouldn't be confused with our ever-changing taste in style – the most ephemeral and fashionable aspect of songwriting.

Songwriting consists of reframing well-loved fragments of melody in the style and rhythm of the day, then embellishing them with lyrics that are totally of the moment. Old melodies are reused all the time, but by changing the harmonies, the tempo and the beat, they frequently pass unrecognised.

In their book *The Manual (How to Have a Number One the Easy Way)*, pop pranksters the Timelords wrote:

Every number one song ever written is only made up from bits of other songs. There is no lost chord. No changes untried. No extra notes to the scale of hidden beats to the bar. There is no point searching for originality. Creators of music who desperately search for originality usually end up with music that has none because no room for their spirit has been left to get through.

In other words, since any new pop song will inevitably contain plagiarism, why not take what you want from other songs to start with? It's a method that's been used by popular songwriters as long as the industry has existed. Listen to the bridge of 'Together Forever' by Rick Astley – isn't that amazingly like the verse of 'The Way You Look Tonight' by Jerome Kern? And the first line of the chorus of 'Last Christmas' by Wham! – doesn't that remind you of 'Reunited' by Peaches & Herb?

What makes these apparent similarities acceptable is the changed framework in which the musical phrase is placed, and the style in which the new song is constructed. Different lyrics change the musical emphasis, so when it comes to words, writers are less likely to plagiarise and more likely to search for originality. Since this is craft rather than art, professional songwriters are usually regarded with less reverence than singers. Yet many of the major figures in rock are even more casual in their approach to songwriting. John Lennon told David Bowie, 'Look, it's very simple – say what you mean, make it rhyme, and put a backbeat to it.'

It was a great formula. Lennon had the knack of writing

songs that sounded like everyday speech set to music. This was mainly because he knew exactly what he wanted to say. Most writers are the opposite. More anxious to avoid the truth rather than state it, they rely on poetic phrases and double meanings. Their songs are often written with no thought of commerciality behind them. Sinead O'Connor claims her songs are simply mental housework. 'Just me tidying my brain ... I just write songs for myself, I don't do them for anybody else.' Black British singer-songwriter Seal agrees. 'All my songs are therapy. I'm giving myself therapy.' And this also seems to be Eric Clapton's approach. 'I only compose songs if I'm in an emotional state, if I'm experiencing extreme happiness, extreme sadness or grief. Then I compose because I have to fix myself. I compose to heal myself from damage.'

Eric's most famous song is 'Wonderful Tonight', seemingly a love song directed at the person who lights up his life. In fact, it was written in anger. Eric and his girlfriend, Patti Boyd, were going out and Patti was taking forever to get ready. Eric, who hates unpunctuality, had been waiting downstairs for over two hours. 'I went back upstairs to see what was going on, and she was up there with one of her girlfriends, still trying on different things. I said, "Well that's nice – what is it, a curtain? You look wonderful."' Eric went back downstairs, picked up his guitar and wrote a song to calm his nerves. 'It wasn't written in the sense of love or affection. It was written just to pass the time, and I was pretty angry.' Nevertheless, when Eric came to record the song he allowed no hint of sarcasm to enter his performance. For all who heard it, it was a love song.

Brilliant recorded performances have often given lyrics a depth of meaning way beyond their original intent. In 1966, when

Vicki Wickham and I wrote the lyrics for 'You Don't Have To Say You Love Me', Dusty Springfield was unsure about them. She gave them to her producer, Johnny Franz, who was also unsure, but he suggested she try them anyway.

Dusty was insecure about her singing ability. When it came to recording she would accept nothing less than perfection and always presumed she could come nowhere near it. The night she recorded our song she complained that the echo on her voice wasn't right. The engineer ran downstairs to the basement to adjust the inputs to the echo chamber. As he did so, he noticed how good the echo sounded in the stairwell of the seven-storey circular staircase. Five minutes later, Dusty was halfway up it, singing into a mike hanging in space in front of her. What she then sang was one of the greatest pop performances of all time. Sheer perfection from the first breath to last.

In the music business, things often come together that way. People mess around fiddling with microphones and being half-serious about lyrics. Then the artist gives an electrifying performance and all the messy pieces turn into a magnificent whole.

Culture Club's first hit was another example of a superb performance endowing ordinary lyrics with extraordinary meaning. On paper, the lyrics for 'Do You Really Want To Hurt Me' look like mundane pop suitable for a young girl. But George's fragile, pleading performance made them a perfect song for a boy faced with the difficulties of being effeminate.

Like many songwriters his songs would often be derived from bits and pieces of other songs he'd heard. Steve Levine who produced 'Do You Really Want To Hurt Me', watched the way George worked. 'Because George wasn't a musician and knew nothing about music technically, he would hear things in a song that were not the strictly musical elements – the atmosphere, or the feel. He'd tell me he was going to write a verse like another well-known song, then he'd sing me something structurally different. He sometimes thought he'd taken something from another song but no one else would have known it because the thing he'd heard in that other song which was so special wasn't necessarily the melody line.'

Songwriters often copy other songs quite intentionally, mixing the verse of one with the chorus of the other, but giving both their own style and arrangement, and perhaps changing the chords. Creating popular songs this way is not to be sneered at – nothing we create comes from nowhere. Although some songwriters think their new song is the result of an overnight visit by God, most realise it's just a composite of a thousand different pieces of music they have heard at some time or other.

Boy George and all other writers who write this way simply believe in getting on with it, rather than waiting for divine inspiration.

Among the more serious-minded writers of the eighties were many who'd come from a background not much different from Boy George's but had been affected by it quite differently, like Matt Johnson, who was angry to the bottom of his working-class boots.

Matt's father had been a docker, but when the docks closed, he'd opened a pub and begun promoting artists in discos. The original culture of anger in the working classes was about being exploited. Once people had climbed the social ladder and ceased to be exploited, they no longer had a clear target for their rage, and this seemed to make them even angrier. Their children adopted their anger, but finding themselves in a middle-class environment were confused as to where they should direct it.

Matt Johnson had a group called The The. 'I felt very angry, like a lot of other people, and I tried to put it into a popular song format.' Matt's words were personal, and just like Paul Weller's with the Style Council, they were much angrier than his music. Somehow this seemed to render them suitable for serious consideration by the critics. But whenever anyone makes a list of the greatest hit songs, the number that seem to have arisen from commercial motivation always seem to outnumber the others. Paul McCartney admits that in the early days he and John Lennon were able to knock things out without too much inspiration. Their stimulus would be the money they could make from a new song. 'John and I literally used to sit down and say, "Now, let's write a swimming pool."'

Surprisingly, even the ultra-credible Van Morrison admits that when he's writing a song, 'I'm making it for the marketplace.' Even more commercially minded are the Bee Gees. 'We never completely do a song just to please ourselves. We bring everybody we can into the studio, even the receptionist, so that we can get their opinions. We put about 30 per cent of what we consider to be art into our records, and about 70 per cent of it is writing for the public.'

Writing for pop success forces most writers to refine their lyrics until they become ambiguous. The Pet Shop Boys wrote great lyrics simply because their experience, coming from being gay, had to be made ambiguous and in line with everyone else's. They found words to describe their own experience that could be interpreted differently by each listener. That's what great pop writing is about. And it's why more *pop* songs have become classics than *rock* songs. Rock stars have the freedom to write songs that are blatantly to the point and self-indulgent, which usually makes them less commercial. During the punk era, Dire Straits encountered the ultimate example of such a song when they were booked to play an outdoor festival. Mark Knopfler was tuning up in the dressing room as the first punk band went on-stage. 'I heard them shout a lightning-fast "1-2-3-4" as they plunged into the first number. Then the first line of the song boomed out across Deptford – "My old man's a cunt".'

In the sixties, many of the established music publishers felt apprehensive about the growing power of the record companies. At United Artists, Noel Rodgers had worked his way up from plugger to head of the publishing division. Having reached the top, he then had to watch as the record division overtook him. He told me, 'Some of us publishers feel the music industry is being stolen from under our feet.' As a result, many publishers went all out to maximise their profits before their slice of the action was taken away from them altogether. The publisher who did best was Dick James, who grabbed the Beatles. The deal he gave them was sharp even by the standards of the day. Naïvely, Brian Epstein thought it was so good he asked, 'Why are you doing this?'

The answer should have been, 'To get your songs tied up tight so I can squeeze every penny out of them.'

In the UK, it was normal for the publisher to take 15 per cent for his work in collecting the money a song earned, then to split the rest of the income with the writer on a 50-50 basis. The end result was: publisher 57.5 per cent, writer 42.5 per cent. Overseas, the publisher sub-published the song to other publishers who worked on the same basis, except that, having taken 15 per cent for collecting the money, they split the remaining 85 per cent half between themselves and half to the UK publisher. For doing nothing more than paying the cheque into the bank, the UK publisher took 15 per cent of what the foreign publisher submitted, then split the balance 50-50 with the writer. On this basis the end result was: foreign publisher 57.5 per cent, UK publisher 24.5 per cent, writer 18 per cent.

But if the UK publisher happened to own the foreign publishing company the split for royalties coming from overseas would be: UK publisher 82 per cent, writer 18 per cent. Music lawyer Irving David explains, 'Most established UK publishers owned and controlled their overseas affiliates and so were, effectively, retaining the lion's share of the publishing income by applying the so-called "salami principle" – the writer got paid after everyone else had taken a slice.'

To writers, this seemed endlessly unfair. Ray Davies of the Kinks wrote a song about it in which he named everyone in the circle of managers and publishers who made money from his songwriting. None of them sued for libel, instead they just took their cut on this song, just as they had on all the others.

Writing songs for stars who themselves are not writers must surely be the easiest job in the music industry. As a songwriter you have no tour schedules, no interviews, no A&R men to tell you what to do. You can get up when you like, work when you want and write whatever songs you fancy.

In the sixties, the idea of writing a song for a particular singer was less common than nowadays. Mostly, writers wrote songs they liked the sound of and decided later who they should give them to. Songs often came about by accident, like when Albert Hammond's songwriting partner was reading out titles of books trying to give Albert some inspiration. When he read out '*The Railways of Southern Califonia*', Albert heard it as '*It never rains in Southern California*'.

Mitch Murray tells how he wrote a song called 'How Do You Do What You Do To Me'. He gave it to EMI's top A&R man, George Martin. 'George was looking for a song for a new group he'd signed called the Beatles. But John Lennon didn't like the song, so when they recorded it they deliberately screwed it up. So Brian Epstein gave it to Gerry and the Pacemakers who had a No. 1 hit with it.

Mitch also had a No. 1 with Georgie Fame's 'Bonnie And Clyde'. 'Pete Callander and I saw the film of *Bonnie and Clyde* and I said, "They blew it – they should have had a No. 1 hit from that film." So we gave them one.'

The most successful writing team of the sixties was Barry Mason and Les Reed. Les remembers, 'One Sunday afternoon we wrote "I'm Coming Home" for Tom Jones, "Everybody Knows" for Dave Clark, and "The Last Waltz" for Engelbert.' A couple of million pounds before tea-time.

In the seventies, the two biggest songwriting teams were Roger Cook with Roger Greenaway, and Nicky Chinn with Mike Chapman. Nick and Mike wrote glam rock songs for most of the glam rock artists while the two Rogers wrote mainstream ballads for artists like the New Seekers and Blue Mink. But it was the eighties that produced the most successful songwriting team ever. From 1984 until the end of the decade, the songs of Stock Aitken Waterman gave British pop its primary identity.

Pete Waterman had been a DJ in the north of England. He is a good-natured down-to-earth man, stocky and slightly scruffy, who looks like he might run a pub or own a sandwich bar. Years of watching people dance had taught Pete what the ordinary person wanted from dance music. 'I'm a Motown fanatic,' he explains, 'so I found myself highly in demand in gay clubs. And it was always the same old story. They wanted a familiar song with a solid four-to-the-bar bass drum.'

Most of the gay clubs had dance-floor lights that were automatically activated by the sounds from the record that was playing. When Pete teamed up with Mike Stock and Matt Aitken they worked on activating these lights to the maximum thus making their records seem more exciting than other people's. Pete explained, 'It was all done with handclaps and cowbells. We put in sharp sounds that cut through – bits of percussion, with a lot of top – and played them frequently and fast, triplets and things like that. If you got it right, you could make the lights go crazy. We cut the bass frequencies down and put what the bass guitar was playing into a higher frequency range. That gave our records more volume too. When one of our records came on, it was louder than the previous one, and the lights would go off like fireworks.'

To begin with Stock Aitken Waterman concentrated on high-energy tracks for the gay market at more than average tempos, mainly remakes of old Motown songs. But having set up shop specifically for that market, they soon found a broader public for what they were doing. Almost effortlessly, they began to turn out hit after hit. First they took on Bananarama, three charming girls who weren't the world's greatest singers and had to play gigs by lip-synching to tapes; then Sinitta; then Mel & Kim; then Rick Astley, a nineteen-year-old tape-operator who reached No. 1 in America even though he sang as if he was gargling. Biggest of all was Kylie Minogue, an Australian soap-opera star whom a British critic described as a 'prancing, dancing antiseptic swab', and Jason Donovan, who sued a magazine for suggesting he was a hypocrite for denying that he was gay. When Donovan won the case and proved he was straight, his popularity declined sharply.

Pete Waterman revelled in his success and loved provoking the rest of the industry by rubbing their noses in it. And he was always ready to oblige the press with a quote that would upset the people in the industry who considered songwriting a serious art. 'What makes a hit record isn't its chart position,' he'd insist. 'What makes a hit record is cash. When you see a cheque come in your bank for a million quid you know that's a real hit.'

Pete, Mike and Matt had started out just to be producers, but they'd soon found it easier to write the songs than to go looking for them. They wrote to a formula that was dictated by their production techniques, and this meant that every song they wrote would be perfectly produced. Soon their writing had become the mainstay of their success but because the songs that pushed the trivial artists whom they produced to the top of the charts came from formula songwriting, many people in the industry put them down. They felt that hit songs should be created with blood, sweat and tears, so they booed when Stock Aitken Waterman went onto the stage to receive their third Ivor Novello award.

Writers who struggled for months to write hits were cheered, even when their songs were of no greater merit. Stock Aitken Waterman preferred to go straight to it without wasting time.

In the music industry there are two copyrights. One is owned by the music publisher and is the copyright of the song performed. The other is owned by the record company and is the copyright of the actual recorded performance.

When Sir George Martin started in the business record companies didn't think of the recordings as having a long-term value. 'Records were made for the moment only. Profits were thought of in terms of an instant mark-up on the manufacturing cost. Song copyrights belonged to the publishers, and not only did nobody in record companies realise their real value, they didn't even realise the value of the new copyrights they were creating by having artists record the songs.'

When record companies started releasing 'Greatest Hits' albums in the mid-seventies, they soon came to realise the value of the recording copyrights they owned. After that, it wasn't long before they started turning their attention to the other copyright – the song copyright owned by the music publishers. Increasingly, major record companies came to resent paying publishers a royalty for their ownership of the song copyright. They began to use large chunks of their profits to buy up publishers and turn themselves into conglomerate record and publishing companies, thus picking up both sets of copyright royalties. Most of the majors already had their own small publishing companies but now they started to buy up the big publishing houses and assimilate them. By the eighties, the biggest music publishers were the record companies.

In the past, music publishers had worked closely with their writers. They helped them develop their songs, made suggestions and then went out and found singers to sing them. But by the eighties the largest publishing companies, now owned by record companies, had virtually stopped helping in this way. They were simply 'buying' writers – giving them advance payments deductible from future royalties and then leaving them to find their own way of writing and exploiting their songs.

The total songwriting earnings from a good-sized worldwide hit could be around £300,000. If an album followed with two or three more hit singles the earnings could be quadrupled. By investing £20,000 in a songwriter at an early stage in his career, a publisher might make millions when the writer had international success. It was a much lower investment than record companies had to make.

But there was a new and insidious habit creeping into the publishing side of the industry. For fixing a deal or for getting a song recorded, someone who helped in the process would demand a share of the songwriting income. The most common situation was for well-known artists to demand a share of the writer's income if they were to record an unknown song. Most writers complained bitterly, but many artists felt justified in their demand. They argued that many songs would have remained unknown if life hadn't first been given to them by a perfect performance.

While most songwriters are cautious of sharing their talents some, thankfully, have been quite the opposite. When Simon

Climie was writing 'I Knew You Were Waiting' for George Michael and Aretha Franklin, he was stuck for a word. The chorus ran, 'Though the river was deep – I didn't ...'

Whatever word Simon tried putting next, it seemed to make the chorus fall flat. From the studio in Detroit he phoned his old friend Don Black, one of Britain's greatest and longest serving songwriters. In a flash Don had given him the word 'falter'. It was this word, as much as anything else, that made the song work, but Don asked for no credit. It was a present from one great songwriter to another.

Sometimes songwriters are less generous to each other. In the mid-seventies George Harrison ended up in court accused of having copied 'He's So Fine', a song first recorded by the Chiffons and written by Ronald Mack. George Harrison's version was 'My Sweet Lord'. The problem was not just that the melody was similar, it was that the musical arrangement was equally so. This made Harrison's song seem even more like the original.

In cases like these, the defence team usually wheel in a musicologist. Seventy years after the death of a songwriter, all the material he ever wrote passes into the public domain – anyone can use it and call it their own. So the job of the musicologist is to confirm that the claimant's melody has indeed been stolen, not just by the defendant, but by the claimant too. 'It was never his in the first place,' the musicologist explains. 'It was the cello counterpoint in the third movement of Saint-Saëns' second symphony, which is now out of copyright.'

Music lawyer Irving David explains, 'The theft is not disproved, it's simply reapplied to something that's there for the taking because it's in the public domain. Both the claimant and the defendant have the right to steal it, and would appear to have done so, though it's possible that neither of them had ever heard the piece of music from which their respective themes originated.'

In George Harrison's case, the musicologist's defence didn't help. The judge ruled that Harrison was guilty of copyright infringement but conceded that it had not been deliberate. George was mystified. 'I still don't understand how the courts aren't filled with similar cases – as 99 per cent of the popular music that can be heard is reminiscent of something or other.'

In the British music business there has always been great importance put on the word 'credible'. From time to time its meaning has changed but usually it has meant that a singer, his performance or his song, has had some element of integrity about it that has set it apart from other more cynically produced commercial music. At the beginning of rock 'n' roll, 'credible' simply meant being young and full of energy. When it became obvious that those qualities were being hijacked by record companies in order to make profits, artists had to show some element of difference or dissent in order to be called 'credible'. The first real step towards achieving that status was to write your own songs. When everybody started doing it, 'credible' began to be applied only to singer-songwriters who transcended the limits of pure pop. The Beatles were 'credible', but sometimes only just. The Rolling Stones were the epitome of it, though in the late seventies even they teetered on the brink when they made a four-to-the-floor disco record.

In the glam era, Bolan was 'cred' only to start with while Bowie was never anything else. Elton started out with little credibility but earned it through the sheer bravado of his outrageous American shows.

In the punk era, the word 'credible' got tied up with the word 'street'. 'Street' and 'cred' were usually interchangeable but sometimes there were subtle fluctuations in meaning. Everyone was 'credible' providing they did amphetamine sulphate, but if they also spat and swore they were probably 'street-cred'.

New Romantics were considered 'street-cred' if they'd started out at the Blitz club or did drugs, like Visage or Culture Club. But if their claim to fame was simply to make classy music outside of the pop mainstream they would be termed 'credible', like Japan or the Eurythmics. If, like Kajagoogoo or Sigue Sigue Sputnik, their image was based on funny haircuts, even copious drug use and classy music would be unable to restore them to 'cred' status.

In the mid-eighties, the ultimate in 'non-cred' was to be associated with the country's biggest hit-makers, Stock Aitken Waterman. Their songs were simply too catchy and too easily remembered. In a backlash to their success, many artists decided that the best route to credibity was to write their own songs but avoid catchy choruses. This would make it immediately apparent they weren't pandering to the lowest common denominator of public taste. As a result, the charts were filled with dull groups like Fairground Attraction, Aztec Camera, the Christians, Everything But the Girl, Curiosity Killed the Cat and Johnny Hates Jazz. For these groups, the trick was to write songs that could be hits while avoiding being truly memorable.

Other artists, unable to resist the lure of good pop tunes, had to find different ways of establishing their 'cred' status. Taking up social issues was one, being black was another, being gay might help and so could being thoroughly boring.

Erasure were a gay/straight duo. They wrote tuneful Italian-type ballads which they sang to a fast techno beat. Journalists dubbed the duo 'credible' simply because of the sheer banality of their stage performance. It was so bad that it led critics to think their songs must have some hidden meaning, as if they were allegorical comments on urban life.

With the media deciding on such tenuous grounds which artists were fit to be called 'credible', it was surprising to find lots of good words written about two new British rock bands, Iron Maiden and Def Leppard. Both these groups wrote their own songs and had their primary success in America, but what gave them their 'cred' status was the circus-like quality of their stage shows. They played heavy metal with a tongue-in-cheek attitude. The sheer extravagance of the sets seemed to suggest they were parodying heavy metal rather than endorsing it. By the mid-eighties British music critics were tying themselves in knots over what was credible and what wasn't. By then, most of them perceived heavy metal as something of a joke, so groups that parodied were surely making a serious statement.

There were three other writer-artists in the mid-eighties whose credibility the music media considered impeccable. Chris Rea, playing the same gentle rock music he'd always played, suddenly found himself becoming fashionable late in his career. Robert Palmer became credible by making the coolest video seen to date – five exquisite female mannequins performing as his band, filmed by fashion photographer Terence Donovan. And Simply Red – a new group who wrote and played perfect soul ballads – managed to perform them without the slightest hint of star quality, which in an age of great flamboyance from other artists confirmed them as the epitomy of 'cred'.

But despite the 'cred' label stuck on them by the industry media, not one of these artists came near to creating songs anywhere near as memorable as those created by the totally 'non-cred' team of Stock Aitken Waterman.

For whatever reasons songs are conceived, once they've been written, their writers like to feel they're getting a fair deal from their publishers. In 1995, Elton decided this wasn't the case. He took his publisher to court and sued for the return of his copyrights.

His publisher was Dick James. At the time Elton originally signed with him it was normal for the publisher to take the writer's songs for the life of the copyright. Elton's contract to supply Dick James Music with songs would eventually come to an end. But all the songs he'd given the company during the period of his contract would remain the company's property until seventy years after Elton John had died. Elton didn't want to wait that long and in 1986 he went to court to get them back.

Elton based his case on the fact that Dick James had operated the standard sixties scam of dividing the royalties in half twice, sub-publishing songs to his own subsidiary companies in other countries on a 50-50 basis. But Elton didn't sue for the money skimmed from him in this fashion, he sued for the return of his songs which had been assigned to Dick James for 'life of copyright'.

In the eighties, publishing deals were still frequently very one-sided. Sting once said, 'Any artist worth his salt has arrogance.' He then revealed the degree of his own arrogance by suing Virgin Music for signing him to a publishing contract which he said was 'onerous and unfair'. After a few days in court it was revealed that the publishing contract with which Virgin signed Sting, and which he claimed was unfair, was almost the same as the one that he was using to sign new writers to his own publishing company.

Sting and Virgin settled out of court. In Elton's case, Dick James won, but shortly after the court case he died of a heart attack.

Dick had once been a pop singer himself and was a jovial man, much liked by everyone who dealt with him, yet as he grew older he simply couldn't understand the changes that had taken place in the industry. In the early seventies he agreed to pay an advance to Junior, my Spanish singer-songwriter, in return for a publishing agreement. The day I took Junior to sign the agreement, Dick was sitting in a huge leather chair, looking well-fed and jovial. His offices left little doubt as to his success as a music publisher, they were lavish, and the walls were covered in gold records. It was just ten years since he'd signed the Beatles from whom he'd made his first ten million or so, and five years since he'd signed Elton John from whom he'd made at least the same amount again. From these young artists, Dick had made himself seriously rich by doing little more than persuading them to sign their names at the bottom of a difficult-to-understand publishing agreement.

As my Spanish songwriter was signing his contract, Dick turned to me in all seriousness and said, 'I think it's about time I had another bit of luck.'

CHAPTER TWENTY-TWO

ADDICTED TO ATTENTION

From the beginning, I saw getting publicity for my stars as one of the primary functions of being a manager. In this I'd been well-trained in the sixties by the likes of Andrew Oldham and Kit Lambert. The problem was knowing where to draw the line.

An artist's craving for attention is the fuel that drives the entertainment business. Without this underlying craving, there would be no stars. But that doesn't mean all stars live easily with their addiction to attention. Some revel in it right from the beginning. Others are confused by it. They resent it, suppress it, deny it or reject it. But if they succeed in this, they'll no longer be stars.

Successful, mature stars are those who have come to terms with their craving for publicity and learned to harness it for their own success. On the way to such maturity, many young stars find themselves confused by their desire for media attention – they want the limelight but feel unworthy of it. Their addiction to attention throws up all the classic love-hate confusions of any addict for his or her source of addiction. Publicity addicts often show enormous aggression towards the journalists whose attention they crave. The journalists have effectively become their drug dealers – desperately needed, but also despised. But like addicts of every type, those who are addicted to attention know how bad the world can look on a day when their dealer doesn't show up.

To Boy George the world looked good, especially when he first saw himself on the front page of a newspaper.

John Reid, Elton John's manager, once described taking his first sniff of cocaine. 'I was very apprehensive, but I took it, and it was an instant falling in love.'

And that's what happened to Boy George when he got his first sniff of the press. He became instantly addicted.

Dr Mark Griffiths, a psychologist at Nottingham Trent University, defines addiction as an activity that takes over somebody's life. 'They will do it to the neglect of everything else, they get withdrawal symptoms if they can't do it. They build a tolerance zone in time, needing more and more of that activity or substance ...'

That was Boy George. Everything he did had to be done with the media on hand, he could get himself into the papers just by washing his hands. 'I knew that if I walked into the ladies' toilet that would make the *Sun* – so I did it.'

From the moment Culture Club had their first hit, George was constantly pushing for more and more column inches. Jon Moss, the group's drummer, was less appreciative of the media's attention. He and George were having an affair, but George was effectively cheating on him by having a simultaneous affair with the media.

Surprisingly, the press made little of Boy George's romance with Jon. Perhaps they thought the public wouldn't like it, or maybe they just didn't notice it. Nevertheless, Jon felt their romance was being conducted under the gaze of the media, and for him it became intolerable. Soon he found himself endlessly squabbling and bitching with George. Then they got violent. Jon hit George with a hammer. George drove over to Jon's house and smashed his car through Jon's brand new electric garage doors.

After that, the couple stopped seeing each other except for business. As a result, George allowed his input of drugs to shoot up. At a photo-shoot in Paris, while the models were taking a break with cocaine, the photographer slipped Boy George some heroin – his first ever. He sniffed it and vomited, but inside of a month he was using a gram a week.

Unlike ecstasy which opens doors of perception and exaggerates physical and mental sensations, heroin simply puts its user inside a beautiful feelingless bubble. Most users get hooked on it in order to escape a wretched existence, which for rock artists often means normal life as compared with being on-stage. For someone as full of life as Boy George, the drug seemed unsuited to his personality, but it had grabbed hold of him during a period of weakness. He admits to having felt guilty at achieving success beyond his own estimation of his self-worth, and then there was the break-up with Jon Moss.

Strangely, there is little evidence that heroin causes serious physical problems in itself. The problems stem mainly from the bad company that addicts keep. And in George's case it wasn't just a matter of being hooked on heroin, he was also being urged by his friends to indulge in just about every other drug. 'As well as smack, coke and spliff, we were starting to take lots of different pills, Valium, Rohypnol, Temazepam, DFs and Temgesics – all downers of one kind or another. The pills came on prescription, or off other junkies. Sometimes we used them for withdrawal, but more often as another way of getting high, defying the warnings not to mix them with alcohol. Getting and taking drugs was a sport, no less dangerous than joy-riding or surfing on the roofs of trains.'

And all the while the press were close at hand.

Bob Dylan once gave a warning to all publicity-seeking

rock stars. 'Being noticed can be a burden. Jesus got himself crucified because he got himself noticed.'

For Boy George it seemed inevitable. In due course he would be crucified ...

Time after time, artists will tell you that their first musical experience was when they were four or five years old, at a party or with a group of adults. They sang something and the grown-ups applauded. They were kids, craving attention, and music got it for them.

Watch any contemporary pop star on-stage, running to one side, leaning over to sing lines to the adoring audience, running back to the other side, preening themselves to sing another line, pointing the mike towards the crowd, offering them a line to sing. Think of a cute little boy showing off in front of a group of fawning adults and that's what you have. Bono, Jagger, George Michael, Boy George, Robbie Williams, you name it – what you are watching is little boys showing off. The difference is simply that over the last forty years it has been developed into an artform.

'I've reported on pop and rock stars for twenty years,' says John Blake, 'and really they're just kids showing off. They're like little kids in a swimming pool who shout to their mum and dad "Watch me, watch me" before they jump in the water. Let's face it, secure well-balanced adults don't need to get on-stage and shout "Watch me, watch me" to an audience of 50,000.'

In the late sixties, Billy Gaff, who later managed Rod Stewart, worked for Robert Stigwood's company as a record plugger. Robert asked him if he would like to become Cream's tour manager.

'What would I have to do?' asked Gaff.

'Have you ever looked after children?' Robert asked him.

Kids showing off will do anything to get attention. The Who smashed their guitars – the Stones dressed up as their mothers and pissed against walls – Marc Bolan covered himself with glitter – David Bowie performed oral sex on-stage with the neck of a guitar – the Sex Pistols vomited at airports and spat at their audience – ABC wore belts of dildos round their waists. But Boy George outdid them all. He dropped in and out of heroin addiction in full public view.

It was the *Daily Mirror* that started it. On the front page they accused Boy George of selling drugs to a photographer, 'Another Rock 'n' Roll Tragedy'. For some years, George's father, Jerry O'Dowd, had been finding it increasingly difficult to make George listen to anything he had to say. Now, watching him sink into heroin addiction, Mr O'Dowd decided to communicate with his son in the one way he knew George would understand – through the press. In an effort to bring him to his senses, George's father called the *Sun* and offered them a story.

Two days later, there it was in two-inch headlines: 'Junkie George Has Eight Weeks To Live'.

Within days, the entire press, both tabloid and broadsheet, had made it their most important ongoing story. To Jon Moss, this confirmed what he'd thought – the press were as addicted to George as George was to them. 'When they discovered he was a junkie, it gave them a whole new angle. And they went completely mad for it.'

George was charged with possession of heroin and fined £250. He tried to explain his downfall to the media. 'The thing that drives people to become celebrities is this need for overwhelming love. Often, when they get the fame they crave, they feel they don't deserve it. So they screw up.'

But things had hardly started. Shortly afterwards, Boy George's friend, Michael Rudetsky, died of a heroin overdose at George's house. George went into a deep depression. He flew to Montserrat, recorded some songs and got even deeper into drugs. When he came back to London, another friend died and he sank even lower.

At Christmas his mother arrived at his house in Hampstead and saw a photographer outside.

'What do you want?' she demanded.

'I'm waiting for George to die,' he told her.

The list of rock and pop stars who have been addicted to heroin is almost as long as the list of stars itself, but George was the first to have his addiction followed by the media, fix by fix.

John Blake admits, 'It was me that started the whole thing with that first headline in the *Mirror*. George never forgave me, which was a pity because I liked him. I suppose I could have pretended that by running the story we were setting him on the path to recovery, but that wouldn't have been true. It was just a great story – and for a tabloid journalist like me, it was just too good to pass up.'

Boy George's addiction to attention meant he simply couldn't stop himself from doing things that got him exposure in the press. It could be as simple as wearing a silly hat or as serious as admitting to drug addiction. But in the end it was this same need for media attention that gave him the strength to kick his heroin habit. He realised how much exposure the press would give him if he managed it and the thought of it was irresistible.

Like most rock artists addicted to heroin, when Boy George talked of kicking his drug habit, he only meant heroin. To help him kick it he used alcohol, ecstasy, marijuana, barbiturates, methadone, amphetamine and Buddhism. But most of all he used publicity.

For a manager, manipulating the press into giving their star vast column inches can become as addictive as it is for the artist. As Wham!'s manager it went further than that – quite frequently the publicity was focused on me rather than the group. I found myself on the managers' chat-show circuit, frequently bumping into Malcolm McLaren who was still living on the fading glory of the Sex Pistols. For me, the purpose of a TV interview was to take the risk of exposing yourself for real, which could be genuinely exciting. Malcolm thought the point was to pull a great con trick.

On one occasion I did *The Ruby Wax Show* with him. In the dressing-room he sipped white wine and talked animatedly. A few days earlier I'd been in the studio with him when he was recording Jeff Beck's guitar counterpointing with an opera singer. Now we discussed it, and everything he had to say was stimulating and provocative. But once he was on camera and joined me on Ruby's interview couch he flopped down, appearing to be stoned out of his head, and talked rubbish. 'Yeah, well Ruby, it's like, er, you know, it's difficult for me, er, to get me 'ead round it.' Yet at that time Malcolm was not only making a fascinating album of opera classics mixed with dance and rock, he was also heading the creative department of one of Hollywood's biggest film studios. The real Malcolm McLaren was permanently interesting. The one he chose to present to the public was usually a bore. But that's what happens to people when they're constantly seeking attention.

Elvis Costello admits to being fascinated by the way people become addicted to fame. 'It's funny to watch someone go through that moment when they want to be real, the moment when they resist fame, and the moment when they give in to it.'

For the music industry it's essential that stars give in to it. A recording artist's need for a daily fix of headlines is the primary motivation for continuing to record and perform. Since the beginning of rock 'n' roll the ultimate aim of every performer has been to be watched and admired. Keith Richards remembers posing in front of the mirror at home. 'I was hopeful. The only thing I was lacking was a bit of bread to buy an instrument. But I got the moves off first, and I got the guitar later.'

David Bowie made it clear that for him stardom was the necessity and music just the means of achieving it. 'I honestly feel there is something incredibly lacking in my life. I've always been keen on being accepted. I want to make a mark.'

In the nineteenth century, Sigmund Freud got near the real truth about the artistic temperament. 'The artist has also an introverted disposition and has not far to go to become neurotic. He is one who is urged on by his instinctual needs which are too clamorous.'

Most artists seem to suffer from a deep insecurity. Before they walk out on-stage, their insecurity makes them terrified of what they are about to do, but it's also the thing that drives them to do it. Endlessly, like kids showing off, they have to prove and re-prove that they can gain people's attention and love. Elton John admits, 'It's my desperate craving for affection.'

From Michael Jackson to Sinead O'Connor, well-known artists have told of being unloved as children. But when they're on-stage, the audience gives these unloved children the affection they've always craved. In doing so it often encourages them to stay emotionally immature and unable to deal with the real world.

The mid-eighties had its usual share of newcomers searching for the public's attention but no one did it more modestly and with better music than the Pet Shop Boys.

In 1984, when I was in Miami for the filming of George Michael's video of 'Careless Whisper', Neil Tennant was there as a journalist for *Smash Hits* and asked me to listen to a tape. Among the people who've given me tapes to listen to there have been taxi drivers, immigration officers, bank managers, doctors, a policeman who stopped me for speeding and a beggar sitting in a doorway with his dog. But for some reason I was very shirty with Neil and refused to listen (I think I was annoyed that a journalist, having been given access to the band, should use it to bother me). Later, having been totally scathing about the possibility of his becoming a pop star, I regretted it. My regret at failing to listen to his tape was nothing to do with wanting to be his manager, it was because the Pet Shop Boys' music was everything I liked – lyrical, cool, intelligent, direct yet complex. The singing, which was laughed at by many people, was perfection – disenfranchised but coolly impassioned. The Pet Shop Boys album *Please* was the first time I'd heard music that demanded to be called 'pop', while simultaneously being recognisable as 'art' – like Lichtenstein's paintings.

A little while later Dusty Springfield arrived in my office and I gave her equally short shrift. Later, I regretted that too.

Dusty said she was unhappy with Vicki Wickham, her manager of fifteen years. Would I manage her?

Vicki was my oldest friend, so to put the idea instantly out of Dusty's head I told her bluntly she was far too old.

'But I'm in my prime,' she protested, shocked. 'I have offers coming in from everywhere. Even the Pet Shop Boys want me to record with them.'

'Listen,' I told her. 'It's about time you faced the facts. If you weren't a dyke, you'd probably be a grandmother by now.'

She left the office in a storm and went straight back to Vicki, which is what I'd hoped she would do. But I felt bad about it. Dusty was having a bad time and wasn't feeling confident about herself. I was rude and it may have crushed her confidence one bit further. Fortunately though, the Pet Shop Boys helped her rebuild it when they asked her to sing on 'What Have I Done To Deserve This?'

In the studio, Dusty asked Neil Tennant, 'How do you want me to sound?'

'Like Dusty Springfield,' he told her.

And magically, she did.

In the autumn of 1985, Wham! agreed to attend that year's CBS conference at Eastbourne. We went by helicopter from Battersea, and left late because George was upset that there was only one pilot. He'd previously said he would only fly by helicopter if there were two pilots.

It was a four-seater with George and Andrew sitting in the back. I sat in the front with the pilot and we'd hardly set off when he told me he was lost. He pulled a road map from a glove compartment and shoved it into my hands. 'We should be following the A22 – look down below, then try to match it with the map.'

Then he had another problem. It was too dark. 'We've only got half an hour. You see that cloud in front – we'll have to fly above it. If when we get there we can't find a hole in the cloud to come down through, we'll have to come back. But by then it will be too dark so we won't be able to come back.'

He pulled over the clouds and went straight ahead. Fifteen minutes later we saw a hole in the cloud and the pilot went straight through it and landed. As he opened the cockpit a horde of children came running towards the helicopter. Wham!, the most wanted group in the UK, travelling with no security, had just landed in the middle of a school playing field.

Later that evening I went back to London with George in a limousine. On the way he said, 'At the end of the year, there'll be no more Wham!. If you want to manage me when I go solo, you'll have to get rid of Jazz.'

I'd already decided, after Wham! broke up, I wouldn't go on working with Jazz. Even though we were great friends I preferred the freedom of working alone. But I didn't want that imposed on me by someone else. So when George told me I should get rid of Jazz, I told him we worked only as a pair. In doing so, I effectively ruled out managing George after Wham! broke up, so I persuaded Jazz we should find a way of selling our management company and taking a profit on what we'd achieved.

In his book *Bare*, George commented on this and said, 'he must have been crazy'. But that presumed I enjoyed being his manager. What he failed to understand was that once I'd pulled off the deal for Wham! to play in China, it was no longer fun. It was a permanent scramble to keep Wham! going against George's will. There was no reason to believe that managing him as an individual would be any more enjoyable.

We sold our management business to a public media company fronted by our UK promoter, Harvey Goldsmith. Unfortunately, although the company was public, it turned out that the largest shareholder was Sol Kerzner who owned Sun City, at that time a target for anti-apartheid feeling across America. American showbusiness newspapers got hold of the story and chastised George for allowing a percentage of his earnings to go towards a company they claimed had links with apartheid.

George dismissed us and from there on things fizzled towards a finish. Although we were no longer Wham!'s managers, there wasn't anything left to manage anyway, they were breaking up. But first there was to be one last concert at Wembley – 'The Final'.

George politely invited us, and politely we went.

So, did I know George was gay?

The answer is no – I hadn't a clue. I saw no reason to investigate the matter. If he'd wished to talk about his sexuality, it wouldn't have been difficult – after all, he knew I was gay.

I'd occasionally heard bitchy rumours from people about George, but those are the sort of things you hear endlessly, both in the gay world and in showbusiness. As far as I was concerned, sexuality was not something you discussed with your artists unless they chose to make it a specific part of their songs or imagery, and George had clearly split himself into two – the public George and the private one. As a result there was no more reason to ask him about his sexuality than there was the tour manager, the sound man or my dentist. Sexuality, I thought, should be private unless a person wishes to make it public, though you could never persuade a tabloid newspaper of that, especially the *Daily Mail*.

Around that time, the *Mail* printed excerpts from Albert Goldman's new book on John Lennon. In the piece they mentioned Brian Epstein and said he was gay. They also printed a photograph of me, under which, to be safe from libel (so they thought), they printed the words 'Simon Napier-Bell, who is *not* homosexual'.

I thought it looked as if I'd asked them to do it, as if I was covering something up, so I went to see my lawyer and we decided to sue for libel. A little way into preparing for the case my lawyer asked, 'I've got to ask you something rather personal – have you ever had sex with girls?'

'Of course,' I told him. 'But that doesn't stop me being primarily gay, does it?'

He looked despondent. 'They'll wheel them into court and say it proves you're *not* homosexual. We'll be humiliated.'

So we had to pull out of the case.

Elton John also had a libel case with the tabloids.

Some years previously, Elton had announced, 'There's nothing wrong with going to bed with somebody of your own sex.' Thereafter, whenever he sat in the directors' box at Watford Football Club, the crowd chanted 'Elton's a poofter'. On 25 Februrary 1987, the *Sun* decided to join the football mob and ran a front-page headline announcing, 'Elton Boys Scandal'.

Graham X had 'confessed' to supplying teenage boys to Elton John. Mr X claimed the youngsters were 'paid a minimum of £100 each plus all the cocaine they could stand'.

Elton sued for libel. The *Sun* printed more details and Elton sued again. Altogether there were seventeen writs.

Elton's initial argument was that a newspaper had no right to intrude into his private life. But lawyers don't like philosophical arguments of that type, so instead they focused on the fact that the *Sun* had got their dates wrong.

Elton told the *Daily Express*, 'They can say I'm a fat old sod, they can say I'm an untalented bastard, they can call me a poof, but they mustn't lie about me.' Then he told journalist John Blake of the *Daily Mirror*, 'I couldn't have done the things they said I did because I was in America, but I don't know how to prove it.'

John says, 'In the Elton case, I was the good guy. I got hold of British Airways flight records and got him the proof he wanted. Then the *Mirror* ran a headline saying the *Sun* had got it wrong.'

The *Sun* fought back with photos taken ten years earlier at a party – one picture, they said, was 'too disgusting to print in a family newspaper'.

The *Sun* had underestimated the genuine affection that their readers felt for Elton. He'd had pink hair long before Johnny Rotten, been the first rock star to play the Soviet Union, was a friend of Princess Diana and a passionate football fan who would fly thousands of miles to see Watford play regular league games. Incredibly, people stopped buying the paper. In just a few weeks the *Sun* lost 200,000 in circulation.

In December the *Sun* said 'Sorry Elton', and climbed down with the first libel apology ever to run as a front-page headline. It finished off, 'We are delighted that the *Sun* and Elton have become friends again.'

For his part Elton said, 'Life is too short to bear grudges,' and graciously accepted a million pounds in damages.

John Blake saw the deal as important. 'Elton did everyone a favour. He got himself a stack of money, bloodied the *Sun*'s nose, and made all of us journalists a lot more careful about peering into the private lives of famous people.'

After the Elton fiasco, the *Sun* recruited gossip journalist Rick Sky from the *Star* specifically 'to make friends with the pop world'. Almost at once, Rick made an enemy of George Michael.

'George was so secretive. I was told to get a story from him, but ever since the Wham! days George had refused to talk to the *Sun*. I tried calling him at his home but he told me to fuck off and slammed the phone down. So I wrote, "Today I called George at his London flat and he poured his heart out to me." Then I used quotes from interviews he'd given some other journalists. That was the normal way we did things in the tabloids.'

George Michael's need for attention was more ambivalent than Elton's or Boy George's. It wasn't just column inches that he wanted; he wanted to establish his self-worth. To some people this made him seem overly self-important, but no matter, it gave him his emotional drive.

He was struggling with the problem of how to present himself to the public as an individual rather than as half of Wham!. Really, he wanted to be as much his real self as he could, but in the end he invented a new persona to hide behind – George Michael, mark II. To the press, it was a puzzle. He seemed to want publicity, yet rejected it – he courted it, then fought it off. One thing they picked up for sure – George Michael and Boy George were having a running battle of words.

Boy George intimated there was a gay side to George Michael's character. For gays who felt their sexuality was a private matter, Boy George was a nightmare, the homosexual equivalent of a lager lout. To them, he could no more be termed typically gay than an English football fan in full vomit could be termed typically straight.

When George Michael was making his video for 'Careless Whisper' in Miami, Culture Club was playing a gig at the local stadium. George asked me if I could arrange for him to go. I called Boy George's tour manager and left a message, saying I'd pop down later to pick up a couple of passes for George. It never occurred to me he'd refuse, but when I drove over to pick them up, there was a message from Boy George saying 'no way'.

Sting once said, 'When you're a rock star you're allowed to be a petulant child ...' Boy George could be that all too easily, but he could also be very funny. When George Michael claimed a certain girl had broken his heart, Boy George said: 'That girl's a fag-hag, everyone knows it. She shared a flat with me once. She broke my Hoover, not my heart.'

Quotes like that made sure the press were never far away, and despite everything he'd been through with journalists, Boy George still liked having them there. Other artists have found it less comfortable. Simon Le Bon complained, 'It's very out of proportion that my haircut got front page next to 30,000 people dying in an Indian disaster. It makes me quite sick.'

Elvis Costello insisted more directly, 'When I'm not working, people should keep their fucking noses out of my life.'

Mick Jagger by this stage had been in the business longer

than all of them. He had none of Costello's anger. Rather, he'd grown sick and tired of the whole game. 'It's wearing. You're on all the time ... With all this attention, you become like a child. It's awful to be at the centre of attention. You can't talk about anything apart from your own experience, your own dopey life.'

As they grow older, many pop and rock musicians seem to grow increasingly shy of their obsessive need for attention. Many of them deny that they have such feelings. Bono of U2 would surely not survive without the benefits of notoriety, yet he seems to persuade himself otherwise. 'There are two definite types of musician who talk to the press. There are those who say "Listen to this wonderful music, aren't I great" and there are those who say "Listen to this wonderful music, isn't it great." We're definitely in the latter.'

Roger Waters of the Pink Floyd came to hate not only the press but his audiences too. He complained they 'were only there for the beer' and saw them as 'one monolithic, insensate, roaring, flailing beast'. Yet he was still there on-stage, still performing for them.

At a show in Montreal, near the front of the crowd, he spotted a particularly devoted fan whose gaze never left his face as he performed. So he seduced him – bit by bit – smiling as he performed, offering him encouragement to push his way through the crowd and come closer to the stage, until eventually the teenager was standing at the very front, ecstatic at having made mental contact with his idol. Then, at the end of the last number, as the song finished, Roger sniffed, hacked, rolled a great gob of mucous from his throat to his mouth and let it fly right in the boy's face.

The object of his anger wasn't really the boy, it was his own self-loathing, the degradation of being addicted to attention. The audience's affection is something all artists crave and many feel guilty about receiving. Marc Almond described the whole experience of being on stage as 'that enormous feeling of energy and adulation from people ... that love rush'. He could have been talking about ecstasy ...

CHAPTER TWENTY-THREE

'E' FOR ENGLAND

It was while I was managing Wham! that I first heard of ecstasy. Over a period of time, I became aware there was a new drug around that caused people who took it to be consumed by a religious fervour for its further promotion, just like acid in the sixties.

The realisation that something new was going on in the drug underground didn't hit everyone in the business simultaneously, it came first to people dealing with pop groups who were happening in the States, particularly those which were into dance music or hanging out in the key New York clubs, most of which were gay. Boy George had latched onto ecstasy early on in New York, and so had Marc Almond and Soft Cell who claimed to have made their first album on it in 1982. So had their weirdo manager, Stevo. All these people were slowly spreading word about it, and for those who'd lived through the acid epidemic of the sixties it was immediately apparent that this drug was somewhat similar. People who took it were inspired into caring for each other and the world in general. It changed their lives and their ability to understand other people's lives (or so they thought).

At first, for seen-it-all cynics like me, E seemed to be nothing amazing. But later that changed. It *was* amazing. The effect the drug had on the teenage population was like that of LSD multiplied a thousand times, and it was because of an added element. Acid had been purely hallucinogenic, ecstasy was a hallucinogenic combined with amphetamine. You didn't just lie back and let your fantasies swirl over you,

you leapt straight into the middle of them and danced like a demon.

Ecstasy is MDMA – methylene-dioxy-meth-amphetamine. It was first synthesised in 1914 and like acid it went through the hands of the CIA before becoming popular. The drug's ability to bond people in friendship made the CIA think it could be an aid to interrogation. It came in the form of a small white pill and was as easy to take as an aspirin.

Journalist Peter Nasmyth perfectly captured the essence of a first-time experience with ecstasy. 'Suddenly I knew I could trust her with my closest secrets ... strange because half an hour before I wouldn't have cared if I never saw her again in my life. I viewed life out of a benign fearlessness – a kind of winter's night, mug-of-Horlicks feeling, "the hug drug".'

A tab of ecstasy not only created empathy and affection for all those around you, it delivered six hours of dance energy. James Horrocks, co-owner of React Records, was one of many people who'd first come across it during summer holidays in Ibiza, where there were three great dance clubs – Amnesia, Ku and Pacha. 'Ecstasy arrived in Ibiza by way of American gays and the hip dance crowd from New York and Miami way back in '82 and '83. Spanish barmen used to slip it in a rum punch they called Coco Loco. At first, the English couldn't understand why they had such a great time whenever they went to Ibiza, they thought it must be the climate or something.'

In the summer of 1987, Brits visiting these clubs had finally worked out what was making them feel so good. The next stage was to bring the Ibiza experience back home. To recreate Ibiza's all-night open-air party atmosphere in the middle of a

British winter should have been impossible, but E overcame the problem.

The first major hangout was a fitness centre's gym near Southwark Bridge, south of the river. Once a week the gym was turned into a disco called Shoom, a word chosen to convey the initial feeling of being hit by ecstasy. The man behind it all was Danny Rampling, a south London soul DJ, who spoke of his experience with ecstasy in Ibiza as if it had been a religious conversion. 'Aquarius was on us, and I wanted to share that with other people.'

The people Danny shared his club with came from all walks of life. Art students and hippies mixed with football hooligans and petty criminals. The crowd took their tabs of E clasping bottles of Lucozade, bubbling over with love and affection for one another. Soon, word got round and aspiring stars of media and fashion began to discover the club too.

At first, the music they danced to was the same sort of happy mixture that had been played on their Balearic holidays. But as time progressed the DJs increasingly incorporated a new type of music into their playlists.

While British holidaymakers had been in Ibiza dancing to everything from 'La Bamba' to Cyndi Lauper, American producers of house and garage records in Chicago and Detroit had been driving round listening to Depeche Mode, New Order and Kraftwerk on their car stereos.

Tony Wilson, who had been the first TV producer to book the Sex Pistols, was now the owner of Factory Records to which New Order were signed. 'People came back from Ibiza turned onto E, but once they got home they found the songs they'd been dancing to on holiday were less easy to dance to without the island atmosphere. So there was this new "E" generation looking for the right music to go with their drug. What they finally found was house and garage music from Detroit and Chicago, which was influenced by Depeche Mode and New Order. The new music started to be played in Manchester on Friday nights at the Hacienda and in Nottingham on Tuesday nights at the Garage, but there was no E in those places. The first person to couple the new music with the new drug was Danny Rampling at Shoom.'

Rampling had stumbled onto something groundbreaking. As people of all types and backgrounds began to discover Shoom and its magic ingredient, Danny realised he'd created the basis for a completely new subculture the likes of which had never been seen before. 'This thing united everyone together. The way I was feeling at that point was the golden age was dawning.'

The new music was soon renamed 'acid house'. At Shoom the flyers asked the question 'Can you pass the acid test?', which was a copy of a flyer given out in California in the sixties by the Merry Pranksters, a group of pagans who turned people on to LSD.

The new music owed a lot to drum machines and samplers which, due to the falling cost of Japanese technology, had recently become affordable for aspiring DJs and musicians. In America, especially in Detroit and Chicago, DJs had used drum machines like the Roland TR-808 to beef up the records they were playing in the underground clubs. It also gave them the opportunity to change records while keeping the beat the same, mixing records and tapes in and out, creating whole new tunes and remixes in the process.

Samplers, like those manufactured by Akai, were machines that could be fed with a short burst of recorded sound and programmed to replay it whenever and wherever the producer wanted. 'Miaoow' wails a cat on the off-beat, and two bars later there it goes again, 'Miaoow' on the off-beat – 'Miaoow' on the off-beat – 'Miaoow' on the off-beat.

Soon these rhythmic repetitions of sound became the distinctive trademark of every dance record. Everyday sounds or phrases recurred every few bars, forcing themselves hypnotically into the listener's brain. A song's hook no longer had to be its chorus, it could be nothing more than a weird laugh. This perfectly suited the trancelike state in which dancers taking ecstasy found themselves.

The boom in sampling and the boom in ecstasy arrived on the scene almost simultaneously. According to journalist Danny Kelly, 'The drum machine and sampler allowed white boys to be nearly as rhythmic as black boys in making music. And ecstasy allowed white boys to dance nearly as rhythmically as black boys.'

The new technology and the new drug interacted together to change the sound of pop music. No longer did you have to pinch bits of other people's songs and rewrite them in the style of the day. Now, using the sampler, you could pinch whole chunks of the original recording. An early example of this was a dance track by MARRS, a couple of DJs who mixed together bits of hundreds of different records to make 'Pump Up The Volume'. In September 1987 it became the first record ever to reach No. 1 in all three singles charts – Indie, Dance and Pop.

The repeated words 'pump up the volume' turned out to be so addictive that when dancers tired of the musical aspects of the record they still wanted to hear the phrase. Since it was now so easy to borrow bits from one record and use them again in another one, it wasn't long before the phrase 'pump up the volume' turned up again. In fact it helped a brand new group get a No. 1 record.

After Wham! had broken up, I'd taken on the management of a group called Blue Mercedes. They were a duo – David Titlow and Duncan Millar – who wrote songs in a slightly ABC mould and had been spotted by Dave Ambrose who by then was the managing director of MCA records. He'd signed them and suggested that Stock Aitken Waterman should produce them.

Blue Mercedes ended up with two of Pete Waterman's most dance-orientated producers, Phil Harding and Ian Curnow. When the album was finished the initial single chosen to promote it was 'I Want To Be Your Property'. Phil and Ian did a dance remix to get the record moving on the club circuit. They sampled the famous phrase 'pump up the volume' and inserted it liberally. The result was amazing. The record went straight to No. 1 in the American dance charts and stayed there for fourteen weeks.

In America's dance-drug culture at that time the principal taste-forming cities were Los Angeles, Miami, New York, Chicago, Detroit and Philadelphia, all of them already swamped with ecstasy. Popular taste in those six cities would determine what was at the top of the national US dance chart. This in turn went on to influence DJs throughout the world, so Blue Mercedes soon found themselves on a worldwide promotion tour of clubs and discos, and I went with them.

We got back to London to find ecstasy had exploded. It

was changing London's regular nightlife beyond recognition. The new centre was Heaven, owned by Richard Branson, underneath the railway arches at Charing Cross Station. It was originally London's biggest gay club. Now something else was happening. For Monday nights, the club, which had a capacity of 3,000, had been renamed 'Spectrum: Theatre of Madness'. It was the biggest thing in London – lasers, pyrotechnics, spaceships descending from the roof. And E. When he saw the success of Spectrum, Danny Rampling moved Shoom to the YMCA in Tottenham Court Road where it immediately became London's number-one centre for anyone dealing in ecstasy. 'Everyone became a drug dealer,' says one of the regulars. 'Whether it was three pills a night or thirty. Unlike other drugs, with E, part of the culture was to buy and sell it. I guess you just wanted other people to join in with you.'

This was also true in Manchester where for years the best club in town had been the Hacienda. DJ Dave Haslam later wrote, 'The "great" club suddenly became a "life-changing experience" ... They'd be dancing on the stairs, in the cloakroom queue, in the toilet queue, the whole building was shaking.' Mike Pickering, a DJ at the Hacienda, remembers how quickly the use of ecstasy spread throughout Manchester. 'Almost like a Mexican wave ... over a week or two weeks.'

It was becoming clear, ecstasy plus house music equalled mass euphoria. Ecstasy was allowing a whole generation of young people to break free from their inhibitions. Ecstasy made people want to congregate in bigger and bigger groups and dance the night away. For the more business-minded clubbers like Tony Colston-Hayter, a regular at Shoom, the financial benefits soon became obvious. People would pay £15 for an all-night rave with a further £15 for a tab of ecstasy.

Grabbing the opportunity, Colston-Hayter set out to promote raves for thousands of people at a time initially using film studios, empty warehouses or unused aircraft hangars. Then he hit on the idea of using the open countryside. He sold a thousand tickets for a Sunrise Mystery Trip, and laid on coaches. The event was held in an equestrian centre at Iver Heath in Buckinghamshire. In his book *Altered States* Matthew Collin wrote, 'Flares burned along the wooded approach road, and as the coaches drew nearer, lasers flashed into the sky.' At the height of the evening, dry ice flooded the dance floor, and as the sun rose people were collecting wild flowers to thread through each other's hair.

The next rave was even bigger. Sunrise Guy Fawkes was for 3,000 people, but by then the media had got hold of the story and were pressuring the police to act. As the guests arrived, so did squads of riot police. They fought till five in the morning before the police gave up and allowed the party to commence. From then on the size of the venues grew and grew. They called the summer of 1988 the 'Summer of Love'. For the kids, it was a summer of endless fun – for the promoters, of endless profits.

For those of us who'd been around in the sixties, it was difficult not to be reminded of the vast congregations who gathered to worship acid at the end of that decade. But most of the older generation seemed to have forgotten their youth. They were soon raising the voice of 'family values'. Why should kids be allowed to have so much fun when the responsibility of running their lives rested on adults?

A police squad was set up specifically to target and search out raves, but the advent of the mobile phone helped evade the 'killjoy' squad. Ken Tappenden was the Kent police divisional commander put in charge of stopping these rave parties. 'The traffic never started until quarter to one in the morning which was a most unusual time to have traffic on your motorways, and I knew then that I had a problem.'

Parties were meticulously organised. Message banks communicating with a thousand mobile phones meant a thousand cars packed with teenagers could be sent in high-speed convoy to a secret destination where, once started, even if the police arrived the party would be too big to stop. Sheryl Garratt, author of *Adventures in Wonderland*, remembers, 'The great thing was finding them. You'd be lost for hours and hours and hours. You'd drive over a hill and suddenly there it was, this fantasy world built specially for you.'

Chris Lowe of the Pet Shop Boys says, 'I used to love going to raves ... I used to enjoy the fact that it was like some sort of mystery tour. Before then, your nightlife was more predictable. You went with certain people and left with certain people. This way you never knew what was going to happen ...'

Later, Jarvis Cocker of Pulp wrote a lyric that summed it all up. 'Mother, I can never come home again 'cos I seem to have left a very important part of my brain somewhere, somewhere in a field in Hampshire.'

By now the media were hot on the trail of each and every party. Police Commander Ken Tappenden used the media to announce, 'This is nothing to do with people wanting to party, this is about people wanting to take drugs.' In June, reporting 'the biggest ever acid party', the *Daily Mail* wrote, 'When 11,000 youngsters descended on a quiet airfield in the middle of the night, drug pushers were waiting to tempt them with an evil selection of narcotics.' It followed this up with a piece that ended, 'Those responsible for this gigantic exercise in hooking our youth on drugs must be brought to book and the stiffest penalties imposed.'

When the police began giving them problems, the organisers printed special fake flyers giving false instructions, and made sure they found their way into police hands. While 500 police were dispatched to Kent, 5,000 partygoers would be heading for Essex. Then the police started using similarly deceptive methods, putting information about non-existent parties on the phone banks. In case the police turned up, party organisers would have an on-site lawyer who would argue the illegality of stopping the event with the policeman in charge. Ken Tappenden complained, 'The minute you touch their equipment they counterclaim for damage ... These organisers fear the VAT man more than they fear us.' But in the end, Tappenden saw it as a victory for the police. 'We won because we stopped it all in eighteen months and we drove it underground ... we drove it into warehouses.'

While millions of teenagers and twenty-somethings were discovering the delights of a new drug, their younger brothers and sisters were discovering Bros, two blond twins and a bass player. Just when the Pet Shop Boys had moved pop music nearer to art, Bros returned it to its basest origins – pretty singers and a screaming sub-teen audience. Bros became the forerunners of a decade in which the industry would be completely dominated by packaged groups of pretty boys.

They were marketed by the manager of the Pet Shop Boys, Tom Watkins, whom Neil Tennant once described as 'a big fat man with a loud voice'. Tom thought that was an unfair comment. 'When they came to me, the Pet Shop Boys were too meek to face the big wicked music industry alone. That's why they needed me. I'm larger than life, dear. That's what artists want from a manager.'

Tom was indeed a huge man, and proud of it. He also enjoyed being aggressively confrontational about his own homosexuality. 'Darling, there's nothing I love more than knowing that some big butch number fancies my arse. Except, perhaps, letting him have it.'

Tom Watkins had once tried to be a pop star himself. 'It was an outrageous idea,' he admits 'A fat bastard like me. How could I be a pop star? I can't sing a fucking note. But I persuaded EMI to give me and a friend a deal and they put a record out. It didn't do much so I wrote a second single – "When Will I Be Famous?" When EMI dropped us, I looked around for a group to sing it. That's how I ended up managing Bros.'

Tom Watkins was the music industry personified – brash, cynical and calculating, but also endlessly amusing. Apart from giving Bros one of his songs, Tom's major contribution to their success was to jam freshly laundered socks down the front of their jeans. 'To give a more appealing shape,' he explained. 'Neither of them, you might be surprised to know, were Mensa members...'

In the music business, Mensa members had always been something of a rarity, but there were always plenty of bright people around. Now, with the prevalence of ecstasy, many of these were becoming less focused. Ministry of Sound marketing manager Mark Rodol explains, 'People at majors who'd previously been hard-working, aggressive promotion men, or rock fans, or marketing whiz kids, went to a few raves, did some

E and suddenly became ultra cool – they'd tell everyone they'd been 'karma'd" and ask to work in the dance department.'

But while the majors stood still in shock at the sudden boom in dance music, the smaller, more nimble independents took a giant step forward. Ecstasy and the dance music with which it was worshipped had given them a new lease of life. In many ways, acid house had achieved what punk never achieved. Punk had proved that any group of energised kids could buy guitars and make a semi-musical statement on-stage. Samplers and synthesisers set up in a bedroom now proved that anyone could become a producer – anyone, that is, with creativity and imagination. For just as punk had weeded out a few real talents from a mass of angry voices, so the dance charts separated the super-imaginative producers from those who simply showed prowess with computers.

But the great thing about the 'bedroom-studio generation' was that they were free of Malcolm McLaren type manipulation. Moreover, the new dance music was rooted in a culture of artistic freedom. Anything heard and liked, from the chorus of a Bach chorale to the flapping of a flag in the wind, could be incorporated into a dance track.

Major record companies were caught on the hop. This new generation of bedroom producers and artists didn't seem to play by the established rules. Without the need for big advances in order to make a record, these kids were making records first and thinking about releasing them afterwards. But then, once a few promo copies had been pressed up and the record was gaining the approval of DJs and clubgoers, why give it to a major? If you did, not only would they skim off the profits, they might fail to make it a hit because they knew nothing about the new dance culture.

Specialised dance labels sprung up all over the country, often owned by the producers themselves. For a major, a sale of 50,000 12-inch records wouldn't amount to much. For someone with no overheads it could mean a profit of £50,000. Enough to move out of a bedroom and buy a proper studio.

The major companies wanted to cash in on this new dance market, but they didn't know how. In fact, the answer was staring them in the face.

A decade previously, Peter Jamieson had been head of EMI in Greece and Spain. For years, he'd been hooked on the idea of putting together compilation albums with the same sort of flow as pop radio, but no one had ever managed to get one off the ground. When he was put in charge of EMI in London in the early eighties he looked at the idea again.

Jamieson's problem was that, individually, even major record companies were unable to provide enough variety to produce compilation albums, and they were unwilling to co-operate with each other. But one day Jon Webster from Virgin turned up in Peter's office and proposed the very same thing. EMI and Virgin linked up on the project and within a year pop compilations had become the mainstay of the industry. Jamieson was not only the man behind the world's most successful compilation series, he was also the person who gave it its name. 'When I was a kid I would be playing the latest Beatles record or whatever, and my dad would come home and put on Richard Crooks's "The Holy City" and say, "Now, that's what I call music." When we were preparing the first compilation album, I was sitting in Virgin's office and I saw a poster on the wall by the Danish Bacon Marketing Board which said "Now, that's what I call bacon". I decided it was fate – so the series was named that way. But in the end, we put the emphasis on the word "NOW".'

From then onwards, the major companies sold their music like bacon – specially selected and shrink-wrapped. But the compilation albums they were selling were mainly pop songs. They should also have been doing the same thing with dance music.

At the end of the eighties when dance music went overground, the majors were wrongfooted. While they floundered, an independent company grabbed the opportunity and headed for the big time.

The Ministry of Sound was in unfashionable Elephant and Castle, but for kids who had grown tired of raving in wet fields it quickly became the most fashionable place in London. Club manager Mark Rodol explains, 'We catered for people who didn't want to stand in the mud all night on a Saturday. Ministry of Sound was civilised raving.'

It was owned and run by Eton-educated James Palumbo whose father was Lord Palumbo, head of the Arts Council under the Thatcher government in the 1980s. The younger Palumbo left university and went to work in the city, selling share options. He worked maniacally and amassed a good lump of capital. A friend who had the idea to start a rave-type club in London asked him for an investment. The Ministry took over a London Transport bus garage underneath the railway arches near Elephant and Castle. All that had to be done was make it waterproof and stop people getting in without paying. Despite success, the club's profitability went downhill. When Palumbo looked like losing his invested capital, he moved in and took over.

From there onwards it was the business success story of the nineties.

In the early nineties the club dominated the London dance scene. It opened at midnight and ran till seven in the morning. Palumbo did well with the local council. Quiet, lightly built and dressed in cuff-linked shirts and dark suits, he looked more like the merchant banker he'd once been than the owner of a dance club about to make his fortune from a boom in an illegal drug. Because ecstasy would drive the dancers, no alcohol was needed and only a dance licence was required. Palumbo overcame the councillors' objections to all-night opening by pointing out that closing at the normal time of three in the morning meant that kids would be left on the street with no public transport to get them home. Since there was no alcohol on sale, surely it wouldn't hurt to let them stay inside the club till the morning tube started running. It was a carbon copy of the arguments used in the fifties by Jeff Kruger, the owner of the Flamingo Club when he sought permission from the West End police. Then, the stimulus for all-night sessions had been rhythm & blues music and amphetamine tablets. Now it was house music and ecstasy.

Journalist Lucian Randall remembers his first visit to the Ministry when he was nineteen. 'The queues could be off-putting and the high-security prison façade was pretty intimidating, but the first time I went was with a *Melody Maker* hack, so it was guest-list all the way. Once inside my *Melody Maker* chum disappeared off to the toilets and scored some E. Having dropped the tab we made our way down a long pitch-black corridor, bumping into people and apologising with such warmth and consideration that you'd think a near-fatal collision had occurred. We emerged into a cavernous room with the loudest sound system of all time – maximum volume, minimum ear hurt – everything vibrant, everyone having a fantastic time.'

Palumbo's shrewd development of the club led to it gaining huge street credibility. Its success was stunning and the overheads were low. Because raves were part of weekend culture, there was no point being open Monday to Thursday. The club opened from midnight to dawn on Fridays and Saturdays. It had the best sound system in the world and the best DJs were flown in each weekend from America, DJs who not only knew music but also knew ecstasy. They would match the tempo of the music to the changing effects of E on the dancers' nervous systems. Even with extra doses, the hallucinogenic effects of ecstasy didn't increase greatly. So as the evening wore on, the effects of the amphetamine contained in the drug started to dominate. To suit the change in mood, DJs gently shifted the music from an ecstasy groove to an amphetamine rave.

Ministry became the dance club of dance clubs. Its name filtered through to clubgoers the world over; its forecourt was jammed with thousands waiting to get in every Friday and Saturday. On the basis of the club's reputation with the rave crowd, Palumbo started a record label and began to release Ministry of Sound compilation albums. Tracks that got the best reaction on the dance-floor were mixed into a perfect dance set by well-known DJs.

For years, clubbers had been buying illegal tapes of this type sold in clubs and markets. But Ministry of Sound now offered them high-quality CDs, with excellent packaging, available at all record stores up and down the country. People who had never been to the club could now have the famous 'Ministry experience' for the price of a record. The club had a door policy that refused admission to people under twenty-one. As a result, in search of the 'Ministry experience', teenagers bought the compilations in their droves. Soon, for many, a record with a Ministry logo became the guarantee of a perfect front-room party. (But don't forget to bring your own E!)

In the midst of all this E culture, I decided on a retro step. I took over the management of Asia, the old progressive rock band from the seventies. Compared with the world of ecstasy, this was like taking up residence in a museum.

For a while it felt comfortable moving back in time. The new Asia had two original members, Steve Howe on guitar and Geoff Downes on keyboards. At the time of their greatest success I'd been dismissive of the music's pomposity and lack of rhythm & blues groove, but now, at the beginning of the nineties I belatedly discovered its technical virtuosity and harmonic depth. Even so, it still remained rock in the classic early-seventies style when volume and grandeur made up for having a groove.

Asia were old-fashioned in every way, but thoroughly charming. Geoff Downes and John Payne, the new singer, liked their booze and cocaine. Steve Howe was rooted in late-sixties hippydom – long hair, health food and marijuana. Vinny and Trevor, the second guitarist and the drummer, were younger and took whatever came, including a smaller weekly pay-check.

The band had long passed the stage of inner tensions and disruptions that rock bands thrive on in their formative years. They had a fixed audience and a defined musical style, most of the songs in the set were their best-known ones from the past and towards the end of the show Steve Howe would play a ten-minute solo spot of his own guitar classics. The group made a new album every eighteen months or so and all the songs would fit the old pattern, even the sleeves continued in the same air-brush tradition. The USA, Japan, Europe – touring with Asia was comfortable and trouble-free, like driving sedately around in an old Rolls-Royce. The biggest problems were just the usual rock trivia – a venue that had been repainted gave off a smell that caused Steve Howe to retire to bed – some of the group got busted for doing coke in Germany and bail money had to be wired quickly from London – someone broke the golden rule of American touring and crapped in the Winnebago toilet.

At the end of each trip, it was surprising to snap out of this museum of rock history and find oneself back in a modern world where young people on ecstasy were scornful of the music played by groups like Asia. 'We don't need it,' said Colin Angus of the Shamen. 'It's redundant, macho, ego-motivated, dominator music. It's had its day – everything has been said in rock 'n' roll.'

In Manchester many people would have disagreed with him.

Manchester was spawning something new, not exactly dance music, but rock with a dance groove. Two new guitar groups, the Stone Roses and the Happy Mondays, were playing this new type of rock and executives of major record companies in London were surprised at its huge local success. What was it, they wondered, that made these groups so special? The answer, of course, was E.

Ian Brown of the Stone Roses was somewhat reticent about the influence of drugs on the group's music. 'They're pretty important is all I'm saying.'

Many critics considered the Stone Roses to be the most influential British guitar band of the late eighties. Musically, they almost certainly were. But that was to miss the point. The late eighties was not about guitars, it was about ecstasy.

The Happy Mondays were the most influential E group. They revolved around singer Shaun Ryder whose dad had been a singer, comedian, bass player, postman, and from the age of sixteen onwards had done every drug there ever was. Shaun was brought up on a tough housing estate in Swinton and had a best mate, Bez, whom he'd met in the dole queue when they were both sixteen. Shaun had done his first drugs at thirteen – a microdot of acid – and by the time he was sixteen he was already hooked on heroin. After he met Bez they would take three or four tabs of acid at a time. Eventually they drifted into music because 'apart from stealing cars, it was the only thing we could do that would let us keep on doing drugs'. They picked other musicians for the band and financed their lives by buying and selling drugs.

It was during this period that Shaun and Bez went to Amsterdam and discovered ecstasy. Bez remembers, 'I'd be there lying awake at night thinking, I wish there was some new fucking drug what would just do this, do that, and do that. The next minute I popped one of these things and it's done everything I wanted.' He started bringing the new drug home with him in volume and selling it all round Manchester.

When Tony Wilson first spotted Shaun Ryder and the Happy Mondays, he knew he'd found something special, but he wasn't sure how to deal with it. He chose a producer to work with them, but the producer walked out on the first day, cursing them: 'Those people are total scumbags... noone should be forced to work with them – they are the worst bastards I have ever come into contact with.'

The group's first album failed miserably. 'It was like flogging a dead horse,' says Tony Wilson. 'But we loved them and we were committed.' The band went back to playing gigs around Britain with Shaun's dad, Derek, driving the van and enjoying the drugs as much as the rest of them. He told a journalist, 'Look – you define the success of a tour by how many drugs you score.'

The group's second album was *Bummed*, recorded entirely on E, and it was a huge success. After it came out, Shaun and the group played the 8,000-capacity G-Mex Centre every Monday. 'Everyone in the place was on E, and it made us look better and sound better. I knew they were all on E because we used to go out in the audience selling E like T-shirts.'

This was the first time the industry had seen the artist as a drug-pusher, but why not? Like amphetamine sulphate in the seventies and acid in the sixties, the drug created the audience. Kids on E wanted E-culture music. To profit from this, all the music industry had to do was to identify the kids who were taking it, then provide them with the right records. It was a cinch! From this basis came the success of the Stone Roses, and the Inspiral Carpets – and then the Happy Mondays, straight in at No. 1 with their album, *Pills, Thrills and Bellyaches*. But none of these groups was on a major label.

For everyone involved in E the joke was on authority. And it got even bigger when the English football squad were persuaded to sing New Order's song for the World Cup, 'E for England'. In the end the band had to change the title, but the lyrics were still crammed with drugs references and it became one of the most successful football songs of all time.

The majors responded to all this the only way they knew how – by buying up the biggest independents: not the new dance labels but old-time independent giants like Chrysalis and Virgin. Being independent, these smaller companies had at least made inroads into the new dance culture, so the majors now found some of it coming their way. It also gave them one or two major artists.

In 1988, PolyGram took over Island Records and with them U2. They then bought America's biggest independent company, A&M.

EMI purchased 50 per cent of Chrysalis Records, then bought out Virgin, which gave them Janet Jackson. They also set about further enlargement of their publishing interests by buying SBK Music, which included the April Music catalogue, obtained ridiculously cheaply from CBS Records. EMI then grabbed Jobete, the company that owned the songs made famous by Motown.

This expansion of the majors sent a clear signal to the new independent dance companies – sooner or later you'll lose your independence, even if you get as big as Virgin or Chrysalis. The world's top five record companies were turning themselves into impregnable fortresses of copyright exploitation.

Ecstasy's effects spread far and wide – and not just in the music industry. Across the country young people everywhere calmed down and found themselves thinking about romance and relationships. It had even quietened down football hooligans. In 1990, John Stalker, the Deputy Chief Constable of Greater

Manchester Police, said, 'It's almost as if hooliganism is not fashionable any more.' Gary, an ex-football gang leader, agreed. 'Ecstasy came along and people got chilled ... Everyone looked at one another and said what a great party, and then violence declined. People were too busy having a good time to care about anything else.'

Author Sheryl Garratt says, 'A lot of the people involved in this did think it was going to change everything ... the Berlin wall *did* come down, Nelson Mandela *did* walk out of prison ... There were huge changes going on in the world which felt like a part of it. It was a very euphoric time.'

And euphoria, like ecstasy, helped sell records of all types.

These new gentle attitudes boosted people's need for several sorts of music other than dance. James Horrocks at React Records had been one of the first to spot a niche market for ecstasy dance, but he also recognised that the drug caused an increase in sales of other types of music. 'People were saying – "If ecstasy is this big, why isn't the chart just dance records and nothing else?" They didn't understand ... Ecstasy made you feel the world was one big happy place. It was great for dancing, and you danced all night, but you didn't necessarily buy the records you danced to. When you went home you felt emotionally concerned with the rest of humanity. You'd made contact with other people's feelings. At home, kids wanted music that reflected their new-found feelings of caring. Ecstasy not only made the dance market boom, it provided a boom in softer, more sentimental music – Lisa Stansfield, maybe even Celine Dion, things like that.'

In London, a thorough working knowledge of E seemed to have become the essential qualification for someone to be given a radio programme or an executive position in the dance department of a major record company.

Judge Jules, formerly a law student, then a club and pirate radio DJ, landed both. He got a BBC Radio One programme on Saturday evenings and a label of his own at PolyGram Records. Previously he'd been a promoter too. 'Some of our one-off events were extremely back-street affairs. Once we'd got word about a place, we then had to break into it, get the generators and the sound systems in and then let everyone know. We relied mostly on word of mouth and pirate radio stations. We'd have ravers listening in for details about where to go the same night as the event.'

Jules found that ravers were addicted to the whole experience – the drugs, the dancing, the illicitness. 'There usually wouldn't be any toilets, and if we couldn't get hold of a hired generator it was a case of getting the power supply to run on a cable from a street light. The police would always turn up, but by the time they arrived, there'd be maybe 1,000, 2,000 ravers on site, so there wasn't much they could actually do. It was a crazy time for the police ... they were having to address a new naughtiness among young people, and they really didn't have the legal powers to deal with it.'

Danny Rampling, the man behind the original Shoom club, was plucked from London's dance music station Kiss FM by Radio One and ended up with 2 million listeners. The *Sun* called it an outrage that a show should be given to 'one of the founders of the drug-ridden acid house craze'. But the truth was, BBC had to accept that the use of ecstasy at weekends had become the primary leisure activity of British youth. Half a million kids were doing a tab of E every Friday night. They had a new style of dressing – fun T-shirts, headbands and double-baggy trousers. They had E-fashion, E-imagery, and E-slang. Adults, seeking to be in tune with their youngsters, happily joined in their drug-related slang without knowing its derivation. Words like 'sorted' passed straight into mainstream English.

Large commercial companies got into it too. Ecstasy users found that alcohol blurred the drug's effects. As a result, rave clubs didn't bother with alcohol and this gave a massive sales boost to bottled waters. Innocent parents were pleased to see their kids drinking less, but brewers were not so happy. As the use of E grew, use of the country's favourite drug declined – beer sales decreased across the UK by 11 per cent. To counter the loss of beer sales, drinks companies began repackaging alcohol in smaller, stronger doses, giving it a 'quick hit' image, like taking a pill or shooting up. These 'alcopops' consisted of a strong shot of alcohol hidden in a traditionally non-alcoholic drink. Lemonhead tasted like lemonade; Red Raw was an alcoholic ginger beer; and Moo was a milkshake that got you drunk. The greatest idea of all was DNA – 'alcoholic spring water'.

Other companies too, seeing these figures, realised the power of E-culture and jumped on the bandwagon. Just as in the days of LSD, major corporations used E-imagery to infiltrate the youth market, and many of the ads were dreamed up by advertising executives who themselves were users of the drug.

In the sixties and seventies, kids went into the rock business then got into drugs. By the beginning of the nineties, kids who'd got themselves into drugs were choosing the music business as a sympathetic career.

In 1992 the Shamen released 'Ebeneezer Goode', about a guy who was the life and soul of the party. In the chorus the backing voices chanted 'Eezer Goode' – ('E's are good'.)

The very same week that the BBC launched a 'Drugs Alert' campaign warning about the dangers of taking E, the Shamen's song reached No. 1 in the Radio One chart. 'E's are good – E's are good', it chanted six times a day, provocatively negating the Beeb's feeble warnings.

The 'records and drugs' business was booming as never before.

CHAPTER TWENTY-FOUR

CHEATING THE CHART

The British music press love labels. When they thought up Britpop they were delighted with themselves.

It started in 1994 when they noticed a couple of new groups emerge – simple guitar groups, playing live music, fresh and uncontrived with intelligent lyrics. Much of the music press had been finding it hard dealing with the pervading DJ culture. As writers and editors what they wanted were stars and guitars like they'd had in the old days.

The first group they championed was Blur who initially entered the charts in 1991; then they created a frenzy about Suede, who turned up in 1993 and didn't even have a record contract at the time. But the next year, when these two were joined by Oasis, the press decided it was a 'movement'. Suddenly *everything* was Britpop. After being pushed out of the spotlight by sampling machines and doped-up DJs, guitar groups were back – Oasis, Blur, Pulp, Suede. Every label had to have one.

Oasis came with a good-sized chip on their shoulder. They were from Manchester – the Gallagher brothers and three friends.

Brought up in an Irish community that saw Dublin as its real capital, the Gallaghers were perfectly primed to be cynical about all things British. Even so, they'd fallen in love with the music of the Beatles and copied it almost note for note. But unlike songwriters who steal melodies and reframe them in the style of the day, the Gallagher brothers did the opposite.

They came up with their own original melodies, then reframed them in the style of thirty years ago, albeit with a bit of punky overdrive. The end result was striking, and although it had no more relevance to contemporary music than the sound of a Dixieland jazz band, it hit a common nerve among British teenagers and took off. 'The most ecstatic live show most of this crowd have ever, and probably will ever, experience,' said the *NME*. But the real key to Oasis's success was their musical sensitivity. As if they were ashamed of this, they compensated with decadent imagery stolen straight from seventies rock – the Rolling Stones and Led Zeppelin.

All this, when combined, made Oasis unique. Yet as 'Britpop' they were lumped together with a bunch of groups from Britain's provincial cities none of which had anything in common with them. Britpop was simply a name dreamed up by the music media. By using a slick ad-agency word the media hoped to create a new musical era. In the end, it simply trivialised the artists to whom it was applied.

Suede came from Haywards Heath, a sleepy middle-class town, not big enough to have a sleazy centre. The atmosphere of their home town summed them up – no attitude, but searching hard to find one. Brett Anderson, the lead singer, told everyone, 'I'm a bisexual who has never had a homosexual experience.' It made a change from gay artists claiming to be bisexual although they'd never had a heterosexual experience.

Melody Maker splashed Suede across the front cover, calling them 'The Best New Band in Britain'. As if he were afraid the music wasn't good enough to do it for him, Brett talked and talked. So did his partner, Mat Osman. 'In London',

he said, 'compared with Haywards Heath, you're on a cloud.'
And he told us what type of cloud, 'the E scene – Heaven, and
places like that'.

Brett Anderson sang love songs which included lines like,
'We kiss in his room to a popular tune.' When the public took
these sentiments to be gay, Brett feigned surprise. Hadn't we
considered, he asked, that he might have been expressing the
'female point of view'?

His naïvety was charming. Or was it deliberate? Or was it
deliberately charming?

Increasingly, record buyers were able to see through
imagery and hype. British teenagers had spent their entire
lives living under a Conservative government obsessed with a
market economy. Young people were cynical of anything they
were asked to buy: nothing marketed by the music business
came in its natural state – each new group had already been
selected, polished, remixed, test-marketed, corrected, and fed
to the media. Suede's guitarist Bernard Butler remembers
meeting a journalist at the time who told him, 'This will be
your year – it was decided at a meeting last week.'

In interviews Suede openly discussed these inner workings
of the image-building process and it worked against them.
Oasis did much better. They simply refused to reveal they
were articulate (except when they wrote lyrics).

Blur sat somewhere in the middle – perfect liberals, with the
courage to be uncommitted both image-wise and musically.
Slowly they moved in a perfect circle, from dance to punk and
back again. They had a pretty singer called Damon Albarn
who told the press, 'There's nothing more up to date and
relevant than us.'

They were from Colchester, more provincial than Manchester but less of a joke than Haywards Heath. Once more, androgyny was in the forefront of their lyrics – 'Girls who are boys who like boys to be girls who do boys like they're girls who do girls like they're boys...' They entered into competition with Oasis by releasing a single on the same day, and won, going straight to No. 1. Then they appeared to fizzle out while Oasis, more confident of what they were really about, made a succession of big hits. Social analysts told us Britpop was the musical fruit of the government's attempt to create a classless nation, but really it was just the same old thing – kids discovering drugs and the big city.

Soon, the media had thrown a fourth group into the mix – Pulp.

Pulp had been around since 1981. Being too young to go into pubs, it was hard to get gigs, so they wrote to John Peel who gave them a radio session. For the next twelve years not much happened, but then John Peel gave them another session. Pushing thirty, the members of the group suddenly found themselves included in Britpop.

Pulp's biggest asset was their singer, Jarvis Cocker. He came with a loud mouth which produced endlessly good copy ('Being skinny is neater and tidier, and it's not got bulges all over'). After Pulp had scored a few hits, Jarvis decided to boost his fame at the 1995 Brit Awards. First he sang 'Sorted for E's and Wizz', a song which some people considered unsuitable for the occasion. Then, while Michael Jackson was singing 'Earth Song', Jarvis ran out on-stage to join him. Jackson had recently settled a legal action involving paedophile allegations. Now he was making a fool of himself pretending to be the new Messiah with a gang of children dressed as deprived third-worlders. Jarvis decided he should protest 'at the way Michael Jackson sees himself as some Christ-like figure with the power of healing'. He clambered on-stage, ran in front of Jackson, lowered his trousers and flashed his bare bottom. At the age of thirty-three, it was past its prime, but to a bored audience it was still a welcome sight.

A year earlier, I'd been at another Michael Jackson concert which would have benefited from such a cheerful distraction. It was in Bangkok just three days after the news of Jackson's paedophile case had been splashed across newspapers round the world. For two days Michael had stayed in his hotel room, sedated, unable to face the world, refusing to perform. On the third night he played a slow, laid-back concert, sometimes crying on-stage, sometimes not appearing when he was meant to, then suddenly being even more brilliant than usual.

The reason I was in Bangkok was because James Palumbo from the Ministry of Sound had called me to say he wanted some advice about Asia.

By now the Ministry of Sound was known as much for being a record label as for being a club. The Ministry's logo on a compilation album was a guarantee of a good record for dance fans. The brand had become the artist. Kids bought the records, not for their content but for their street-credibility. Ministry's albums had found a niche not catered for by the majors and not requiring the heavy level of TV advertising that the majors needed to sell their dance albums.

James Palumbo felt it was time to extend the Ministry's influence beyond London. He wanted to set up Ministry clubs in Asia and sell records on the back of them, just as he was doing in Britain. In return for a smaller split of the profits as he could give them, he would find partners to finance him. Japan seemed the obvious target but James preferred the idea of Thailand.

I took him to Bangkok and introduced him to the best people, Grammy Records, owned by a sophisticated grey-haired smoothie called Paiboon. Grammy had more than half the entire Thai market under their control and was expanding in all directions. Paiboon was lobbying the government to allow Grammy to open shops selling school equipment and youth-oriented products in every school in Thailand. When Paiboon realised he was being asked to participate in a club whose success had been built entirely on the boom in ecstasy, he was horrified. Just to be seen talking to James Palumbo could lose him his deal for school shops. The lunch was polite but very short. So I took James to meet Itthyvat.

Itthyvat is a big belly of a man – Buddha himself in a loose-cut grey suit with thick horn-rimmed glasses and a smile like a Halloween pumpkin. He's as canny as they come, which means maybe as canny as James Palumbo. From Bangkok, Itthyvat had made himself part of the history of almost every British rock group that ever made it, and many that didn't. For a long time he'd been the top promoter in Thailand and also owned the principal pop radio stations. In the seventies and eighties he got rich going to the UK, choosing unknown British groups of quality and booking them to do shows in Bangkok for a few hundred pounds.

The groups would expect to play in a pub or a small club but Itthyvat would fly back to Bangkok and put their records on all his radio stations. At the end of a month the group would be the hottest ticket in town and might arrive to find themselves playing two nights in a 10,000-seater hall.

Bob Geldof remembers how it was when the Boomtown Rats played there. 'We were No. 1 in Thailand when we arrived. We learned later that this was no great achievement as the character who promoted the concert also controlled seventy-two hours a week of national radio and virtually declared by personal fiat what was No. 1 at any given time. For weeks before we arrived all the unfortunate Thais heard on their radio was the Boomtown Rats.'

But groups never complained about this treatment. They stayed in five-star hotels, were provided with unlimited girls and felt like superstars.

Itthyvat was more than a sharp promoter, he was a policeman too. One of his principal police activities was to keep an eye on foreign artists bringing drugs in and out of the country.

To top even this, in the seventies Itthyvat persuaded Warners they would never get anywhere in the local market without him as their local partner. They made him chairman and gave him half their shares. He then persuaded Sony to do much the same. Later, he did it for a third time with BMG. Itthyvat was a clever and charming man, but nevertheless, James Palumbo thought he might get the better of him.

For their first meeting Itthyvat invited James to a Thai restaurant where the meal began with raw jellyfish in a fiery sauce. 'What a wonderful texture,' James commented enthusiastically.

It was going to be a good contest.

Back in London, Britpop soon proved to be nothing but a gimmick. It was just a label, something with which the British music industry had hoped to sell a new batch of artists to America. Of all the groups termed 'Britpop', only Oasis came near to success in the States, though in the end they too failed, unable to adopt the required professionalism.

In the States, Oasis toured for a bit and built up a wave of expectation. Their gig at West Hollywood's Whiskey A Go-Go would be attended by everyone who mattered. But the group blew it. Their manager explained why. 'Every fucking fucker in the fucking band and crew had been up for two days straight solid doing coke and crystal meths, right up to showtime ...'

Oasis deliberately played up a lifestyle of drug excess for the benefit of the media. But in playing it up, they became trapped in it. Liam and Noel Gallagher found it more fun to overdo drugs than to worry about success in the States. So they gave up, came back to Britain and carried on being self-indulgent. To keep themselves in the headlines, Liam confessed to sprinkling cocaine on his breakfast cereal and Noel announced that doing drugs was as normal as 'getting up and having a cup of tea in the morning'.

It caused a stir, but it was hard to see why – most people already knew it was true. Most people also knew that Oasis had blown their chances of being the biggest British group in the States in twenty years.

Journalists who'd been whipping up a battle between Oasis and Blur began to realise that the real battle in the British record market was between Take That and East 17 – two boy groups, both aimed at young teen audiences. These groups had been packaged and marketed to the last degree and they set a path the music business would follow to the end of the decade.

East 17 were managed by Tom Watkins and the group's creative strength came from its songwriter, Tony Mortimer. It was Tony who first went to Tom. 'You walk into Tom's office and you know you're walking into a management office. I've met lots of managers, and you don't get that … overpowering aura, and I think that's important. It's all about egos and auras, this industry.'

East 17 had come together naturally at school. They left without an O-level between them and later admitted they were better known at the local police station than by their fans. On videos they copied the body movements of America's black ghetto kids – ugly and intimidating – shoulders shrugged towards camera, fingers prodding threateningly towards the lens.

Watkins was obsessed with style and design. He had the idea of taking these movements and repackaging them prettily, like a Disneyland trip to the ghetto. He remodelled the group, re-dressed them, gave them a logo, and made them fit for a Habitat window.

For a while they were hugely successful playing pop music with an angry thrust. They disintegrated when the singer Brian Harvey was pushed out of the group. Manager Tom Watkins said, 'It wasn't so much the drugs he did, it was his talking about them. After a while, he just completely pissed me off … And when he went public and said that he took "X" amount of ecstasy pills and that it was OK to do it … and then made some kind of apology the next day, smoking a joint – I found that absolutely unacceptable.'

As with most of his artists, Tom wasn't over-generous in his praise of East 17 once they'd parted company with him. 'Tony Mortimer was one of my all-time favourites, but most of the band were just numb-nuts.'

The truth is, Tom never saw any of his artists as anything more than a source of income, and he admits it. 'Nineteen Andy Warhols, a Picasso, a couple of Dalis – that's what the music business has meant to me.'

Take That were managed by Nigel Martin-Smith and were built around Gary Barlow, slightly plump and rather dull. Nigel Martin-Smith considered his singing and songwriting worth promoting, so he put the group around him.

In the *Daily Mail* Marcus Berkmann called them 'barely pubescent boys' and questioned their intelligence. His assessment of their pubescence seemed somewhat faulty – their imagery was pure gay porn. Young men stripped to the waist, lying around on beaches, hands touching, muscles rippling, crotches bulging. In *Gay Times*, Richard Smith described one of their videos as 'a billion-dollar Cadinot skinflick with only the cocks and the come-shots cut out'.

But under the erotic front, manager Martin-Smith demanded they keep a pure image. All signs of sex, drinking, smoking and drugs had to be hidden, and members of the group were formally forbidden to have steady relationships. Punishable misdemeanours included going out without a security man or being photographed coming out of a pub. If a group member acquired three strikes against him he was summoned to a 'Behaviour Meeting'. Here an official warning of dismissal could be given.

For a while it worked. Take That found themselves one of the most successful British pop groups for years, breaking sales records that had been set by the Beatles. They had a vast fanbase and had No. 1 after No. 1.

But with the world at their feet there was no way five

healthy young lads could stay that pure for long. Eventually one member, Robbie Williams, was pushed into leaving for having committed sins which had always previously been considered absolute requisite behaviour for pop stars – drinking, sleeping with girls, doing the odd drug or two, and generally having fun.

'Having fun' was the way James Palumbo saw business deals, and 'having fun' meant 'winning'. James never thought of business deals in terms of mutual benefit and he presumed everyone else perceived them in the same way.

In Bangkok, he decided at once that Itthyvat was looking to get one over on him. Itthyvat, sensing this, immediately perceived Palumbo in the same light. From then on it was an endless fencing match. In the other's eyes, both sides overestimated the value of what they were bringing to the deal. Palumbo considered the Ministry's name and expertise in running a club had a greater value than 50 per cent. Itthyvat felt the same about his ability to find finance and get police approval. In the end, despite their differences, the two of them arrived at a working arrangement.

I went with Palumbo's people to check out proposed sites – disused railway sheds, a burnt-out nightclub on top of a skyscraper, warehouses on the outskirts of town. Part of Palumbo's tough stance with Itthyvat was that during the period between agreeing the deal and finally opening the club, Itthyvat would make a substantial monthly payment to Ministry in London which was intended to prove his seriousness. This meant, if the project were to collapse, James would be a guaranteed winner.

There was something about James that reminded me of George Michael.

*

George Michael once said to me, 'I have never done anything which I could regret.' This may have meant he never had any regrets, or it could have meant he was cautious beyond belief. More likely, it simply meant he enjoyed making statements that rang with self-confidence and personal belief. In this he reminded me enormously of James Palumbo.

In 1992, we'd heard that George Michael was suing Sony to get out of his contract with them. The contract was the one he'd entered into with CBS as a member of Wham! after his court case with Innervision. It had now been extended by Sony to cover the individuals in the group after they ceased to play together.

George had a legal problem. His real anger with Sony wasn't so much about the terms of the contract as the company's attitude towards him. It was rumoured that George had heard a senior executive of Sony in America speaking negatively about him. This was on top of the dispute regarding George's insistence on a low-key promotion for his second solo album. As a result, George wanted to be released from his contract. George's lawyers advised him he would never get out of the contract on the basis of Sony being disrespectful to him, therefore he should fight them on the basis that his contract was unfair. But since he'd worked with Sony under that same contract for so long, the courts were likely to say he'd 'affirmed' it.

At the peak of Wham!'s success George had broken up the group. Then, as a solo artist he'd refused to appear in videos to promote his own records. Now, having made himself some £50 million, he'd decided he didn't like his recording agreement. Some people were saying he was an unreasonable person.

Paul Russell, head of Sony Europe, said, 'The industry has to avoid going to court if it doesn't want to self-destruct.'

What he really meant was, 'If it wants to carry on as it always has done.'

But why should anything carry on as it always had done? Least of all the British record business.

For forty years, success for British record companies had been largely based on the idea of manipulating the chart. In the fifties, the creation of a Top Ten singles chart had given record companies the power to run the industry, but since then they'd been enslaved by it. From the moment Brian Epstein revealed that the first Beatles single had been bought into the chart, the public's innocence was destroyed. After that, bribes were replaced by 'freebies', cheating became legitimate and confidence tricks were admired.

In a statement in 1987, the BPI admitted that its constant attempts to stop hyping were largely ineffective. 'It is not only record companies, but friends of groups, grannies, etc. buying large amounts of one record.' But mostly, of course, it was the very same record companies that formed the BPI committee.

In the mid-eighties, Peter Jamieson, as chairman of the British Phonograph Industry, who'd been so successful with the *NOW* compilations, was chairman of the BPI's weekly meeting and saw it as increasingly farcical. 'Week after week, heads of major record companies sat around the BPI conference table thinking up new rules that would stop any one company getting an advantage over the others. Then, the meeting over, they rushed back to their offices where their marketing people tried to find a way round the very rules they had just helped impose.'

From the seventies onwards, albums were the industry's

primary source of income. Perversely, a place in the singles chart was still the root of all promotion. But with over 200 singles a week being released and only 3 per cent of them selling, record shops became fed up with having cluttered shelves. They refused to stock any record that was not already in the chart. As a result, knowing how to 'influence' the chart became the essential quality required of every record company executive.

Tony Powell, who is now managing director of Pinnacle Records, was then head of marketing at Polydor. 'There were only 350 shops that made returns to the charts so all the companies employed "strike forces" who targeted those few shops. If you could move a dozen copies of an artist's single across the counter in those shops on a Monday, it would show up high in the national chart when it came out on Tuesday.'

One method was to give the shops a dozen singles by a new artist together with a dozen free albums by a major star like Queen or Diana Ross. Each time the shop sold one of the albums they would slip a copy of the unknown single into the bag as a free giveaway. To satisfy the rules of the chart, which insisted that all records must be paid for, the shop could assign one pound of the money received for the album as the selling price of the unknown single. By this method singles of unknown artists came from nowhere and went straight into the Top 40.

It seemed that to get anywhere in the industry people had to accept the concept of chart manipulation. It was so commonplace that no one in the industry saw it as dishonest or unfair – it was just a game. But the tradition of achieving success through these means spilled over into everything else. For a record company, taking advantage of a chart that could be manipulated was only a short step from taking advantage of an artist – and it was this attitude that led George Michael to take a stand against Sony.

The general argument in court was along the lines that, although since the sixties both publishers and managers had moved towards more equitable agreements, major record companies had not. When they signed new artists, they demanded contracts of six to ten albums, effectively eight to fourteen years of an artist's life. This sort of enslavement was on a par with the old Hollywood system of restricting film stars to one studio.

Moreover, record companies continued to pepper their contracts with outrageous clauses. Contracts said that the choice of songs and producer would be by mutual agreement with the artists, but hidden away around page fifty in the same agreement would be a clause that said, 'Should the record company and artist disagree, the record company's decision will be final.'

The public were mostly unaware that artists had to pay the costs of making their own records which the record companies then owned in perpetuity. Imagine a film star not only having to pay the cost of the film he appears in, but also having to assign the ownership of it to the film company. Other outrages, still found in contracts in the nineties, were...

- 'At the record company's discretion, royalties for the sale of records in any one country may be calculated on the selling price of the same record in any other country.' (In other words, your 10 per cent royalty for 100,000 records sold in Germany at the equivalent of £14 is going to be calculated as if they'd been sold in Thailand at £2 each.)

- 'At the record company's discretion, royalties becoming due in any six-monthly period can be carried forward to the next period.' (In other words, 'You ain't never gonna get paid!')
- 'In the event that an album is subject to a TV advertising campaign, royalties can be reduced by 50 per cent.' (Half royalties could be triggered by a fifteen-second slot in the middle of the night on Channel 5 at a cost of around £250. For the record company, the saving on a million-selling album would be around £750,000.)

Good lawyers always found these clauses and threw them out. But for artists, the fact that they were there in the first place was enough to create a permanent distrust of the record company's motives. On the other hand, when record companies used similar underhandedness to get a record into the chart, the artist never complained.

Being in the chart created records sales. Marketing departments didn't 'sell records to get into the chart', they 'got into the chart to sell records'. Traditionally, the methods they used were called hyping rather than cheating. And in order to excuse themselves from accusations of dishonesty or downright illegality, those working in the industry preferred to think of getting records into the chart as a game.

In 1996, John Kennedy, a lawyer who'd made a substantial name for himself representing artists, was seduced away from private practice by an offer to become chairman of PolyGram.

Some of what he found he didn't like. 'There was a certain amount of hyping going on. In a meeting with the managing directors of our various companies, I asked whether any of them were doing it. They all remained silent, which gave me the impression that perhaps some of them were. So I told them, 'One thing is absolutely clear. If you're doing it, you're not very good at it, because our chart positions are fairly terrible.''

Kennedy knew something had to change at PolyGram. 'I had two choices – one, to teach them to do it better, or two, to take the moral high ground and decide we would have nothing more to do with hyping in the future.'

Kennedy admits that his decision to start a campaign against it was taken purely on pragmatic grounds. 'My morality was definitely influenced by the fact that we were not very good at it.'

He decided to do something that should have been done years before, but which no member of the BPI had ever dared to do. 'I went to the BPI meeting and asked, 'Can I assume that as a council we would be horrified if anyone sitting at this table were to be involved in hyping the charts?'

'Everyone shuffled in their seats so I said, 'I take that to mean you're all in agreement. And if that's the case, can I propose that if anyone at this table were to be caught hyping the charts we would jointly ask for the most serious possible sanctions against them?'

'All the BPI members started spluttering into their coffee, so I added, 'Either we're against hyping or we're not. And if we're against it, shouldn't we agree as a council that if we find chart hyping taking place we should ask the police to investigate it and urge the prosecutor to demand a prison sentence?''

After forty years, the game was up.

CHAPTER TWENTY-FIVE

SPICE AND VICE

The Spice Girls blew Britpop out of the window. They were the first beneficiaries of the industry's switch from chart hype to all-out marketing. In the nineties they became role models for teenage girls just as the Beatles had become role models for all young people in the sixties. But by the nineties the nature of role models had changed out of all recognition.

In the sixties the Beatles had been seen as talented, as having worked to get what they'd got. Other young people wished that they too had been bold enough to walk out of school, stick it out in Hamburg for two years and now be in the limelight reaping the benefit. The Beatles had struck gold, but although they'd been lucky, people felt they'd earned it.

The nineties was the lottery age. The Spice Girls weren't seen as musicians who'd earned their success, they were seen as lottery winners. To win the lottery was everyone's dream. Lottery winners were the new upper class. When teenagers aspired to being a Spice Girl, it was because those five girls had picked the lucky ticket. Unable to dance, unable to dress themselves with style, unable to sing, they'd nevertheless moved to the top.

It was their very ordinariness that made them so popular. They'd had luck. They'd bucked the system.

But when it came to bucking the system, it was the music business itself that took the prize. By the end of 1996 it was earning Britain over a billion pounds a year in exports and the new Labour government recognised it as a major industry, just like iron and steel, or insurance. But anyone who earned their living in the music industry knew how wrong they were.

At the 1997 Brit Awards I sat surrounded by A&R men and record company executives paying homage – not to the stars on-stage – but to the contents of bottles and capsules and small paper packets that were hidden around their person. A group picked up an award then walked straight from the stage to the toilets to sniff a quick celebration of coke. They did this in the presence of the Minister for Culture, the deputy Prime Minister and the Prime Minister's wife, all under the watchful eye of the TV cameras. But why not? It was expected of them, and it was expected of the industry – even politicians knew that. After all, it wasn't just artists who were up to their eyeballs in drugs, nor was it just the managers, the record producers, the A&R men and the company executives – it was also the record-buyers they were targeting, some of them the children of politicians.

Teenagers now saw drugs as a normal part of everyday life, like alcohol, football, video games or going to school. Young people in Britain had become drug literate. The average teenager knew more about the ups and downs of recreational drugs than his own family doctor.

By and large, they'd also learnt to take these drugs with some element of responsibility – no more, perhaps, than a teenager would show for anything else, but at least on a par with alcohol. Drug counsellors and social workers investigating drug use found a regular pattern among teenagers. In the minority, drug abuse and addiction on a worse scale than ever before. But in the majority, responsible drug use. Social workers didn't like to call it that because it appeared to condone drugs (which wasn't the official policy of the people who paid their wages), but an understanding of drugs and a sensible attitude towards their use had appeared among teenagers. They used the right drug for the right mood – laying off them when studying for exams, or taking amphetamines to keep alert for late night swotting – smoking joints for an evening at home listening to music, or taking an E for a Saturday night's clubbing. A report commissioned by the Joseph Rowntree Foundation said, 'Most young people who use drugs are as sociable, sensible, and morally aware as others of their age, and not the reckless, alienated, oblivion-seeking losers of popular myth.'

Hospitals now saw Saturday nights not only in the traditional image of alcohol and pub-fight victims, but also in terms of clubbing and drugs. In the main it wasn't overdoses that caused the casualties. *The Times* medical column reported that there were several altogether new symptoms now listed by urban hospitals.

Clubber's Nipple – *a friction burn suffered by girls dancing without a bra while waving their hands in the air* ... Clubber's Bottom – *a friction burn caused by dancing in PVC trousers without underwear* ... Clubber's Eye – *usually sustained as a result of dancers waving cigarettes in the air.*

Although selling drugs was still illegal, making money from talking about them certainly wasn't. Drugs now consumed volumes of newsprint and commanded a substantial service industry. Magazines and papers like *The Face*, *Mixmag* and *NME* endlessly quoted people talking about different drugs and suggesting music and style accessories to match. Pop stars, more than ever, were reported to be enjoying the benefits of cocaine, amphetamines, ecstasy and acid. Artists talked cheerfully to the press about the drugs they took.

Elastica told us, 'Speed is cheap and cheerful, it's a laugh and it makes you psychotic – which sums up the music, really.'

An artist known as Hooligan suggested that 'speed should be put in the water supply'.

The Boo Radleys admitted that their main objective in getting into music was to 'get famous and takes loads of drugs'.

George Michael let us know that his new album, *Older*, was 'pretty much recorded on cannabis – I wasn't drinking, because I was too stoned.'

Even tabloid journalists, whose job was to report these stories as if they were shocked, had quite different attitudes in private. Music writer Rick Sky admitted, 'If you like alcohol you're going to like drugs too, aren't you? Heroin feels good, cocaine feels good, amphetamine feels good. That's why drugs exist, because they feel so good.'

As the nineties moved on and the boom in ecstasy diminished, many club owners who'd benefited from its popularity now wanted to clear their names and claim their clubs had always been drug free. But the truth was no secret. Why would kids have gone into alcohol-free clubs at midnight planning to dance until dawn, if they hadn't been able to find the stimulants they needed inside?

The first club to head for respectability and disown its past was Ministry of Sound which was now primarily a record label. James Palumbo had been the success story of the nineties. He'd grabbed the opportunity to finance himself from the dance culture based on the boom in ecstasy and turned a small dance club into a self-sufficient industry. In doing so, he'd proved what everyone had suspected for years – major record companies' need for an across-the-board selection of contemporary music caused them to be unfocused and wasteful. Palumbo was never a modest man and was certainly not impressed by the quality of people in record companies with whom he had to do business. He told me, 'I've only come across two top executives with enough brains to justify their absurd salaries.'

After I'd taken him to Thailand, I took James to Japan. Selling the Ministry of Sound to the Japanese should have been a cinch, but the club's obvious connection with drug culture proved a drawback. Even so, everyone we talked to was longing to take the plunge.

I took James to meet not just those companies that had record interests like Sony and Toshiba, but to Japan's huge multi-faceted companies that dabbled in everything that was profitable in the Japanese economy – Mitsubishi, Sumitomo, Fuji. In each one of them we got as far as the boardroom but at Sumitomo we got the furthest. They were desperate to expand their hold of the Japanese youth market and needed Ministry's imagery to plug product sales through cable TV. They wanted it, but they were terrified of Ministry's connection with drug culture. Of all the world's great capitalist countries, the Japanese government had the strictest attitudes against youth drug use. It also had the oldest people in government – most of them ex-World War II soldiers, once sent to war on handfuls of amphetamines.

As usually happened in Japan, the attraction of profit won through. The boards of several major companies slowly overcame their qualms about the drug connection, but as they did so James slowly withdrew from making a deal. When he was offered finance to open Ministry bars all over Japan, he refused it.

In Britain, Ministry's greatest asset was its street-cred image – it was not part of the commercial establishment, it could be trusted, it was an arbiter of good taste in dance music and style. All the Japanese companies we spoke to intended to use Ministry's street-cred name to underwrite mainstream commercial sales projects. They were going to turn Ministry into a Disney-like trade name for late teens, and their plans were good. But once they'd convinced James Palumbo of the value of using Ministry's street-credibility in a more commercial way, he realised they needed him more than he needed them, and it might as well be him who reaped the profits. So he turned his sights back on Britain.

Meanwhile, the arrival of ecstasy in Japan and South East Asia opened up the market for Ministry without them having to waste time with opening clubs there. Tom Foley at React saw an immediate difference. 'We used to find it difficult to sell our product in Asia, but then they started getting ecstasy and suddenly the kids wanted house music. Our Asian exports went up ten times within two years.'

While the overseas markets looked after themselves, Ministry started a compilation dance album series that would challenge EMI's *NOW* in terms of sales. The name was *Dance Nation*, and as soon as James Palumbo discovered no one had copyrighted it, he realised he was about to hit the jackpot.

Ministry of Sound began building itself into the most successful independent record company in Europe. James embraced the idea of power. His instinct was to buy other companies and assimilate them, not to be assimilated into anyone else's set-up. He talked about wanting to be Prime Minister. 'How could you be?' I asked him. 'You know nothing about politics. You don't have a point of view on anything political, not even Left or Right.'

'But I don't need one yet, do I?' he insisted. 'When the time comes, I'll read up on it and decide where I ought to stand on the crucial issues.'

It reminded me of David Sylvian writing *Tin Drum* from a book of photos of China and planning to make an album about politics on the basis of buying a copy of *The Times*. There was much more of the creative artist in James than his business opponents realised. If used correctly against him, it could prove to be his weak spot. Artists can never make rational decisions about their artistic creations, which is what the Ministry of Sound is to James Palumbo.

In the run-up to the election James befriended the Labour party, lent them a limo, and met with Tony Blair. Later he told the press, 'I helped draft the government's anti-drugs bill. Really, it should go further.' In stark contrast he then started *Ministry*, a magazine that gave its readers the low-down on every aspect of dance, drugs and sex. 'GHB is said to increase sensuality and can lead to great sex.' 'LSD (about 300 micrograms in the form of five 'chocolate hearts") with four St John's Wort tablets ... one of the best drugs 'n' sex combos'.

Very quickly, *Ministry* magazine established itself as a success, an important reference point for late-teen culture.

Early-teen culture in the mid-nineties was still dominated by the Spice Girls. Virgin's managing director Paul Conroy had once worked with Madness at Stiff Records. From them he'd learned about projecting the image of a gang and had used it as the basis for the Spice Girls' image. Certainly, that's what the group now looked like. Where thirty years earlier, the Beatles had projected the image of the world's most exclusive gentleman's club, the Spice Girls projected the image of a female East End gang – five streetwise vamps, rampaging disdainfully through the record industry, whooping it up.

At the beginning of 1996 Take That split up. By July the Spice Girls had taken their place as the biggest band in the UK. By December they were the biggest act in the world. Geri Halliwell explained what it was like. 'You do the Brits, and then suddenly you'd be flying to New York and doing something equally fantastic, then you'd go to Cannes, then you'd do the Prince's Trust, then you'd start a movie, during which you'd write your second album, then you'd fly to Istanbul, rehearse for a tour, go to India, go to Australia for two days ... It was just so manic that you were fighting to take it all in, desperately wanting to absorb every special moment as well as being professional, doing your job, keeping the group together emotionally, and fighting jet lag.'

By the nineties, what pop and rock fans expected from their stars had changed significantly since the sixties. People no longer wanted manic rock stars, they wanted clever ones. In the post-ecstasy age, if it was drug-fuelled decadence you wanted, you didn't need a pop star to live out your fantasy for you – you could do it yourself. Pop stars were no longer admired for their anti-establishment integrity. Instead, they were respected for the sophistication with which they made themselves wealthy. For the industry, this was a dream come true – pop stars could now be coerced into every possible profit-making venture without losing credibility or record sales.

In the course of two years, the Spice Girls did promotions for Pepsi-Cola, Levi's, Poloroid and dozens of other companies. They had two hit albums, five hit singles, toured in thirty-three countries, made a movie and then fired their manager, seemingly to try and prove they could have done it all without him in the first place.

Financially, the girls had done well for themselves, but EMI, who owned Virgin, had done even better. By the end of 1998, the group had sold more than 35 million albums and 18 million singles.

For EMI, the cost of pressing a CD was not more than 20p. The cost of packing it in a plastic case with a paper inlay would have been deducted from the artist's royalties, an extraordinary anomaly which still persists in all contracts with major record companies. In the UK, EMI owned its own distribution company which sold records to retailers at what is known as PPD (Price Paid by Dealer). This varied, but at that time was usually around £7. From this was calculated the artist's royalty – a highish one might have been 18 per cent, or £1.25, but deducted from this was the cost of packaging the CD in its plastic box, usually calculated at 15–20 per cent of the total royalty.

After pressing costs and the payment of artists' royalties, this left a minimum of £5 per record in EMI's hands, approximately five times the amount that reached the artists. From 35 million albums, this would have come to £130 million, from which EMI would have paid the cost of worldwide marketing, which was unlikely to have exceeded £10 million. Meanwhile, with all their other earnings added in, the Spice Girls themselves were reported to be worth £19 million pounds each. An amount which had taken the Beatles fifteen years to make.

*

This was the nineties – the 'lottery age', the 'in-yer-face' age. Modesty and reticence were out. Seal told us, 'Five years ago I would get annoyed when my welfare cheque arrived a day late. The next thing I know, I'm pissed off if my limo didn't turn up.'

In the nineties, that's the way you were meant to be. If you made money you were meant to rise to the occasion and revel in it. But there was more to it than that – pop fans required their artists to be clever with their money too. The Spice Girls impressed their fans by getting themselves set up with top financial advisors. They were not going to blow the fortune they were earning.

In 1987 Joe Cocker was broke. His father, rummaging in Joe's living room, found a sixteen-year-old uncashed cheque from A&M Records for $197,000. At the time, pop and rock fans found the story endearing. Five years later, in the nineties, things had changed. When Sting discovered seven million pounds missing from his bank account, even though the culprit was his trusted accountant, the public's perception towards him seemed negative. 'Not clever with money, eh? What a loser!'

To modern teenagers, to be careless with money looked plain stupid. Nineties rock 'n' rollers had to be shrewder than that. Pop fans were no longer impressed by the extravagance of a group who paid $20,000 for a week's supply of cocaine. Nowadays they were more likely to be impressed by a group who could con their record company into buying it for them.

Similarly, when people said the Spice Girls couldn't sing, it wasn't a putdown, it was said in admiration. It was the

Spice Girls' ability to achieve wealth and stardom despite being perceived as unable to sing that so impressed their young fans. Once again it proved that kids on the street think the greatest heroes in the music industry are the people who take it for the biggest ride. Yet in reality the Spice Girls hadn't taken the industry for a ride at all, on the contrary, they were the first major success of the industry's shift towards more sophisticated marketing.

Paul Conroy, who had signed them to Virgin, explained, 'The way things work now is that marketing and A&R move hand in hand. We ask, can the company create something the company can sell? Does the singer and the song have what it takes to make a hit? How much impact will the artist make on TV? Extraordinarily, until very recently none of those questions was ever asked, it was just the A&R department choosing what music they liked.'

With the success of the Spice Girls the music industry was bursting with a new confidence. Damon Albarn of Blur put it down to something else. 'There's a blizzard of cocaine in London at the moment, and I hate it. It's stupid. Everyone's so blasé, thinking they're so ironic and witty and wandering round with this stupid cokey confidence.'

Drugs expert Harry Shapiro explains: 'In the music business, people thrive on aggression and hard partying. Cocaine is the ultimate creator of bullshit talk and action. Cocaine causes the body to release adrenalin and other natural substances that help it react swiftly in moments of danger or anger. In normal situations, when the danger has passed the body reabsorbs the chemicals. Cocaine prevents it from doing so. It's the perfect drug, not only for company executives, producers and managers, but for performers too. It imbues the user with supreme self-confidence, an illusion of clear-mindedness and manipulative power over others. It throws out etiquette and comes straight to the point.'

By the time the Spice Girls had hit the top, cocaine had become the music industry's official badge. DJ Lisa Loud has been around since the early days of Ibiza and was one of the first successful female house DJs. She thinks the universal shift to cocaine was simply the E generation growing up and changing their habits. 'It's almost stereotypical. People think, I go to these places now, I drive this car, so I've got to be spending £50 a night on my drug.'

Manager Tom Watkins was less enthusiastic. 'What with cocaine and the rest of it, half the industry has scrambled eggs for brains.'

Scrambling their brains nightly in the line of duty, junior A&R staff from the major companies went talent-spotting. In the late nineties no one working as an A&R scout could be employed if they didn't bring with them a working knowledge of contemporary drugs. Drugs were now the central core of youth culture and young people were using them in a purely cultural way rather than for making political statements. Teenagers moved trendily from designer drugs, like ecstasy, to golden oldies, like pot and pep pills. Ten years previously different dance clubs would have been inhabited by different groups of teenagers, each dedicated to their own type of drug and style of music. Now, on different evenings the same groups of teenagers moved from venue to venue, changing their drug-and-music combination according to the suitability of the occasion in which they were participating.

Pop and popular dance music, as always, was trying to follow the trend in drugs, but with ecstasy waning there was no dominant drug and therefore no dominant type of music. Dance mixes could promote records cross-culturally – rap music, techno, house or garage could each be remixed in the style and tempo of the other. The principal objective of an A&R man was to find music that could be crossed over from one specialist audience to another until it had expanded sufficiently to become mainstream.

Among all this musical diversity, one division of music never crossed the borders into popular dance. As a counter-balance to cocaine and manic Spice Girls optimism, there was a growing number of bands playing miserable anthems of despair. Top sellers were Radiohead, the Verve, Travis, and the Manic Street Preachers. Of these four, the Manics had originally started out looking quite promising. 'We're nihilistic,' they'd announced, 'it's a really positive thing.' Their subsequent path to stardom became as confused as their philosophy. Their principal member carved his arm with a razor blade, then disappeared, probably committing suicide. The most likely cause seems to have been a premonition of the group's future musical direction – mainstream 'glum rock'.

For people who didn't like dancing, these bands seemed to be the answer. For a while the Verve moved ahead of Oasis to be considered the biggest group in the country but the problem for this type of group was that record companies were no longer prepared to build new acts over two or three albums. Jazz Summers, now their manager, summed up the problem. 'The Verve only became popular with their third album. But now, with record companies spending to the hilt on marketing first albums, something like this is unlikely to happen again.'

There were still plenty of big acts around that had been built in the traditional style, emerging over a period of several albums, slowly creating a solid fanbase that could subsequently keep them at the top: Simply Red, Jamiroquai, M People – these were all acts that had originally been invested in by record companies with sufficient funds to let them develop over a period of time. But in the future, this would no longer be the case. Mounting corporate pressure for quick profits, coupled with the expense of the new marketing techniques, meant that an act's first album had to hit maximum sales. If not, the group would be dropped.

Record companies began to be criticised by the media for their lack of long-term commitment to new artists, but many people in the industry thought the situation was an improvement. Peter Jamieson, formerly chairman of BPI, has no regrets for the days when new artists received contracts guaranteeing them two or three albums. 'Groups get launched and they either happen or they don't. If they don't, they're dropped. For the record company it's a lot better than having to pay for pot-smoking layabouts to sit around the studio making second and third albums which everyone knows will get nowhere.'

By 1997, the upper levels of the charts were no longer manipulated by cheap trickery but by expensive marketing techniques, a situation that had come about directly as a result of the BPI's decision to reject chart fixing, as Tony Powell explains. 'Hyping in the Top 20 was impossible. The BPI had given the chart compilation to an independent source. There was now a computerised chart return machine from virtually every shop in the UK – more than 6,000 of them. To hype a record or to cheat the chart would be more expensive than the benefit it gave.'

But to think hyping wasn't taking place would be naïve. Clive Banks, manager of Mike Oldfield, pointed out, 'You can call it what you like, but if you've got the money to give Woolworths 20,000 free copies of your single and you can afford to pay them to give you a window, and you make a £200,000 video, you'll get into the charts. Isn't that still hyping?'

John Kennedy, who'd instigated the end to hyping, was more concerned with aggressive price-cutting. 'By 1997 the only way to get an advantage was by discounting. But managing directors got reports every Monday morning listing the prices that every single was selling at. Every company could see what the other was doing.'

But the problem with marketing and discounting is that they cost. With their expenditure rising so much, record companies were unwilling to spread the publicity for a new single over more weeks than necessary. Singles were now marketed ahead of release and had to sell straight into the Top Ten in the first week of release. When he was working as a lawyer, John Kennedy remembers going to a client's office on a Monday morning and waiting anxiously with him to see if his record entered the Top 75. 'Now, if it's not in the Top Ten it's hardly worth having marketed it. S Club 7 for instance has had a marketing spend of more than £1,000,000.'

By the late nineties, with a million pounds of marketing money needed on top of the original cost of signing and recording the artist, the major companies began to back away from anything that couldn't be turned into instant pop. In this new streamlined record business there would be no room for manoeuvre. Artistic temperament was 'out'; formula was 'in'. Everything would be planned, programmed and perfectly executed. Artists would have to enter quickly and willingly into the commercial pop machine. The record company's decision would be final.

In terms of aggressive, marketing-based pop the Spice Girls had shown the way and other girl groups like All Saints and B*witched had done well too. But really, ever since the fifties, the British music industry had always preferred working with boys. Their egos were bigger, they were more easily seduced by the rewards of success, and they didn't get pregnant. So for the last three years of the decade, company after company invested in four-and five-piece boy groups in the mould of Take That. The essential requirements were the ability to accept orders, a willingness to take dancing lessons, and good teeth.

CHAPTER TWENTY-SIX

BOYS, BOYS, BOYS

Boyzone, Westlife, 911, Code Red, 5ive, A1 – never before had the industry seen so many artists with so little attitude. By the end of the nineties, mediocrity was the order of the day. Westlife got four consecutive No. 1s with their first four records, but *Melody Maker* called them 'a bunch of karaoke monkeys barely able to scratch their empty testicles'.

Fabricated groups all used the same producers, the same writers, the same marketing techniques, the same video directors. The quality of production was more important than the artist – as were the songs, the clothes, the promotion, the videos, and the budget.

Everyone sang the same, danced the same, and moved the same. Vocal coaches now came to the studio and sang the song for the vocalist to copy. Everyone used the same vocal coaches so all the singers sounded the same. Boys for boy groups were chosen to appeal to young teenagers, then groomed and dressed accordingly. Groups were styled to produce fanatical young fans and purchasing records was simply a way of buying into their dream.

Frank Musker, Chairman of the British Academy of Songwriters, complained, 'A&R departments are no longer in the business of Artists and Repertoire. They have become high-level concept merchants who can't sell a new artist to their own record company unless there is a clear-cut marketing angle to be exploited ... In the past the singer would make the record and then the record company would devise a marketing campaign around it. Now the tail is wagging the dog and the music is the last element of the equation to be put into place.'

It was as if the film industry were to hire advertising agencies to come up with great posters, then try to make movies to go with them. Jonathan King thought it was the lowest ebb to which the industry had ever sunk. 'Artists are responsible for only a tiny amount of the reason that the record is a hit. Even in the case of those boy groups where someone can actually sing, the song will still have been written by someone else, plugged by someone else, promoted, marketed and put into packaging by somebody else, and all the so-called artist does is to stand in front of a camera and sing to it in the style his voice coach taught him. Yet they still get the full credit.'

Manager Stevo put it even more succinctly. 'The people who have the talent are the people backing the bands.'

Captain Sensible, now an ageing punk rocker, found it unbelievable anyone would want to watch a boy group. 'You want to see a group on stage that means it, like dangerous, like they're about to autodestruct, like next week they might be in prison for something or other – you wanna know they've got personality defects.'

The Prodigy perfectly fitted this description. They'd started out as an electronic dance group doing raves at the height of the ecstasy era. They played tough, futuristic music, rather mad but clearly 'rock' in attitude. Although devoid of guitars, the group miraculously ended up not only on the front covers of techno dance magazines but also of *Kerrang!*, the heavy-metallist's bible. Prodigy had fans from every side of the spectrum. Their live shows looked like rock while their records were mad amphetamine dance, and for a while they seemed to be everything the nineties was meant to be. They also made the best video of the decade – a creepy-crawly sex-and-drug horror movie in a crocodile-infested bed-sitting-room.

'The most important band this country has produced in the past five years,' said Daniel Miller, head of Mute Records, pointing out that originality could still sell. 'Oasis may sell well and be huge in Britain, but they sound so English. The Prodigy have truly international appeal.'

But all too soon, even Prodigy were being carefully packaged for export to America.

Stuart Watson, managing director of Jive Records, confirmed the worst fears of those who liked their pop with a little attitude when he admitted, 'We are selling branded goods like Mars bars or Colman's mustard.'

By the end of the nineties, the sheer volume of crass boy group pop music caused anything outside the mainstream to be termed 'alternative'. If you didn't copy Steps or Boyzone, you were probably 'alternative'. If you showed a little anti-establishment bile – if you were unable to pass the offices of a major record company without spitting or cursing – you were probably 'underground'.

To many, 'alternative dance' music was the new rock. The traditional rock-loving music press realised that if they were going to have to deal with hordes of knob-twiddling electronic musicians, they might as well support ones like the Prodigy, the Chemical Brothers and Fatboy Slim, who neatly injected rock music into their dance tracks. At its best, music like this had no record company input and no A&R man's influence. It reflected youth culture in the raw.

As always the music press had a tendency to overhype each new group to arrive on the scene. When, over a brief period in the mid-nineties, a few successful groups emerged from the Bristol area, *NME* immediately talked about a 'Bristol sound'. Londoners held their breath. What next? Torquay?

For the principal group that came from Bristol at the time, it couldn't have been more insulting. It was Massive Attack who defined the sound of the nineties – innovative music based on dance. It could be both pop and have depth. It could be easy-listening background music or mind-blowingly up-front loud. It could be slick and complex, or astonishingly simple. It frequently used the sounds and phrases of everyday life with hypnotic repetition. And it soon set the style for other musicians to follow. *Melody Maker* said of their single 'Unfinished Sympathy': 'It will unquestionably stand as one of the greatest soul records of all time. Utterly glorious.' And fans of all genres of music would vote it their favourite single of all time again and again.

Acts like Massive Attack, the Orb, Leftfield, Underworld and Goldie created something that straddled pop, dance and easy listening. Working with keyboards and computers, painting with sound and rhythm, they could create an aural collage that could be considered on a par with the best contemporary art of all sorts. Like all seriously considered art, the imagery contained in it was often obsessive and personal.

The stars of this music were not the singers but the producers. When the music required a singer, they used one who fitted the track rather than work consistently with the same voice. And at doing all these things, Massive Attack led the way. Many others followed, and in the face of the growing trend for boy groups, the British music industry found itself occasionally turning out some of the most mature and creatively worthy music it had ever produced.

The major record companies, however, could take no credit. At best, they came in belatedly, helping to finance the promotion of these artists by offering them marketing expertise and hugely expensive videos. In nearly all cases, they could take no credit for developing them. The major companies wanted quick hit music, not artistic concepts. They wanted popular imagery for the promotion of musical copyrights that they would own. They became more interested in marketing music than in recording it. As a result, even the most successful alternative dance acts found their promotion budgets being cut by the record company in favour of investing in the latest manufactured boy group. The British music business had become a totally pop industry.

As long ago as 1957 artist Richard Hamilton came up with a perfect definition of what pop should be:

Popular (designed for a mass audience) – Transient (short term solution) – Expendable (easily forgotten) – Low cost – Mass produced – Young (aimed at youth) – Witty – Sexy – Gimmicky – Glamorous – Big Business.

With the high cost of marketing and production, there was no possibility of pop in the nineties being low cost, but other than that Richard Hamilton's criteria were followed to the letter. One of the new areas in which record companies hoped to sell records was the sub-teen market where children were targeted as young as seven. Descending the cultural ladder to reach them were Steps and S Club 7, airbrushed replicas of humanoid youth, attempting something that scientists had always maintained was impossible – the attainment of absolute zero.

One girl group, All Saints, tested the boundaries of the new pop culture by grinding their crotches into the faces of their subteen audience. Soon, at weddings and family get-togethers, it became quite normal to see seven- and eight-year-old kids taking to the dance-floor and pumping themselves sexually in a carbon copy of All Saints' on-stage erotica. The *NME* called their act 'uncut lunacy ... living proof that pop stars are chosen at random.'

Sometimes the media commented with surprise that there were no solo stars coming out of these carefully stage-managed groups. But stars are difficult people. When groups were being put together the difficult ones were always left out.

Robbie Williams was one that got through. While he'd been with Take That, Robbie's off-stage exuberance had been suppressed by their manager. Within weeks of leaving, his fans found out that Robbie wasn't as squeaky clean as the rest of the group. Robbie drank, took drugs, screwed around and did all the other things expected of a competent pop star. He also had talent. He threw off Take That's plastic packaging, wrote his own songs, made his own mistakes and emerged as a star of the top order. But it was unlikely to happen again. The music industry no longer had time to take in renegades like Robbie and tame them.

Keith Richards once said, 'Record companies would love to get rid of musicians entirely, those bothersome things that talk back and want to do it better.' Now, what Keith had forecast was coming true. Record companies were no longer looking for musicians and singers, they wanted actors

– people who could learn their lines and play the role that was given them. Neil Tennant, in the midst of setting up a new tour for the Pet Shop Boys, complained that pop was being taken over by graduates of second-rate stage schools. 'If you do an audition for dancers or singers in London, there's a shortage of them. And these pop groups aren't really doing pop music at all, they're doing some weird kind of show-businessy thing, which is really anodyne and pre-Beatles in its inspiration. There is no darkness in Steps. The only darkness within that whole phenomenon is the sheer ambition in it, which has a cruel quality about it. Calculating, like Boyzone. It's an astonishingly calculated thing.'

If there was a plus side to this crassness it was that the videos these pop groups made were always politically correct. Whereas in the seventies and eighties it had been avant-garde musicians and political activists who'd stressed racial equality and social acceptance, it was now one of the principal themes of mainstream pop. Black or white, Chinese or Indian, gay or straight – everyone was sold as one big happy family. Sometimes it came across as pure kitsch, but by setting standards for children as young as seven, it was doing more for future racial harmony than any protest song had ever done.

By now the music industry included a substantial presence of the new generation of black youth. Black artists like Mark Morrison, Gabrielle and Eternal, as British as their white counterparts. It had been a long time coming – for, however talented they might have been, black artists had always struggled to find a way in the UK charts.

In the early eighties there'd been Amazulu, a black Bananarama (except that they could sing better). They'd mixed Caribbean attitude with happy British pop but finally drifted into a haze of heroin.

Billy Ocean had done better. He was the first British black artist to happen in America. He'd learnt the ukelele, completed a course in tailoring, worked in Savile Row, released a flop single, lost his job, found another in a Ford factory, got a break in the seventies and had sporadic small-time hits. But in the eighties he re-emerged with huge hits on both sides of the Atlantic, like 'Caribbean Queen' and 'When The Going Gets Tough'.

Although he was the first black artist from Britain to become a valuable export commodity, Billy was overlooked by British critics, mainly because he sang pop. I remember sitting in the 1987 annual ASCAP awards (the American Society of Composers and Publishers), watching Billy Ocean scoop award after award for his sales in the USA – best singer, best male artist, biggest selling song. In the States he was acclaimed as a great soul singer and *Billboard*, the leading music industry magazine, dubbed him 'that incredible voice'. Yet Britain didn't give him too much respect.

Seal, born in Paddington, found success through a year in Asia that changed his musical perspective. His first album was sixty-three weeks in the US album charts, his second stayed there for two years. His song, 'Kiss From A Rose', won him Grammy awards in 1996 as Record of the Year, Song of the Year, and Best Male Pop Vocal Performance. That year, he was the best-selling British pop artist in the world. But in Britain he was hardly even thought about.

Sade suffered the same fate. In America, in 1986, she was dubbed the 'Queen of Cool' and made the cover of *Time* magazine. Her second album, featuring 'The Sweetest Taboo', was No. 1 in the States and she won a Grammy for Best New Artist. Her first two albums sold 15 million worldwide and *Billboard*'s review of her third album called it 'simmering with style and substance'.

But in Britain, 'Your Love Is King' was her only hit single and that was it.

Sections of the British music media, always concerned with credibility, had taken the attitude that for someone black to sing pop was selling out. While Billy Ocean, Sade and Seal stormed America these sections of the British press still preferred Aswad, 'the most important voice in British reggae'.

They were. But if other British artists chose to sing pop, why couldn't the media give them the same sort of support?

In the early eighties, by looking after a young British soul singer called Junior Giscombe, Keith Harris became one of a very small select group – successful black British managers. As a kid, he'd always been aware of one or two black artists making it on the British pop scene. 'In the sixties there was Shirley Bassey, Kenny Lynch and Madeline Bell with Blue Mink. At the beginning of the seventies there were mixed groups like the Foundations and Hot Chocolate, then the 2-Tone groups, though the biggest-selling black British singer was Liz Mitchell who sang the lead with Boney M.'

Nevertheless, until the late nineties, large numbers of black artists had been unable to slip comfortably into the current chart scene and just be a part of it – despite the often huge success of their US counterparts. This highlighted the different attitudes of media and record companies on either side of the Atlantic. There was prejudice of a kind in record companies, but Keith Harris thinks it wasn't as simple as the staff being anti-black. 'It was more of a feeling among A&R men that black music should fit into a certain slot. They still thought of black people as being of a certain "type". Like when Carl McIntosh from Loose Ends went to visit his A&R man at Virgin. He walked over to the reception desk and said, "Tell them Carl's here." When the girl looked up and saw a black face she called upstairs and said, "Your minicab's arrived."'

But by the nineties attitudes had changed considerably. Soul II Soul had won a Grammy and sold six million albums in the USA. In Britain, new black pop singers were emerging who were much more integrated in the general pop scene. In the late nineties, there was a huge explosion of R&B and garage music bubbling up from the clubs and straight to the top of the charts.

Things seemed to be working out as they should do. Black artists were no longer being marginalised, they were simply being perceived as artists.

The same was also true of gays, and someone who did much to help in that direction was George Michael.

Really, we would all prefer that George hadn't been caught doing something in a toilet, and I'm sure he would too. But once it had happened, he took it as an opportunity to emphasise the very ordinariness of being gay.

By this time George had brought to near perfection the art of balancing personal publicity with the creation of pop music. For both, he deserved a place in the superstar elite – the aristocracy of the British music industry. But his cool bravado on CNN after his arrest confounded all those people who felt that having one's sexual feelings exposed required a subsequent period of head-hanging and shame. 'I don't feel any shame,' he insisted. 'I feel stupid and reckless and weak for having allowed my sexuality to be exposed this way. But I don't feel any shame whatsoever.'

In an interview with Michael Parkinson on BBC television, he again shrugged off the idea that he should be ashamed for having responded to the overtures of an undercover cop sent to provoke him. Wouldn't every heterosexual man have responded in the same way to an equally attractive female?

George's openness and humour were convincing. People who had liked him before the interview seemed to like him even more afterwards. But when George turned his arrest into a joke by shooting his next video in a laser-flashing disco-toilet he re-aroused the hatred of America's huge homophobe population. The Californian cop who'd set up his entrapment in the first place even tried to sue George for causing him emotional distress.

Wow!

It was fascinating, from the sixties onwards, to see how often gays and their lifestyle had cropped up in the history of the British music business. The number of gay people in major record companies has been negligible. Even the number of gay artists has been very small. Yet their importance seems to outweigh their numbers. In one form or another, the influence of gays on the British industry has been on a par with the influence of blacks and black music on the American industry.

Mick Jagger's provocative male-to-male sexual attractiveness was a fundamental part of the Rolling Stones' early success. So was Brian Epstein's gayness on the way the Beatles were presented and sold. And from the seventies onwards, many artists gained promotional benefits from outing themselves. Yet there were all too few British pop stars who just said openly and honestly from the beginning that they were gay – Tom Robinson was one, Jimmy Somerville another and there was also Andy Bell of Erasure. All three of them, like George Michael, presented themselves in a reasonably normal manner. On the other side of the fence were Marc Almond and Boy George, taunting the world with their obvious effeminacy.

Marc Almond went the full way and presented himself as an attractive sex object for straight men, the most dangerous thing any gay could ever do. When straight men found themselves fancying him, it made them hate both him and themselves. 'I was spat at in the street,' recalls Marc, 'punched in the face by strangers, insulted and ridiculed both in public places and on radio, on television and in the press, and it was all done in the most homophobic way imaginable.'

Boy George tackled the problem of his sexuality quite differently. He turned himself into a music-hall joke by making himself look as if he was at a fancy-dress party. As a result he came across as less sexual and straight men felt less intimidated.

David Bowie and Elton John came out more diffidently. Bowie, who was bisexual, went for the maximum publicity by announcing he was gay. Elton, who was gay, hedged his bets by saying he was bisexual. Both of them dressed outrageously when they were on-stage and rather normally when they were off it. To some extent this lessened the impact of their statements. When Elton put on normal clothes and turned up in the directors' box at Watford Football Club it was as if his declaration of bisexuality had just been an extension of his need to dress up on-stage, just a part of being in showbusiness.

George Michael didn't worry straight men too much. He didn't go out of his way to make them fancy him and he caused them no confusion about their own sexuality. And when George spoke on TV about his arrest, he almost made them understand. One man's dick stands up for blondes, another for brunettes, another for good-looking blokes. What's the difference? We're all in the same boat, none of us can control what our dick takes a liking to.

George even won round the British tabloids. To a man, they renounced gay bashing forever. And in return for publicising his pet charity, NetAid, George even gave an interview to his old enemy the *Sun* in which he admitted that their pursuit of Elton twelve years earlier had helped the cause of gay acceptance: 'the exposure of various celebrities' private lives over the last ten years ... I don't think it was meant to, but in its own way it has increased tolerance as well as selling newspapers'.

He was right. The next pop star to hit the headlines for being gay was Stephen Gately of Boyzone. The tabloids' new-found tolerance was quite sickening, particularly as it was later disclosed that Stephen had only gone public about himself because a Sunday paper had threatened to run a story on his love life if he didn't.

But the good thing was, the public just couldn't care less.

In 1999, I saw a report by Andrew Potter, chairman of PRS, reporting on the healthy state of the world music market.

> *We are currently collecting from around the world into the UK – £200,000,000 a year. In 1915 it was £4,000. In 1930 when we had a thousand members it was £173,000.*

In 1970 when there were 5,000 members it was £9 million pounds. In 1980, it was 13,000 members and £39,000,000. Now we are at 36,000 members.

Strangely, at that very same time, major British record companies were complaining that things were not as profitable as they should be. It seemed absurd – with the world's capitalist economies booming and young people everywhere spending more money than ever – that record companies were feeling the pinch. Of course, they were spending more than ever on marketing. But a glance through the annual report of any of the majors would reveal something else – they were also suffering the consequences of excessively high salaries.

At the top of EMI there were several executives who had no day-to-day connection with the running of the UK record company yet between them their salaries came to more than the combined salaries of all the people who ran the day-to-day business of the company that funded them.

Before becoming managing director of Andrew Lloyd Webber's Really Useful record company, Tris Penna was head of A&R at EMI's Parlophone label. 'Top executives were brought in, sometimes completely unconnected with music, and were paid huge salaries. Shortly after Jim Fifield arrived, we were all stopped from using couriers, which everyone presumed was because of his salary. You were actually restricted on how well you could do your job because the money was being siphoned off to pay all these salaries.'

At the same time that Tris Penna ran Parlophone at EMI, the general manager of the whole company was Clive Black. 'Simple things piss people off in companies – you can't do this, you can't do that, you can't get a cab. At EMI it caused quite a lot of resentment that certain executives would have a cab waiting outside all day just in case they wanted to go out. It's not good for morale when an executive's cab bill is larger than a junior member's salary.'

Marketing man Tony Powell thinks the industry is unusually bad at building careers for people. 'Instead of slowly promoting people from bottom to top, most managing directors, when they get a vacancy at the top end, look outside the company for a replacement. They buy people in at hugely inflated salaries. But managing directors themselves are usually on short-term contracts, just two or three years. So their thinking is short-term and self-centred. When they leave there are often half a dozen senior executives they brought into the company who are paid far too much for both their ability and the work they have to do. It's a big drain on a company's resources, and the next thing you know they're cutting the marketing budgets.'

In 1998, this is what happened to PolyGram. In 1997 they had a hugely successful ten-million-selling record by U2 which left the books looking good. But a year later, things had taken a turn for the worse and they found themselves top-heavy with executive pay demands. As a result Philips, the owners of the company, decided to sell the company to American drinks company Seagram.

Warners and BMG found themselves similarly pressured by costs and started making plans to consolidate and streamline. For the majors it was the beginning of the end of their slapdash history – an industry built on a boom in record sales of rock 'n' roll forty-five years earlier.

*

In the fifties, to escape the dreary parental attitudes of postwar Britain, the young protested with raucous rock 'n' roll. Record companies eagerly recorded the new music and released the resulting songs as vinyl singles. Twenty years later, albums of rock music were being packaged and sold with sophisticated marketing techniques. What had once been the sound of teenage protest had become a solid and respectable source of income. By 1999 real rock music was dying and unlikely to be revived. Paul McCartney said, 'Ballads and babies – that's what happened to me.' And that's what had happened to the British music industry. It had gone through its childhood, had a mad adolescence, struggled to bring up the kids, reached middle age and had at last got the hang of life. The result was a service industry which provided the public with a backing track to live by, but little more.

Even rock artists who had once been the industry's greatest renegades were beginning to see the music business in the same light. Pete Townshend admitted, 'Being famous through rock music is very insubstantial. It's an annoyance, an irritant. In twenty years I'm sure that sewage is going to be our main problem, and then the guy who takes away your rubbish and gives us a glass of clean water, he's going to be the great hero of our time. Pop music is a service industry, and when you get famous it's monumentally boring. I wouldn't go through it again.'

Despite Pete's outspoken disillusionment, the nineties produced the usual crop of dedicated young musicians hoping for success but unwilling to be groomed as boy groups. For them, the struggle to the top would be even tougher than it had been in the sixties. The public no longer welcomed new artists with the enthusiasm it once had. Rick Witter of

Shed Seven summed it up perfectly. 'I was working at York Sainsbury's, and people were walking past saying, "What a wanker." Now, because I'm in a group, people are going to be saying that in national magazines. It's the next step.'

CHAPTER TWENTY-SEVEN

NETTING THE PROFITS

I can tell you right now, there's no doom and gloom at the end of this book. The music industry is booming. And although it's grown up and become serious, you can still find lucky producers and songwriters becoming overnight millionaires, artists' managers making a healthy living outside the corporate structure, and record company middle-managers picking up £300,000 a year for doing little more than avoiding any decision that might connect them with something that fails.

While none of those things are as common as they used to be, it's still as easy as ever for junior A&R people to hang out each night in trendy clubs and put in petty cash vouchers for the 'extras' incurred. Corporate acceptance of sex 'n' drugs 'n' rock 'n' roll has never been higher. Only recently I received an Internet flyer from an A&R department of one of the world's four major record companies, consisting of a game where Es fell from the ceiling and dancers had to try and catch them.

Yes, the British music industry, Britain's greatest contribution to world culture in the twentieth century, is alive and well and doing more drugs than ever.

But business-wise, how are things changing? To find out I had a quick round of dinners and conversations.

Sir George Martin thinks, in ten years' time, record companies as we know them will have ceased to exist. 'Music is being disseminated by new methods – by digital TV, by endless local radio stations, but most importantly on the Internet. Record companies will simply become huge distribution companies acquiring copyrights for exploitation, distributing through electronic means.'

Pete Waterman goes one step further. He sees a change in the way record companies make their profits altogether. 'With producers finishing new mixes and immediately putting them onto the Internet, the recorded copyright is going to become less important and songs will be the future of record companies' income. That's why record companies are buying publishers as fast as they can.'

Manager Clive Banks agrees. 'There'll be no more vast profiteering from vinyl resold at twenty times its physical value. Record companies are effectively becoming publishers. By releasing songs as a digital file on the Internet they are effectively publishing them. They'll make their money by charging a small fee each time someone copies a recording from the Internet or listens to it on digital TV.'

This is exactly the way music publishers earned their money before record companies took over the industry in the mid-fifties. So has the music business come full circle?

'Yes!' says John Kennedy, Universal's UK president, the man who tried to end hyping. 'But despite the drop in income when the Internet becomes the chief form of distribution, our high marketing spends will still continue. For kids bought up with videos and MTV, even the best artists have to be marketed with all the tools of the trade, the same tools you might use for less talented artists.' Like many people within the UK industry, EMI chairman Rupert Perry sees things broadly remaining as they are. 'The biggest changes that are taking place are internal administrative ones. Despite the Internet, for most record buyers, things are little different now from how they were in the sixties, and that's probably how it will stay. Radio and TV will continue to be the principal methods of plugging popular music. And record shops will continue to be happy social centres where recorded music is obtained in one form or another as well as being available over the Internet.'

At Jive Records, Stuart Watson too thinks that promotion and marketing will stay as it is, but he admits distribution channels will probably change. 'Singles will be announced for downloading on a certain day at a certain time and promoted ahead of time. When downloading becomes the major way of purchasing product, millions of downloads will be made the first couple of days of release.'

'Won't that affect the chart?' asks Jeremy Marsh, managing director of BMG Records. 'At the moment, to be in the chart, singles have to be sold at a chart return shop. With record companies running their own websites there will be no policing mechanism ... I think the Web is the beginning of the end for the chart system.'

'Not a bad thing if it is,' says Roger Greenaway, chairman of ASCAP. 'The fact is that at the moment the chart is a promotional and marketing tool which the majors can exploit with high marketing spends. If the chart were to disappear, the majors might have to compete on an equal footing with smaller independent companies.'

Jonathan King looks forward to this turning of the tables with relish. He hopes that by using the Internet artists will turn the clock back. 'One of the things I always loved about this industry was being able to make your own records at home for £50. It was a very positive thing – you could find a second-hand guitar, you could write a hit and become a millionaire.'

Many people ask: if artists can make their own records and put them onto their own Internet sites, will record companies be needed at all?

'Of course they will,' says Clive Black. 'An artist sitting at home sending his music out over the Net doesn't feel like a star. He wants to be loved and acclaimed. The record company provide him with a limo outside his front door, welcome him to the office, take him out to lunch, give him a line of coke.'

During the last year, whenever I've found myself in a group of music industry people, these are the sort of arguments and discussions I hear. From listening to them, one thing seems to have become clear. In the twenty-first century the emphasis in the industry will be on the exploitation of copyrights, not on the sale of vinyl.

My own forecast is that the industry will be divided into two – a copyright creation industry, which finds and markets artists – and a copyright exploitation industry, run by accountants, lawyers and bankers. At the top end, the exploitation of recorded copyrights will be lumped together with the exploitation of copyrights in films, videos, games, books and all manner of other things – effectively, all one industry.

Bertelsmann have already moved further than anyone else in this direction. They not only own BMG Entertainment, which includes Arista and RCA Records and BMG Music Publishing, but they also own Random House, one of the world's major book publishers. And they own investments in telecommunications, the Internet and mobile phones. Overall, Bertelsmann have 65,000 employees in 45 countries and turn over $29 billion a year in revenue. The result of all this is that the key people in the record division are less important than they used to be in the overall league of BMG executives. The whole entertainment division of BMG accounts for only 30.1 per cent of its turnover, while book publishing accounts for 30.8 per cent.

The same applies to the huge conglomerate now composed of WEA and AOL.

At Sony too, records are just a division of something infinitely larger. Even at Universal, which is specifically an entertainment company, records are outshone by movies, TV and other interests, and in 2000 the whole of Universal became just another division of a conglomerate company whose main businesses are mobile phones and water purification.

To me, despite these changes, British pop music has never sounded better nor been better produced. Someone else who thinks the same is Daniel Miller of Mute, who's had his ears open to the best avant-garde pop music for the last thirty years. 'It's the most creative time for music,' he says. 'There's a huge ground swell of great music being made.'

I agree. I find that much of today's computerised dance and trance music manages to be both meaningful and fun in the way of good modern painting or architecture. Without the fun, so does the music of Radiohead, who might once have been described as rock but have now moved on to something else.

On the other hand, traditional rock music will soon be consigned to musical history like bebop, Dixieland and Gilbert & Sullivan. At present, it survives only because it's still the greatest music there is for live concerts and achieves a rapport with large audiences that is completely different from dance or pop music. Dance rhythms turn people in on themselves and make them introverted. Rock rhythms bring them out of themselves, arouse them, and provide a bond between performer and listener. So in the UK rock survives, but only just. To promote it, the industry has had to integrate it with the pop market. Rock can no longer exist away from pop as it did in the days of Led Zeppelin.

Nowadays, when we see concerts featuring guitar groups like Travis on the same bill as teeny-bop crotch-jerkers like All Saints, it becomes abundantly clear that whether it's called rock, hip-hop, dance or teeny-bop, it's *all* just pop music. All the artists are in the same industry, marketing themselves in the same way, like so many ice-creams in a supermarket freezer. Magnum, Solero, Bounty or Crunchie – Westlife, Oasis, the Corrs or B*witched – each has its own imagery and style but is packaged, marketed and distributed by the same teams of people.

At the beginning of the twenty-first century, young Britain is almost a classless society. In the mid-fifties, as a teenage bandboy for the Johnny Dankworth Orchestra, I found having a public-school accent an embarrassment – not because I was laughed at, but because it got me unwarranted respect. Nowadays, it's commonplace for teenagers from an upper-class background to downgrade their accents to gain equal opportunities in normal society. Bono once described Neil Tennant's voice as having 'the quality of a Toyota commercial'. Although it was meant as an insult it was actually a compliment. Television ads are aspirational. The voice on a Toyota ad seems a voice worth having. It's one more homogenising factor in modern life, and the same homogenisation spills over into public taste in music. As time passes, the musical differences between different acts seems to diminish rather than increase.

Until a decade ago, the artists that record companies wanted were the ones with the greatest musical individuality. Now it's the ones who can subtly change their image to match current fashion and turn out the least pigeonholed music. With no social significance attached to an artist's image the music is free to make its own statement. More importantly, it can be used for advertising or endorsing a variety of products without conflicting with what the artist stands for. The value to the record company grows accordingly. From now on, the big money will come from licensing records to advertisers, using records in film scores or playing them as title music for TV programmes or sports events. Some people in A&R departments still kid themselves they're looking for musical artists, but they're not. They're looking for marketable faces with which to exploit copyrights. But it's not an artistic disaster, it's just a shift in emphasis.

Like many people, I miss the excitement of the days when a group could make a record on Monday, hear it played on the radio on Tuesday and see it in the shops on Friday. But at the same time, it's good to see things change. Record companies now have real marketing departments with a thorough understanding of promotion, something that in the past was all too often thrown at the manager to deal with.

The British music business has at last turned itself into a real industry, something approaching what America has had for the last twenty years. Bullshit is down and quality is up. But with packaging and marketing on a par with any other industry, stars have to accept being turned into products. If a major campaign creates no record sales, the artists will be instantly dropped – there'll be no second and third albums. The music business is tougher, better organised and more professional than it's ever been before, but in such a competitive environment record companies no longer have the time or the money for artist development – profit is all that matters.

On a recent trip to America I bumped into Ed Bicknell, Dire Straits' manager. He'd just been to a meeting at Reprise where someone told him, 'We don't sell music anymore – we sell shares! We need hits, not artists.'

When we refer to Elton John, or Sting, or George Michael as superstars, it's not simply because of their music, it's because they've taken the raw material of their ordinary selves and sculpted it into superstar imagery. The irony is that although the back catalogues of artists like these are hugely valuable assets, record companies are no longer sure they want to create such megastars. They can be too difficult and self-centred.

When I talked to Tom Watkins, flamboyant manager of East 17 and Bros, he told me he'd seen the star of the future. It's a computer-generated pop star called Kukali. 'Anything you can imagine, you can make him do. He's my favourite artist already because he simply doesn't answer back. He hasn't got a lawyer, he's not going to go on the strop, he's not going to phone me stoned in the middle of the night to say he wants to give up being a pop star and become a Buddhist monk.'

So in the modern climate, Tom's no longer a manager – he's the owner of a copyright.

The multinational owners of the world's record business hierarchy – BMG, Universal, Warner and Sony – look down on their new acquisitions and see, all too clearly, the value of these copyrights. But while copyright exploitation will undoubtedly become the main focus of the major record companies, the boardrooms of the multinational corporations that own them will be wary of connecting themselves too closely with the potentially drug-ridden world of pop music. It's likely that the 'copyright exploitation departments' will separate themselves from the 'copyright creation departments' (the old A&R departments). These will be broken up and scattered around to create a broader net. As a result, young entrepreneurs will find more sources of finance and be given greater freedom.

For those of us who like work to be fun, the A&R half of this new two-tier music business is the place to be. That's where you'll find entrepreneurs, managers and artists. But from upstairs, in the 'copyright exploitation departments' there'll be a fair number of starstruck executives who like to come downstairs occasionally to see how things are going. As always, these top executives will be unable to resist the odd evening out with the artists – getting drunk, checking out the latest music, checking out the latest drugs.

Personally, when it comes to drugs, my own experience extends only to smoking a few joints and once having taken a single amphetamine tablet. But like me, most people in the industry who don't use drugs are nevertheless quite unfazed by their all-pervasiveness. Martin Mills of Beggars Banquet admits, 'For some artists drugs seem to play a necessary part in their creativity. It's up to them how they use them. I have never ever taken them myself but I can't really say I disapprove of them.'

Well how could he? How could any of us?

Like everyone who profits from the music business, I

have to accept that I'm profiting from an industry inexorably intertwined with the promotion of recreational drugs of all sorts. For many people, doing the right ones with the right people at the right time has led to a fortune or even being knighted. Sir Elton John openly admits to twenty years of drug-taking as he made his way to a knighthood. Sir Paul McCartney owns up to having used all manner of drugs and has been busted and jailed on several occasions. And if Sir Elton and Sir Paul represent the 'acceptable' face of the industry, what about the others?

Sting once said, 'The term rock star is pejorative; it means maniac – drug addict ...' And he was right. Think of a name in British popular music and the facts about drug-taking are there, interview after interview, confession after confession, biography after biography.

Since the beginning of rock 'n' roll, the interrelationship between drugs and music has been commercially and creatively beneficial to the industry. Drugs helped the music industry invent itself and at different times have sustained it, revitalised it and even refinanced it. Drugs can help create the right conditions for music to be made and for record sales to thrive. As Jarvis Cocker points out, 'Part of the reason that people listen to music is that it gives them a picture of another world, and that's the same thing that happens when people take drugs.'

Within the industry, when people express disapproval of drugs they're often objecting not so much to them being used as to them being used irresponsibly. Factory Records boss Tony Wilson loathes cocaine when it's taken into the recording studio. 'Nothing destroys creativity like cocaine,' he warns. 'Never work, think or try to create on it.'

But when work isn't involved, he thoroughly enjoys the stuff. 'We all do it at weekends,' he happily admits. 'It's a party drug.'

Even Ken Tappenden, the Kent police commander who spent two years of his life trying to close down the E scene, has now come to see that raves were not the evil he once thought they were. 'I often wonder why we bothered. Super lights, lovely people, and I wish them well for the future.'

In October 2000, I attended the annual Roll of Honour dinner held by the Music Managers Foundation where the person being honoured was Genesis's manager, Tony Smith. In the past, the names have included manager Ed Bicknell, Universal MD John Kennedy, publisher Peter Reichart, Warner chief executive Rob Dickins, and promoter Harvey Goldsmith. The award they are presented with is 'The Peter Grant Award'.

Bearing in mind the reputation of Led Zeppelin's manager for violence and drug addiction, some people might find this outrageous – like giving someone in the drinks industry 'The Al Capone Award' – or presenting a politician with 'The Saddam Hussein Award'. But to most people, Peter Grant's druggy image seems happily in tune with the industry they know and love. And no one who has ever been offered the award has turned it down.

The honouring of key music business figures with an award bearing Peter Grant's name not only shows respect for a great manager, it also emphasises the industry's easy acceptance of the part that drugs have played in its history. The reverence and good humour with which the Peter Grant Award is presented and received each year is a timely reminder that attitudes in the British music industry are much the same as they always have been.

Black vinyl may have gone. White powder seems here to stay.

CAST OF CHARACTERS

Abrams, *Stephen* American psychology graduate doing research into ESP at Oxford University in the 60s

Adam Ant Grubby 70s punk who turned himself into an immaculate 80s teen idol

Aitken, *Matt* One of the Stock Aitken & Waterman songwriting/production partnership

Albarn, *Damon* Lead singer of 90s group Blur

Albert, *Ted* Owner of Australian publishing and record company

Aldred, *Michael* Co-compere of *Ready Steady Go!*, 1963–68

Almond, *Marc* Singer with Soft Cell; early user of ecstasy

Altham, *Keith* Features editor for *NME* in early 60s, then publicist to pop and rock stars

Amadeo Owner and door policy controller of Sombrero club, High Street, Kensington

Ambrose, *Dave* Bass player in the 60s; A&R for EMI in the 70s; ran MCA Records in the 80s

Ames, *Roger* Founder of London Records, then head of PolyGram, then Warner

Anderson, *Brett* Lead singer of 90s group Suede

Angus, *Colin* Member of 80s/90s group The Shamen

Antonioni One of Italy's greatest filmmakers: *L'Aventura, Blow-Up, Zabriskie Point*

Arden, *Don* Tough-guy East-End manager in the 60s, 70s and 80s: Nashville Teens, Small Faces, Amen Corner, ELO, Black Sabbath, Lynsey de Paul

Asher, *Jane* Paul McCartney's first girlfriend as a Beatle

Astley, *Rick* Tape operator at Pete Waterman's studio who got the chance to sing

Bacall, *Lauren* Great 30s and 40s Hollywood film star

Bacharach, *Burt* One of America's greatest living composer-songwriter-producers

Bacon, *Francis* One of Britain's great twentieth-century painters

Baez, *Joan* Politically minded American folk singer in the 60s and 70s

Baker, *Adrian* One of Britain's most sought-after session singers in the 60s and 70s

Baker, *Ginger* Fiery red-haired rock drummer; one of 60s rock group Cream

Baldry, *Long John* Tall British blues singer; now living in Canada

Ball, *Kenny* Moustachioed Dixieland jazz trumpeter

Bangs, *Lester* Much respected American music critic and commentator

Banks, *Clive* 60s and 70s plugger who became 80s and 90s manager

Barber, *Chris* Dixieland jazz trombonist and band leader

Barbieri, *Richard* Keyboard player with 70s/80s group Japan

Barlow, *Gary* Lead singer and songwriter with 90s boy group Take That

Barrett, *Syd* Pink Floyd singer/guitarist who became a recluse

Barrie, *Jack* In the 60s, manager of the Marquee club; in the 70s also manager of Bangs disco

Barry, *John* 60s arranger/producer who became film composer: James Bond movies, *The Ipcress File*

Bart, *Lionel* Songwriter and creator of musical *Oliver!*

Bassey, *Shirley* Britain's first great black singing diva

Batt, *David* Singer with 70s group Japan; changed his name to David Sylvian

Batt, *Steve* Drummer with 70s group Japan; changed his name to Steve Jansen

Baverstock, *Jack* Head of A&R at Philips Records in the 60s

Beaton, *Cecil* Photographer and friend of the royal family from the 40s to the 60s

Beck, *Jeff* Britain's greatest blues guitarist; once a member of the Yardbirds

Beerling, *Johnny* Producer at BBC Radio One; then overall programme controller

Belcher, *Muriel* Lesbian owner of Colony Club, Soho's showbiz meeting place of the 50s and 60s

Bell, *Madeline* Black American singer who came to London in the 60s and stayed

Benjamin, *Louis* Head of Pye Records during its heyday in the 60s

Bennett, *Tony* Great American singer of the pre-rock 'n' roll generation

Berkmann, *Marcus* Journalist and columnist in the *Daily Mail*

Bertelsmann Founder of BMG Records and the Bertelsmann group of companies; started as door-to-door magazine salesman in Germany after the war

Best, *Pete* The drummer the Beatles fired just before they became successful

Bez Dancer/band-member of late 80s/early 90s E-influenced Manchester group the Happy Mondays

Bicknell, *Ed* Manager of Dire Straits

Bilk, *Acker* Dixieland clarinet player and band-leader

Billings, *Vic* Manager of Dusty Springfield in the 60s

Birkin, *Jane* Actor and wife of French musician Serge Gainsbourg

Black, *Cilla* Brash 60s Liverpool singer managed by Brian Epstein

Black, *Clive* Former general manager of Warner, then EMI, and son of Don Black

Black, *Don* One of Britain's top songwriter/lyricists since the 60s

Blackburn, *Tony* Radio DJ who started on pirate Radio London, then moved to BBC Radio One

Blackwell, *Chris* White Jamaican founder/owner of Island Records

Blaikley, *Alan* Co-manager of 60s groups the Honeycombs and Dave Dee, Dozy, Beaky, Mick & Tich

Blake, *John* Tabloid journalist and gossip columnist, now a publisher of showbiz books

Blanchflower, *Robin* Record company employee

Bloom, *John* 60s tycoon who flooded Britain with cheap washing machines

Bogart, *Neil* Flamboyant owner of Casablanca Records, America's most successful independent record company in the 70s

Bolan, *Marc* Made his name as a 60s hippy singer on a rug, then became a glam rock megastar

Bond, *Graham* Substantially girthed 60s jazz-funk keyboard player and bandleader

Bonham, *John* Drummer with Led Zeppelin

Bono Public moraliser and proselytiser and lead singer with Irish rock band U2

Booth, *Stanley* American journalist who toured with the Rolling Stones in the 60s

Boothby, *Lord Bob* A politician. In the 20s, Churchill, commenting on why Boothby always picked such unattractive girlfriends, famously said 'Buggars can't be choosers'

Bowie, *Angie* American girl who married David Bowie

Bowie, *David* Probably Britain's most influential solo pop/rock star ever

Boy George Tall, jokey, fun, camp, outspokenly gay superstar of 80s pop

Boyd, *Patti* Beatle George Harrison's first wife who later married Eric Clapton

Bragg, *Billy* Politically minded, socially committed 80s folk singer

Branson, *Richard* Businessman with a hippy image but a thoroughly capitalistic business empire

Brown, *Ian* Lead singer with 90s Manchester E-influenced rock group the Stone Roses

Brown, *James* One of the all-time great black American soul singers

Brown, *Jericho* Flatmate of record producer Steve Rowland in the 60s

Brown, *Joe* One of Larry Parnes's stable of 50s rock 'n' roll singers

Brown, *Pete* Songwriter for Cream and other 60s and 70s rock groups

Bruce, *Jack* Bass player with 60s supergroup Cream

Bruce, *Tommy* 60s rock 'n' roll singer

Burdon, *Eric* Singer with 60s pop/rock group the Animals

Burgess, *Anthony* One of Britain's great twentieth-century authors: *A Clockwork Orange, Malayan Trilogy*, etc.

Burgess, *Guy* 50s gay spy who defected to Russia; half of the Burgess–MacLean scandal

Burgess, *John* Record producer with EMI in the 60s and with Air; George Martin's company thereafter

Burns, *Hugh* One of Britain's leading session guitarists since the early 70s

Burroughs, *William* American author who emerged from the Beat Generation and wrote *The Naked Lunch*

Burton, *Richard* Welsh Shakespearean actor, drunk and husband, first to Sybil, then to Elizabeth Taylor

Burton, *Sybil* First wife of Richard Burton

Bush, *Kate* Quirky, skinny 80s pop star

Calder, *Tony* Was once a teddy boy, then a partner in Immediate Records, then a resident of Antigua and manager of reggae star Eddy Grant

Callander, *Pete* Wrote songs with British songwriter Mitch Murray

Capone, *Al* Leading American Mafia mobster of the 20s prohibition era

Captain Sensible Leader of the 70s punk band the Damned

Carrà, *Raffaella* Italian disco singer in the late 70s

Carducci, *Joe* American author of the book *Rock and the Pop Narcotic*

Carroll, *Ronnie* 50s British romantic pop singer

Cash, *Johnny* American country and western singer

Cass, *Mama* Big lady from the American singing group the Mamas & Papas

Chandler, *Chas* Bass player with the Animals, then manager of Jimi Hendrix and Slade

Chapman, *Michael* Half of the 80s songwriting team Chapman & Chinn

Charles, *Prince of Wales* Heir to the British throne

Checker, *Chubby* American black singer who made the Twist famous with his record 'Let's Twist Again'

Chelita Wife of Tony Visconti; producer of Marc Bolan and other 70s hit acts

Cher American female singer

Chinn, *Nicky* Half of the 80s songwriting team Chapman & Chinn

Chou, *Mr* Opened a showbiz Chinese restaurant in London where the waiters were all Italian

Clapton, *Eric* A great British guitarist

Clark, *Dave* A 60s pop star, drummer and group-leader

Clark, *Petula* British actress and pop singer who went to live in France

Cleave, *Maureen* Journalist and regular *Evening Standard* feature writer in the 60s and 70s

Climie, *Simon* Songwriter and singer; part of 80s group Climie Fisher

Coachworth, *Frank* A music publisher in London since the 50s

Cocker, *Jarvis* Lead singer with 90s Britpop group Pulp

Cocker, *Joe* Coarse-voiced and odd-moving 60s rock singer who still keeps going

Cohn, *Nik* Newcastle-born journalist and novelist

Cole, *Nat King* American black pop star and jazz pianist of the 40s and 50s

Cole, *Richard* The tour manager for Led Zeppelin throughout their career

Collier, *Mike* Briton producing records in the States in the 50s; became music publisher in London in the 60s, 70s and 80s

Collins, *Gerry* DJ and disco entrepreneur

Collins, *Phil* Child actor turned Genesis drummer turned solo singer

Como, *Perry* 50s American soft romantic singer

Conroy, *Paul* Ex-manager who gave it up to run Virgin Records

Conway, *Russ* Nine-fingered 60s pop pianist who lost a digit in the navy

Cooke, *Sam* One of America's great black soul singers of the 50s and 60s

Cooper, *Alice* American rock star who dressed funny and played with snakes on-stage

Copeland, *Miles* Manager of the Police, and the brother of their drummer

Cosimo, *Piero di* Florentine painter renowned for painting fauns and centaurs and for living off hard-boiled eggs which he cooked while boiling his glue to save fuel costs

Costello, *Elvis* British rock poet who emerged during the punk era

Cotton, *Billy* 40s and 50s bandleader with regular radio variety show

County, *Wayne* 70s glam rock star who changed his sex

County, *Jayne* The person he became

Coward, *Noël* Great British author, playwright and wit

Cribbins, *Bernard* Popular English comedian of the 60s and 70s

Crooks, *Richard* One of the twentieth century's greatest operatic tenors, at his peak in the 20s and 30s

Crosby, *David* American singer-songwriter, member of 70s rock group Crosby, Stills & Nash

Crowley, *Aleister* Victorian author and adventurer, heavily into drugs, sex and black magic

Curnow, *Ian* A producer working with Pete Waterman's team in the 80s

Currie, *Billy* Keyboard player with New Romantic groups Visage and Ultravox

Currie, *Steve* Bass player with Marc Bolan during the time of his greatest success

Dagger, *Steve* Manager of 80s New Romantics Spandau Ballet

Dali, *Salvador* Spanish painter with funny moustache

Daltrey, *Roger* Singer with the Who

Dankworth, *Johnny* Respected British jazz musician

Dannen, *Fredric* American author of *Hit Men*, about the US music industry

David, *Irving* London-based music business lawyer

Davies, *Dave* A member of 60s group, the Kinks; brother of lead singer Ray

Davies, *Ray* Singer/songwriter and leader of the 60s pop group the Kinks

Davis, *Clive* American record executive; ran CBS in the 70s, Arista in the 80s and 90s

Davis, *Miles* Black American jazz trumpeter

Davis, *Spencer* Leader, but not singer, of the 60s British rhythm & blues band the Spencer Davis Group

Day, *Doris* American film star and pop singer, 50s and 60s

Dean, *James* Legendary American film star

Dean, *Mark* Whizz-kid young record man who signed Wham! in the early 80s

Dean, *Rob* Played guitar with Japan

Dee, *Dave* In the 60s, one fifth of Dave Dee, Dozy, Beaky, Mick & Tich; in the 80s, a record company A&R man

Deedes, *William* In 1964 an Old Harrovian, member of the Cabinet and minister in charge of the government's information services

Dee Generate Minor British punk star of the 70s

Defries, *Tony* Manager of David Bowie in the 70s

Des Barres, *Pamela* Groupie, chiefly with Led Zeppelin, and author of *Rock Bottom*

Diana, *Princess* Princess of Wales; wife of Prince Charles

Digance, *Richard* Quirky British folk singer in the 70s and early 80s

Dion, *Celine* Canadian megastar ballad singer

Domino, *Fats* Black American rhythm & blues singer of the 40s and 50s

Donegan, *Lonnie* Perpetrator of the skiffle craze in Britain in the 50s

Donner, *Clive* British film director: *Here We Go Round the Mulberry Bush*, *What's New Pussycat*, *Nothing But the Best*

Donovan Donovan Leitch: folksy British pop singer loosely modelled on Bob Dylan

Donovan, *Jason* Australian soap star from *Neighbours*, turned into British pop star

Donovan, *Terence* Jason's father, a great fashion photographer

Doonican, *Val* An Irish singer with endless droning hits in the 60s

Dorsey, *Gerry* Original stage name for Anglo-Indian singer Englebert Humperdinck

Downes, *Geoff* Keyboardist with Buggies and Asia

Driberg, *Tom* Gay Labour cabinet minister in the 60s

Duncan, *Jake* Tour manager with Ozzy Osbourne, Wham! and others

Dylan, *Bob* Legendary American folk-rock-pop singer

Eager, *Vince* One of Larry Parnes's stable of 50s rock 'n' roll singers

East, *Dolly* Wife of Ken East

East, *Ken* Australian managing director of EMI London, then of Decca

Eastman, *Lee* American businessman; father of Linda

Eastman, *Linda* Amateur photographer who married Paul McCartney

Ecstasy *Cindy* Backing singer and drug supplier to the 80s group, Soft Cell

Eddy, *Duane* 50s and 60s American rock 'n' roll guitarist

Egan, *Rusty* DJ at the Blitz club in early 80s; became part of the hit group Visage

Elliott, *Tony* Publisher of *Time Out* in the mid-70s

Elms, *Robert* British music journalist

Emerson, *Eric* American music journalist for *Rolling Stone* in the 70s

Emerson, *Keith* Keyboardist with Emerson, Lake & Palmer

Englemann, *Franklin* Staid old-fashioned BBC radio presenter in the 40s and 50s

Entwistle, *John* Bass player with the Who; started out playing trumpet in a Dixieland jazz band

Epstein, *Brian* Manager of the Beatles

Eppy *see* Brian Epstein

Ertegun, *Ahmet* One of two Turkish brothers who went to the USA in the 50s and started a record label, Atlantic Records, which became one third of WEA records

Evans, *Sir Richard* The British ambassador to China in the 80s

Everett, *Derek* A&R man at EMI in the 60s, CBS in the 70s, and then of his own company

Everett, *Kenny* Liverpool-born DJ in the 60s and 70s; TV comic in the 80s

Everett, *Lee* Girlfriend of Billy Fury in the 50s, then wife of comedian Kenny Everett

Faith, *Adam* 50s and 60s pop star; 70s manager; 80s and 90s actor

Faithfull, *Marianne* 60s pop star, actress and girlfriend of Mick Jagger

Fame, *Georgie* Jazz-funk keyboardist and pop star with hit singles in the 60s

Farian, *Frank* German record producer – Boney M, Meat Loaf, Milli Vanilli, etc.

Farlowe, *Chris* A 60s kid around town with a great voice, no star quality, and one big hit

Farson, *Dan* Famous in the 50s and 60s as writer, journalist, TV raconteur and drinker

Fatboy Slim A DJ/record producer/songwriter

Featherstone, *Roy* General manager of EMI in the 60s; ran MCA in the 70s

Feldman, *Charlie* One of Hollywood's greatest ever agents (40s and 50s), then a film producer: *Casino Royale*, *What's New Pussycat*

Feliciano, *José* Spanish-American superstar soul singer

Fenton, *John* 60s co-manager of the Moody Blues; part of consortium who bought the Beatles merchandising

Ferraz, *Diane* Black British singer in the 60s, part of Nicky Scott & Diane Ferraz duo

Fifield, *Jim* Top executive at EMI in the 90s

Filippello, *Connie* Publicist for superstars in the 80s and 90s, from George Michael to Giorgio Armani

Fish, *Michael* Designed trendy clothes in the 60s

Flippo, *Chet* American writer and author of books on music stars

Fonda, *Peter* Hollywood film star, son of Henry Fonda

Formby, *George* Ukelele-playing British film comedian of the 40s and 50s

Franklin, *Aretha* One of the all-time great black American soul singers

Freed, *Alan* An American radio DJ in the 50s

Freeman, *Alan* An Australian DJ who came to Britain in the 60s and introduced *Pick of the Pops*

Frewin, *Gordon* London gay club DJ and executive for Motown Records in the 60s

Fruin, *John* Executive of Warner Records and head of the British Phonograph Industry until dismissed for chart irregularities

Fry, *Martin* Singer with the New Romantic group ABC

Fury, *Billy* Larry Parnes's favourite in his stable of 50s rock'n' roll singers

Gabrielle Black British pop star of the 90s

Gaff, *Billy* Manager of the Faces, and then of Rod Stewart

Gainsbourg, *Serge* French musician/actor, married to Jane Birkin

Gallagher, *Liam* Singer with 90s rock group Oasis; brother of Noel Gallagher

Gallagher, *Noel* Songwriter with 90s rock group Oasis; brother of Liam Gallagher

Gamble, *Kenny* Half of the 70s American soul duo Gamble & Huff

Garbo, *Greta* American actress of the 20s and 30s

Garland, *Judy* American singer and actress of the 40s and 50s

Garratt, *Sheryl* Music journalist and author of a book on the ecstasy era: *Adventures in Wonderland*

Garrick, *David* A short-time recording artist in the 60s

Gary An ex-football gang member

Geldof, *Bob* Singer with the 70s/80s group Boomtown Rats and the man behind Live Aid

Gentle, *Johnny* One of Larry Parnes's stable of 50s rock 'n' roll singers

Gerrie, *Malcolm* Producer of 80s cult pop TV show *The Tube*

Gibb, *Andy* The younger pop-star brother of the three Bee Gees

Gibb, *Barry* A Bee Gee

Gibb, Maurice A Bee Gee

Gibb, *Robin* A Bee Gee

Gielgud, *John* Great British Shakespearean actor

Ginsberg, *Allen* An American poet

Glitter, *Gary* Glam rock star of the 70s

Goddard, *Geoff* A session keyboard player of the 50s and 60s

Godfrey, *Raymond* An early manager of the singer Tom Jones

Godley, *Kevin* Member of 10cc; left to form duo with Lol Creme; first they made hit songs, then they became video directors

Goffin, *Gerry* Half of the American songwriting team Goffin & King

Goldie American singer who came to London and formed Goldie & the Gingerbreads in the 60s

Goldman, *Albert* American author of books on John Lennon, Elvis Presley and disco music

Goldsmith, *Harvey* British concert promoter

Gomelsky, *Giorgio* Ran the Crawdaddy in Richmond in the 60s where the Rolling Stones and the Yardbirds were discovered

Good, *Jack* TV producer; the first man to get rock 'n' roll on to British TV in the 50s

Goode, *Johnny* One of Larry Parnes's stable of 50s rock 'n' roll singers

Gordy, *Berry* Owner and founder of Motown Records

Gore, *Martin* Songwriter and founding member of British techno group Depeche Mode

Gormley, *Peter* Long-time manager of Cliff Richard

Graham X Man who sold story to the *Sun* newspaper about Elton John's sex life

Grainer, *Ron* Australian film and TV composer, resident in London from the 60s onwards

Grant, *Cary* Hollywood film star

Grant, *Jimmy* BBC producer of *Saturday Club*, a pop/rock show in the 60s

Grant, *Peter* Heavyweight manager of Led Zeppelin

Grasso, *Francis* Legendary DJ at the Sanctuary Club in New York in the 70s

Grayson, *Larry* British camp TV comedian

Green, *Derek* Head of A&M in London when they dropped the Sex Pistols

Green, *Ian* A musical arranger and session conductor

Greene, *Graham* One of the twentieth century's greatest British authors

Greenfield, *Robert* A journalist

Griffiths, *Dr Mark* A psychiatrist

Griffiths, *Captain Emlyn* Manager of the Springfields, folky British pop group in the early 60s

Grundy, *Bill* Grumpy TV presenter who made the Sex Pistols say 'fuck' on TV

Gunnell, *John* Brother of Rik Gunnell, 60s agent, manager and hard man

Gunnell, *Rik* Brother of John Gunnell, 60s agent, manager and hard man

Hadley, *Tony* Lead singer with 80s pop group Spandau Ballet

Haley, *Bill* American singer who brought rock 'n' roll to the world

Hall, *Tony* British radio DJ in love with Motown music in the 60s; then a record company executive, publisher and manager

Hall and Oates American pop singer/songwriting duo

Hamilton, *David* A DJ on pirate radio, then on BBC

Hamilton, *Richard* One of the original pop artists of the 50s

Hammond, *Albert* British songwriter and singer

Harding, *Phil* Record producer, part of the Stock Aitken Waterman team in the 80s

Harris, *Bob* Whispering Bob Harris was compere of long-running TV rock show *The Old Grey Whistle Test*

Harris, *Jet* A member of the Shadows in the 50s, then half of a duo with Tony Mehan

Harris, *Keith* A pop manager

Harris, *Lee* A social worker

Harris, *Richard* An actor

Harris, *Rolf* An Australian who became a British TV personality

Harris, *Wee Willie* A 50s rock 'n' roll star

Harrison, *George* A Beatle

Harvey, *Brian* The singer with 90s pop group East 17

Harvey, *Laurence* A British actor who made it big in Hollywood in the 60s and 70s

Haslam, *Dave* A Manchester writer and journalist

Hatton, *Billy* A member of the 60s pop group the Fourmost

Hawken, *John* Keyboard player with 60s group the Nashville Teens

Hemmings, *David* Actor who played the lead in Antonioni's film *Blow-Up*

Hendrix, *Jimi* Legendary black American guitarist

Hewlett, *John* Bass player in 60s group John's Children

Hickey, *William* A gossip column in the *Daily Express*

Hicks, *Tommy* A cabin boy who became a pop star; *see* Tommy Steele

Hitler, *Adolf* A dictator

Hockney, *David* A painter

Hofmann, *Dr Albert* The scientist who discovered LSD

Holiday, *Billie* Legendary black American soul singer of the 30s and 40s

Holland, *Dave* A British session bass player who joined the Miles Davis band

Hollingsworth, *John* A British writer of film music

Hooligan A minor pop star in the 90s

Hopkin, *Mary* A singer from Wales who gave the Beatles the first hit on their own record label in the 1968

Horn, *Trevor* First sang with progressive rock group Yes, then became a top record producer

Horrocks, *James* Joint owner of dance-compilation label React Records

Howard, *Ken* Co-manager of 60s groups the Honeycombs and Dave Dee, Dozy, Beaky, Mick & Tich

Howe, *Sir Geoffrey* A one-time Conservative Chancellor of the Exchequer

Howe, *Steve* Guitarist with 80s rock group Asia

Howlin' Wolf American blues singer

Huff, *Leon* Half of the 70s American soul duo Gamble & Huff

Hughes, *Jimmy* Black American soul singer in the 50s

Hughes, *Patrick* A painter

Hulanicki, *Barbara* The owner of Biba, a department store in London in the 70s

Humperdinck, *Engelbert* An Anglo-Indian singer who was managed by the same person as Tom Jones

Hurst, *Mike* A member of the Springfields, folky British pop group in the early 60s, then became a record producer

Hynde, *Chrissie* Singer and leader of the Pretenders since the late 70s

Iglesias, *Julio* Spanish singer who made it big worldwide

Isaacs, *Jeremy* Controller of Channel Four TV in the 80s

Itthyvat, *Bhiraleus* A concert promoter in Thailand

Jack the Ripper Legendary nineteenth-century sex criminal

Jackson, *Michael* Legendary American superstar

Jackson, *Tony* A member of the 60s British pop group the Searchers

Jacobs, *David* A TV and radio presenter in the 60s and 70s

James, *Dick* Music publisher who signed the Beatles and Elton John and had once been a pop singer himself

Jamieson, *Peter* One-time head of EMI Records and of the British Phonograph Industry

Jansen, *Steve* Drummer with 70s/80s group Japan

Jarman, *Derek* Gay film director and diarist

Jarratt, *Jeff* A record producer

Jeffery, *Mike* Manager of 60s group the Animals

Jenner, *Peter* First manager of the psychedelic rock group Pink Floyd in the 60s

Jewell, *Derek* Celebrated British writer and journalist

Johansen, *David* Lead singer with the New York Dolls, American glam rock group in the 70s

John, *Sir Elton* British superstar singer/songwriter/pianist since the early 70s

Johnson, *Holly* Singer with Frankie Goes To Hollywood, 80s British disco group

Johnson, *Matt* Singer/songwriter with The The

Johnson, *Paul* A political columnist

Jolson, *Al* White American soul singer of the 20s and 30s who blacked his face to gain acceptance for the imitation black voice he sung with

Jones, *Brian* Guitar player with the Rolling Stones

Jones, *Howard* Minor 80s pop star

Jones, *John Paul* Bass player with Led Zeppelin

Jones, *Tom* British superstar singer since the mid 60s

Jordan *see* Rooke, Pamela

Judge Jules Promoter of rave concerts turned DJ turned record company executive

Junior Junior Giscombe, a black British singer of the 70s and 80s

Junior Antonio Morales, a Spanish pop star of the 60s and 70s

Kane, *Eden* A pop singer in the Adam Faith mould in the early 60s

Karn, *Mick* Bass player with 70s/80s group Japan

Kass, *Ron* American record executive appointed by the Beatles to do A&R at Apple Corps

Kelly, *Danny* A journalist

Kemp, *Gary* Lead singer with 80s group Spandau Ballet

Kennedy, *Bobby* Brother of President John F. Kennedy

Kennedy, *President John F.* American president who got shot

Kennedy, *John* New Zealander who came to England and became co-manager of 50s rock 'n' roll singer Tommy Steele

Kennedy, *John* London music business lawyer of the 80s who became head of Universal Records (London) in the 90s

Kent, *Nick* British writer and journalist, now living in France and writing for TV

Kerr, *Jim* Singer with 70s/80s group Simple Minds

Kerzner, *Sol* A South African businessman, one-time owner of Sun City

Kidd, *Johnny* Early British rock 'n' roller who performed with a group called the Pirates and wore a black eye-patch

King, *Carole* Great American songwriter of the 60s, 70s and 80s

King, *Jonathan* British music business personality of the 60s, 70s, 80s and 90s; singer, producer, journalist and TV presenter

Kirchherr, *Astrid* Photographer and leader of the existentialist art movement in Hamburg in the 50s

Klein, *Allen* American showbusiness lawyer who took over the management of both the Beatles and the Rolling Stones in the late 60s

Knight, *Gladys* Classic American pop/soul singer

Knopfler, *Mark* Guitarist and singer/songwriter with Dire Straits

Kramer, *Billy J* 60s pop singer from Liverpool managed by Brian Epstein

Kray, *Reggie* An East End gangster in the 50s and 60s, one of the Kray Twins

Kray, *Ronnie* An East End gangster in the 50s and 60s, one of the Kray Twins

Kruger, *Jeff* Owner of the Flamingo Club in London in the 50s and 60s, then of Ember Records

Kunze, *Michael* A German record producer working at MusicLife Studios in Munich in the 70s

LaBelle, *Patti* American pop/soul/gospel singer

Laing, *R.D.* Scottish psychologist who believed that insanity was a 'creative resolution of emotional conflicts'

Lake, *Greg* Bass player with King Crimson left to form Emerson Lake & Palmer, 60s and 70s progressive rock group

Lake, *Veronica* 30s Hollywood film star

Lambert, *Constant* A classical composer; father of Kit Lambert

Lambert, *Kit* Co-manager of the Who

Lauper, *Cyndi* American rock/pop singer of the 80s and 90s

Laurie, *Cy* British Dixieland clarinettist and band-leader in the 50s and 60s

Leahy, *Dick* British record company executive at Philips in the 60s, at GTO (his own company) in the 70s, and Morrison-Leahy in the 80s (music publishers for Wham!)

Leander, *Mike* Session keyboardist, arranger and record producer

Leary, *Timothy* The high-priest of psychedelia; preached the taking of acid to American youth in the 60s with the slogan 'Turn on. Tune in. Drop out'

Le Bon, *Simon* Singer with Duran Duran

Lee, *Peggy* Great American pop singer of the 40s and 50s

Legend, *Bill* Drummer with Marc Bolan during the time of his greatest success

Leiber, *Jerry* Half of the American songwriting team of Leiber & Stoller

Leitch, *Donovan see* Donovan

Lemmy Ian Kilmister, bass player with Hawkwind and Motörhead

Lennon, *Cynthia* First wife of John Lennon

Lennon, *John* A Beatle

Lennox, *Annie* Singing half of the British duo Eurythmics

Lenny the Leaper A popular Soho character of the 50s and 60s

Lesley, *John* Head of Rank Leisure's dance hall division in the 70s

Levine, *Steve* Record producer for Culture Club and others

Lewis, *Jerry Lee* Legendary American rock 'n' roll singer/pianist

Lewis, *Sir Edward* Chairman and founder of Decca Records

Leyton, *John* 50s small-time British film actor, then pop singer, then film director

Liberace Flamboyant camp American pop showman/pianist of the 50s, 60s and 70s

Lichtenstein, *Roy* Great American pop art painter

Lillywhite, *Steve* British record producer of rock groups

Lindsay-Hogg, *Michael* Director of 60s TV show *Ready Steady Go!*

Little Richard Legendary black American rock 'n' roll artist

Lloyd-Elliott, *Martin* Contemporary British psychologist to music artists

Lloyd Webber, *Sir Andrew* Writer of stage musicals: *Jesus Christ Superstar*, *Evita*, *Cats*, etc.; founder/owner of The Really Useful group of companies

Locking, *Licorice* A joining member of The Shadows in the late 50s

Lockwood, *Sir Joseph* Chairman of EMI group in the late 50s and 60s

Lovelace, *Linda* Star of classic American porn film *Deep Throat*

Lowe, *Chris* One of the two Pet Shop Boys, formerly an architect

Luce, *Henry* Founder of Time Inc.

Lulu Scottish singer on the British pop scene since the 60s

Lydon, *John* Became Johnny Rotten, lead singer of the Sex Pistols, then went back to being John Lydon of PIL

Lynch, *Kenny* Black British singer/comedian/music business personality since the 50s

Lyttelton, *Humphrey* British dixieland jazz trumpeter and band-leader since the 50s

MacCallum, *Alison* 70s Australian pop singer

McCartney, *Mike* Brother of Paul McCartney, member of 60s group the Scaffold

McCartney, *Sir Paul* A Beatle

McCrae, *George* American soul singer

McCulloch, *Jimmy* Guitarist with Paul McCartney's 70s group Wings

McGough, *Roger* Poet and member of 60s group Scaffold

McGowan, *Cathy* Co-compere of *Ready Steady Go!*, 60s TV show

MacInnes, *Colin* British author and novelist

Maclean, *Donald* 50s spy; half of the Burgess–Maclean scandal

McIntosh, *Carl* Member of 80s British soul group Loose Ends

McIntosh, *Robbie* Drummer with the Average White Band

McLagan, *Ian* Keyboard player with the Small Faces, then the Faces

McLaren, *Malcolm* Manager of the Sex Pistols

Magic Alex Inventor employed by Apple Corps in the 60s and for a while John Lennon's best friend

Maharishi Mahesh Yogi An Indian guru with many British and American showbusiness as his clients

Manilow, *Barry* American pop singer

Mao, *Chairman* Leader of Communist China

Margaret, *Princess* British princess

Marilyn British drag-queen and pop star

Marriott, *Steve* Lead singer of the Small Faces

Marsden, *Gerry* Lead singer with 60s group Gerry & the Pacemakers

Marsh, *Jeremy* British record company executive

Martin, *Dean* American crooner and best friend of Frank Sinatra

Martin, *Sir George* Producer of the Beatles

Martin-Smith, *Nigel* Manager of Take That

Marvin, *Hank* Guitarist with the Shadows

Marx, *Groucho* Old-time American film comedian, one of the Marx Brothers

Mason, *Barry* British songwriter in the 60s and 70s

Matthew, *Brian* Compere of BBC radio programme *Saturday Club* in the 60s

Mathis, *Johnny* American black singer in the 50s and 60s

Mature, *Victor* Old-time toughman Hollywood actor

Maud, *Chris* Journalist writing for *Melody Maker* in the 80s

May, *Phil* Vocalist with 60s group the Pretty Things

Maybank, *Leon* Society photographer in the 50s

Meat Loaf Large American rock star

Meek, *Joe* 50s/60s British record producer

Meisel, *Peter* German owner of Hansa Records

Meisel, *Trudi* Peter Meisel's noisy wife

Mel & Kim 80s pop duo

Melly, *George* British music business personality since the 50s; singer, author, journalist, raconteur

Mendl, *Hugh* A pop record executive at Decca Records in the 50s, 60s and 70s

Mercury, *Freddie* Singer with Queen

Michael, *George* At first, the singing half of Wham!, then a solo pop singer

Michael, *John* A trendy clothes shop owner in the 60s and 70s

Millar, *Duncan* Keyboardist/songwriter with 80s group Blüe Mercedes

Miller, *Daniel* Record producer and owner of Mute Records

Millings, *Dougie* Tailor to the stars in the 60s

Mills, *Gordon* Manager of Tom Jones, Engelbert Humperdinck and Gilbert O'Sullivan

Minogue, *Kylie* Australian soap actress who turned pop star in the 80s

Mitchell, *Guy* American 50s pop singer

Mitchell, *Liz* Lead singer with Boney M

Money, *Zoot* 60s British rhythm & blues artist

Monro, *Matt* Smooth British ballad singer of the 60s and 70s

Monroe, *Marilyn* Hollywood film star

Montenegro, *Hugo* American pop orchestra leader in the 60s and 70s

Moon, *Keith* Drummer with the Who

Morali, *Jacques* French record producer of the Village People

Morley, *Paul* Sardonic British journalist and music business commentator who was also joint-manager of Frankie Goes to Hollywood

Moroder, *Giorgio* German-Italian record producer of disco hits throughout the 70s and 80s

Morrison, *Bryan* Once an agent and manager, then a partner in Morrison Leahy – music publishers for Wham!

Morrison, *Mark* 90s British black rap artist/singer

Morrison, *Van* Irish rock/rhythm & blues singer since the 60s

Morrissey British pop singer, originally with the Smiths

Mortimer, *Tony* Writing member of 90s pop group East 17

Moss, *Jerry* American chief executive and joint owner of A&M Records before its sale in the 90s to PolyGram/Universal

Moss, *Jon* Drummer with punk group London, then with the Damned, then with Culture Club

Most, *Mickie* Britain's most successful pop record producer in the 60s

Motown, *Pamela see* Fruin, Gordon

Moyet, *Alison* British pop singer, big in the 80s

Mulcahy, *Russell* Top director of music video clips throughout the 80s

Mulligan, *Mick* British dixieland trumpeter and bandleader in the 50s and 60s

Murray, *Charles Shaar* A British music writer and journalist

Murray, *Mitch* British songwriter, wit and after-dinner speaker

Murray, *Pete* British radio DJ

Musker, *Frank* Songwriter and chairman of the British Academy of Songwriters

Myers, *Laurence* 70s manager of the Sweet and Gary Glitter

Nash, *Graham* Lead singer with British group the Hollies in the 60s, then with American group Crosby, Stills & Nash

Nasmyth, *Peter* British journalist

Newell, *Norman* British producer/arranger/songwriter and lyricist

Nixon, *Richard* An American president

Noone, *Peter* Lead singer with Herman's Hermits

Novello, *Ivor* Pretty-faced British songwriter of the 40s and 50s whom Winston Churchill claimed to have slept with in order to make sure he couldn't be aroused by a man

Nutter, *Tommy* Tailor to the stars in the 60s

Oakey, *Phil* Lead singer of 80s group the Human League

Oberstein, *Maurice* American record executive resident in London since the 60s; head of CBS London, then PolyGram, and of the BPI

Obie *see* Oberstein, Maurice

Ocean, *Billy* Black British pop singer with big hits in America in the 80s

O'Connor, *Des* British pop singer, comedian and chat-show host since the 50s

O'Dowd, *George* Boy George

O'Dowd, *Gerry* Father of Boy George

Oldfield, *Mike* Composer/producer of bestselling album *Tubular Bells*

Oldfield, *Rex* Record executive who left EMI in the 60s to open MGM Records in London

Oldham, *Andrew* First manager of the Rolling Stones

Olga Singer with punk group the Toy Dolls

Ono, *Yoko* Second wife of John Lennon

O'Rahilly, *Ronan* Originator of the pirate ship Radio Caroline and manager of 60s Soho club The Scene

Orton, *Joe* British playwright

Osbourne, *Ozzy* Manic British rockstar

Osman, *Mat* Member of Britpop group Suede

O'Sullivan, *Gilbert* 70s pop singer/songwriter managed by Gordon Mills

Page, *Jimmy* Guitarist with the Yardbirds and Led Zeppelin

Page, *Patti* 50s American pop singer

Paiboon Damrongchaitham Owner of Grammy Entertainment, a giant Thai music, records, television, films and retail business

Palmer, *Carl* Drummer with Emerson, Lake & Palmer, then Asia

Palmer, *Robert* Classy British soul singer

Palumbo, *James* Owner and chief executive of Ministry of Sound

Palumbo, *Lord Peter* James Palumbo's father, head of the Arts Council in the 80s

Paramor, *Norrie* Bandleader and record producer with successes in the 50s and 60s

Parkinson, *Michael* British TV chat-show host and interviewer

Parnes, *Larry* First British rock 'n' roll manager; died rich in the 80s, but afraid of poverty, the inquest heard he'd eaten nothing but boil-in-the-bag fish for months

Paul, *Leslie* Manager of songwriter Lionel Bart in the 50s

Peel, *John* British radio DJ and supporter of non-commercially motivated music

Pendleton, *Harold* Owner of the Marquee Club

Penna, *Tris* Record company executive at Parlophone, then the Really Useful Company

Peter and Gordon 60s pop singing duo

Phillips, *Frank* Old-fashioned, posh-voiced BBC announcer from the 50s

Phillips, *Ray* Member of 60s group the Nashville Teens

Pickering, *Mike* A DJ at the Hacienda Club, Manchester in the 80s

Pierre A French-Canadian pianist at a dockside pub in Montreal in the later 50s

Pitt, *Ken* Manager of 60s pop star Crispian St. Peters, and of David Bowie until 1971

Plant, *Robert* Singer with Led Zeppelin

Plaster Caster, *Cynthia* An American groupie famed for leading a gang of girls who made plaster-casts of rock stars' penises

Poly Styrene A punk singer/songwriter in the 70s

Pop, *Iggy* Long-penised, self-flagellating American rock star

Potter, *Andrew* Chairman of the British Performing Rights Society in the late 90s

Powell, *Clive see* Fame, Georgie

Powell, *Enoch* Conservative politician

Powell, *Tony* Record company marketing executive

Power, *Duffy* One of Larry Parnes's stable of 50s rock 'n' roll singers

Powers, *Kid Congo* Guitarist in the Gun Club, the Cramps and the Bad Seeds

Presley, *Elvis* American singer

Preston, *Billy* American keyboardist

Price, *Jim* American horn player

Pride, *Dickie* One of Larry Parnes's stable of 50s rock 'n' roll singers

Prince, *Peter* British record company executive

Prince, *Viv* Member of the 60s rock fraternity and drummer with the Pretty Things

Quant, *Mary* Leading designer of women's clothes in the 60s

Quatro, *Suzi* American who became British glam rock star

Rampling, *Danny* Club DJ who opened the first E club, Shoom

Randall, *Lucian* A journalist

Rank, *Lord* J. Arthur Rank, a zealous Methodist who founded Britain's first major leisure industry corporation – the Rank Organisation

Raven, *Paul see* Glitter, Gary

Ray, *Johnnie* Gay, tortured, American heart-throb crooner of the 50s who cried as he sang

Rea, *Chris* British soft-rock singer/songwriter

Read, *John* Sir Joseph Lockwood's successor as chairman of the EMI group

Reed, *Les* A songwriter

Reed, *Lou* Gay American cult rock star who hung out in London in the 70s

Regan, *Riff* Singer with the punk group London

Reid, *John* Manager of Elton John

Relf, *Keith* Singer with the Yardbirds

Richard, *Cliff* British pop singer since the 50s

Richards, *Keith* Guitarist with the Rolling Stones

Ridgeley, *Andrew* The guitar-playing half of Wham!

Ridley, *Wally* Songwriter and EMI staff record producer in the 50s, 60s and 70s

Roberts, *Michael* Journalist with the *Sunday Times* in the 70s

Robinson, *Tom* Singer/songwriter/bandleader of the Tom Robinson Band

Rock, *Mick* Fashion and showbusiness photographer

Rodgers, *Noel* Head of United Artists Music in London in the 60s

Rodney Bennett, *Richard* British classical and film composer, and jazz pianist

Rodol, *Mark* Marketing director of Ministry of Sound

Rollins, *Henry* American writer, critic and music commentator

Ronson, *Mick* Guitarist with David Bowie's band during the height of glam rock in the 70s

Ronstadt, *Linda* American pop/rock/country singer

Rooke, *Pamela* Manager of Sex, the kinky Kings Road clothes shop owned by Malcom McLaren in the 70s

Ross, *Diana* Black American singer, once a member of the Supremes

Rossi, *Francis* Guitarist/vocalist with Status Quo

Rotten, *Johnny see* Lydon, John

Rowe, *Dick* The Decca A&R man in the 60s who turned down the Beatles

Rowland, *Steve* American record producer resident in the UK since the beginning of the 60s

Roza, *Lita* English big-band singer with the Ted Heath Band in the 50s

Rudetsky, *Michael* A friend of Boy George

Russell, *Paul* A record executive for CBS/Sony

Rutherford, *Paul* A member of 80s group Frankie Goes to Hollywood

Ryder, *Shaun* Lead singer/songwriter with the Happy Mondays

St John-Stevas, *Norman* Once a member of the Conservative government

St Peters, *Crispian* A singer, a two-hit wonder in the 60s

Samwell-Smith, *Paul* Bass player with the Yardbirds, then a record producer

Sarstedt, *Peter* Anglo-Indian British pop star of the late 60s

Sarstedt, *Rick* Peter Sarstedt's older brother who had his big hits in the early 60s as Eden Kane

Sarstedt, *Robin* Peter and Rick Sarstedt's younger brother who had his big hit in the 70s

Sassoon, *Vidal* A hairdresser

Satie, *Erik* A classical composer

Savage, *Jon* A writer

Savile, *Jimmy* A DJ

Sayer, *Leo* A 70s pop star

Scabies, *Rat* A punk drummer with the Damned

Scamell, *H.E.* A member of the teaching staff at Yale University in the 70s

Scargill, *Arthur* The leader of the National Union of Mineworkers during their strike in the 80s

Schmolzi, *Horst* A German record company executive sent to London to oversee the opening of Polydor Records in the 60s

Scott, *Nicky* A 60s pop singer; one of the Nicky Scott & Diane Ferraz duo

Scott, *Norman* A boyfriend of Liberal leader Jeremy Thorpe

Scott, *Norman* A club DJ at Bangs disco in the 70s

Scott, *Tommy see* Jones, Tom

Seal Paddington-born British black soul singer

Secunda, *Tony* Manager of 60s group the Move

Sesto, *Camilo* A Spanish singing star

Shampan, *Harold* An old Tin Pan Alley music publisher

Shapiro, *Harry* Drug historian, social worker and writer

Shapiro, *Helen* London schoolgirl who had hits in the 50s

Shaw, *Sandie* 60s pop star

Shelton, *Anne* 50s pop star

Sheridan, *Tony* A 50s pop singer who used the Beatles as his backing group before they were famous

Shostakovitch, *Dmitri* A Russian composer

Shuman, *Mort* A songwriter

Simon and Garfunkel An American pop duo

Sinatra, *Frank* A singer

Singer, *Ray* An aspiring pop star in the 60s who became a record producer

Singleton, *Steve* A member of the 80s group ABC

Sinitta A disco pop singer in the 80s

Sioux, *Siouxsie* A punk singer in the 70s

Sizer, *Alan* An A&R person at RCA in the mid 70s

Sky, *Rick* A tabloid journalist

Slater, *Terry* An A&R man for EMI during the 70s and 80s

Small, *Millie* A pop singer in the 60s

Smith, *Bessie* The greatest American blues singer

Smith, *Reg* Chauffeur to Andrew Oldham, the Rolling Stones' manager, in the 60s

Smith, *Richard* Journalist and writer on gender issues

Smith, *Trixie* American blues singer in the 20s

Snowdon, *Lord* Photographer and one-time husband of Princess Margaret

Solomon, *Phil* Irish businessman prominent in the 60s; part owner of Radio Caroline and Major Minor Records

Somerville, *Jimmy* British white soul singer and gay activist

Sommerville, *Brian* Publicist to the Beatles, the Who, and many others

Spector, *Phil* American record producer of great hits of the 50s and 60s

Spot, *Jack* Notorious East End and Soho gangster of the 40s and 50s

Springfield, *Dusty* British soul singer

Springfield, *Tom* Dusty's brother; a singer/songwriter

Stalker, *John* Deputy Chief Constable of Greater Manchester Police in the 80s

Stamp, *Chris* Co-manager of the Who

Stansfield, *Lisa* A white British soul singer of the 80s and 90s

Stardust, *Ziggy* David Bowie in disguise in the 70s

Starr, *Ringo* A Beatle

Steele, *Tommy* Britain's first rock 'n' roll star

Steinman, *Jim* An American record producer

Stephen, *John* Owner of clothes shops in Carnaby Street and elsewhere

Stevens, *Cat* A 60s pop singer turned devout Muslim

Stevo The weirdo manager of Soft Cell and The The

Stewart, *Amii* Black American singer made famous by Hansa Records in Germany

Stewart, *Dave* Producer/guitarist half of the British duo Eurythmics

Stewart, *Rod* A rock singer

Stigwood, *Robert* Manager of the Bee Gees and a theatre and movie producer

Stiggy *see* Stigwood, Robert

Sting First, a singer with the Police, then by himself

Stock, *Mike* A member of the 80s production team of Stock Aitken Waterman

Stoller, *Mike* Half of the American songwriting duo Leiber & Stoller

Strange, *Steve* Singer with the New Romantic group Visage

Stratton-Smith, *Tony* Manager of the Herd and Genesis and owner of Charisma Records

Street-Porter, *Janet* TV executive and journalist

Strummer, *Joe* Guitarist/singer/songwriter with the Clash

Sugerman, *Danny* Manager of Iggy Pop

Suggs Lead singer with Madness

Sullivan, *Peter* Staff record producer at EMI in the 60s

Summer, *Donna* LaDonna Gaines, black American singer who married a German called Sommers and made her first hit in Munich, produced by Giorgio Moroder

Summers, *Jazz* British manager (Lisa Stansfield, the Verve) and co-manager (Wham!)

Sutch, *David* 50s rock 'n' roll singer known as Screaming Lord Sutch who stood for parliament at every bi-election for over thirty years representing the Monster Raving Loony Party

Sylvian, *David* Singer with 80s group Japan

Tappenden, *Ken* Kent police commander who stamped out raves in the 90s

Taylor, *Derek* Journalist and press officer for the Beatles

Taylor, *Elizabeth* Film star with lots of husbands

Taylor, *Roger* Drummer with Queen

Teller, *Al* American top record executive, head of Epic Records in New York in the 80s

Tennant, *Neil* One of the two Pet Shop Boys, formerly a journalist with *Smash Hits* and *NME*

Tharpe, *Sister Rosetta* American black gospel and blues singer

Thatcher, *Margaret* British Prime Minister in the 80s

Thornton, *Big Mama* 40s and 50s black blues singer from the American South

Thorpe, *Jeremy* Gay Liberal politician who found it hard dealing with his private life when he was made leader of the party in the 70s

Titlow, *David* Singer/songwriter with 80s group Blue Mercedes

Took, *Steve Peregrine* Half of 60s hippy duo T Rex together with Marc Bolan

Townshend, *Pete* Guitarist and songwriter with the Who

Townsley, *Bill* General manager of Decca Records under its chairman, Sir Edward Lewis, throughout the 50s and 60s

Tredinnick, *Miles* Punk singer of the group London in the 70s, known as Riff Regan

Troy, *Doris* Black American pop/soul singer prominent in the late 50s and 60s

Trudeau, *Pierre* Canadian Prime Minister in the late 60s

Turner, *Tina* American black rock and soul singer, originally married to Ike

Tynan, *Ken* Theatre critic and intellectual prominent in the 60s and 70s; the first person to say the word 'fuck' on British TV

Valentine, *Dickie* British heart-throb romantic singer of the 50s

Vanda, *Harry* Dutch songwriter who went to live in Australia and formed the Easybeats with Australian George Young and others

Vaughan, *Frankie* 50s British smoothie singer who always appeared with a hat and a cane

Vincent, *Gene* American singer who came to London in the late 50s and stayed to become part of the British rock 'n' roll scene

Visconti, *Tony* American producer who came to London in the late 60s and stayed to become producer of Marc Bolan, David Bowie and others

Wace, *Robert* Co-manager of the 60s group the Kinks

Wagner, *Richard* A German composer

Wakeman, *Rick* Keyboardist with Yes, a progressive rock group in the 70s

Walden, *Brian* TV interviewer and political analyst

Wale, *Michael* Music business journalist since the 60s, now mostly a sports journalist

Walker, *Scott* American teenager who came to London in the 60s to escape the draft and became a part of a pop trio with two other Americans – the Walker Brothers

Warhol, *Andy* American pop artist who made his workshop, The Factory, a New York centre for artists, dropouts and freaks

Warwick, *Dionne* American female singer launched in the 60s by the writing and production of Burt Bacharach

Washington, *Geno* 60s British rhythm & blues artist

Waterman, *Pete* Former Northern DJ who became Britian's most successful record producer and songwriter in the 80s

Waters, *Muddy* Black American blues guitarist and singer

Waters, *Roger* An original member of Pink Floyd

Watkins, *Tom* One of Britain's most eccentric living pop managers

Watson, *Stuart* Record company executive with Zomba Records

Watts, *Charlie* The drummer with the Rolling Stones

Wax, *Ruby* American chat-show hostess mainly resident in the UK

Webb, *Harry* A skiffle singer before he decided to become Cliff Richard

Webster, *John* A record executive at Virgin Records in the 80s

Welch, *Chris* A music business journalist since the 60s

Weller, *Paul* Earnest political activist/singer who made brilliant music with his groups the Jam and the Style Council

Wexler, *Jerry* Legendary American record producer of nearly all the hits on Atlantic Records

White, *Barry* Gravel-voiced black American soul singer

Whitehouse, *Mary* Public moralist who campaigned against bad words and thoughts in British TV programmes

Whitfield, *David* 50s British crooner focusing on songs with a religious bent

Wickham, *Vicki* Booked all the acts for classic 60s TV programme *Ready Steady Go!*, then became manager of American soul group Labelle, and of Dusty Springfield

Wilde, *Marty* One of Larry Parnes's stable of 50s rock 'n' roll singers originally named Reg Smith

Wilde, *Oscar* An Irish playwright

Williams, *Hank* American country & western guitarist and singer

Williams, *Kenneth* Camp British comedian with big nostrils

Williams, *Richard* One-time editor of *New Musical Express* and journalist for *The Times*

Williams, *Robbie* A member of British boy band Take That who emerged as a solo star

Williams, *Tennessee* American playwright

Williamson, *Sonny Boy* A black American blues and harmonica player

Wilson, *Brian* A member of the American vocal group the Beach Boys

Wilson, *Harold* British Prime Minister in the 60s

Wilson, *Tony* Manchester-based TV producer, journalist and record company owner

Winwood, *Stevie* Soulful British singer, originally with the Spencer Davis Group

Wood, *Len* General manager of EMI Records in the 60s

Wood, *Ronnie* Guitarist with the Faces who then joined the Rolling Stones in the 70s

Wood, *Roy* Singer/composer with 60s and 70s bands the Move, ELO and Wizzard

Young, *George* Australian songwriter

Young, *John Paul* Australian pop singer

Young, *Muriel* Radio and TV producer of music shows in the 50s, 60s and 70s

Young, *Paul* Soulful British pop singer of the 80s

Zanetta, *Tony* Ex-member of Andy Warhol's staff employed by David Bowie's manager to run his New York office in the 70s

INDEX OF QUOTATIONS

The vast majority of quotations and anecdotes in this book come directly as a result of my working in the music industry for the last forty years; from meeting, working and partying with those involved. In the course of writing this book over the past two and a half years I have, in many instances, gone back to these original sources to corroborate facts, quotes and stories through a large number of personal interviews.

I have also read a whole stack of books, magazines and newspapers for research. In some instances I found material of which I had been previously unaware. Many of these sources have been invaluable and are credited below.

In some instances the material from the interviews and the material from books have collided. Repeating stories *verbatim* seems to be a classic music industry trait. Where this has occurred I have credited the written source and noted that a personal interview also took place.

Note: Full details of published sources can be found in the Bibliography.

Page

6   'We were called the Cavemen ...' (Tommy Steele in Leigh, 1996)

6   'a thoroughly English singer' (MacInnes, 1959)

6   'a pale-blue bellboy outfit' (Jack Good in Leigh, 1996)

6   'his eyes twinkled ...' (ibid.)

7   'Tommy Steele is a better performer than Elvis' (Larry Parnes in Rogan, 1988)

10   'He thrashed me six times on my hand. ...' (Billy Fury in Ellis, 1961)

12   'It is sexualistic, unmoralistic ...' (White Citizens Council in Obstfeld and Fitzgerald, 1997)

14   'We went into the studio ...' (Lonnie Donegan in Leigh, 1996)

16   'You come from the same county ...' (Larry Parnes in Leigh, 1996)

16   'Some of the gigs were miles apart ...' (Joe Brown in Leigh, 1996)

22   'The A&R man would say ...' (Mickie Most in Leigh, 1996; Most also told me this in a personal interview)

23   'because I was the youngest person ...' (Jack Good in Leigh, 1996 and Palmer, 1976; Good also told me this in a personal interview)

23   'I decided that rock 'n' roll ...' (Jack Good in Leigh, 1996 and Palmer, 1976; Good also told me this in a personal interview)

23   'he always wore a suit ...' (Tommy Steele in Palmer, 1976; Steele also told me this in a personal interview)

24   'I could hardly remain on two feet ...' (Jack Good, *Disc Magazine*, 5/8/61)

26   'I was a carbon copy of Elvis ...' (Cliff Richard in Leigh, 1996)

26   'It was a real drippy song ...' (Jack Good in Leigh, 1996)

26   'If this record had been a product of Sun Records ...' (Jack Good, *Disc Magazine*, 9/8/58)

27   'He didn't want me to be too much like Elvis ...' (Cliff Richard in Leigh, 1996)

60 'It should have been called "Speeding London" ...' (Shapiro, 1990)

61 'One day they'll be greater than Presley' (Brian Epstein in Epstein, 1965)

62 'We'd heard that Brian was queer ...' (Paul McCartney in Miles, 1997)

66 'My Beatles hat which cost me a fortune ...' (Jarman, 1994)

69 'One, two, three ...' (Paul McCartney in Miles, 1997)

70 'I knew what I was looking at ...' (Andrew Oldham in Ewing, 1996)

70 'energy and three chords' (Mick Jagger in Obstfeld and Fitzgerald, 1997)

70 'I remember when I was very young ...' (ibid.)

70 'You don't have to hear what Bob Dylan's saying ...'(John Lennon in Obstfeld and Fitzgerald, 1997)

77 'The young are rejecting ...' (William Deedes, address to City of London Young Conservatives)

77 'While the music is performed ...' (Paul Johnson, *New Stateman*, February 1964)

77 'smooth as liquid paraffin ...' (Jack Good in Leigh, 1996)

78 'Perhaps I'm being cruel ...' (David Jacobs in Leigh, 1996)

80 'I was quite often sent for ...' (Jonathan King in Watkinson and Anderson, 1994)

81 'a shocking scene of debauchery ...' (*News of the World*, July 1966)

83 'It gave me the creeps ...' (McLagan, 2000)

84 'The taxman's taken all my dough' ('Sunny Afternoon'; words and music by Ray Davies © 1966 Davray Music Ltd and Carlin Music Corp, London NW1 8BD; all rights reserved)

110 'There was a large ashtray on the table ...' (ibid.)

110 'I just took a little of my Rolling Stones money ...' (Andrew Oldham, ibid.)

111 'There wasn't anything to stop you ...' (Andrew Oldham in interview with Oldham and Calder, *Q* magazine)

111 'We had the Beach Boys' publishing ...' (Tony Calder, ibid.)

112 'The best work I ever had ...' (Jimmy Savile in Leigh, 1996)

113 'That's when your fucking instruments go ...' (Keith Moon in Obstfeld and Fitzgerald, 1997)

115 'In my little music room at Cavendish Avenue ...' (Paul McCartney in Miles, 1997)

117 'I was out doing a show ...' (Chris Farlowe in Burdon, 1986)

118 'I am all for audiences going mad ...' (Coward, 1982)

119 'You sleep in sunlight ...' (Cohn, 1989)

120 'He was doing all kinds of really small deals...' (Burdon, 1986)

123 'My visual field wavered ...' (Albert Hofmann in Tyler, 1988)

124 'In ten minutes I lived a thousand years' (George Harrison in *The Beatles Anthology*, 2000)

128 'It's quite funny to think ...' (Hulanicki, 1982)

129 'The lead singer ... rolled on-stage ...' (letter in *Melody Maker*)

131 'He transcended all his pettiness ...' (Faithfull, 1995)

133 'Dylan politely asked him ... taken it as his own (story in Faithfull, 1995)

133 'What good's the bloody Parthenon without LSD!' (John Lennon in Brown and Gaines, 1983)

134 'I took Mick through the trees ...' (Beaton and Buckle, 1979)

160 'You do the music, and I'll take care of everything else ...' (Peter Grant in *Mr Rock 'n' Roll*, Channel 4, produced by Virtual Television Company)

160 'Peter lived, breathed and slept beside the band ...' (Malcolm McLaren, ibid.)

161 'we want people to get stoned on the show, not on acid.' (Hawkwind interview in *Melody Maker*)

162 'If Wagner were alive today ...' (Richard Williams, King Crimson review, *Melody Maker*)

164 'the guy was unbearable' (Mick Jagger in Jackson, 1997)

164 'I hope people will understand ..' (ibid.)

165 'Much of Mick's speech clanged in my head ...' (Phil May in Jackson, 1997)

166 'I wasn't gonna shoot' (reported at the inquest of the young man murdered by Hell's Angels at Altamont)

166 'We rubbed his back up and down ...' (ibid.)

169 'sheer power, invention, and brilliance of performance ...' (Leonard Bernstein in Giuliano, 1996)

169 'pompous, crazy, ridiculous ...' (Pete Townshend in Giuliano, 1996)

171 'Oh well,' he said. 'If he's living with his manager ...' (Dick James in Norman, 1991)

178–9 'Young Americans were concerned ...' (Pete Townshend in Giuliano, 1996)

179 'Peace ... is only got by peaceful methods ...' (John Lennon in Denselow, 1989)

180 'If I was a Jewish girl in Hitler's day ...' (Yoko Ono in Denselow, 1989)

181 'once you are dead you are made for life' (Jimi Hendrix in Obstfeld and Fitzgerald, 1997)

221 'Their inability to play coupled with their determination to play ...' (John Peel, *Peel Night*, Channel 4, 2000)

222 'The Sex Pistols are like some contagious disease.' (Malcom McLaren in Obstfeld and Fitzgerald, 1997)

228 'They were the last band on ...' (Paul Weller in Reed, 1997)

229 'I plagiarised the whole album ...' (ibid.)

229 'Whatever happened to the great empire ...' (ibid.)

229 'All I did in the beginning was to take a gamble ...' (Maurice Oberstein in Savage, 1991)

230 'Don't think that sticking your boobs out ...' (Chrissie Hynde in Obstfeld and Fitzgerald, 1997)

230 'Look, this is what you have done to me ...' (Poly Styrene in Savage, 1991)

231 'We may not have anarchy in the streets ...' (Siouxsie Sioux in Savage, 1991)

232 'For all the anarchy in the UK ...' (Geldof, 1986)

246 'I went to the Masquerade ...' (Pamela Rooke in Savage, 1991)

248 'Grasso invented the technique ...' (Goldman, 1992)

256 '£300 million empire was sheltering ...' (William Hickey Column, *Daily Express*)

257 'processed and designed for dancing ...' (Carducci, 1995)

274 'Jagger, Wood, and Richards were all going off ...' (Kent, 1994)

274 'It wasn't really anything special ...' (Mick Jagger in Obstfeld and Fitzgerald, 1997)

274 'continued to watch with cold dead eyes ...' (Kent, 1994)

274 'Drugs were an elitist, chic commodity ...' (Greenfield, 1974)

275 'Every minute spent off the road ...' (Keith Richards in Charone, 1979)

284 'He cut off a chunk of the opium ...' (McLagan, 2000)

285 'He sort of perfected the technique of slapping you ...' (John Bettie in *Mr Rock 'n' Roll*, Channel 4, produced by Virtual Television Company)

285 'They were like Noddy people in Toyland ...' (Malcolm McLaren, ibid.)

285 'Peter was hugely overweight ...' (Don Arden, ibid.)

287 'I'm really over this ...' (Jimmy Page in Des Barres, 1996)

287 'It looks like the shit hit the purse.' (John Bonham in Des Barres, 1996)

292 'I find politics the single most uninspiring ...' (Adam Ant in Obstfeld and Fitzgerald, 1997)

292 'this showbusiness crap ...' (Paul Weller, *Record Mirror*)

292 'None of the ideas are mine' (Adam Ant, *Smash Hits*, June 1981)

296 'Steve Strange was the best doorman ...' (Robert Elms, *Top Ten New Romantics*, Channel 4)

298 'Who wants to save the bloody world?' (Simon Le Bon in Obstfeld and Fitzgerald, 1997)

298 'My job is to make it all look as if it's coming from them' (Hill, 1986)

299 'We wanted to do something different ...' (Gary Kemp, *Top Ten New Romantics*, Channel 4)

299 'We wanted fame' (Tony Hadley, ibid.)

300 'My flat's got character ...' (Gary Kemp, *Record Mirror*, August 1983)

300 'soaring joy of immaculate rhythms ...' (sleeve notes of Spandau Ballet's *Journeys to Glory*)

300 'We wanted to touch what is "human" ...' (press release for Thompson Twins' first album, quoted in Hill, 1986)

342 'I think he's the worst thing the miners could have ...' (George Michael, *Today*, 1989; quoted in Goodall, 1995)

343 'We must thank Mrs Thatcher ...' (Billy Bragg in Denselow, 1989)

343 'As a perfectionist, you surely reject ...' (Morley, 1986)

344 'Relax, don't do it ...' (lyrics of 'Relax', Frankie Goes to Hollywood)

344 'Although Boy George and Bowie are gorgeous boys ...' (Holly Johnson, *Him Monthly*)

346 'If someone wrote a song saying "shoot the Queen" nobody would mind ...' (Billy Bragg in Denselow, 1989)

347 'If you ask us all questions ...' (Paul Weller in Denselow, 1989)

348 'Wham! are just a little too belligerent ...' (Morley, 1986)

352 'The tax scheme had fallen through ...' (Geldof, 1986)

357 'If most of those groups at Live Aid ...' (Chris Maud, *Melody Maker*)

357 'We were the first band on ...' (Francis Rossi, *Q Magazine*)

357 'I never once stopped to consider what happened next ...' (Geldof, 1986)

358 'Famine is above politics' (ibid.)

359 'Politicians have no idea how to save the world ...' (Barry Gibb in Obstfeld and Fitzgerald, 1997)

359 'Cheer up ... socialism is supposed to be fun' (Billy Bragg in Denselow, 1989)

359 'Get that grease outta your hair ...' (Henry Rollins in *NME*, 1995)

360 'One can have great concern for the people of Ethiopia ...' (Morrissey, interview with Simon Garfield, *Time Out*, March 1985)

360 'I'm not in a position to be seen as a spokesman ...' (Bono in Obstfeld and Fitzgerald, 1997)

385 'As well as smack, coke and spliff ...' (Boy George, 1995)

387 ' "What would I have to do?" asked Gaff. 'Have you ever looked after children?" Robert asked him' (Coleman, 1994)

387 'The thing that drives people ...' (Boy George in Obstfeld and Fitzgerald, 1997)

388 ' "What do you want?" she demanded. 'I'm waiting for George to die", he told her.' (Mick Brown, *Sunday Times Magazine*, 1987)

390 'It's funny to watch someone ...' (Elvis Costello, NME, 1995)

390 'I was hopeful ...' (Keith Richards in Ewing, 1996)

390 'I honestly feel there is something incredibly lacking in my life ...' (Miles, 1980)

390 'It's my desperate craving for affection.' (Elton John in Black, 1993)

392 ' "How do you want me to sound?" 'Like Dusty Springfield..."' (Neil Tennant speaking at Dusty Springfield's funeral)

393 'he must have been crazy' (George Michael in Michael and Parsons, 1990)

395 'There's nothing wrong with going to bed ...' (Elton John in Black, 1993)

396 'paid a minimum of £100 each ...' (Graham X, *Sun*)

396 'They can say I'm a fat old sod ...' (Elton John, *Daily Express*)

396 'I couldn't have done the things they said I did ...' (Elton John, *Daily Mirror*)

396 'too disgusting to print in a family newspaper' (*Sun*)

396 'Sorry Elton ... We are delighted that the *Sun* and Elton have become friends again.' (ibid.)

423 'Some of our one-off events ...' (Judge Jules, Profile, *Sunday Times Magazine*)

423 'There usually wouldn't be any toilets ...' (ibid.)

423 'one of the founders of the drug-ridden acid house craze' (on Danny Rampling, *Sun*)

428 'The most ecstatic live show ...' (*NME*)

428 'The Best New Band in Britain' (*Melody Maker*)

429 'We kiss in his room ...' (Brett Anderson and Bernard Butler, 'The Drowners', © 1992, Universal Publishing Ltd)

429 'There's nothing more up to date ...' (Damon Albarn in *NME*, 1995)

430 'Girls who are boys ...' (Damon Albarn, 'Girls & Boys', *Parklife*, Blur, 1994)

430 'Being skinny is neater and tidier, and it's not got bulges all over' (Jarvis Cocker in Aston, 1996)

434 'Every fucking fucker in the fucking band ...' (Marcus Russell in Robertson, 1996)

435 'You walk into Tom's office ...' (Tony Mortimer in *Mr Rock 'n' Roll*, Channel 4, produced by Virtual Television Company)

436 'barely pubescent boys ...' (Marcus Berkmann, *Daily Mail*)

436 'a billion-dollar Cadinot skinflick ...' (Richard Smith, *Gay News*)

439 'It is not only record companies ...' (BPI Statement, 1987)

447 'Most young people who use drugs ...' (Joseph Rowntree Foundation, *Guardian*, 5/11/97)

447 *'Clubber's Nipple* – a friction burn ...' (*The Times* medical column)

448 'Speed is cheap and cheerful ...' (Elastica in *NME*, 1995)

468 'that incredible voice' (*Billboard*)

469 'simmering with style and substance' (*Billboard*)

471 'I don't feel any shame ...' (George Michael, interview with CNN)

472 'I was spat at in the street ...' (Almond, 1999)

473 'the exposure of various celebrities' private lives ...' (George Michael, *Sun*)

473 'We are currently collecting from around the world ...' (Andrew Potter, PRS report, 1999)

476 'Ballads and babies – that's what happened to me' (Paul McCartney in Obstfeld and Fitzgerald, 1997)

476 'Being famous through rock music ...' (Pete Townshend in Giuliano, 1996)

477 'I was working at York Sainsbury's ...' (Rick Witter in *NME*, 1995)

481 'At the moment, to be in the chart ...' (Jeremy Marsh, MD of BMG Records, interview, *Music Week*)

484 'the quality of a Toyota commercial' (Bono in *NME*, 1995)

488 'The term rock star is pejorative ...' (Sting in Clarkson, 1996)

488 'Part of the reason that people listen ...' (Jarvis Cocker, *NME*, 15/2/97)

489 'I often wonder why we bothered ...' (Ken Tappenden, *Top Ten, 1990*, Chrysalis TV)

BIBLIOGRAPHY

Aldridge, John (1984) *Satisfaction: The Story of Mick Jagger*, Proteus.

Almond, Marc (1999) *Tainted Life*, Sidgwick & Jackson.

Anthony, Wayne (1999) *Spanish Highs*, Virgin.

Aston, Martin (1996) *Pulp*, Pan.

Barnes, Richard (1979) *Mods!*, Eel Pie.

Bean, J.P. (n.d.) *Joe Cocker, With a Little Help from My Friends*, Omnibus.

Beatles, The (2000) *Anthology*, Cassel.

Beaton, Cecil and Richard Buckle (1979) *Self-Portrait with Friends – The Selected Diaries of Cecil Beaton*, Weidenfield & Nicolson.

Benson, Richard (1997) *Night Fever*, Boxtree.

Berry, Chuck (1987) *Chuck Berry: The Autobiography*, Harmony.

Black, David (1998) *Acid*, Vision Paperbacks/Satin Publications.

Black, Susan (1993) *Elton John, In His Own Words*, Omnibus.

Blake, John (1985) *His Satanic Majesty Mick Jagger*, Holt.

Bockris, Victor (1992) *Keith Richard: The Biography*, Hutchinson.

Bockris, Victor (1995) *Lou Reed: The Biography*, Vintage.

Booth, Stanley (1985) *The True Adventures of the Rolling Stones*, Heinemann.

Bowie, Angela, with Patrick Carr (1992) *Backstage Passes*, Orion.

Boy George (1995) *Take It Like a Man* (with Spencer Bright), Pan.

Bracewell, Michael (1997) *England is Mine, Pop Life in Albion from Wilde to Goldie*, HarperCollins.

Braun, Michael (1964) *Love Me Do*, Jonathan Clowes.

Brown, Peter and Steven Gaines (1983) *The Love You Make*, Macmillan.

Burdon, Eric (1986) *I Used to Be an Animal but I'm Alright Now*, Faber & Faber.

Carducci, Joe (1995) *Rock and the Pop Narcotic*, Redoubt Press.

Charone, Barbara (1979) *Keith Richards*, Futura.

Clarke, Donald (1990) *The Penguin Encyclopaedia of Popular Music*, Penguin.

Clarke, Gary (1995) *Elton My Elton*, Smith Gryphon.

Clarke, Martin (1997) *Manic Street Preachers*, Plexus.

Clarkson, Wensley (1996) *Sting*, Blake.

Clayson, Alan (1997) *Hamburg*, Sanctuary.

Cohn, Nick (1989) *Ball the Wall*, Picador.

Cohn, Nick (1969) *Awopbopaloobopalopbamboom*, Weidenfield & Nicolson.

Coleman, Ray (1994) *Rod Stewart*, Pavilion.

Coleman, Ray (1985) *Clapton*, Warner.

Collin, Matthew and John Gregory (1998) *Altered State*, Serpent's Tail.

County, Jayne (1995) *Man Enough to Be a Woman*, Serpent's Tail.

Coward, Noël (1982) *The Noël Coward Diaries*, Graham Payn.

Cunningham, Mark (1996) *Good Vibrations*, Sanctuary.

Dannen, Fredric (1990) *Hit Men*, Random House.

David, Hugh (1997) *On Queer Street: A Social History of British Homosexuality*, HarperCollins.

Davies, Dave (1996) *Kink: An Autobiography*, Boxtree.

Denselow, Robin (1989) *When the Music's Over*, Faber & Faber.

Des Barres, Pamela (1996) *Rock Bottom: Dark Moments in Music Babylon*, St Martin's Press.

Driver, Jim (1994) *Rock Talk*, The Do Not Press.

East 17 (1995) *Talkback*, Omnibus.

Ellis, Royston (1961) *The Big Beat Scene*, New English Library.

Epstein, Brian (1965) *A Cellarful of Noise*, Souvenir Press.

Ewing, Jon (1996) *The Rolling Stones, Quote Unquote*, Paragon.

Faithfull, Marianne (1995) *Faithfull* (with David Dalton), Penguin.

Fiegel, Eddi (1998) *John Barry: A Sixties Theme – From James Bond to Midnight Cowboy*, Constable.

Flippo, Chet (1997) *Your Cheatin' Heart: A Biography of Hank Williams*, Plexus.

Frame, Pete (1979) *The Complete Rock Family Tree*, Omnibus.

Frith, Simon and Andrew Goodwin (1990) *On Record*, Routledge.

Frith, Simon (1978) *The Sociology of Rock*, Constable.

Geldof, Bob (1986) *Is That It?*, Sidgwick & Jackson.

Gillett, Charlie (1983) *The Sound of the City: The Rise of Rock and Roll*, Souvenir.

Gillman, Peter and Leni Gillman (1986) *Alias David Bowie*, Hodder & Stoughton.

Giuliano, Geoffrey (1996) *Behind Blue Eyes: A Life of Pete Townshend*, Coronet.

Goldman, Albert (1971) *Freakshow: The Rocksoulbluesjazzsickjewblackhumorsexpoppsych Gig and other scenes from the Counter-Culture*, Atheneum.

Goldman, Albert (1992) *Sound Bites*, Abacus.

Goodall, Nigel (1995) *George Michael, In His Own Words*, Omnibus.

Gosling, Ray (1980) *Personal Copy*, Faber & Faber.

Greenfield, Robert (1974) *A Journey Through America with the Rolling Stones*, Dutton.

Hadleigh, Boze (1999) *Sing Out*, Robson.

Herman, Gary (1984) *Rock 'n' Roll Babylon*, Plexus.

Hildred, Stafford and David Gritten (1998) *Tom Jones*, Sidgwick & Jackson.

Hill, Dave (1986) *Designer Boys Material Girls: Manufacturing the 80s Pop Dream*, Blandford Press.

Hodkinson, Mark (1991) *Marianne Faithfull: As Tears Go By*, Omnibus.

Hodkinson, Mark (1995) *Queen: The Early Years*, Omnibus.

Hoskyns, Barney (1998) *Glam!*, Faber & Faber.

Hulanicki, Barbara (1982) *From A to Biba and Back Again*, Comet.

Jackson, Laura (1997) *Heart of Stone*, Blake.

James, Martin (1997) *The Prodigy*, Ebury Press.

Jarman, Derek (1994) *Dancing Ledge*, Quartet.

Jones, Alan, and Jussi Kantonen (1999) *Saturday Night Fever*, Mainstream Publishing.

Kent, Nick (1994) *The Dark Stuff*, Penguin.

Leigh, Spencer (1996) *Halfway to Paradise: Britpop 1955–1962*, Finbarr.

Macdonald, Ian (1995) *Revolution in the Head*, Pimlico.

MacInnes, Colin (1959) *Absolute Beginners*, Allison & Busby.

MacInnes, Colin (1959) *England, Half English: Pop Songs and Teenagers*, McGibbon & Kee.

McLagan, Ian (2000) *All the Rage: My High Life with the Small Faces, the Faces, the Rolling Stones and Many More*, Pan.

Matlock, Glen, with Pete Silverton (1990) *I Was a Teenage Sex Pistol*, Faber & Faber.

Martin, George (1994) *The Summer of Love*, Pan.

Melly, George (1970) *Revolt into Style*, Penguin.

Michael, George and Tony Parsons (1990) *Bare*, Michael Joseph.

Middles, Mick (1996) *From Joy Division to New Order: The Factory Story*, Virgin.

Miles, Barry (1978) *The Clash*, Omnibus.

Miles, Barry (ed.) (1980) *David Bowie, In His Own Words*, Omnibus.

Miles, Barry (1997) *Paul McCartney: Many Years From Now*, Secker & Warburg.

Morley, Paul (1986) *Ask: The Chatter of Pop*, Faber & Faber.

Murray, Charles Shaar (1991) *Shots from the Hip*, Penguin.

NME (1995) *Big Mouth Strikes Again – The Book of Quotes*, New Musical Express.

Norman, Philip (1991) *Elton*, Hutchinson.

Norman, Philip (1982) *The Road Goes On Forever*, Corgi.

Norman, Philip (1984) *The Stones*, Hamish Hamilton.

Obstfeld, Raymond and Patricia Fitzgerald (1997) *Jabberrock*, Cannongate.

Oldham, Andrew Loog (2000) *Stoned*, Secker & Warburg.

Olcese, Andrea (1985) *Internationalists, Introducing The Style Council*, Riot Stories.

Orton, Joe (1987) *The Orton Diaries*, Methuen.

Paglia, Camille (1990) *Sexual Personae: Art and Decadence from Nefertiti to Emily Dickinson*, Yale University Press.

Palmer, Tony (1976) *All You Need Is Love: The Story of Popular Music*, Weidenfield & Nicolson.

Pandit, S.A. (1996) *From Making to Music*, Hodder & Stoughton.

Paytress, Mark (1992) *Twentieth Century Boy*, Sidgwick & Jackson.

Quant, Mary (1967) *Quant*, Pan.

Reed, John (1997) *Paul Weller: My Ever-Changing Moods*, Omnibus.

Robertson, Ian (1996) *Oasis: What's the Story?*, Blake.

Robb, John (1999) *The Nineties*, Ebury Press.

Rogan, Johnny (1984) *Van Morrison: A Portrait of the Artist*, Elm Tree Books.

Rogan, Johnny (1988) *Starmakers and Svengalis: The History of British Pop Management*, Macdonald, Queen Anne Press.

Savage, Jon and Hanif Kureishi (eds) (1995) *The Faber Book of Pop*, Faber & Faber.

Savage, Jon (1991) *England's Dreaming: Sex Pistols and Punk Rock*, Faber & Faber.

Savage, Jon (1997) *Time Travel*, Vintage.

Shapiro, Harry (1990) *Waiting for the Man: The Story of Drugs and Popular Music*, Helter Skelter.

Shapiro, Harry (1996) *Alexis Korner: The Biography*, Bloomsbury.

Shaw, Sandie (1992) *The World at My Feet*, Fontana.

Sky, Rick (1993) *The Take That Fact File*, HarperCollins.

Smith, Richard (1995) *Seduced and Abandoned*, Cassell.

Stump, Paul (1997) *The Music's All That Matters*, Quartet Books.

Thompson, Ben (1998) *Seven Years of Plenty*, Victor Gollancz.

Timelords, The (1988) *The Manual: How to Have a Number One the Easy Way*, Curfew Press.

Tremlett, George (1996) *David Bowie: Living on the Brink*, Carroll & Graff.

Turner, Steve (1994) *Cliff Richard: The Biography*, Lion Publishing.

Tyler, Andrew (1988) *Street Drugs*, New English Library.

Vyner, Harriet (1999) *Groovy Bob*, Faber & Faber.

Wale, Michael (1972) *Vox Pop: Profiles of the Pop Process*, Harrap.

Watkinson, Mike and Pete Anderson (1994) *Scott Walker: A Deeper Shade of Blue*, Virgin.

Welch, Chris (1981) *Adam & The Ants*, Star.

White, Charles (1985) *The Life and Times of Little Richard*, Pan.

White, Timothy (1990) *Rock Lives*, Holt.

Wiener, Jon (1985) *Come Together: John Lennon in His Time*, Faber & Faber.

Wood, Ron, with Bill German (1987) *Ron Wood*, Harper & Row.

Wyman, Bill (1990) *Stone Alone*, Penguin.

Yorke, Richie (1974) *Led Zeppelin*, Virgin.

INDEX